The Home
How-To Sourcebook

The Home How-To Source Book

Mike McClintock

Charles Scribner's Sons • New York

Copyright © 1984 Mike McClintock

Library of Congress Cataloging in Publication Data

McClintock, Michael, 1945-
   The home how-to sourcebook.

   Includes index.
   1. House construction—Amateurs' manuals.   2. Dwellings—
Remodeling—Amateurs' manuals.   I. Title.
TH4813.M3   1984   643   83-20219
ISBN 0-684-18015-4
ISBN 0-684-18045-6 (pbk.)

1 3 5 7 9 11 13 15 17 19   F/C   20 18 16 14 12 10 8 6 4 2

1 3 5 7 9 11 13 15 17 19   F/P   20 18 16 14 12 10 8 6 4 2

Printed in the United States of America.

for Sidney Hertzberg

CONTENTS

ABOUT THE SOURCES

When you find a book like this, with hundreds of entries in dozens of different how-to and home consumer fields, several questions are likely to pop into your mind, for instance: how did the sources that are listed get listed, what about the ones that aren't here, and what does a listing mean—that the source has passed some test or other? Here are some answers.

• Not every home consumer source is here. If it was, your fingers would now be cramping from holding up the book. The listing is selective.

• Every source included here received a letter or a phone call and responded to several questions about its products or services, its consumer literature, how it can help consumers, and more. Any potential source that did not answer (no matter how promising) did not get listed.

• I tried for the best possible geographic coverage. For example, when two sources in the same area were similar, I tried to find something special about one of them, dropped the other, and looked further in a different part of the country.

• A listing is not a recommendation, unless you read that I have used the source and have nothing but good things to report. Conversely, firms and groups not listed are not necessarily bad sources to be avoided. They may have been dropped because another company offers better literature, literature at no cost, a more comprehensive warranty, or just happens to be in the right part of the country. And I may have missed a few good ones. However, it is fair for you to assume that

I went looking for good sources and that I included materials and mail-order firms I have had success with, companies, associations, and agencies that are responsive to consumer inquiries, and so forth. I did not go looking for the bad apples. So in all honesty a listing is a kind of implied endorsement, at least a preliminary screening, unless, again, something to the contrary is mentioned. And in some instances, when there were some negatives to report, you'll hear about them.

• Not every product or service of every source is included in its entry. The entries are not mini-catalogs. The aim was to cover some of the variations, some of the fine points and special features, even some of the ideas and attitudes behind the products and services—enough so you will know whether or not you should use the source.

• None of the sources listed provided products or other goodies to sweeten their own name as opposed to a competitor's. Where products and services are described as though I have used them, I *have* used them somewhere along the line, in the course of building houses for ten years, doing repair and renovation work, writing six books and about 250 magazine articles in home consumer fields, and doing a home consumer question-and-answer program on the radio every week for the last three years.

• Where descriptions of firms or groups are quoted, I have let the people who provide the product or service speak for themselves. They are actual quotes, included to help you get a feeling for these people and how they view themselves.

• I considered for a long time whether to include prices and fees. Is it better to include them, or leave them out so you're not disappointed when the entry says $10 but the most current price list is $12.50? At the risk of creating some disappointment I have included average, representative costs where possible—for a simple reason: in the real world of consumer decision making, money is (and should be) part of your consideration. When one company offers a little more than another but at twice the price, money can be the deciding factor. And comparatively, source to source, price ratios are unlikely to change much no matter what happens to the rate of inflation. Blue chip companies with blue chip prices rarely switch to bargain basement, mass market production. So the most expensive source is likely to stay the most expensive, even if everyone's price goes up some. Costs are part of the picture and part of this book.

• Finally, if you know a good source in any of the fields covered in *The Home How-To Sourcebook* that I missed, I welcome your letter giving the source's name and address, and a few words to recommend them. Write to me in care of the publisher: Charles Scribner's Sons, 597 Fifth Ave., New York, NY 10017.

AUTHOR'S NOTE

As I started this book I was curious about the outcome—not how the book would turn out, but how I would react to an unnatural and prolonged exposure to a sea of products and services and to overdoses of the wondrous language of marketing and sales: self-adjusting hinges proven with "300,000 slam tests" and "Executive Series" prefabricated log homes.

The endless superlatives and advertising hype that seemed to take life and practically spring from the stuffed mailbox every morning made less and less of an impression the more I read them. But since this is a source-book, not a book you will read cover to cover to get an overview, I do want to tell you what my lasting reaction was after all the products and services and facts and figures and evaluations went into the manuscript and the slogans went into the wood-stove.

By letter or phone I talked to thousands of companies, associations, and agencies across the country until I began to feel that I was on some kind of home consumer national tour. What stuck out, at first, was all the companies with massive amounts of literature, product specs, technical reports from independent testing labs, national retail networks, and consumer affairs departments; also, some of the amorphous government agencies with a hundred barely connected departments, churning out reports and regulations, with publication lists thicker than most company catalogs. But what stuck in the end was the character of many of the small firms and agencies operating in between the big ones. None of them are indispensable cogs in the national economic wheel, but the more I saw the more they seemed to be like glue holding the whole

system together, even though times have been too tough for many small companies that didn't have the lawyers and the pull and the nerve to ask Congress to bail them out.

I began to picture the big organizations dividing and multiplying like cultures in a petrie dish, with the small organizations serving as the fluid in the dish, the seemingly nondescript but essential medium for growth. More than glue, there was a lot of life in there. The small outfits seemed to give the whole system a little heart. Without the need to stake out a big chunk of territory, they found room in the system for small-scale initiative and human-scale ideas, and even some peculiar ideas.

Conventional rules of sales and growth and success say there is no room for a company that continues to sell only a hundred hand-operated masonry block fabricating machines every year. But there is a company that does it and makes a profit, because to the few homesteaders and others who do buy the machines they are invaluable. And there is room in the system for people who have combined their life's love and their life's work—quite an accomplishment—whether it's rescuing structural beams from two-hundred-year-old New England barns or turning a small music box and lamp repair service into The Musical Museum, complete with an antique mechanical bird in a cage that rocks back and forth and chirps on command.

People I didn't know who had never heard of me explained in their letters how they had started their businesses from scratch. Some have pictures of their toddlers in the company catalog. And some explained how their parents or grandparents started the business, what has changed since then, and what they have kept the same. There's still a little room left for that too.

Who knows how long it will last; if mom and pop hardware stores, and third generation lumber mills, and understaffed community self-help groups will be squeezed out of the space between big firms and big agencies. From what I see it's not about to happen. And the saving grace is not people pulling themselves up by their own bootstraps (even though they do), or bullet biting; not financial or legal or business wizardry (although that can help). The real find, for me, was what I discovered behind the facts and figures—heart, plain and simple—and I hope that, with all the practical information in this book, some of it shows through.

The Home How-To Sourcebook

PLANNING
AND
DESIGN

PRIVATE FIRMS

New Construction

Architectural Design—Construction

Northern Design Builders
28 Elm St.
Montpelier, VT 05602
(802) 223-3484

This firm provides general contracting, architectural planning, and design services and has experience in rehab and historic restoration work. They are also the state franchise for prestigious Lord & Burnham greenhouses. The principal, Lawrence Atkin, reports, "Major changes we have noted over the past few years include greater interest in greenhouses, awareness of solar benefits in design, energy consciousness, and wood heat," and accordingly offers plans for a solar home (for $250). Northern responds to inquiries with brochures and specific costs and will provide résumés of their construction firm, Northern Design, and architectural arm, Lawrence Atkin Associates.

Business operation Works in design and construction regionally and statewide handling and installing Lord & Burnham greenhouses.

Architectural Design—Woodworking

Louis Mackall & Partner/Breakfast
   Woodworks, Inc.
50 Maple St.
Branford, CT 06405
(203) 488-8364

Since these firms share the same building and the same phone and work on the same projects regularly, they are sharing the same entry. Louis Mackall & Partner is a small architectural firm that designs, among other things, distinctive, imaginative homes. The style is difficult to pin down, but it is a bit like modern Colonial; there is a lot of exposed timber framing and a lot of glass. The style is exemplified by a house on Nantucket for which Mr. Mackall received citation in Architectural Record's Houses of the Year awards program. Wood shakes are used on the outside of the house and inside, tie-rods are used as collar beams, an ingenious modern twist that reminds me of Charles Eames's "factory catalog" house. It is definitely not the antiseptic "chemical factory" type of modern architecture lambasted so nicely in Tom Wolfe's *From Bauhaus to Our House*. The other side of this operation, Breakfast Woodworks, fabricates much of the woodwork used in Mackall's projects and works for other architects and clients as well. There is no catalog of stock items. In fact, Duo Dickinson writes, "People are growing blankly nauseated by the imposition of the Catalog in daily life. We are purveyors of an aesthetic notion of the life that lies dormant in every object and material." While their prose gets a little carried away, their woodwork is concise; sculptural but not taken beyond the reality of everyday, household conditions into the art gallery. For instance, they made beautiful, functional, hardwood door-closing hardware for the Nantucket house.

Business operation All work is custom. Both firms welcome inquiries, and have many excellent samples of their work to show.

Energy and Solar Design/ Consulting

Ensar Group Energy and Design Services
3710 Hwy. 82
Glenwood Springs, CO 81601
(303) 945-6503

This company provides a wide range of energy-related services dealing with both conventional and alternative hardware systems. Formerly called Solar Pathways, Ensar now operates or has a controlling interest in the following companies:

Ensar, Inc., deals mainly in energy consulting, working with computer models and integrating architecture and engineering requirements.

Insulshutter, Inc., manufactures insulated shutters and skylight louvers and is beginning to produce windows fabricated with Heat Mirror transparent insulation.

Alpen Products, Inc., is a separately incorporated firm making insulated glass and several types of sophisticated glazing ranging from solar heating to solar control products.

Sunspool, Inc., in Palo Alto, makes drain down valves and other solar-related hardware.

Details, product information, and addresses for all these companies can be obtained by writing Ensar at the above address. Examples of their projects with energy-saving results and more are available on request.

Homebuilding Plans and Books

Garlinghouse Company
320 S.W. 33 St.
PO Box 299
Topeka, KS 66601
(913) 267-2490

Garlinghouse sells stock blueprints for new homes nationally by mail order. They will provide a list of available plans in book form, which cover design alternatives that may help in making a final selection of working blueprints. Write for basic information first, and always try to obtain a sample, even a single page, of a plan before ordering full sets.

Home Building Plan Service, Inc.
2235 N.E. Sandy Blvd.
Portland, OR 97232
(503) 234-9337

HBPS has been in the plan business since 1946, and they have literally thousands of what they call predesigned stock home plans. They present the plans in book form, so you can churn through many varieties of the same basic type of plan (hillside, vacation, earth sheltered, passive solar, etc.) to find one you like. Full working blueprints are available for each plan. Other extras include a structural materials list and typical plumbing, wiring, and solar heating diagrams.

Business operation Advertising regularly in the national how-to magazines, HBPS has all materials open for inspection in their Portland retail outlet. They will send you a brief color brochure outlining their service.

Pricing Survey plan books for vacation, hillside, and other homes are about $3 each. Blueprint prices on request. Supporting mechanical drawings are about $8 to $10. For plan orders or current price quotes on plan prices, they offer a toll-free line: 1 (800) 547-5570.

Home Planners, Inc.
23761 Research Dr.
Farmington Hills, MI 48024
1 (800) 521-6797

This firm sells plan books with full illustrations and sample layouts, all of which are backed with complete construction blueprints. The plan books are categorized by size and style, and each group of about 300 or 400 designs costs $5 or $6 in book form. The complete design collection is $15. However, the blueprints, which include landscape sketch, foundation plan, cross sections, elevations, and a materials list, are $75, and $15 for additional copies. Considering what an architect would charge, this is inexpensive. Of course an architect might come up with a design that suited you better than one of 200 or 400 or even 1000 stock plans.

Business operation   Home Planners will send an informative brochure, which includes a look at the plan books and blueprints, on request.

I. M. Bruinier & Associates, Inc.,
  Designers
1304 S.W. Bertha Blvd.
Portland, OR 97219
(503) 246-3022

This firm offers a variety of plan books showing floor plans, well-rendered perspective views, and complete construction blueprints for every plan shown. The plan books are inexpensive, averaging $2 or $3 for, say, an 80-page booklet with 250 to 350 designs. The blueprints (you get four copies because the building department and others must have their own copies) are expensive, about $150 to $200 and up. That's bargain basement compared with what an architect would charge you. But your own architect might come up with a plan that better meets your individual needs and tastes. The idea of the plan books is to cover so much ground, so many styles, and so many situations that you will get, or almost get, the equivalent of a custom design.

Business operation   You can write for a list of plan books, which are grouped according to house type and site; Sloping and View Sites and Duplex Incoms Homes, for instance. Complete blueprints include as standard equipment many features that sev-

eral companies in this field treat as extras and charge extra for—things like material specs and lumber lists, and printing the plans in reverse, so the garage could be on one side of your lot instead of the other. The plan book artwork shows no construction details but is rendered in a modern style with perspective shadows—a small point, but a realistic touch not found in many similar books.

National Plan Service
435 W. Fullerton Ave.
Elmhurst, IL 60126
(312) 833-0640

National sells a wide variety of plans, ranging from sixteen different kinds of garages, to decks, gazebos, storage buildings, waterbeds, clocks, and so forth, books filled with complete home plans (some billed as energy-saving designs, some as "country-rustic," etc.), and a moderate list of how-to books by Better Homes and Gardens, Sunset, and Gardenway.

Business operation   All plans are available by mail order, direct to the consumer, and are also available in some retail lumber and building supply outlets. Write for National's 4-page flyer that briefly covers it all.

Pricing   Plan prices are modest, for example, $15 each (5 sets for $50) for garages, $10 for smaller utility sheds.

Outbuilding Specialties
Sun Designs
PO Box 206
Delafield, WI 53018
(414) 567-4255

Sun sells plan books and blueprints of privys, bridges, cupolas, and gazebos. Most have a moderately ornate Victorian style, although there is a lot of variation, including Colonial. They present their many designs in study plan books that lay out the building in place in a very nice sketch and include some details of construction. Each design is available in complete blueprint form.

Business operation   Sun sells via mail order worldwide. They will send you free three small brochures that describe the plan books and the blueprints.

Pricing   Plan books are about $7. Blueprints range from $12 to about $20.

Solar and Earth-Sheltered Homes
Malcolm Wells
PO Box 1149
Brewster, MA 02631

This architect concentrates in an area that is becoming more and more popular. As he writes, "The smokier our skies, the filthier our rivers, the more eroded and asphalted our land, the busier I become." Mr. Wells specializes in the design of solar and earth-sheltered buildings, and sells several books on the subject via mail order.

Business operation   A brochure listing the books with descriptions and prices is sent on request at no charge. Titles include underground design and plan books, passive solar energy, and more.

Restoration and Remodeling

Fireplace/Garden Design
Halsted S. Welles & Associates, Inc.
287 E. Houston St.
New York, NY 10002
(212) 777-5440

What fireplaces and gardens have in common in this case is masonry work. The firm designs for both new construction and restoration and renovation work on existing fireplaces and gardens.

Business operation   The interesting thing about this company is that it offers a variety of design and consulting services and also keeps a staff of masons and other craftsmen "in house." Most companies give you one or the other, and sometimes you get stuck in the middle trying to explain who said what to whom and what they meant by it. Working in the New York City area, the firm has been written up several times in area newspapers and magazines. You can write for some of the press clippings and other information about the company.

Historic Preservation/Restoration
The Ehrenkrantz Group, P.C.
Building Conservation Technology, Inc.
1555 Connecticut Ave. NW
Washington, DC 20036
(202) 387-8040

This firm works nationally in architecture and has a subsidiary specializing in historic preservation, restoration, and rehabilitation work. Some of its more prestigious clients include the New York Public Library and the New York Parks Department for work on the Central Park Conservancy, and it has done work on the Chrysler Building, Union Station in Pittsburgh, and many more.

Business operation   You can contact one of the firm's four offices (in New York, Washington, Nashville, and San Francisco) for brochures on its work, staff, schedule, and costs. The Washington office works almost exclusively on preservation projects.

James Thomas Wollon, Jr., A.I.A.
600 Craigs Corner Rd.
Havre de Grace, MD 21078
(301) 879-6748

This architect specializes in historic structures. Services include traditional practice of preparing drawings and specifications, helping with contractor selection, and inspecting work during construction. Unique services include consultation on architectural history, building condition, code compliance, and nomination to the National Register of Historic Places. The architect is registered to practice in Maryland, Virginia, Pennsylvania, Delaware, and North Carolina. Consulting services are possible in New Jersey and West Virginia as well. Mr. Wollon notes the growing interest in the continued use of old buildings, adding, "The Bicentennial gave this movement a great boost. New awareness of conservation in more recent years has further sustained the movement."

Landscape and Garden
James W. Gibbs, L.A., and Associates
340 E. 93 St.
New York, NY 10028
(212) 722-7508

This firm specializes in the restoration and reconstruction of period landscape designs —gardens that have gone to seed.

Business operation The firm works along the eastern seaboard up to Indiana and Illinois. Write for costs and the range of specific services. Jamie Gibbs writes, "Not all designers are interested in limited projects. Our firm prides itself in our ability to both serve our clients and create spaces we are proud of."

Restoration and Renovation Planning
Don A. Swofford, Architect
Woodbrook Village
1843 Seminole Trail
Charlottesville, VA 22901
(804) 973-3155

In addition to conventional architectural services, this firm specializes in residential restoration and recycling. The principal, Mr. Swofford, notes "a major trend toward emphasizing the value of recycling earlier built structures. The restoration cycle is now giving us a renaissance cycle of tastefully done new buildings."

Business operation The firm works regionally, and will answer inquiries by sending a brochure describing its services. After consultation, it will provide written proposals.

Restoration Architecture Consulting
Clio Group, Inc.
3961 Baltimore Ave.
Philadelphia, PA 19104
(215) 386-6276

The Clio Group specializes in social, architectural, planning, and land use research and the combination of these factors to create a sound environment. Using a backlog of information on architecture of the mid-Atlantic region, the group can provide historical services that include researching and documenting existing buildings and preparing applications for National Registration and local certification. Environmental impact studies, seriated paint analysis, and architectural services that include design, restoration, and preservation counseling can also be provided. Some recent projects include historic site surveys for the city of Philadelphia and restoration consultation for the University of Pennsylvania.

Business operation Write for a brochure briefly describing their services, including the training and specialties of the partners.

Inspection and Evaluation

Home Inspection

Claxton Walker & Associates
10000 Falls Rd.
Potomac, MD 20854
(301) 299-2755

Claxton Walker provides comprehensive inspection services regionally and offers clients helpful literature on fuel cost comparisons, typical water usage of household fixtures, how to figure lifecycle costs of appliances, and more. The company is a member of ASHI, the American Society of Home Inspectors.

G. C. Oberndorfer & Associates, Inc.
1979 Quarry Rd.
Yardley, PA 19067
(215) 968-6463

A home inspection firm operating in Pennsylvania, New Jersey, and Delaware, Oberndorfer & Associates provides written reports covering eight areas in the home: roofing, basement, plumbing, cooling, kitchen, electrical system, structure, and heating system. A member of the American Society of Home Inspectors, its literature goes well beyond the limited ASHI guidelines and does not contain the many exclusions from inspection noted in ASHI literature. Additionally, they offer a service warranty that provides "unlimited phone consultation, on-site emergency service, and inspection of major, contracted work done on the inspected property." As far as I can tell, this is a unique warranty.

Pricing Oberndorfer states that its fees average only about one-tenth of one percent of the home purchase price.

Guardian National Inspection and
    Warranty Corporation
55 Cedar Lane Rd.
Orleans, MA 02653
(617) 255-6609

Represented nationwide, this engineering company does nothing but inspect buildings —a service for buyers prior to purchase, sellers prior to sale, and homeowners who must document faulty construction or who want supervision of new construction. Specific inspections covering preventive maintenance and energy conservation are available. Noting a radical increase in demand for homeowner consumer protection in the last decade, Guardian provides three kinds of inspection reports: verbal only; a condensed (10 pages on average) written report; and a much more detailed written report, all of which are based, on the average, on a 3-hour site inspection including the structure and mechanical systems. To their credit, they do not report by checklist (preprinted forms covering, theoretically, all possibilities), which they correctly characterize as "ambiguous and usually uninformative." They warranty their work and offer buyers rating reports on different home components, predicting 1-, 2-, and 3-year levels of performance and the maximum maintenance costs. Always ask for a sample report to determine if you really need a professional to discover the kind of information it contains. Write Guardian (member of the American Society of Building and Construction Inspectors) for a brochure describing its services and for regional office locations.

Business operation Representatives should be prepared to furnish descriptive brochures, copies of completed inspection reports, and references on request.

Pricing On a case by case basis.

Old House Inspection Company, Inc.
140 Berkeley Place
Brooklyn, NY 11217
(212) 857-3647

All inspectors working for Old House are licensed architects and engineers. They provide prepurchase inspections, checking plumbing, heating, electrical structure, roof, and more. They encourage their clients to go along on their inspection tour. And why not? It makes a lot of sense as the idea is to determine areas that need immediate repairs (which can become strong bargaining points before going to contract), as well as those requiring long term solutions. Old House does submit written reports, generally 5 to 7 days after inspection. The principal, Hal Einhorn (member of the American Institute of Architects) writes, "One trend in prepurchase house inspection seems to be more of a concentration on energy-saving guides, especially for old houses."

Business operation Old House works predominantly in the New York metropolitan area and generally on houses 50 years old or more. Its inspectors will be happy to talk to you over the phone about services.

Pricing Fees range from $200 to $300 depending on the size and type of house.

Wm. J. Warren & Son, Inc.
300 S. Howes St.
Fort Collins, CO 80521
(303) 482-1976

Warren & Son is a general contracting firm specializing in renovating old and historic structures, it also operates a home inspection service. Let one of their recent jobs speak for the firm. It took $4000 and many hours of research for Mr. Warren to uncover the original contract for a home in Fort Collins, a contract between a noted Colorado architect, Montezuma Fuller, and the original owner. Then Warren uncovered the original design, published with full material specs in a 1902 edition of *Carpentry & Building* magazine. Restoration began while applications were filed to get historical landmark status for the building. Off came siding and all interior work except original bearing supports. New mechanical systems were installed, and painstaking finishing work started, guided in part by a 1902 family photograph showing the original detailing. On went some 200 corbels and fourteen different exterior mouldings. The "before" and "after" pictures are remarkably similar —even down to finials and downspout locations.

Business operation Mr. Warren writes, "I will send a descriptive brochure about our inspection services free to anyone who requests it. I will also estimate any project, consult on any construction matters, and perform a variety of supervising and management jobs on an hourly basis. I will travel anywhere!"

Soil Testing
Sudbury Laboratory, Inc.
6 October Hill Rd.
Holliston, MA 01746
(617) 429-7900

Sudbury manufactures several soil test kits, sold at lawn and garden centers and some hardware stores, for evaluating pH and nutrient levels. You add a little soil to the vials, shake, and compare the resulting colors to a chart on the package. It tells what you have and what to do about it. A brief pamphlet is available from the company, which will sell the products direct if you cannot find them locally.

TRADE ASSOCIATIONS

Energy-Efficient Framing
Western Wood Products Association
  (WWPA)
Yeon Building
Portland, OR 97204
(503) 224-3930

This trade association for western lumber manufacturers is a valuable source of detailed technical information on wood characteristics, including grading, design values, rafter spans, and more. They can provide a booklet that explains how lumber is graded, sized, and rated according to appearance, use, capacity, and so forth. Also, they support the Plen-Wood system of floor framing that uses bays between joists and a heavily insulated, climate controlled crawl space below them to deliver heat. WWPA will sell you a rafter and joist span calculator (a device similar to a slide rule that accurately converts horizontal measurements to angled rafter lengths at various degrees of roof pitch) for about $2. Write for a list of publications.

Fire Prevention/Protection
National Fire Protection Association
  (NFPA)
Batterymarch Park
Quincy, MA 02269
(617) 328-9230

NFPA is *the* place to go for information about all phases of fire prevention, protection, and fighting, although a caution must accompany the latter: fire fighting is a complicated business that should be handled by professionals, and even though it is a natural reaction to fight a house fire when it breaks out, to protect your family and your property all fire fighting professionals advise you to get out and leave the job to them. That said, there is still a lot to know about fires. The NFPA produces the National Fire Codes, a set of about 250 standards and codes on fire safety. But note that state, county, and local fire codes may supersede these national codes and each other. For example, portable kerosene heaters are outlawed in New York City, allowed in some single-family dwellings but not in some multiple dwellings outside the city, and banned in some townships but not in others. The NFPA, which has a lot of valuable literature for consumers and fire professionals, notes that, "With woodstoves and coal-burning stoves gaining in popularity, people should be especially careful with these installations." In this regard, two pieces of their literature are appropriate: *Home Heating Fact Sheet*, and *Save Home Energy The Firesafe Way*.

Business operation Write the address above for a complete list of publications. Ask also for information on a new trend in home fire protection, residential sprinkler systems.

Home Evaluation
National Association of Realtors (NAR)
430 N. Michigan Ave.
Chicago, IL 60511
(312) 440-8000

In addition to conventional association activities furthering the interests of the

400,000-plus member realtors, NAR approves a limited number of companies offering warranties on existing homes. The warranty is based on an inspection of structural soundness, mechanical systems, roofing, and other components at the time of sale and costs roughly one percent of the sale price. The guidelines provide a basis for evaluating cost-effective home repairs and improvements and deciding which ones will add the most value to your home or best prepare it for sale. Write the NAR for a list of approved companies.

Home Insurance
American Insurance Association
85 John St.
New York, NY 10038
(212) 669-0400

A source for many publications on loss prevention that cover such topics as safety guides for electrical appliances, hand tools, and construction work of all kinds. Write for their publications list. Most are moderately priced.

Manufactured Housing (Mobile Homes)
Manufactured Housing Institute (MHI)
1745 Jefferson Davis Hwy.
Arlington, VA 22202
(703) 979-6620

"A mobile home is a cheap, temporary place to live, probably in a crowded, substandard site." This is the kind of bum rap that led trade organizations like the MHI not to call themselves the Mobile Home Institute. Today, particularly when mortgage money is expensive and scarce, mobile homes are the only reasonable option for many families who want some equity in the place where they live but can't afford fixed-site housing. Many of these units look as fixed and permanent as any development house. And many are sold fully equipped with all major appliances, lamps, carpeting, and more. Furthermore, all mobile/manufactured homes produced after June 15, 1976 have been built to the guidelines of the National Manufactured Home Construction and Safety Standards Act of 1974, established and enforced by HUD. Now there are some 10,000 mobile/manufactured home retailers in the United States, almost 25,000 mobile/manufactured home communities, and some 1.8 million sites. For information on construction and safety standards, such as which units have or do not have urea formaldehyde foam insulation in the walls, write MHI for their brochure, *Quick Facts.* (Send a SASE.) They can direct you to your state association as well. It pays to work at the state level with people who have familiarity with dealers in your area.

Plywood Design/Specifications/ Grading
American Plywood Association (APA)
7011 S. 19th St.
PO Box 11700
Tacoma, WA 98411
(206) 565-6600

APA is a nonprofit trade association that is the most abundant and one of the best-informed sources on the design, performance, and installation of plywood products. It represents mills that produce about 80 percent of all structural wood panel products manufactured in the United States. They make extensive information available to consumers, some of it very basic, some of it quite technical. Among APA's most important functions is the development of industry-wide guidelines for product specs and performance, including stringent grading rules. APA maintains eight quality testing labs and a research center in Tacoma to this end. Other functions and services include conducting regional seminars on design and performance, publishing an extensive list of books and brochures, sponsoring an annual design competition for architects, builders, students, *and* do-it-yourselfers. They also have a limited number of home plans using plywood products.

Business operation   First, write for the APA Publications Index. Most of the titles listed are available at the rate of five different titles for $1 to cover postage and handling. Of particular interest to builders and do-it-yourselfers is booklet No. C20D, *Grades & Specifications*, which fully explains the variety of structural panels, their markings, performance, sizes, uses, and more; booklet No. F405, *Performance-Rated Panels*, on the variations of plywood and composite board; and booklet No. X505J, *Panel Handbook & Grade Glossary*, a 40-page handbook with illustrations.

PROFESSIONAL SOCIETIES

Construction Contracts

American Institute of Architects (AIA)
1735 New York Ave. NW
Washington, DC 20006
(202) 785-7300

Of particular interest to anyone planning a major home repair, renovation, or addition project is AIA Document A107, which is really a series of documents entitled *Abbreviated Form of Agreement Between Owner and Contractor*. This standardized form is suited to projects of modest scale (like a kitchen remodeling with new cabinets, appliances, flooring, etc.), up to and including major additions. Generally a more detailed document is used for new homes built from start to finish. Write the AIA for a complete list of contract documents. A107 is several pages long and contains much of the protective language you want. It is written in a way that will stand up in court if you ever get there. Spaces are left for the details of your job—names, dates, materials, and so forth. Also, AIA contracts are helpful as general guidelines for writing your own contract as an informal letter of agreement. These forms are industry standards. No contractor should refuse, or even hesitate, to use them.

Standards

American Society for Testing and
    Materials (ASTM)
1916 Race St.
Philadelphia, PA 19103
(215) 299-5585

ASTM is a nonprofit organization that establishes what they call "voluntary consensus standards," which cover test methods, specifications, definitions, practices, and product classifications. The current membership of ASTM is some 28,000 organizations and individuals worldwide working on 138 technical committees, which turn out some 6700 standards and numerous technical publications. The most efficient way to get an insight into ASTM operations is to write for their Publications Catalog. Its index covers adhesives, electrical insulating materials, fire standards, paints, pest control—you name it. A short description of all ASTM materials on the subject is provided with an order form and price list.

Structural and Earthquake Engineering

Applied Technology Council (ATC)
2150 Shattuck Ave., Suite 806
Berkeley, CA 94704
(415) 540-0223

ATC was formed in 1971 through the efforts of the Structural Engineers Association of California. Its purpose is to encourage research in structural and earthquake engineering and to translate research results into formats useful to engineers. Many of its reports may prove too taxing for laymen, but I've included it here because earthquakes are a special concern that merits the closest possible study, even if some of the information you come across is technical. Of particular interest among reports with very exotic, academic titles are: ATC-4, *A Methodology for Seismic Design and Construction of Single-Family Dwellings* (available through HUD, 451 Seventh St. SW, Washington, DC 20410 as HUD Report No. HUD–PDR–248–1). It runs 576 pages. A condensation (57 pages) available from ATC is *The Home Builders Guide for Earthquake Design*. Write ATC for synopses of other reports.

GOVERNMENT AGENCIES

Climate/Solar/Storms

U.S. Department of Commerce
National Oceanic and Atmospheric
    Administration (NOAA)
Environmental Data and Information
    Service
National Climatic Center
Federal Building
Asheville, NC 28801
(704) 258-2850

A bonanza of information on all aspects of climate for serious homesteaders, those in rural areas, seacoasts, or sites with severe weather—or for people like me who are simply interested. I lost a good hour of work time on this book when the large bundle of booklets, brochures, reports, and the like arrived from NOAA. I got hooked reading the booklet on tsunamis, the great ocean waves, which has incredible pictures, one sequence showing a wave hitting the shore; computer simulations; even a travel time chart for the waves. Then I had to go through the storm surge booklet, which has a North Atlantic hurricane tracking chart. This stuff is fabulous. It takes a little work and some imagination to apply directly to specific sites but is worth it, particularly for those folks I mentioned above. You can write for free, detailed reports on wind chill, computing and using degree day information, local climate data, and more. Other publications are for sale. Write for the list. A little-known, abundant source of specific, technically supported, practical environmental information.

Consumer How-To Information

State and County Consumer Offices

Every state has a consumer office; some states have many local branches as well. The trouble is, a lot of people contact them only when they have a serious complaint, for example, about a product or a home improvement contractor. But as a rule these agencies are able to supply a lot of information (usually free) on product and material standards, health and safety codes, and more. For instance, if you are deciding how to heat a new addition, don't spend a lot of time matching your R values and U factors to the BTU ratings of kerosene heaters—at least not until you know it is legal to use them where you live. They are banned in many cities and a surprising number of local communities (town codes can supersede state codes) as well. Call your local consumer agency and ask before plunging ahead.

(Note that if you have a fire loss stemming from a code-banned heater, your insurance company won't pay off.) Write or call your local consumer agency for its publications list. Local agencies are included here because they are better able to provide specific information on local issues (like codes, permits, and licenses) than a statewide agency. However, state agencies are likely to have a wider selection of literature. It is good policy to write a letter first requesting general information on publications and services and then, when you see what they have and what they can do, go back with very specific requests. The state by state listing follows.

ALABAMA

State Office
Consumer Protection Division
Office of Attorney General
560 S. McDonough St.
Montgomery, AL 36104
(205) 832-5936
(800) 392-5658 (Alabama only)

ALASKA

State Office
Consumer Protection Section
Office of Attorney General
1049 W. Fifth Ave., Suite 101
Anchorage, AK 99501
(907) 279-0428

Branch Offices
Office of Attorney General
State Court Office Building
604 Barnette St., Room 228
Fairbanks, AL 99707
(907) 465-8588

Office of Attorney General
Pouch K, NBA Building
217 Second St.
Juneau, AL 99811
(907) 465-3692

Office of Attorney General
415 Main St., Room 304

Ketchikan, AL 99901
(907) 225-6120

ARIZONA

State Office
Office of Attorney General
207 State Capitol Building
Phoenix, AZ 85007
(800) 354-8431 (Arizona only)

Branch Office
Office of Attorney General
403 W. Congress St.
Tucson, AZ 85701
(602) 882-5501 (Fraud only)

County Offices
Cochise County Attorney's Office
PO Drawer CA
Bisbee, AZ 85603
(602) 432-5703 ext. 470

Consumer Protection/Economic Crime Unit
Pima County Attorney's Office
111 W. Congress, 9th Floor
Tucson, AZ 85701
(602) 792-8668

Yuma County Attorney's Office
PO Box 1048
Yuma, AZ 85364
(602) 782-4534 ext. 55

City Offices
Mayor's Citizens Assistance Office
251 W. Washington
Phoenix, AX 85003
(602) 262-7777

Supervising Attorney
Tucson City Attorney's Office
PO Box 27210
2302 E. Speedway, Room 202
Tucson, AZ 85726
(602) 791-4886

ARKANSAS

State Office
Consumer Protection Division
Office of Attorney General
Justice Building
Little Rock, AR 72201
(501) 371-2341
(800) 482-8982 (Arkansas only)

CALIFORNIA

State Office
California Department of Consumer Affairs
1020 N St.
Sacramento, CA 95814
(916) 445-1254 (Consumer information)

Public Inquiry Unit
Office of Attorney General
555 Capitol Mall, Suite 350
Sacramento, CA 95814
(800) 952-5225 (California
only)

Branch Offices
California Department of
Consumer Affairs
107 S. Broadway, Room 8020
Los Angeles, CA 90012
(213) 620-4360

California Department of
Consumer Affairs
455 Golden Gate Ave., Room
2091
San Francisco, CA 94102
(415) 557-0966

County Offices
Alameda County District
Attorney's Office
24405 Amador St., Room 103
Hayward, CA 94544
(415) 881-6150

Contra Costa County District
Attorney
Special Operations Division
PO Box 670
725 Court St.
Martinez, CA 94553
(415) 372-4500 ext. 4620

Del Norte County Division of
Consumer Affairs
2650 Washington Blvd.
Crescent City, CA 95531
(707) 464-2716 or 3756

Fresno County District
Attorney's Office
Courthouse
1100 Van Ness Ave.
Fresno, CA 93721
(209) 488-3141

Kern County Consumer Unit
1215 Truxton Ave.
Bakersfield, CA 93301
(805) 861-2421

Consumer and Environment
Protection Division
Los Angeles County District
Attorney's Office

320 W. Temple St., Room 540
Los Angeles, CA 90012
(213) 974-3970

Los Angeles County Department
of Consumer Affairs
500 W. Temple St., Room B-96
Los Angeles, CA 90012
(213) 974-1452

Consumer Protection Unit
Madera County Weights and
Measures
902 N. Gateway Dr.
Madera, CA 93637
(209) 674-4641

Consumer Division
Mendocino County District
Attorney's Office
Ukiah, CA 95482
(707) 468-4211

Consumer Affairs Division
Napa County District Attorney's
Office
1125 Third St.
Napa, CA 94558
(707) 253-4427

Major Fraud/Consumer
Protection Unit
Orange County District
Attorney's Office
PO Box 808
700 Civic Center Dr. West
Santa Ana, CA 92702
(714) 834-3600

Orange County Office of
Consumer Affairs
Building C
1300 S. Grand Ave.
Santa Ana, CA 92705
(714) 834-6100

Economic Crime Division
Riverside County District
Attorney's Office
PO Box 1148
4080 Lemon St.
Riverside, CA 92502
(714) 787-6372

Sacramento County District
Attorney's Fraud Division
PO Box 749
Sacramento, CA 95804
(916) 440-6823

San Diego County District
Attorney's Office
PO Box X–1011
San Diego, CA 92112
(714) 236-2474

Consumer Fraud/Economic
Crime Unit
San Francisco District
Attorney's Office
880 Bryant St., Room 320
San Francisco, CA 94103
(415) 553-1821

San Joaquin County District
Attorney's Office
PO Box 50
Stockton, CA 95201
(209) 944-3811

Consumer Unit
San Luis Obispo County District
Attorney's Office
302 Courthouse Annex
San Luis Obispo, CA 93408
(805) 549-5800

Consumer Fraud Unit
San Mateo County District
Attorney's Office
Hall of Justice and Records
Redwood City, CA 94063
(415) 363-4656

Consumer/Business Law Section
Santa Barbara County District
Attorney's Office
118 E. Figueroa
Santa Barbara, CA 93101
(805) 963-6158

Santa Clara County Department
of Consumer Affairs
1553 Berger Dr.
San Jose, CA 95112
(408) 299-4211

Santa Clara County District
Attorney's Office
70 W. Hedding St., West Wing
San Jose, CA 95110
(408) 275-9651

Division of Consumer Affairs
Santa Cruz County District
Attorney's Office
701 Ocean St., Room 240
Santa Cruz, CA 95060
(408) 425-2054

Consumer Fraud Unit
Solano County District
    Attorney's Office
600 Union Ave.
Fairfield, CA 94533
(707) 429-6451

Consumer Affairs Coordinator
Stanislaus County Office of
    Consumer Affairs
1100 H St., 2d Floor
Modesto, CA 95354
(209) 523-7707

Stanislaus County District
    Attorney's Office
PO Box 442
Modesto, CA 95353
(209) 577-0570

Ventura County District
    Attorney's Office
800 South Victoria Ave.
Ventura, CA 93009
(805) 654-3110

Yolo County District Attorney
Consumer Fraud Division
PO Box 1247
Woodland, CA 95695
(916) 666-8521

City Offices
Consumer Protection Section
Los Angeles City Attorney's
    Office
200 N. Main St.
1700 City Hall East
Los Angeles, CA 90012
(213) 485-4515

Consumer Protection Unit
San Diego Attorney's Office
City Administration Building
202 C St., 3d Floor
San Diego, CA 92101
(714) 236-6007

Consumer Division
Santa Monica City Attorney's
    Office
1685 Main St., Room 310
Santa Monica, CA 90401
(213) 393-9975 ext. 321

COLORADO

State Offices
Antitrust and Consumer
    Protection Enforcement
    Section

Office of Attorney General
1525 Sherman St., 2d Floor
Denver, CO 80203
(303) 866-3611

Consumer and Food Specialist
Colorado Department of
    Agriculture
1525 Sherman St., 4th Floor
Denver, CO 80203
(303) 866-3561

County Offices
District Attorney for Archuleta,
    Laplata and San Juan
    Counties
PO Box 3455
Durango, CO 81301
(303) 247-8850

Boulder County District
    Attorney's Consumer Office
PO Box 471
Boulder, CO 80306
(303) 441-3700

Denver District Attorney's
    Consumer Office
1544 York St.
Denver, CO 80206
(303) 333-4224
(303) 333-7723 (Complaints)

El Paso District Attorney's
    Consumer Office for El Paso
    and Teller Counties
El Paso and Teller Counties
27 E. Vermijo, Suite 413
County Office Building
Colorado Springs, CO 80903
(303) 471-5861

District Attorney's Consumer
    Office for Larimer County
Larimer County
Rocky Mountain Bank Building
PO Box 1489
Fort Collins, CO 80522
(303) 221-7200

Pueblo District Attorney's
    Consumer Office for Pueblo
    County
Pueblo County
Courthouse
10th and Main Sts.
Pueblo, CO 81003
(303) 544-0075

Weld District Attorney's
    Consumer Office for Weld
    County
Weld County
PO Box 116
Greeley, CO 80632
(303) 356-4000 ext. 743

CONNECTICUT

State Offices
Department of Consumer
    Protection
State Office Building
165 Capitol Ave.
Hartford, CT 06115
(203) 566-4999
(800) 842-2649 (Connecticut
    only)

Antitrust/Consumer Protection
Office of Attorney General
30 Trinity St.
Hartford, CT 06115
(203) 566-5374

City Office
Office of Consumer Protection
Middletown
City Hall
Middletown, CT 06457
(203) 347-4671 ext. 216

DELAWARE

State Offices
Delaware Division of
    Consumer Affairs
Department of Community
    Affairs and Economic
    Development
820 N. French St., 4th Floor
Wilmington, DE 19801
(302) 571-3250

Economic Crime and Consumer
    Rights Division
Department of Justice
820 N. French St.
Wilmington, DE 19801
(302) 571-3849

DISTRICT OF COLUMBIA

D.C. Office of Consumer
    Protection
1424 K St., NW, 2d Floor
Washington, DC 20005
(202) 727-1158

FLORIDA

State Offices

Division of Consumer Services
110 Mayo Building
Tallahassee, FL 32301
(904) 488-2221
(800) 342-2176 (Florida only)

Consumer Protection Division
Office of Attorney General
State Capitol
Tallahassee, FL 32301
(904) 488-3266

Office of the Comptroller
State Capitol
Tallahassee, FL 32301
(904) 488-0286

Department of Business
   Regulation
The Johns Building
5 S. Bronough St.
Tallahassee, FL. 32304
(904) 488-7114

Branch Offices

Office of Attorney General
401 N.W. Second Ave., Suite
   820
Miami, FL 33128
(305) 377-5441

Office of Attorney General
1313 Tampa St., 8th Floor
Park Trammell
Tampa, FL 33602
(813) 272-2670

Office of the Comptroller
111 E. Coastline Dr., Room 610
Jacksonville, FL 32202
(904) 359-6085

Office of the Comptroller
401 N.W. Second Ave., Suite
   870
Miami, FL 33128
(305) 377-5213

Office of the Comptroller
400 W. Robinson St., Room 501
Orlando, FL 32801
(305) 423-6115

Office of the Comptroller
160 Governmental Center,
   Suite 701
Pensacola, FL 32501
(904) 436-8520

Office of the Comptroller
1861 N.E. Capital Circle
Tallahassee, FL 32308
(904) 488-0027

Office of the Comptroller
1313 Tampa St.
Tampa, FL 33602
(813) 272-2565

Office of the Comptroller
111 Georgia Ave., Suite 211
West Palm Beach, FL 33401
(305) 837-5054

County Offices

Brevard County Consumer
   Fraud Division
State Attorney's Office
County Courthouse
Titusville, FL 32780
(305) 269-8401

Broward County Consumer
   Affairs Division
236 S.E. First Ave., 6th Floor
Fort Lauderdale, FL 33301
(305) 765-5306

Metro Dade County Consumer
   Protection Division
140 W. Flagler St., 16th Floor
Miami, FL 33130
(305) 579-4222

Consumer Protection Division
South Dade County Government
   Center
10710 S.W. 211th St.
Miami, FL 33189
(305) 232-1810 ext. 285

Dade County Consumer Fraud
   Division
Office of State Attorney
1351 N.W. 12th St.
Miami, FL 33125
(305) 547-5200

Consumer Advocate
Metropolitan Dade County
44 W. Flagler St., Room 2301
Miami, FL 33130
(305) 579-4206

Assistant State Attorney for
   Manatee, Sarasota, and
   DeSota Counties
Office of State Attorney

2070 Main St.
Sarasota, FL 33577
(813) 955-0918

Duval County Division of
   Consumer Affairs
Department of Human
   Resources
614 City Hall
Jacksonville, FL 32202
(904) 633-3429 or 3940

Hillsborough County
   Department of Consumer
   Affairs
305 N. Morgan, Suite 707
Tampa, FL 33602
(813) 272-6750

Palm Beach County
   Department of Consumer
   Affairs
Commerce Building
324 Datura St., Suite 300
West Palm Beach, FL 33401
(305) 837-2670

Palm Beach County Economic
   Crime Division
Office of State Attorney
PO Drawer 2905
West Palm Beach, FL 33402
(305) 837-2391

Pasco County Consumer Affairs
   Division
530 Sunset Rd.
Newport Richey, FL 35552
(813) 847-8110

Pinellas County Office of
   Consumer Affairs
801 West Bay Dr., Suite 601
Largo, FL 33540
(813) 448-3801

Seminole County Consumer
   Fraud Division
Office of State Attorney
Seminole County Courthouse
Sanford, FL 32771
(305) 322-7534

City Offices

Lauderhill Consumer Affairs
   Committee
1080 N.W. 47th Ave.
Lauderhill, FL 33313
(305) 583-1045

Tamarac Board of Consumer
  Affairs
5811 N.W. 88th Ave.
Tamarac, FL 33321
(305) 722-5900 ext. 27

GEORGIA

Governor's Office of Consumer
  Affairs
205 Butler St. SE, Suite 356
Plaza Level East Tower
Atlanta, GA 30334
(404) 656-3790
(800) 282-4900 (Georgia only)

Attorney for Deceptive Practices
Office of Attorney General
228 State Judicial Building
Atlanta, GA 30334
(404) 656-3357

City Offices
Atlanta Mayor's Office of
  Community and Consumer
  Affairs
City Hall
68 Mitchell St., S.W.
Memorial Dr. Annex
Atlanta, GA 30303
(404) 658-6105

HAWAII

State Offices
Governor's Office of Consumer
  Protection
250 S. King St.
PO Box 3767
Honolulu, HI 96812
(808) 548-2560 (Administrative
  and Legal—Hawaii only)

Branch Offices
Governor's Office of Consumer
  Protection
PO Box 191
Lihue, Kauai, HI 96766
(808) 245-4365

Governor's Office of Consumer
  Protection
PO Box 1098
Wailuku, Maui, HI 96793
(808) 244-4387

Governor's Office of Consumer
  Protection
75 Aupuni St.

Hilo, HI 96720
(808) 961-7433

IDAHO

State Office
Business Regulation Division
Office of Attorney General
State Capitol
Boise, ID 83720
(208) 334-2400

ILLINOIS

State Offices
Governor's Office of Interagency
  Cooperation
160 N. LaSalle St., Suite 2010
Chicago, IL 60601
(312) 743-2773

Consumer Protection Division
Office of Attorney General
500 S. Second St.
Springfield, IL 62706
(217) 782-9011

Consumer Protection Division
Office of Attorney General
228 N. LaSalle, Room 1242
Chicago, IL 60601
(312) 793-3580

Branch Offices—Downstate
Office of Attorney General
210 William St.
Alton, IL 62002
(618) 465-2711

Office of Attorney General
Association of Commerce and
  Industry Building
210 Southeast St.
Bloomington, IL 61701
(309) 829-6344

Office of Attorney General
103 S. Washington, Suite 12
Carbondale, IL 62901
(618) 457-7831

Office of Attorney General
113 N. Neil St., Suite 308
Champaign, IL 61820
(217) 333-7691

City Hall
520 Jackson, Box 99
Charleston, IL 61920
(217) 345-5651

Office of Attorney General
Chamber of Commerce Building
PO Box 1031
Decatur, IL 62525
(217) 429-5167

Office of Attorney General
818 Martin Luther King Dr.
East St. Louis, IL 62201
(618) 874-2238

Office of Attorney General
500 Main St.
Peoria, IL 61602
(309) 671-3191

Office of Attorney General
813 E. State St.
Rockford, IL 61104
(815) 965-1060

Office of Attorney General
1800 Third Ave., Room 220
Rock Island, IL 61201
(309) 788-7820

Branch Offices—Upstate
Office of Attorney General
Community Center
1616 N. Arlington Heights Rd.
Arlington Heights, IL 60004
(312) 259-7730

Office of Attorney General
403 W. Galena Blvd., Room 203
Aurora, IL 60506
(312) 892-4341

Office of Attorney General
1339 W. Irving Park Rd.
Bensenville, IL 60106
(312) 595-2374 or 2375

Office of Attorney General
4750 N. Broadway, Room 216
Chicago, IL 60640
(312) 769-3742

Office of Attorney General
1104 N. Ashland Ave.
Chicago, IL 60622
(312) 793-5638

Office of Attorney General
7906 S. Cottage Grove
Chicago, IL 60619
(312) 488-2600

Office of Attorney General
Chamber of Commerce Building
800 Lee St.
Des Plaines, IL 60016
(312) 824-4200

Office of Attorney General
71 N. Ottawa St.
Joliet, IL 60434
(815) 722-0433 or 0434

Office of Attorney General
6101 Capulina St.
Morton Grove, IL 60053
(312) 965-4658

Office of Attorney General
5127 Oakton St.
Skokie, IL 60065
(312) 674-2522 or 673-0500

Office of Attorney General
414 N. Sheridan Rd.
Waukegan, IL 60085
(312) 249-3802

County Offices
Cook County Office of State's
  Attorney
303 Daley Center
Chicago, IL 60602
(312) 443-8425

Madison County Office of State's
  Attorney
103 Purcell St., 3d Floor
Edwardsville, IL 62025
(618) 692-4550

City Offices
Chicago Department of
  Consumer Services
121 N. LaSalle St., Room 808
Chicago, IL 60602
(312) 744-4090

Des Plaines Consumer
  Protection Commission
1420 Miner St.
Des Plaines, IL 60016
(312) 297-1200 ext. 258

INDIANA

State Office
Consumer Protection Division
Office of Attorney General
219 State House
Indianapolis, IN 46204
(317) 232-6330 or 6331
(800) 382-5516 (Indiana only)

County Offices
Lake County Prosecuting
  Attorney
2293 N. Main St.
Crown Point, IN 46307
(219) 738-9055

Marion County Prosecuting
  Attorney
560 City–County Building
Indianapolis, IN 46204
(317) 633-3522

Vanderburgh County
  Prosecuting Attorney
First Judicial Circuit
Courts Building, Room 220
Civic Center Complex
Evansville, IN 47708
(812) 426-5150

City Office
Gary Office of Consumer Affairs
Annex East
1100 Massachusetts
Gary, IN 46407
(219) 944-6475

IOWA

State Offices
Consumer Protection Division
Office of Attorney General
1300 E. Walnut, 2d Floor
Des Moines, IA 50319
(515) 281-5926

Iowa Citizens' Aide/
  Ombudsman
515 E. 12th St.
Des Moines, IA 50319
(515) 281-3592

KANSAS

State Office
Consumer Protection and
  Antitrust Division
Office of Attorney General
Kansas Judicial Center, 2d
  Floor
Topeka, KS 66612
(913) 296-3751
(800) 432-2310 (Kansas only)

County Offices
Consumer Fraud Division
Johnson County District
  Attorney's Office

Johnson County Courthouse,
  Box 728
Olathe, KS 66061-0728
(913) 782-5000 ext. 317, 318

Consumer Fraud and Economic
  Crime Division
Sedgwick County District
  Attorney's Office
Sedgwick County Courthouse
Wichita, KS 67203
(316) 268-7921

Shawnee County District
  Attorney's Office
212 Shawnee County
  Courthouse
Topeka, KS 66603
(913) 295-4340

City Offices
Kansas City Department of
  Consumer Affairs
701 N. Seventh St., Room 969
Kansas City, KS 66101
(913) 371-2000 ext. 230, 231

Topeka Consumer Protection
  Division
City Attorney's Office
215 E. Seventh St.
Topeka, KS 66603
(913) 295-3883

KENTUCKY

State Office
Consumer Protection Division
Office of Attorney General
209 St. Clair St.
Frankfort, KY 40601
(502) 564-2200
(800) 432-9257 (Kentucky
  only)

County Office
Jefferson County Consumer
  Protection Department
208 S. Fifth St., Room 401
Louisville, KY 40202
(502) 581-6280

City Office
Owensboro Consumer Affairs
  Commission
101 E. Fourth St.
Owensboro, KY 42301
(502) 684-7251 ext. 8230

LOUISIANA

State Offices

State Office of Consumer
  Protection
2610A Wooddale Blvd.
PO Box 44091, Capitol Station
Baton Rouge, LA 70804
(504) 925-4401
(800) 272-9868 (Louisiana
  only)

Consumer Protection Section
Office of Attorney General
1885 Wooddale Blvd., Suite
  1205
Baton Rouge, LA 70806
(504) 925-4181

Office of Marketing
Department of Agriculture
PO Box 44184, Capitol Station
Baton Rouge, LA 70804
(504) 292-3600

Branch Office

Consumer Protection Section
Office of Attorney General
234 Loyola Ave., 7th Floor
New Orleans, LA 70112
(504) 568-5575

County Office

Consumer Protection and
  Commercial Fraud Division
Jefferson Parish District
  Attorney's Office
New Courthouse Annex,
  5th Floor
Gretna, LA 70053
(504) 368-1020

MAINE

State Offices

Consumer Fraud Division
Office of Attorney General
State House Station No. 6
Augusta, ME 04333
(207) 289-3716

Bureau of Consumer Protection
Department of Business
  Regulation
State House Station No. 35
Augusta, ME 04333
(207) 289-3731

MARYLAND

State Offices

Consumer Protection Division
Office of Attorney General
26 S. Calvert St.
Baltimore, MD 21202
(301) 659-4300

Office of Licensing and
  Consumer Services
Motor Vehicle Administration
6601 Ritchie Hwy. N.E.
Glen Burnie, MD 21061
(301) 768-7420

Branch Offices

Metro Branch Office
Maryland Attorney General's
  Consumer Protection Division
5112 Berwyn Rd., 3d Floor
College Park, MD 20740
(301) 474-3500

Western Maryland Branch Office
Maryland Attorney General's
  Consumer Protection Division
138 East Antietam St.
Hagerstown, MD 21740
(301) 791-4780

Eastern Shore Branch Office
Maryland Attorney General's
  Consumer Protection Division
State Office Complex
Salisbury, MD 21801
(301) 546-4407

County Offices

Anne Arundel County Board of
  Consumer Affairs
Arundel Center
Annapolis, MD 21401
(301) 224-6750 ext. 7300
  Baltimore)
(202) 261-8250 ext. 7300
  (Washington, D.C.)

Howard County Office of
  Consumer Affairs
Carroll Building
3450 Courthouse Dr.
Ellicott City, MD 21043
(301) 992-2176

Montgomery County Office of
  Consumer Affairs
611 Rockville Pike

Rockville, MD 20852
(301) 279-1776

Prince George's County
  Consumer Protection
  Commission
1142 County Administration
  Building
Upper Marlboro, MD 20870
(301) 952-4700

City Office

Baltimore Major Fraud Unit
309 Court House
Baltimore, MD 21202
(301) 396-4997

MASSACHUSETTS

State Offices

Self-Help Consumer
  Information Office
Executive Office of Consumer
  Affairs
John W. McCormack Building
One Ashburton Pl., Room 1411
Boston, MA 02108
(617) 727-7780

Consumer Protection Division
Department of Attorney General
One Ashburton Pl., 19th Floor
Boston, MA 02108
(617) 727-8400

Branch Office

Consumer Protection Division
Department of Attorney General
20 Maple St.
Springfield, MA 01103
(413) 785-1951

County Offices

Franklin County Consumer
  Protection Agency
District Attorney's Office
Courthouse
Greenfield, MA 01301
(413) 774-5102

Hampden County Consumer
  Action Center
17 Wilbraham Rd.
PO Box 1449
Springfield, MA 01101
(413) 737-4376

Consumer Protection Agency
Hampshire County District
  Attorney's Office
Courthouse
15 Gothic St.
Northampton, MA 01060
(413) 584-1597

Worcester County Consumer
  Rights Project
399 Main St., Room 200
Worcester, MA 01608
(617) 752-3718

City Offices
Boston Mayor's Office of
  Consumer Affairs and
  Licensing
1 City Hall Plaza, Room 703
Boston, MA 02201
(617) 725-3320

Consumer Division
Lowell Community Team Work,
  Inc.
167 Dutton St.
Lowell, MA 01852
(617) 459-0551 or 6161

MICHIGAN

State Offices
Office of Attorney General
690 Law Building
Lansing, MI 48913
(517) 373-0573

Michigan Consumers Council
414 Hollister Building
106 W. Allegan St.
Lansing, MI 48933
(517) 373-0947
(800) 292-5680 (Michigan
  only)

County Offices
Bay County Consumer
  Protection
Bay County Building
Bay City, MI 48706
(517) 893-3594

Genesee County Consumer
  Affairs
206 S. Center Rd.
Burton, MI 48529
(313) 257-3161

Macomb County Office of
  Prosecuting Attorney
Macomb Court Building, 6th
  Floor
Mt. Clemens, MI 48043
(313) 469-5600

Consumer Action Center
Washtenaw County Office of
  Prosecuting Attorney
120 Catherine St.
PO Box 8645
Ann Arbor, MI 48107
(313) 994-2420

City Office
Citizens Resources Department
4500 Maple
Dearborn, MI 48126
(313) 943-2285 or 2143

City of Detroit Consumer
  Affairs Department
1600 Cadillac Tower
Detroit, MI 48226
(313) 224-3508

MINNESOTA

State Offices
Consumer Protection Division
Office of Attorney General
Room 200
117 University Ave.
St. Paul, MN 55155
(612) 296-3353

Governor's Office of Consumer
  Services
128 Metro Square Building
Seventh and Roberts Sts.
St. Paul, MN 55101
(612) 296-4512
(612) 296-2331 (Complaints)

Branch Office
Duluth Regional Office
Governor's Office of Consumer
  Services
320 W. Second St., Room 610
Duluth, MN 55802
(218) 723-4891

County Office
Hennepin County Citizen
  Protection and Economic
  Crime Unit
C2100 County Government
  Center

Minneapolis, MN 55487
(612) 348-8105
(612) 348-4528 (Complaints)

City Office
Minneapolis Department of
  Licenses and Consumer
  Service
101 A City Hall
Minneapolis, MN 55415
(612) 348-2080

MISSISSIPPI

State Offices
Consumer Protection Division
Office of Attorney General
PO Box 220
Jackson, MS 39205
(601) 961-4244

Consumer Protection Division
Department of Agriculture and
  Commerce
High and President Sts.
PO Box 1609
Jackson, MS 39205
(601) 354-6258

MISSOURI

State Offices
Trade Offense Division
Office of Attorney General
Supreme Court Building
PO Box 899
Jefferson City, MO 65102
(314) 751-2616

Missouri Department of
  Consumer Affairs, Regulation
  and Licensing
PO Box 1157
Jefferson City, MO 65102
(314) 751-4996

Branch Offices
Trade Offense Division
Office of Attorney General
431 Missouri Office Building
615 E. 13th St.
Kansas City, MO 64106
(816) 274-6686

Trade Offense Division
Office of Attorney General
111 N. Seventh St.
St. Louis, MO 63101
(314) 444-6815

MONTANA

State Office
Consumer Affairs Unit
Department of Commerce
1424 Ninth Ave.
Helena, MT 59620
(406) 449-3163

County Office
Missoula County Attorney
County Courthouse
Missoula, MT 59801
(406) 721-5700

NEBRASKA

State Office
Consumer Protection Division
Department of Justice
605 S. 14th St.
Lincoln, NE 68509
(402) 471-2682

County Office
Douglas County Attorney's
Office
909 Omaha–Douglas Civic
Center
Omaha, NE 68183
(402) 444-7625

NEVADA

State Offices
Consumer Affairs Division
Office of Attorney General
State Mail Room Complex
Las Vegas, NV 89158
(702) 386-5293

Consumer Affairs Division
Department of Commerce
State Mail Room Complex
Las Vegas, NV 89158
(702) 386-5293

Branch Office
Consumer Affairs Division
Department of Commerce
201 Nye Building
Capitol Complex
Carson City, NV 89710
(702) 885-4340
(800) 992-2973 (Nevada only)

County Office
Washoe County Consumer
Protection Division

District Attorney's Office
PO Box 11130
Reno, NV 89520
(702) 785-5652

NEW HAMPSHIRE

State Office
Consumer Protection and
Antitrust Division
Office of Attorney General
State House Annex
Concord, NH 03301
(603) 271-3641

NEW JERSEY

State Offices
Division of Consumer Affairs
Department of Law and Public
Safety
1100 Raymond Blvd., Room 504
Newark, NJ 07102
(201) 648-4010

Department of Public Advocate
PO Box 141
Trenton, NJ 08625
(609) 292-7087
(800) 792-8600 (State agency
action only)

Division of Law
1100 Raymond Blvd., Room 315
Newark, NJ 07102
(201) 648-4732

New Jersey Office of Consumer
Protection
1100 Raymond Blvd., Room 405
Newark, NJ 07102
(201) 648-4019

County Offices
Atlantic County Consumer
Affairs
1601 Atlantic Ave., 7th Floor
Atlantic City, NJ 08401
(609) 345-6700 ext. 475

Bergen County Consumer
Affairs
332 Main St.
Hackensack, NJ 07601
(201) 646-2650

Burlington County Consumer
Affairs
54 Grant St.
Mount Holly, NJ 08060
(609) 261-5054

Camden County Consumer
Affairs
Camden County Administration
Building
600 Market St. (Lower Level)
Camden, NJ 08101
(609) 757-8387

Cape May County Consumer
Affairs
Central Mail Room
Cape May Court House
Cape May, NJ 08210
(609) 465-7111 ext. 399

Cumberland County Consumer
Affairs
788 E. Commerce St.
Bridgeton, NJ 08302
(609) 451-8000

Essex County Consumer
Services
900 Bloomfield Ave.
Verona, NJ 07044
(201) 226-1571

Gloucester County Consumer
Affairs
The Cotton Building
One S. Broad St.
Woodbury, NJ 08096
(609) 845-1600

Hudson County Consumer
Affairs
County Administration Building
595 Newark Ave.
Jersey City, NJ 07306
(201) 792-3737 ext. 252, 219

Hunterdon County Consumer
Affairs
PO Box 198
Califon, NJ 07830
(201) 832-5621

Mercer County Consumer
Affairs
640 S. Broad St.
Trenton, NJ 08611
(609) 989-6671

Middlesex County Consumer
  Affairs
841 Georges Rd.
North Brunswick, NJ 08902
(201) 745-2787

Monmouth County Consumer
  Affairs
Hall of Records
Main St.
Freehold, NJ 07728
(201) 431-7900

Morris County Consumer
  Affairs
Court House
32 Washington St.
Morristown, NJ 07900
(201) 285-2811

Ocean County Consumer Affairs
C.N. 2191, County Administration Building, Room 225
Toms River, NJ 08753
(201) 929-2105 or
  (609) 693-5011

Passaic County Consumer
  Affairs
County Administration Building
309 Pennsylvania Ave.
Paterson, NJ 07503
(201) 881-4547

Salem County Consumer Affairs
County Administration Building
PO Box 24
Salem, NJ 08079
(609) 935-7510 ext. 301

Somerset County Consumer
  Affairs
County Administration Building
Somerville, NJ 08876
(201) 725-4700 ext. 306

Union County Consumer Affairs
PO Box 186
300 N. Ave. East
Westfield, NJ 07091
(201) 233-0502

Warren County Consumer
  Affairs
Court House Annex
Belvidere, NJ 07825
(201) 475-5361 ext. 353

City Offices
Belleville Consumer Affairs
Municipal Building
Belleville, NJ 07109
(201) 759-9100

Brick Consumer Affairs
Municipal Building
Brick, NJ 08723
(201) 477-3000 ext. 201

Cedar Grove Consumer Affairs
Town Hall, 525 Pompton Ave.
Cedar Grove, NJ 07009
(201) 239-1410

Cinnaminson Consumer Affairs
Municipal Building
1621 Riverton Rd.
Cinnaminson, NJ 08072
(609) 829-6000

Clark Consumer Affairs
Municipal Building
Westfield Ave.
Clark, NJ 07066
(201) 388-3600

Clifton Consumer Affairs
City Hall, 900 Clifton Ave.
Clifton, NJ 07015
(201) 473-2600 ext. 297

Cranford Consumer Affairs
Municipal Building
8 Springfield Ave.
Cranford, NJ 07016
(201) 276-8900

Denville Consumer Affairs
Municipal Building, Main St.
Denville, NJ 07834
(201) 627-8900

Deptford Township Consumer
  Affairs
542 Penn Blvd.
Woodbury, NJ 08906
(609) 845-5300 ext. 262, 375

Dunellen Consumer Affairs
Borough of Dunellen
PO Box 174
Dunellen, NJ 08812
(201) 752-0009

East Brunswick Consumer
  Affairs
Municipal Building, Ryder La.
East Brunswick, NJ 08816
(201) 254-4600

Edison Consumer Affairs
Municipal Building
Edison, NJ 08817
(201) 287-0900

Elizabeth Consumer Affairs
City Hall
60 W. Scott Pl.
Elizabeth, NJ 07203
(201) 353-6000 ext. 376

Englewood Consumer Affairs
Municipal Building
9 West St.
Englewood, NJ 07631
(201) 567-1800 ext. 208

Fort Lee Consumer Affairs
Borough Hall
Fort Lee, NJ 07024
(201) 947-5235

Freehold Consumer Affairs
Municipal Plaza
Schanck Rd.
Freehold, NJ 07728
(201) 462-7900

Garwood Consumer Affairs
Borough Hall, Center St.
Garwood, NJ 08027
(201) 789-0689

Glen Rock Consumer Affairs
Borough Hall, Harding Plaza
Glen Rock, NJ 07452
(201) 447-2555

Hackensack Consumer Affairs
Municipal Building
65 Central Ave.
Hackensack, NJ 07602
(201) 342-3000 ext. 216

Hoboken Consumer Affairs
City Hall
Washington St.
Hoboken, NJ 07030
(201) 420-2038

Kearny Consumer Affairs
26 N. Midland Ave.
Kearny, NJ 07032
(201) 991-9282

Linden Consumer Affairs
City Hall, N. Wood Ave.
Linden, NJ 07036
(201) 486-3800

Livingston Consumer Affairs
Township Hall
357 S. Livingston Ave.
Livingston, NJ 07039
(201) 992-2244

Lodi Consumer Affairs
Borough Hall, 59 Main St.
Lodi, NJ 07644
(201) 777-9100 ext. 234

Long Branch Consumer Affairs
Municipal Building, 344
   Broadway
Long Branch, NJ 07740
(201) 222-7000

Madison Consumer Affairs
Hartley Dodge Memorial
Madison, NJ 07940
(201) 377-8000

Matawan Consumer Affairs
Borough Hall
150 Main St.
Matawan, NJ 07747
(201) 566-2113

Middlesex Borough Consumer
   Affairs
1200 Mountain Ave.
Middlesex, NJ 08846
(201) 356-8090

Millburn Consumer Affairs
Town Hall, 375 Millburn Ave.
Millburn, NJ 07041
(201) 376-2030

Morristown Consumer Affairs
Municipal Building
110 South St.
Morristown, NJ 07960
(201) 538-2637

Mountainside Consumer Affairs
Municipal Building
1385 Route 22
Mountainside, NJ 07092
(201) 232-2400

Newark Office of Consumer
   Action (for North and East
   Wards)
City Hall

920 Broad St., Room B–23
Newark, NJ 07102
(201) 733-8000

Newark Office of Consumer
   Affairs (for Central, South
   and West Wards)
598 S. 11th St.
Newark, NJ 07103
(201) 733-8000

New Milford Consumer Affairs
Borough Hall
930 River Rd.
New Milford, NJ 07640
(201) 262-6100

New Providence Consumer
   Affairs
Borough Hall
New Providence, NJ 07974
(201) 665-1400

Nutley Consumer Affairs
City Hall, 228 Chestnut St.
Nutley, NJ 07110
(201) 667-3300

Paramus Consumer Affairs
Borough Hall, Jockish Square
Paramus, NJ 07652
(201) 265-2100

Parsippany Consumer Affairs
Municipal Building
1001 Parsippany Blvd.
Parsippany, NJ 07054
(201) 263-7152

Passaic City Consumer Affairs
City Hall, 330 Passaic St.
Passaic, NJ 07055
(201) 365-5520

Perth Amboy Consumer Affairs
City Hall, 44 Market St.
Perth Amboy, NJ 08861
(201) 826-0290 ext. 39

Plainfield Consumer Affairs
City Hall
Watchung Ave.
Plainfield, NJ 07701
(201) 842-6110

Red Bank Consumer Affairs
Municipal Building
32 Monmouth St.
Red Bank, NJ 07701
(201) 842-6110

Rockaway Township Consumer
   Affairs
Municipal Building
19 Mount Hope Rd.
Rockaway, NJ 07866
(201) 627-7200

Rutherford Consumer Affairs
176 Park Ave.
Rutherford, NJ 07070
(201) 939-1444

Secaucus Consumer Affairs
Municipal Building
1203 Paterson Plank Rd.
Secaucus, NJ 07094
(201) 330-2000

Sparta Consumer Affairs
65 Main St.
Sparta, NJ 07870
(201) 729-6174

Summit Consumer Affairs
City Hall
512 Springfield Ave.
Summit, NJ 07901
(201) 273-6400

Teaneck Consumer Affairs
Municipal Building
818 Teaneck Rd.
Teaneck, NJ 07666
(201) 837-1600

Union City Consumer Affairs
507 26th St.
Union City, NJ 07087
(201) 866-2255 ext. 42

Union Township Consumers
   Affairs
Municipal Building
1976 Morris Ave.
Union, NJ 07083
(201) 688-2800 ext. 240

Wayne Township Consumer
   Affairs
Municipal Building
475 Valley Rd.
Wayne, NJ 07470
(201) 694-1800 ext. 246

Weehawken Consumer Affairs
City Hall, 400 Park Ave.
Weehawken, NJ 07087
(201) 861-7000 ext. 230

West New York Consumer
Affairs
Municipal Building
428 60th St.
West New York, NJ 07093
(201) 661-7000 ext. 230

West Orange Consumer Affairs
Municipal Building
66 Main St.
West Orange, NJ 07052
(201) 325-4121

Wildwood Action Line
4400 New Jersey Ave.
Wildwood, NJ 08260
(609) 729-4444

Willingboro Consumer Affairs
Municipal Complex, Salem Rd.
Willingboro, NJ 08046
(609) 877-2200

Woodbridge Township
Consumer Affairs
Municipal Building
One Main St.
Woodbridge, NJ 07095
(201) 634-4500 ext. 231

NEW MEXICO

State Office
Consumer and Economic Crime
Division
Office of Attorney General
PO Box 1508
Santa Fe, NM 87503
(505) 982-6916

County Office
Consumer Affairs Division
Bernalillo County District
Attorney's Office
15 Tijeras
Albuquerque, NM 87102
(505) 848-1000

NEW YORK

State Offices
New York State Consumer
Protection Board
99 Washington Ave.
Albany, NY 12210
(518) 474-8583

Consumer Frauds and
Protection Bureau
Office of Attorney General

State Capitol
Albany, NY 12224
(518) 474-8686

Branch Offices
Office of Attorney General
110 Genesee St., Room 23
Auburn, NY 13021
(315) 253-9765

Office of Attorney General
38 Riverside Dr.
Binghamton, NY 13905
(607) 773-7823

Office of Attorney General
65 Court St.
Buffalo, NY 14202
(716) 842-4396

Office of Attorney General
State Office Building
Veterans Memorial Hwy.
Hauppage, NY 11788
(516) 979-5190

New York State Consumer
Protection Board
2 World Trade Center
Room 8225, 82nd Floor
New York, NY 10047
(212) 488-5666

Consumer Frauds and
Protection Bureau
Office of Attorney General
2 World Trade Center
New York, NY 10047
(212) 488-7450

Office of Attorney General
70 Clinton St.
Plattsburgh, NY 12001
(518) 563-8012

Office of Attorney General
40 Garden St.
Poughkeepsie, NY 12601
(914) 452-7744

Office of Attorney General
900 Reynolds Arcade
116 E. Main St.
Rochester, NY 14614
(716) 454-4540

Office of Attorney General
333 E. Washington St.
Syracuse, NY 13202–1471
(315) 473-8181

Office of Attorney General
207 Genesee St.
Utica, NY 13501
(315) 797-6120 ext. 2225

Office of Attorney General
317 Washington St.
Watertown, NY 13601
(315) 782-0100 ext. 444

County Offices
Broome County Bureau of
Consumer Affairs
PO Box 1766, Governmental
Plaza
Binghamton, NY 13902
(607) 772-2868

Erie County District Attorney's
Office
25 Delaware Ave.
Buffalo, NY 14202
(716) 855-2424

Erie County Consumer
Protection Committee
95 Franklin St.
Buffalo, NY 14202
(716) 846-6690

Consumer Frauds and Economic
Crimes Bureau
Kings County District
Attorney's Office
210 Joralemon St.
Brooklyn, NY 11201
(212) 834-5000

Nassau County Office of
Consumer Affairs
160 Old Country Rd.
Mineola, NY 11501
(516) 535-3100

Nassau County Commercial
Frauds and Environmental
Investigations Bureau
262 Old Country Rd.
Mineola, NY 11501
(516) 535-2164

Oneida County Consumer
Affairs
County Office Building
800 Park Ave.
Utica, NY 13501
(315) 798-5601

Onondaga County Office of
Consumer Affairs
County Civic Center
421 Montgomery St.
Syracuse, NY 13202
(315) 425-3479

Orange County Department of
Weights and Measures and
Consumer Affairs
99 Main St., Courthouse Annex
Goshen, NY 10924
(914) 294-5151 ext. 162

Orange County District
Attorney's Office of Consumer
Affairs
County Government Center
Goshen, NY 10924
(914) 294-5471

Putnam County Department of
Consumer Affairs
County Office Building
Carmel, NY 10512
(914) 225-3641 ext. 215

Rensselaer County Citizens
Affairs
1600 Seventh Ave.
Troy, NY 12180
(518) 270-5444

Rockland County Office of
Consumer Protection
County Office Building
18 New Hampstead Rd.
New City, NY 10956
(914) 425-5280

Steuben County Department of
Weights and Measures and
Consumer Affairs
40 E. Steuben St.
Bath, NY 14810
(607) 776-4949

Suffolk County Department of
Consumer Affairs
Suffolk County Center
Hauppage, Long Island, NY
11787
(516) 360-4618

Ulster County Consumer Fraud
Bureau
285 Wall St.

Kingston, NY 12401
(914) 339-5680 ext. 240, 243,
244

Warren County Weights and
Measures and Consumer
Protection
Municipal Center
Lake George, NY 12845
(518) 792-9951 ext. 264

Westchester County District
Attorney's Office
County Courthouse
111 Grove St.
White Plains, NY 10601
(914) 682-3300

City Offices
Babylon Consumer Protection
Board
200 E. Sunrise Hwy.
Lindenhurst, NY 11757
(516) 957-3021

Brookhaven Citizens' Advocate
Town of Brookhaven
475 E. Main St.
Patchogue, NY 11772
(516) 654-7929

Colonie Consumer Protection
Board
Memorial Town Hall
Newtonville, NY 12128
(518) 783-2790

Cortlandt Consumer Affairs
Bureau
Municipal Building
Croton-on-Hudson, NY 10520
(914) 271-6651

Huntington Consumer
Protection Board
100 Main St.
Town Hall
Huntington, NY 11743
(516) 351-3012

Islip Town Citizens Action
Bureau
Islip Town Hall
50 Irish La.
East Islip, NY 11730
(516) 224-5510

Mt. Vernon Office of Consumer
Affairs
City Hall

Mt. Vernon, NY 10550
(914) 668-6000 ext. 231

New York City Department of
Consumer Affairs
80 Lafayette St.
New York, NY 10013
(212) 566-5456

Bronx Neighborhood Office
New York City Department of
Consumer Affairs
1932 Arthur Ave.
Bronx, NY 10457
(212) 299-1400

Brooklyn Neighborhood Office
New York City Department of
Consumer Affairs
209 Joralemon St., Room 6
Brooklyn, NY 11201
(212) 596-4780

Harlem Neighborhood Office
New York City Department of
Consumer Affairs
227 E. 116th St.
New York, NY 10029
(212) 348-0600

Queens Neighborhood Office
New York City Department of
Consumer Affairs
120–55 Queens Blvd.
Room 203
Kew Gardens, NY 11424
(212) 261-2922 or 2923

Staten Island Neighborhood
Office
New York City Department of
Consumer Affairs
Staten Island Borough Hall
Staten Island, NY 10301
(212) 390-5154 or 5155

Orangeburg Consumer
Protection Board
Orangeburg Town Hall
26 Orangeburg Rd.
Orangeburg, NY 10962–1798
(914) 359-5100

Oswego Office of Consumer
Affairs, Weights and
Measures
City Hall
Oswego, NY 13126
(315) 342-5600 ext. 66

Ramapo Consumer Protection
Board
Ramapo Town Hall
Route 59
Suffern, NY 10901
(914) 357-5100 ext. 267

Schenectady Bureau of
Consumer Protection
22 City Hall
Jay St.
Schenectady, NY 12305
(518) 382-5061

Syracuse Consumer Affairs
Office
422 City Hall
223 E. Washington St.
Syracuse, NY 13202
(315) 473-3240

White Plains Department of
Weights and Measures
279 Hamilton Ave.
White Plains, NY 10601
(914) 682-4273

Yonkers Office of Consumer
Protection
201 Palisade Ave.
Yonkers, NY 10703
(914) 965-0707
(914) 963-3980 ext. 301

NORTH CAROLINA

State Offices
Consumer Protection Division
Department of Justice Building
PO Box 629
Raleigh, NC 27602
(919) 733-7741

Office of Consumer Services
Department of Agriculture
PO Box 27647
Raleigh, NC 27611
(919) 733-7125

NORTH DAKOTA

State Offices
Attorney General for the State
of North Dakota
State Capitol Building
Bismarck, ND 58505
(701) 224-2210

Consumer Fraud Division
Office of Attorney General
State Capitol Building
Bismarck, ND 58505
(701) 224-3404
(800) 472-2600 (North Dakota
only)

Consumer Affairs Office
State Laboratories Department
Box 937
Bismarck, ND 58505
(701) 224-2485
(800) 472-2927 (North Dakota
only)

County Office
Quad County Community
Action Agency
27½ S. Third St.
Grand Forks, ND 58201
(701) 746-5431

OHIO

State Offices
Consumer Frauds and Crimes
Section
Office of Attorney General
30 E. Broad St., 15th Floor
Columbus, OH 43215
(614) 466-8831 or 4986
1 (800) 282-0515 (Ohio only)

County Offices
Franklin County Office of
Prosecuting Attorney
Hall of Justice
369 S. High St.
Columbus, OH 43215
(614) 462-3248

Greene County Community
Action Committee
194 E. Church St.
Xenia, OH 45385
(513) 376-1351

Consumer Protection Division
Lake County Office of
Prosecuting Attorney
Lake County Court House
Painesville, OH 44077
(216) 352-6281 ext. 281

Medina County Prosecutor's
Office
219 E. Washington St.

Medina, OH 44256
(216) 723-3641 ext. 38

Montgomery County Fraud
Section
County Courts Building
41 N. Perry
Dayton, OH 45422
(513) 228-5126

Portage County Prosecutor's
Office
247 S. Chestnut St.
Ravenna, OH 44266
(216) 296-4593

Summit County Bureau of
Investigations
53 E. Center St.
Akron, OH 44308
(216) 379-5510

City Offices
Akron Division of Weights and
Measures and Consumer
Protection
1420 Triplett Blvd.
Akron, OH 44306
(216) 375-2878

Canton City Sealer and
Commissioner of Consumer
Protection
919 Walnut Ave. NE
Canton, OH 44704
(216) 489-3065

Cincinnati Consumer Protection
Division
City Solicitor's Office
236 City Hall
Cincinnati, OH 45202
(513) 352-3971

Cleveland Office of Consumer
Affairs
119 City Hall
601 Lakeside Ave.
Cleveland, OH 44114
(216) 664-3200

Columbus Community Services
50 W. Gay St., 4th Floor
Columbus, OH 43215
(614) 222-7144

Youngstown Division of
  Consumer Affairs
Mill Creek Community Center
496 Glenwood Ave.
Youngstown, OH 44502
(216) 747-3561

OKLAHOMA

State Offices
Department of Complaints,
  Investigation and Mediation
Oklahoma Corporation
  Commission
Jim Thorpe Building, Room 680
Oklahoma City, OK 73105
(405) 521-4113

Assistant Attorney General for
  Consumer Protection
Office of Attorney General
112 State Capitol Building
Oklahoma City, OK 73105-4894
(405) 521-3921

OREGON

State Offices
Consumer Protection and
  Services Division
Department of Justice
500 Pacific Building
520 S.W. Yamhill St.
Portland, OR 97204
(503) 229-5522

Consumer Affairs Advisor
Oregon Department of
  Agriculture
635 Capitol St., N.E.
Salem, OR 97310
(503) 378-4665
(800) 452-7813 (Oregon only)

Branch Office
Consumer Protection and
  Services Division
Department of Justice
111 Labor and Industries
  Building
Salem, OR 97310
(503) 378-4320

PENNSYLVANIA

State Offices
Bureau of Consumer Protection
Office of Attorney General

Strawberry Square—15th Floor
Harrisburg, PA 17120
(717) 787-9707

Office of Consumer Advocate-
  Utilities
Office of Attorney General
1425 Strawberry Square
Harrisburg, PA 17120
(717) 783-5048 (Utilities only)

Branch Offices
Bureau of Consumer Protection
Office of Attorney General
27 N. Seventh St.
Allentown, PA 18101
(215) 821-6690

Bureau of Consumer Protection
Office of Attorney General
919 State St., Room 203
Erie, PA 16501
(814) 871-4371

Bureau of Consumer Protection
Office of Attorney General
333 Market St., 17th Floor
Harrisburg, PA 17120
(717) 787-7109

Bureau of Consumer Protection
Office of Attorney General
1405 Locust St., Suite 825
Philadelphia, PA 19102
(215) 238-6475

Bureau of Consumer Protection
Office of Attorney General
300 Liberty Ave., Room 1405
Pittsburgh, PA 15222
(412) 565-5135

Bureau of Consumer Protection
Office of Attorney General
1405 State Office Building
Pittsburgh, PA 15222
(412) 565-5395

Bureau of Consumer Protection
Office of Attorney General
507 Linden St., 1st Floor
Scranton, PA 18503
(717) 961-4913

Executive Deputy Attorney
  General for Public Protection
Office of Attorney General

1511 Strawberry Square
Harrisburg, PA 17120
(717) 787-9716

County Offices
Beaver County Alliance for
  Consumer Protection
Public Works Building
Route 51
Fallston, PA 15066
(412) 728-5700 ext. 422

Bucks County Department of
  Consumer Protection
Administration Annex
Broad and Union Sts.
Doylestown, PA 18901
(215) 348-2911

Chester County Bureau of
  Weights and Measures and
  Consumer Affairs
326 N. Walnut St.
West Chester, PA 19380
(215) 431-6150

Cumberland County Office of
  Consumer Affairs
114 N. Hanover
Carlisle, PA 17013
(717) 249-5802

Delaware County Office of
  Consumer Affairs, Weights
  and Measures
Toal Building
Second and Orange Sts.
Media, PA 19063
(215) 891-4865

Indiana County Consumer
  Affairs Bureau
PO Box 187
Indiana, PA 15701
(412) 465-5531

Lancaster County Consumer
  Protection Commission
PO Box 3480
50 N. Duke St.
Lancaster, PA 17603
(717) 299-7921

Montgomery County Consumer
  Affairs Department
County Courthouse
Norristown, PA 19404
(215) 278-3565

City Offices
Mayor's Office of Consumer
  Services
121 City Hall
Philadelphia, PA 19107
(215) 686-7595

Economic Crime Unit
Philadelphia District
  Attorney's Office
1300 Chestnut St.
Philadelphia, PA 19107
(215) 875-6038

RHODE ISLAND

State Offices
Consumer Protection Unit
Department of Attorney General
72 Pine St.
Providence, RI 02903
(401) 277-3163

Rhode Island Consumers'
  Council
365 Broadway
Providence, RI 02909
(401) 277-2764

SOUTH CAROLINA

State Offices
Office of Citizens Service
Office of the Governor
PO Box 11450
Columbia, SC 29211
(803) 758-3261

Department of Consumer
  Affairs
600 Columbia Building
PO Box 5757
Columbia, SC 29250
(803) 758-2040
(800) 922-1594 (South
  Carolina only)

Consumer Fraud and Antitrust
  Section
Office of Attorney General
PO Box 11549
Columbia, SC 29211
(803) 758-3040

State Ombudsman
Office of Executive Policy and
  Program
1205 Pendleton St., Room 412
Columbia, SC 29201
(803) 758-2249

SOUTH DAKOTA

State Office
Division of Consumer
  Protection
Office of Attorney General
Insurance Building
Pierre, SD 57501
(605) 773-4400
(800) 592-1865 (South Dakota
  only)

TENNESSEE

State Offices
Division of Consumer Affairs
Department of Agriculture
Box 40627 Melrose Station
Nashville, TN 37204
(615) 741-1461
(800) 342-8385 (Tennessee
  only)

Antitrust and Consumer
  Protection Division
Office of Attorney General
450 James Robertson Pkwy.
Nashville, TN 37219
(615) 741-2672

City Office
Nashville Mayor's Office of
  Consumer Affairs
107 Metro Courthouse
Nashville, TN 37201
(615) 259-6047

TEXAS

State Office
Consumer Protection and
  Antitrust Division
Office of Attorney General
PO Box 12548, Capitol Station
Austin, TX 78711
(512) 475-3288

Branch Offices
Office of Attorney General
1607 Main St., Suite 1400
Dallas, TX 75201
(214) 742-8944

Office of Attorney General
4824 Alberta St., Suite 160
El Paso, TX 79905
(915) 533-3484

Office of Attorney General
1220 Dallas Ave., Suite 202
Houston, TX 77002-6986
(713) 650-0666

Office of Attorney General
312 County Office Building
806 Broadway
Lubbock, TX 79401
(806) 747-5238

Office of Attorney General
4309 N. 10th, Suite B
McAllen, TX 78501
(512) 682-4547

Office of Attorney General
200 Main Plaza, Suite 400
San Antonio, TX 78205
(512) 225-4191

County Offices
Dallas County Consumer Fraud
  Division
Special Crime Division
2700 Stemmons Expressway
500 Stemmons Tower East
Dallas, TX 75207
(214) 630-6300

Harris County Consumer Fraud
  Division
Office of District Attorney
201 Fannin, Suite 200
Houston, TX 77002
(713) 221-5836

Tarrant County Economic
  Crimes
200 W. Belknap St.
Fort Worth, TX 76102
(Criminal Consumer Fraud)
(817) 334-1897

Travis County Consumer Affairs
  Office
Suite 624B
N. Pleasant Valley Rd.
Austin, TX 78702
(512) 473-9133

District Attorney for Austin,
  Fayette, and Waller Counties
PO Drawer 10
Bellville, TX 77418-0010
(713) 865-3693

City Offices
Dallas Department of Consumer
  Services
1500 W. Mockingbird,
  Room A–19
Dallas, TX 75235
(214) 670-6414

Fort Worth Office of Consumer
  Affairs, Weights and Measures
1800 University Dr.
Room 208
Fort Worth, TX 76107
(817) 870-7570

San Antonio Housing
  Counseling Program
Department of Human
  Resources
410 S. Main St.
San Antonio, TX 78204
(512) 299-7857

UTAH

State Offices
Division of Consumer Affairs
Utah State Trade Commission
Department of Business
  Regulation
330 E. Fourth South
Salt Lake City, UT 84111
(801) 533-6441

Office of Attorney General
124 State Capitol
Salt Lake City, UT 84114
(801) 533-4262

VERMONT

State Offices
Consumer Protection Division
Office of Attorney General
109 State St.
Montpelier, VT 05602
(802) 828-3171
(800) 642-5149 (Vermont
  only)

VIRGINIA

State Offices
Division of Consumer Counsel
Office of Attorney General
11 S. 12th St., Suite 308
Richmond, VA 23219
(804) 786-4075

State Office of Consumer
  Affairs
Department of Agriculture and
  Consumer Services
Box 1163, Washington Blvd.
Richmond, VA 23209
(804) 786-2042

Branch Office
State Office of Consumer
  Affairs
3016 Williams Dr.
Fairfax, VA 22031
(703) 573-1286 (Complaints)

County Offices
Arlington County Office of
  Consumer Affairs
2049 15th St., North
Arlington, VA 22201
(703) 558-2142

Fairfax County Department of
  Consumer Affairs
4031 University Dr.
Fairfax, VA 22030
(703) 691-3214

Prince William County Office
  of Consumer Affairs
15960 Cardinal Dr.
Woodbridge, VA 22191
(703) 221-4156

City Offices
Alexandria Office of Consumer
  Affairs
PO Box 178
City Hall
Alexandria, VA 22313
(703) 838-4350

Norfolk Division of Consumer
  Affairs
804 City Hall Building
Norfolk, VA 23501
(804) 441-2821

Roanoke Consumer Protection
  Division
353 Municipal Building
215 Church Ave., S.W.
Roanoke, VA 24011
(703) 981-2583

Virginia Beach Division of
  Consumer Protection
City Hall

Virginia Beach, VA 23456
(804) 427-4421

WASHINGTON

State Offices
Consumer Protection and
  Antitrust Division
Office of Attorney General
1366 Dexter Horton Building
Seattle, WA 98104
(206) 464-7744
(800) 552-0700 (Washington
  only)

Office of Consumer Services
Washington State Department
  of Agriculture
406 General Administration
  Building, AX41
Olympia, WA 98504
(206) 753-0929

Branch Offices
Consumer Protection Division
Office of Attorney General
Temple of Justice
Olympia, WA 98504
(206) 753-6210

Spokane Office of Attorney
  General
960 Paulsen Professional
  Building
Spokane, WA 99201
(509) 456-3123

Office of Attorney General
949 Market St.
Tacoma, WA 98402
(206) 593-2904

County Office
King County District Attorney's
  Office
E531 King County Courthouse
Seattle, WA 98104
(206) 583-4513

City Offices
Everett Weights and Measures
  Department
City Hall
3002 Wetmore Ave.
Everett, WA 98201
(206) 259-8845

Seattle Department of Licenses
and Consumer Affairs
102 Municipal Building
Seattle, WA 98104
(206) 625-2536
(206) 625-2712 (Complaints)

WEST VIRGINIA

State Offices
Consumer Protection Division
Office of Attorney General
1204 Kanawha Blvd. East
Charleston, WV 25301
(304) 348-8986

Consumer Protection Division
Department of Labor
1900 Washington Street East
Charleston, WV 25305
(304) 348-7890

City Office
Charleston Consumer Protection
Department
PO Box 2749
Charleston, WV 25330
(304) 348-8173

WISCONSIN

State Offices
Office of Consumer Protection
Department of Justice
PO Box 7856
Madison, WI 53707-7856
(608) 266-1852

Division of Trade and Consumer
Protection
Department of Agriculture,
Trade, and Consumer
Protection
PO Box 8911
801 W. Badger Rd.

Madison, WI 53708
(608) 266-9837
(800) 362-3020 (Wisconsin
only)

Northwest District Office
Department of Agriculture,
Trade, and Consumer
Protection
1727 Loring St.
Altoona, WI 54720
(715) 836-2861

Northeast District Office
Department of Agriculture,
Trade, and Consumer
Protection
1181 A Western Ave.
Green Bay, WI 54303
(414) 497-4087

Southeast District Office
Department of Agriculture,
Trade, and Consumer
Protection
10320 W. Silver Spring Dr.
Milwaukee, WI 53225
(414) 257-8962

Office of Consumer Protection
Milwaukee State Office Building
819 N. Sixth St., Room 520
Milwaukee, WI 53203
(414) 224-1867

County Offices
Kenosha County Consumer
Investigator
912 56th St.
Kenosha, WI 53140
(414) 656-6480

Marathon County District
Attorney's Office
Marathon County Court House
Wausau, WI 54401
(715) 842-0471

Milwaukee County Consumer
Fraud Unit
821 W. State St.
Room 604
Milwaukee, WI 53233–1487
(414) 278-4628

Portage County District
Attorney's Office
Consumer Fraud Unit
Portage County Court House
Stevens Point, WI 54481
(715) 346-3393

WYOMING

State Office
Office of Attorney General
123 Capitol Building
Cheyenne, WY 82002
(307) 777-7841 or 6286

PUERTO RICO

Department of Consumer Affairs
Minillas Governmental Center
Torre Norte Building
De Diego Ave., Stop 22
PO Box 41059
Santurce, PR 00940
(809) 726-6090

Department of Justice
Box 192
Old San Juan, PR 00902
(809) 722-5217

VIRGIN ISLANDS

Consumer Service
Administration
Golden Rock
Christiansted, St. Croix
U.S. VI 00820
(809) 773-2226

Consumer Information—General

Consumer Information Center
Pueblo, CO 81009
Consumer Information Center
General Services Administration
Washington, DC 20405

Two of the most accessible sources for many different kinds of consumer information. Start by asking for the *Consumer Information Catalogue* (available from both sources), which introduces hundreds of publications available from the government on insulation, residential framing, fire safety, you name it. The catalog is updated quarterly.

Consumer Information— Regulations and Standards

Federal Trade Commission
Bureau of Consumer Protection
Sixth and Pennsylvania NW
Washington, DC 20580
(202) 523-3667

FTC's List of Publications contains an extensive listing of booklets and brochures, many at no charge, on such subjects as woodstoves, home siding, R values, warranties, sun reflective film, and more. The list is free and a good place to start looking for specific information sources. FTC also publishes a *Consumer's Resource Handbook* (also available from the Consumer Information Center, Pueblo, CO 81009), which is a 90-page listing of government agencies (state by state and even county by county), including services for the handicapped, state utility commissions, Better Business Bureaus, state and local consumer protection agencies, and more. Regional offices of the FTC follow.

ATLANTA

1718 Peachtree St., N.W.
Suite 1000
Atlanta, GA 30367
(404) 881-4836

Alabama	North Carolina
Florida	South Carolina
Georgia	Tennessee
Mississippi	Virginia

BOSTON

150 Causeway St., Room 1301
Boston, MA 02114
(617) 223-6621

Connecticut	New Hampshire
Maine	Rhode Island
Massachusetts	Vermont

CHICAGO

55 E. Monroe St., Suite 1437
Chicago, IL 60603
(312) 353-4423

Illinois	Minnesota
Indiana	Missouri
Iowa	Wisconsin
Kentucky	

CLEVELAND

118 St. Clair Ave., Suite 500
Cleveland, OH 44114
(216) 552-4207

Delaware	Ohio
Maryland	Pennsylvania
Michigan	West Virginia
New York (West of Rochester)	

DALLAS

2001 Bryan St., Suite 2665
Dallas, TX 75201
(214) 767-0032

Arizona	Oklahoma
Louisiana	Texas
New Mexico	

DENVER

1405 Curtis St., Suite 2900
Denver, CO 80202
(303) 837-2271

Colorado	North Dakota
Kansas	South Dakota
Montana	Utah
Nebraska	Wyoming

LOS ANGELES

11000 Wilshire Blvd.
Los Angeles, CA 90024
(213) 824-7575

Arizona	
Southern California	

NEW YORK
26 Federal Plaza
Room 2243–EB
New York, NY 10278
(212) 264-1207
New Jersey
New York (East of Rochester)

SAN FRANCISCO
450 Golden Gate Ave.
San Francisco, CA 94102
(415) 556-1270
Hawaii
Nevada
Northern California

SEATTLE
915 2nd Ave., 28th Floor
Seattle, WA 98174
(206) 442-4655
Alaska   Oregon
Idaho   Washington

Consumer Prices/Trends

U.S. Department of Labor
Bureau of Labor Statistics
441 G St. NW
Washington, DC 20212
(202) 523-1913

This is one agency of the government that keeps track of who buys what and for how much. It may be of value when you are planning to build, buy, or relocate. Its monthly newsletter, which is free, covers just about all phases of consumer spending and trends and may help you with long-term purchases—such as hurrying or waiting with your $10,000 order for building materials to save a few percentage points.

Business operation You can get your name on the department's list by calling (202) 523-1222 or by writing: Chief, Branch of Inquiries and Correspondence, at the address above.

Consumer Product Protection

U.S. Consumer Product Safety
   Commission
Washington, DC 20207
(800) 638-8326 (Toll-free)
(800) 492-8363 (Toll-free Maryland
   only)
(800) 638-8333 (Toll-free Alaska,
   Hawaii, Puerto Rico, Virgin Islands
   only)

Before you invest in tools, construction equipment, major appliances, and many other products used in and around your home, contact this agency for information about the product—not necessarily a specific recommendation such as you would find in *Consumer Reports*, for example, but for information that will help you evaluate the alternatives. The CPSC covers most consumer products used in and around homes, schools, and recreation areas. The commission sets and enforces minimum safety standards and may if required, ban dangerous products. It has an extensive list of publications on topics ranging from children's furniture, flammable products of all kinds, poisonous paints and other materials to safety planning guides. You can write to the headquarters for this list, for information on recently made rules, to inquire about specific product types, and more, or contact your regional or district office.

CPSC, 1330 W. Peachtree St., Atlanta, GA 30309; (404) 881-2231
CPSC, 100 Summer St., Room 1607, Boston, MA 02110; (617) 223-5576
CPSC, 230 S. Dearborn St., Room 2945, Chicago, IL 60604; (312) 353-8260
CPSC, Metro Square, Suite 580, Seventh and Roberts Sts., St. Paul, MN 55101; (612) 725-7781
CPSC, Plaza Nine Building, Room 520, 55 Erieview Plaza, Cleveland, OH 44114; (216) 522-3886
CPSC, 1100 Commerce St., Room 1C10, Dallas, TX 75242; (214) 767-0841

CPSC, Midland Building, Suite 1000, 1221 Baltimore Ave., Kansas City, MO 64105; (816) 374-2034

CPSC, Guaranty Bank Building, Suite 938, 817 17th St., Denver, CO 80202; (303) 837-2904

CPSC, 3660 Wilshire Boulevard, Suite 1100, Los Angeles, CA 90010; (213) 688-7272

CPSC, 6 World Trade Center, Vesey St., 6th Floor, New York, NY 10048; (212) 264-1125

CPSC, 400 Market St., 10th Floor, Philadelphia, PA 19106; (215) 597-9105

CPSC, U.S. Customs House, 555 Battery St., Room 416, San Francisco, CA 94111; (415) 556-1816

CPSC, 3240 Federal Building, 915 Second Ave., Seattle, WA 98174; (206) 442-5276

Consumer Protection

Federal Trade Commission
Office of Public Affairs
Sixth and Pennsylvania Ave. NW
Washington, DC 20580
(202) 523-3598

Program information: Distribution Branch, Room 270, Washington, DC 20580; (202) 523-3667

Consumer education: Bureau of Consumer Protection, Washington, DC 20580; (202) 724-1870

Rulemaking, funding: Office of the General Counsel, Washington, DC 20580; (202) 357-0258

Warranties: (202) 523-1642 (FTC, Washington, DC 20580)

Warranty complaints: (202) 523-1670 (FTC, Washington, DC 20580)

Advertising claims: (202) 724-1499 (FTC, Washington, DC 20580)

Energy-saving claims. (202) 724-1515 (FTC, Washington, DC 20580)

New home warranties: (202) 523-3911 (FTC, Washington, DC 20580)

These are just a few of the sources for home consumers at the Federal Trade Commission. Write to the FTC Washington, DC, address and print CONSUMER INFORMATION on the envelope to get a list of their programs, specific information on specific programs, an extensive list of free booklets on such subjects as home insulation, woodstove safety, warranties, and more. This agency, unlike grass roots community groups and industry consumer groups, does have teeth. This is the place that can put the bad apples out of business, if, and only if, enough people write or call and tell them who the bad apples are and what they're doing that should be stopped. FTC also has several regional offices:

FTC, 150 Causeway St., Boston, MA 02114; (617) 223-6621

FTC, 26 Federal Plaza, New York, NY 10007; (212) 264-1207

FTC, 118 St. Clair Ave., Cleveland, OH 44114; (216) 522-4207

FTC, 1718 Peachtree St. NW, Atlanta, GA 30367; (404) 881-4836

FTC, 450 Golden Gate Ave., San Francisco, CA 94102; (415) 556-1270

FTC, 55 E. Monroe St., Chicago, IL 60603; (312) 353-4423

FTC, 1405 Curtis St., Denver, CO 80202; (303) 837-2271

FTC, 2001 Bryan St., Dallas, TX 75201; (214) 767-0032

FTC, 11000 Wilshire Blvd., Los Angeles, CA 90024; (213) 824-7575

FTC, 915 Second Ave., Seattle, WA 98174; (206) 442-4655

Energy Conservation
Office of Building Research and
   Development
Conservation and Renewable Energy
Department of Energy
Washington, DC 20585
(202) 252-1650

The Residential Conservation Service (RCS) is a program mandated by the 1978 National Energy Conservation Policy Act. Its principal feature is one that many home consumers still do not know about, called *energy audits*. The law states that all large electric and natural gas utility companies must provide a range of services to their consumers, all geared to saving energy. This means that if you call your local utility company, it is required to perform this service and is not allowed to charge you more than $15. In many cases the service is offered free. A representative from the utility company will come to your home and work through a checklist covering caulking, weatherstripping, insulation, furnace efficiency, and more to evaluate what you have, how much it would cost to make improvements, and how much energy you would save if the improvements were made. In many cases low-cost financing can be arranged.

Business operation   Write to the Department of Energy at the above address for information on the program. Ask for the RCS Fact Sheet, which covers the basics of the program; and also the RCS Publications List. The special phone number for this program is (202) 252-1650; address letters Attention Mr. Jeff Gibson.

Energy-Related Inventions
U.S. Department of Commerce
National Bureau of Standards

Office of Energy-Related Inventions
   (OERI)
Building 225-A46
Washington, DC 20234
(301) 921-3694

One of the most interesting uses of taxpayers' money I've found is this unique office that serves people, not scientists or experts or universities, but just people, who have an idea about how to save energy. The purpose of this program is to evaluate and then select promising energy-related inventions for recommendation to the Department of Energy as candidates for government support. Certain specific procedures must be followed to submit your idea and disclose its details under protection. To do this, write for OERI Form 1019 and complete details of the program. The program covers inventions that involve energy conservation and alternative sources of energy. It is necessary that the idea, and the savings, be calculated in detail. A very interesting way to take your idea out of the shop and into the real world. Maybe it will work out there.

Government Operations Reports
U.S. General Accounting Office (GAO)
Washington, DC 20548

Many of the subjects listed with a condensed description in the publication called *Monthly List of GAO Reports* will not have anything to do with house and home—claim settlements with navy shipbuilders, for instance. However, since the mailing is free on request, and does cover energy, housing, and other such subjects, it is worth writing for. Write to the Document Handling and Information Services Facility, PO Box 6015, Gaithersburg, MD 20877.

Handicapped

National Center for a Barrier Free
    Environment
1140 Connecticut Ave. NW
Washington, DC 20036
(202) 466-6896

One of the best sources of information for planning and design that will not create barrier hardships for handicapped persons. You can write for extensive and detailed information, including home design guidelines and other specific plans. For additional help in this field also contact the Clearinghouse on the Handicapped, Office of Special Education and Rehabilitation Services, U.S. Department of Education, 400 Maryland Ave. SW, Washington, DC 20202; (202) 245-0080.

Historic Preservation

Office of Archeology and Historical
    Preservation
National Park Service, Department of
    the Interior
Washington, DC 20240

A source of general information on restoration and identifying architecturally significant structures. This office will provide a current list of names and addresses for all state historical preservation officers, a bibliography of reference books and periodicals, and preliminary planning information for restoration projects. Act quickly, as the emphasis at this department under Secretary James Watt has swung to making money off the real estate heritage of the country and away from preserving what has managed to survive.

Industry/Labor Statistics

U.S. Department of Labor
Bureau of Labor Statistics
441 G St. NW
Washington, DC 20212
(202) 523-1222

This agency produces statistics on the economy, industry, and labor, makes employment projections, evaluates housing costs (write for the booklet *Rent or Buy?: Evaluating Alternatives in the Shelter Market*, $1.50), provides listings, membership figures, and other information about national labor unions and employee associations, and more. It produces so much information that the most sensible place to start is with its Report No. 552, *Major Programs Bureau of Labor Statistics*. Another report, published every 2 years, of particular interest to those seeking information on education and training, is *Occupational Outlook Handbook* ($9), which covers what workers do on the job, average earnings, training and education required, places of employment, and the outlook for employment for over 400 occupations in 40 major industries.

Information Services

National Technical Information Service
    (NTIS)
5282 Port Royal Rd.
Springfield, VA 22161
(703) 487-4600

This may be the most important source in this book, particularly if you are interested in accumulating a wide variety of information from many different sources on a particular technical subject. NTIS is an agency of the U.S. Department of Commerce and is the little known but central source for public sale of U.S. government sponsored research, development, and engineering reports, foreign technical reports, and other analyses prepared by national and local governments and the agencies that work for them. Here's how the system works. First, write the NTIS for a free (at least for now), massive catalog entitled *Current Published Searches*. This is a bargain, even if you have to pay for it (my information is that there will soon be a $5 charge). Inside is an almost endless listing of subjects, including the R&D of some 350 federal agencies, and under each subject is a list of reference bibliographies you can order. This listing (with synopses) is called a published search and represents about 100 or more publications on that single subject. Some of the more general and more arcane subjects covered are acoustic surface waves, air conditioning, cryogenics, consumer affairs, fuel cells, furnaces, molecular sieves, and mobile homes. It's endless. A great way to acquire the current technical data on just about any home consumer subject.

Mobile Homes/Manufactured Housing

U.S. Department of Housing and Urban
 Development
Manufactured Housing Standards Division
Washington, DC 20410

By now a significant part of the housing market in this country, mobile/manufactured housing is beginning to get greater attention. That means rules and regulations and also some long-needed construction and health standards covering issues like ventilation and insulation gases. Probably the most authoritative and complete source on the subject is the Fourth Report to Congress on Mobile Homes, HUD document HUD–NVACP–564. It is voluminous, covering fire starts, accidents, common defects and solutions, research and test data, rule making, and status of research grants—undoubtedly more than you really need. Another, smaller HUD reprint (from the Federal Register) may also help. It is called *Mobile Home Construction and Safety Standards*. Following is a state by state listing of approved state administrative agencies where you can get information and answers on all aspects of mobile and manufactured housing.

ALABAMA

Department of Insurance
Fire Marshal's Office
445 S. McDonough St.
Montgomery, AL 36130
(205) 832-5844

ARIZONA

Office of Manufactured Housing
1645 W. Jefferson
Phoenix, AZ 85007
(602) 255-4072

ARKANSAS

Manufactured Home
  Commission
1022 High St., Suite 505
Little Rock, AR 72202
(501) 371-1641

CALIFORNIA

Manufactured Housing Section
Division of Codes & Standards
Department of Housing and
  Community Development
PO Box 31
Sacramento, CA 95801
(916) 445-9471

COLORADO

Division of Housing
Department of Local Affairs
1313 Sherman St., Room 523
Denver, CO 80203
(303) 839-2033

FLORIDA

Department of Highway Safety
  and Motor Vehicles
Division of Motor Vehicles
2900 Apalachee Pkwy.
Tallahassee, FL 32301
(904) 488-7657

GEORGIA

State Fire Marshal's Office
Office of the Comptroller
  General
7 Martin Luther King, Jr. Dr.
  SW
Atlanta, GA 30334
(404) 656-2064

IDAHO

Department of Labor and
    Industrial Services
317 Main St., Room 400
Boise, ID 83720
(208) 334-3896

INDIANA

Administrative Building Council
429 N. Pennsylvania St.
Indianapolis, IN 46204
(317) 232-1437 (Eder)

IOWA

Building Code Bureau
Division of the State Fire
    Marshal
Department of Public Safety
Wallace State Office Building
Des Moines, IA 50319
(515) 281-3807 (Appell)
(515) 281-3780 (Weisner)

KENTUCKY

Department of Housing,
    Building and Construction
U.S. 127 South
Frankfort, KY 40601
(502) 564-3626

LOUISIANA

Mobile Home Division
Office of the State Fire Marshal
1033 N. Lobdell Ave.
Baton Rouge, LA 70806
(504) 921-4911

MAINE

Manufactured Housing Board
Department of Business
    Regulation
State House Station 35
Augusta, ME 04333
(207) 289-2955

MARYLAND

Division of Codes
    Administration
Department of Economic and
    Community Development
2525 Riva Rd.
Annapolis, MD 21401
(301) 269-2701

MICHIGAN

Department of Labor
Bureau of Construction Codes
State Secondary Complex
7150 Harris Dr.
PO Box 30015
Lansing, MI 48909
(517) 373-9600

MINNESOTA

Department of Administration
Building Code Division
Light Building Section
408 Metro Square Building
Seventh and Robert Sts.
St. Paul, MN 55101
(612) 296-4628

MISSISSIPPI

Office of the Fire Marshal
416 Woolfolk Building
PO Box 22542
Jackson, MS 39205
(601) 354-6306

MISSOURI

Public Service Commission
Mobile Homes and Recreational
    Vehicles Division
PO Box 360
Jefferson City, MO 65101
(314) 751-2557

NEBRASKA

Department of Health
Division of Housing and
    Environmental Health
301 Centennial Mall South
PO Box 95007
Lincoln, NE 68509
(402) 471-2541

NEVADA

Manufactured Housing Division
Nevada Department of
    Commerce
Capitol Complex
Carson City, NV 89710
(702) 885-4290

NEW JERSEY

Bureau of Construction Code
    Enforcement
Department of Community
    Affairs

PO Box 2768
Trenton, NJ 08625
(609) 292-6254 (Sachdeva)

NEW MEXICO

Commerce and Industry Dept.
Mobile Housing Division
Bataan Memorial Building
Santa Fe, NM 87503
(505) 827-5571

NEW YORK

Housing and Building Codes
    Bureau
Division of Housing and
    Community Renewal
2 World Trade Center
New York, NY 10047
(212) 488-7138 (Selekof)
(212) 488-4910 (Jordan)

NORTH CAROLINA

Department of Insurance
Engineering and Building
    Codes Division
PO Box 26387
Raleigh, NC 27611
(919) 733-3901

OREGON

Department of Commerce
Building Codes Division
MHRV Section
401 Labor and Industries
    Building
Salem, OR 97310
(503) 378-3986 (Galloway)
(503) 378-3176 (Jacobson)

PENNSYLVANIA

Division of Industrialized and
    Mobile Housing
Department of Community
    Affairs
PO Box 155
Harrisburg, PA 17120
(717) 787-9682

RHODE ISLAND

Department of Community
    Affairs
Building Commission
12 Humbert St.
North Providence, RI 02911
(401) 277-3033

SOUTH CAROLINA

Budget and Control Board
Division of General Services
300 Gervais St.
Columbia, SC 29201
(803) 758-5378

SOUTH DAKOTA

Department of Commerce
Division of Commercial
  Inspection and Regulation
State Capitol
Pierre, SD 57501
(605) 773-3697

TENNESSEE

Department of Insurance
Division of Fire Prevention
Sudekum Building
Sixth and Church Sts.

Nashville, TN 37219
(615) 741-7170

TEXAS

Texas Department of Labor and
  Standards
PO Box 12157, Capitol Station
Austin, TX 78711
(512) 475-5712

UTAH

Department of Business
  Regulation
Mobile Homes and Recreational
  Vehicles Division
5159 State Office Building
Salt Lake City, UT 84114
(801) 533-4242

VIRGINIA

Division of Building Regulatory
  Services

Department of Housing and
  Community Development
205 N. Fourth St.
Richmond, VA 23219
(804) 786-4846

WASHINGTON

Department of Labor and
  Industries
Factory Assembled Structures
300 W. Harrison St.
Seattle, WA 98119
(206) 464-6580

WISCONSIN

Department of Industry, Labor
  and Human Relations
Safety and Building Division
PO Box 7969
Madison, WI 53707
(608) 266-1748

Real Property/Fixtures

General Services Administration
Centralized Mailing List Services—8BRC
Denver Federal Center, Building 41
Denver, CO 80225

For information on this unique service provided by the federal government, which helps the public discover and offer bids for surplus government property, you should start with a request for information from your local General Services Administration branch. You should also be able to get a directory of GSA regional offices from the following: GSA, Real Estate Division, Disposal Branch (4PED), 75 Spring St. SW, Atlanta, GA 30303. Once you locate the branch covering the area of the country you are interested in (and it need not be the area you live in), the next step is to write requesting a mailing list application card. When this arrives, follow instructions to list the type of property you are interested in and the price range, and you will begin to receive regular mailings on government property fitting your description that becomes surplus. Types of property include agriculture, timber, grazing, and minerals; commercial and industrial property; buildings and other improvements for off-site use; and residential and waterfront resort property, all in price categories from under $50,000 to over $100,000. A few recent goodies included 3.39 acres with one building formerly known as Blaine Air Force Station in Washington State and a fully operational work camp with sixty-five modular buildings 75 miles east of Point Barrow, Alaska.

Soil/Water/Environment

U.S. Department of Agriculture
Soil Conservation Service (SCS)
PO Box 2890
Washington, DC 20013
(202) 447-4525

In 1935 Congress established the SCS in reaction to the erosion of topsoil from much of America's farmland. Now SCS covers three areas: soil and water conservation, natural resource surveys, and rural community protection and development. It provides an almost overwhelming number of services to landowners, groups, communities, and states, working through some 3000 districts that roughly follow county lines. Nearly every county in the country has a branch office of SCS that can be found in the phone book under the "Government" listing. And every state has a state conservationist. In addition, SCS maintains four technical service centers and a technical staff and resources center at the national level. Your local office is best equipped to tell you the details of local programs. Generally they cover the following: watershed protection; flood prevention; technical and financial assistance to landowners for reclaiming abandoned surface-mined coal lands; appraisal of soil and water resources; assistance to landowners on land management, pollution control, and water quality; snow surveys for water supply forecasting; environmental education; and more.

Business operation Check with your local office or write the national headquarters for a publications list. Generally the titles are thorough and interesting and cover a fascinating collection of subjects: house drainage, grass and tree growing, pond design, evaluating soil on building sites, "inviting birds to your home," windbreak design, and much more. A rich resource.

Standards

National Center for Standards and
  Certification Information (NCSCI)
National Bureau of Standards
Department of Commerce, Technology
  Building, Room B166
Washington, DC 20234
(301) 921-2587

NCSCI maintains a reference collection of engineering and related standards, including some 240,000 specific standards, specifications, test methods, codes, and recommended practices. The agency responds to over 5000 individual inquiries every year, providing the source for standards on specific subjects. That's the key—being specific. For example, if you ask about residential housing you won't get anywhere. You will get a meaningful response if you ask for information on wood frame construction or concrete masonry foundations. The agency can also send you information on their computer-produced keyword context (KWIC) so that you can use punch cards to track down standards on electric toasters, the properties of fireclay brick, and so forth.

Topography

National Cartographic Information
  Center (NCIC)
U.S. Geological Survey
507 National Center
Reston, VA 22092
(703) 860-6045

NCIC offers a wealth of mapping and topographical information for homeowners, homesteaders, and others who want help with evaluating rural land, water resources, and so forth. They will search their vast holdings, including aerial photographs and local detail maps, offered for sale at very modest prices through the USGS or other government agencies. Of particular interest are the following booklets: *Mini Catalogue of Map Data*, which explains in detail all available services, including land use, slope, digital terrain, and other types of maps available and Landsat imagery maps (from a satellite 570 miles up); *Topographic Maps*, which explains local maps in great detail; and a short, direct, informative booklet that may help if you're investigating the outer reaches of your property, called *Finding Your Way with Map and Compass*.

Wood Research
USDA Forest Service, Forest Products
   Laboratory
PO Box 5130
Madison, WI 53705
(608) 264-5600

Probably the best source for information on the latest efforts and results in wood research, the Forest Products Lab publishes a Directory of Research Programs, supplied on request, that lists major work in areas such as biodegradation of wood, engineered wood structures, and fire design engineering. This is only one of the Forest Service's offerings to consumers and builders. Write for their publications list as well.

CONSUMER EDUCATION

Information and Services

Appalachian Community
Highland Research and Education Center
Rte. 3, Box 370
New Market, TN 37820
(615) 933-3443

Highland began in 1932 as a community school and through the years has trained local union leaders and worked with grass roots black civil rights groups. It now cooperates with community groups and individuals on a variety of community issues, for example, land reform and energy development. They regularly conduct workshops and seminars.

Business operation Write for free brochures describing the center and the many subjects it covers. Workshops are informal and oriented toward the practical.

Appropriate Technology
Rain Community Resource Center
2270 N.W. Irving
Portland, OR 97210
(503) 227-5110

Rain is an active proponent and educator in the field of appropriate technology—in the broad sense of that beginning-to-be-overworked phrase. It publishes a bimonthly magazine; responds to direct consumer inquiries; sells a variety of books; conducts research projects; assists in the development of community networks and coalitions; conducts workshops on renewable energy resources, fund raising and program planning; and more. It has some experience in administering projects in these areas as well. In 1981, for example, Rain Umbrella coadministered the DOE's Appropriate Technology Small Grants Program for the state of Oregon. If you are interested in community or individual self-reliance, particularly in the area of energy, using small-scale technology and ecologically sound materials and methods, contact Rain. Bob Baird of Rain writes,

"*Rain Magazine* and some of our publications deal with renewable and alternative energy (i.e., solar, wind power), and on gardening alternatives (i.e., organic, solar greenhouse). The resource center responds to written and phone info requests on these and other issues. A contribution to cover costs is appreciated." Rain is nonprofit.

Arbitration

American Arbitration Association
140 W. 51st St.
New York, NY 10020
(212) 484-4000

In a letter of agreement or a more formal and detailed construction contract (or contract for design services or remodeling, etc.), all possibilities are supposed to be covered. But that's not the way it works. In some cases, whether problems start because of personalities, timing, money, or quality, some form of mediation is necessary. Smart consumers provide for this contingency in their contract. One way to do it is to write to the American Arbitration Association for guidelines and for specific contract language that will get you and your contractor, for example, into arbitration as a last resort before the courts. Costs for this service are moderate, charged on a sliding scale according to the value of your job. The association has branches and facilities in most major cities and experienced volunteer arbitrators, many of whom are established engineers and architects. Write for their literature before you go to contract.

Construction Language

U.S. Department of Housing and Urban
  Development (HUD)
HUD Publication Service Center,
  Room B258

451 Seventh St. SW
Washington, DC 20410

To understand what all the brochures, warranties, plans, estimates, contractors, and product specifications really mean, write HUD for their, *Homeowner's Glossary of Building Terms.*

Consumer Action

Indiana Public Interest Research Group
  (InPIRG)
406 N. Fess St.
Bloomington, IN 47405
(812) 335-7575

One of the many state PIRGs, InPIRG provides information on solar equipment, utility companies, consumer rights, energy conservation, and consumer rip-offs in general. Although they have no specific authority over government agencies or manufacturers, InPIRG handles consumer complaint referrals, can make a referral to an attorney, and publishes various consumer materials such as a guide to small claims court operations. Terry Wilson writes for InPIRG, "When your readers become irritated at the amount of their utility bill or angered at the waste and inefficiency of their public utilities, your readers should contact their state PIRG and get involved. It takes action."

Consumer Education

Director for Consumer Education
Bureau of Consumer Protection
Federal Trade Commission
Washington, DC 20580
(202) 724-1870

This source inside FTC can provide information on the wide range of consumer information and education programs in the federal system. There are many. It can also make referrals to local agencies near you.

Consumer Information

Better Business Bureaus (headquarters)
1150 17th St. NW
Washington, DC 20036
(202) 862-1200

The 150-plus branches of this organization handle about 8 million inquiries and complaints every year. Locally (see the listing that follows for the office nearest you), a BBB office will generally be able to help you in several ways: it can tell you if the manufacturer or service firm you are going to deal with has a satisfactory business record and meets the many BBB standards for business operation, including very specific guidelines on advertising practices and how long the firm has been in business, which can be a deciding factor when comparing alternatives, and likely indicates a track record of some kind that can be checked. BBB does not, however, make specific recommendations. In many cases it offers arbitration services and has an extensive list of interesting consumer publications.

ALABAMA

2026 Second Ave. North,
   Suite 2303
Birmingham, AL 35203
(205) 323-6127

Central Bank Building, Suite 410
West Side Square
PO Box 383 (35804)
Huntsville, AL 35801
(205) 533-1640

307 Van Antwerp Building
Mobile, AL 36602
(205) 433-5494

60 Commerce St., Suite 810
Montgomery, AL 36104
(205) 262-2390

ARIZONA

4428 N. 12th St.
Phoenix, AZ 85013
(602) 264-1721

100 E. Alameda St., Suite 403
Tucson, AZ 84701
(602) 622-7651 (Inquiries)
(602) 622-7654 (Complaints)

ARKANSAS

1216 S. University
Little Rock, AR 72204
(501) 664-7274

CALIFORNIA

705 18th St.
Bakersfield, CA 93301
(805) 322-2074

1265 N. La Cadena
Colton, CA 92324
(714) 825-7280

413 T. W. Patterson Building
Fresno, CA 93721
(209) 268-6424

639 S. New Hampshire Ave.,
   3d Floor
Los Angeles, CA 90005
(213) 383-0992

El Dorado Building, 360 22nd
   St.
Oakland, CA 94612
(415) 839-5900

74–273½ Highway 111
Palm Desert, CA 92260
(714) 346-2014

1401 21st St., Suite 305
Sacramento, CA 95814
(916) 443-6843

4310 Orange Ave.
San Diego, CA 92105
(714) 283-3927

2740 Van Ness Ave., #210
San Francisco, CA 94109
(415) 775-3300

PO Box 8110
San Jose, CA 95155
(408) 298-5880

20 N. San Mateo Drive
PO Box 294
San Mateo, CA 94401
(415) 347-1251, 52, 53

PO Box 746
Santa Barbara, CA 93102
(805) 963-8657

1111 N. Center St.
Stockton, CA 95202
(209) 948-4880

17662 Irvine Blvd., Suite 15
Tustin, CA 92680
(714) 544-5842 (Inquiries)
(714) 544-6942 (Complaints)

COLORADO

524 S. Cascade
Colorado Springs, CO 80903
(303) 636-1155

841 Delaware St.
Denver, CO 80204
(303) 629-1036

CONNECTICUT

Fairfield Woods Plaza, 2345
  Black Rock Turnpike
Fairfield, CT 06430
(203) 368-6538

250 Constitution Plaza
Hartford, CT 06103
(203) 247-8700

35 Elm St.
PO Box 2015
New Haven, CT 06506
(203) 787-5788

DELAWARE

20 S. Walnut St.
PO Box 300
Milford, DE 19963
(302) 856-6969

1901-B W. 11th St.
PO Box 4085
Wilmington, DE 19807
(302) 652-3833

DISTRICT OF COLUMBIA

Prudential Building
1334 G St. NW, 6th Floor
Washington, DC 20005
(202) 393-8000

FLORIDA

8600 N.E. Second Ave.
Miami, FL 33138
(305) 757-3446

3015 Exchange Court
West Palm Beach, FL 33409
(305) 686-2200

GEORGIA

212 Healey Building
57 Forsyth St., NW
Atlanta, GA 30335
(404) 688-4910

PO Box 2085
Augusta, GA 30903
(404) 722-1574

Martin Theatre Building
1320 Broadway, Suite 250
Columbus, GA 31902
(404) 324-0712, 13

PO Box 13956
Savannah, GA 31406
(912) 234-5336

HAWAII

677 Ala Moana Blvd., Suite 602
Honolulu, HI 96813
(808) 531-8131, 32, 33

PO Box 11414
Lahaina, Maui, HI 96761
(808) 877-4000

IDAHO

Idaho Building, Suite 324
Boise, ID 83702
(208) 342-4649

ILLINOIS

35 E. Wacker Dr.
Chicago, IL 60601
(312) 346-3868 (Inquiries)
(312) 346-3313 (Complaints)

109 S.W. Jefferson St., Suite 305
Peoria, IL 61602
(309) 673-5194

INDIANA

118 S. Second St.
PO Box 405
Elkhart, IN 46515
(219) 293-5731

Old Courthouse Center,
  Room 310
Evansville, IN 47708
(812) 422-6879

1203 Webster St.
Fort Wayne, IN 46802
(219) 423-4433

2500 West Ridge Rd., Calumet
  Township
Gary, IN 46408
(219) 980-1511

15 E. Market St.
Indianapolis, IN 46204
(317) 637-0197

204 Iroquois Building
Marion, IN 46952
(317) 668-8954

Ball State University BBB
Whitinger Building, Room 160
Muncie, IN 47306
(317) 285-6375

230 W. Jefferson Blvd.
South Bend, IN 46601
(219) 234-0183

105 S. Third St.
Terre Haute, IN 47801
(812) 234-7749

IOWA

619 Kahl Building
Davenport, IA 52801
(319) 322-0782

234 Insurance Exchange
  Building
Des Moines, IA 50309
(515) 243-8137

Benson Building, Suite 645
Seventh and Douglas Sts.
Sioux City, IA 51101
(712) 252-4501

KANSAS

501 Jefferson, Suite 24
Topeka, KS 66607
(913) 232-0454

300 Kaufman Building
Wichita, KS 67202
(316) 263-3146

KENTUCKY

1523 N. Limestone
Lexington, KY 40505
(606) 252-4492

844 S. Fourth St.
Louisville, KY 40202
(502) 583-6546

LOUISIANA

2055 Wooddale Blvd.
Baton Rouge, LA 70806
(504) 926-3010

300 Bond St.
Box 9129
Houma, LA 70361
(504) 868-3456

804 Jefferson St.
PO Box 3651
Lafayette, LA 70502
(318) 234-8341

1413 Ryan St., Suite C
PO Box 1681
Lake Charles, LA 70602
(318) 433-1633

141 De Siard St.
141 ONB Building, Suite 503
Monroe, LA 71201
(318) 387-4600

301 Camp St., Suite 403
New Orleans, LA 70130
(504) 581-6222

320 Milam St.
Shreveport, LA 71101
(318) 221-8352
(214) 792-7691 (Texarkana
  residents)

MARYLAND

401 N. Howard St.
Baltimore, MD 21201
(301) 685-6986

6917 Arlington Rd.
Bethesda, MD 20014
(301) 656-7000

MASSACHUETTS

8 Winter St.
Boston, MA 02108
(617) 482-9151

The Federal Building, Suite 1
78 North St.
Hyannis, MA 02601
(617) 771-3022

316 Essex St.
Lawrence, MA 01840
(617) 687-7666

908 Purchase St.
New Bedford, MA 02745
(617) 999-6060

293 Bridge St., Suite 324
Springfield, MA 01103
(413) 734-3114

32 Franklin St.
PO Box 379
Worcester, MA 01601
(617) 755-2548

MICHIGAN

150 Michigan Ave.
Detroit, MI 48226
(313) 962-7566

One Peoples Building
Grand Rapids, MI 49503
(616) 774-8236

Holland/Zeeland
(616) 772-6063
Muskegon
(616) 722-0707

MINNESOTA

1745 University Ave.
St. Paul, MN 55104
(612) 646-4637

MISSISSIPPI

PO Box 2090
Jackson, MS 39205
(601) 948-4732

MISSOURI

906 Grand Ave.
Kansas City, MO 64106
(816) 421-7800

Mansion House Center, 440 N.
  Fourth St.
St. Louis, MO 63101
(314) 241-3100

Hollard Building, Park Central
PO Box 4331, GS 319 65806
Springfield, MO
(417) 862-9231

NEBRASKA

719 N. 48th St.
Lincoln, NE 68504
(402) 467-5261

417 Farnam Building
1613 Farnam St.
Omaha, NE 68102
(402) 346-3033

NEVADA

1829 East Charleston Blvd.
  Suite 103
Las Vegas, NV 89104
(702) 382-7141

372-A Casazza Dr.
PO Box 2932
Reno, NV 89505
(702) 322-0657

NEW HAMPSHIRE

One Pillsbury St.
Concord, NH 03301
(603) 224-1991

NEW JERSEY

836 Haddon Ave.
PO Box 303
Collingswood, NJ 08108
(609) 854-8467

Mercer County
Cranbury, NJ 08512
(609) 586-1464

Monmouth County
(609) 536-6306

Middlesex, Somerset, and
  Hunderton Counties
(201) 297-5000

34 Park Pl.
Newark, NJ 07102
(201) 643-3025

2 Forest Ave.
Paramus, NJ 07652
(201) 845-4044

1721 Rte. 38 East
Toms River, NJ 06753
(201) 270-5577

NEW MEXICO

2921 Carlisle, N.E.
Albuquerque, NM 87110
(505) 844-0500

2120 E. 20th St.
Farmington, NM 87401
(505) 325-1136

Santa Fe Division, 227 E. Palace
Ave., Suite C
Santa Fe, NM 87501
(505) 988-3648

NEW YORK

775 Main St.
Buffalo, NY 14203
(716) 856-7180

435 Old Country Rd.
Long Island (Westbury), NY
11590
(516) 334-7662

257 Park Ave., South
New York, NY 10010
(212) 533-6200 (Inquiries &
Complaints)
533-7500 (Other)

257 Park Ave., South (Harlem)
New York, NY 10010
(212) 533-6200

1122 Sibley Tower
Rochester, NY 14604
(716) 546-6776

120 E. Washington St.
Syracuse, NY 13202
(315) 479-6635

209 Elizabeth St.
Utica, NY 13501
(315) 724-3129

158 Westchester Ave.
White Plains, NY 10601
(914) 428-1230, 31

120 E. Main
Wappinger Falls, NY 12590
(914) 297-6550

NORTH CAROLINA

29½ Page Ave.
Asheville, NC 28801
(704) 253-2392

Commerce Center, Suite 1300
Charlotte, NC 28202
(704) 332-7152

3608 W. Friendly Ave.
PO Box 2400
Greensboro, NC 27410
(919) 852-4240, 41, 42

100 Park Dr. Building, Suite 203
PO Box 12033
Research Triangle Park, NC
27709
(919) 549-8221

The First Union National Bank
Building
Winston-Salem, NC 27101
(919) 725-8348

OHIO

PO Box F 596
Akron, OH 44308
(216) 253-4590

500 Cleveland Ave., North
Canton, OH 44702
(216) 454-9401

26 E. Sixth St.
Cincinnati, OH 45202
(513) 421-3015

1720 Keith Building
Cleveland, OH 44115
(216) 241-7678

527 S. High St.
Columbus, OH 43215
(614) 221-6336

15 E. Fourth St., Suite 209
Dayton, OH 45402
(513) 222-5825

405 N. Huron St.
Toledo, OH 45604
(419) 241-6276

903 Mahoning Bank Building
PO Box 1495 44501
Youngstown, OH 44503
(216) 744-3111

OKLAHOMA

606 N. Dewey
Oklahoma City, OK 73102
(405) 239-6081, 82, 83

4833 S. Sheridan, Suite 412
Tulsa, OK 74145
(918) 664-1266

OREGON

623 Corbett Building
Portland, OR 97204
(503) 226-3981

PENNSYLVANIA

Dodson Building
528 N. New St.
Bethlehem, PA 18018
(215) 866-8780

53 N. Duke St.
Lancaster, PA 17602
(717) 291-1151
846-2700 (Toll free, York
County resident)

1218 Chestnut St.
Philadelphia, PA 19107
(215) 574-3600

610 Smithfield St.
Pittsburgh, PA 15222
(412) 456-2700

Brooks Building
Scranton, PA 18503
(717) 342-9129

PUERTO RICO

PO Box BBB, Fernandez Juncos
Station
San Juan, PR 00910
(809) 724-7474
Cable: BEBUSBU

RHODE ISLAND

248 Weybosset St.
Providence, RI 02903
(401) 272-9800

TENNESSEE

716 James Building
735 Broad St.
Chattanooga, TN 37402
(615) 266-6144

PO Box 3608
Knoxville, TN 37917
(615) 522-2139

1835 Union, Suite 202
Box 41406
Memphis, TN 38104
(901) 272-9641

506 Nashville City Bank
Building
Nashville, TN 37201
(615) 254-5872

TEXAS

465 Cypress Duffy Building
Box 3275
Abilene, TX 79604
(915) 677-8071

518 Amarillo Building
Amarillo, TX 79101
(806) 374-3735

American Bank Tower, Suite
720
Austin, TX 78701
(512) 476-6943

PO Box 2988
Beaumont, TX 77704
(713) 835-5348

202 Varisco Building
Bryan, TX 77801
(713) 823-8148

109 N. Chaparral, Suite 101
Corpus Christi, TX 78401
(512) 888-5555

1511 Bryan St.
Dallas, TX 75201
(214) 747-8891

2501 N. Mesa St., Suite 301
El Paso, TX 79902
(915) 533-2431

709 Sinclair Building, 106 W.
Fifth St.
Fort Worth, TX 76102
(817) 332-7585

PO Box 7499
Houston, TX 77008
(713) 868-9500

1015 15th St.
PO Box 1178
Lubbock, TX 79401
(806) 763-0459

Air Terminal Building
PO Box 6006
Midland, TX 79701
(915) 563-1880
563-1882 (Complaints)

337 W. Twohig
San Angelo, TX 76903
(915) 653-2318

400 W. Market St., Suite 301
San Antonio, TX 78205
(512) 225-5833

608 New Rd.
PO Box 7203
Waco, TX 76718
(817) 772-7530

First National Bank Building,
Suite 600
Wichita Falls, TX 76301
(817) 723-5526

UTAH

40 N. 100 East
Provo, UT 84601
(801) 377-2611

1588 S. Main
Salt Lake City, UT 84115
(801) 487-4656

VIRGINIA

105 E. Annandale Rd., Suite 210
Falls Church, VA 22046
(703) 533-1900

First & Merchants Bank
Building, Suite 620
300 Main St., East
PO Box 3548
Norfolk, VA 23514
(804) 627-5651
Peninsula area
(804) 851-9101

4020 W. Broad St.
Richmond, VA 23230
(804) 355-7902

646 A Crystal Tower, 145 W.
Campbell Ave., SW
Roanoke, VA 24011
(703) 342-3455

WASHINGTON

2332 Sixth Ave.
Seattle, WA 98121
(206) 622-8067, 68

N. 214 Wall
Spokane, WA 99201
(509) 747-1155

950 Pacific Ave.
Tacoma, WA 98402
(206) 383-5561

424 Washington Mutual
Building
PO Box 1584
Yakima, WA 98907
(509) 248-1326

WISCONSIN

740 N. Plankinton Ave.
Milwaukee, WI 53203
(414) 273-1600

NATIONAL HEADQUARTERS FOR CANADIAN BUREAUS

2 Bloor St., East, Suite 3034
Toronto, ON M4 W 3J5
(416) 925-3141

ALBERTA

630 Eighth Ave., SW, Suite 404
Calgary, AL T2P 1G6
(403) 269-3905

600 Guardian Building
10240 124th St.
Edmonton, AL T5N 3W6
(403) 482-2341

Grande Prairie, AL
(Open 8:30 to 4:30)
(403) 532-7778

Red Deer, AL
(403) 343-3280

BRITISH COLUMBIA

100 West Pender St., 12th Floor
Vancouver, BC V6B 1S3
(604) 682-2711

635 Humboldt St., Room M–37
Victoria, BC V8W 1A7
(604) 386-6348

MANITOBA

365 Hargrave St., Room 204
Winnipeg, MA R3B 2K3
(204) 943-1486

NEW BRUNSWICK

331 Elmwood Dr., Suite 2
Box 1002
Moncton, NB E1C–8P2
(506) 854-3330

NEWFOUNDLAND

2 Adelaide St.
PO Box 516
St. John's NF A1C 5K4
(709) 722-2222

NOVA SCOTIA

1722 Granville St.
PO Box 2124
Halifax, NS B3J 3B7
(902) 422-6581

ONTARIO

170 Jackson St., East
Hamilton, ON L8N 1L4
(416) 526-1119

354 Charles St., East
Kitchener, ON N2G 4L5
(519) 579-3080

71 Bank St., Suite 503
Ottawa, ON K1P 5N2
(613) 237-4856

321 Bloor St., East, Suite 901
Toronto, ON M4W 3K6
(416) 961-0088

2055 Peel St., Suite 460
Montreal, PQ H3A 1V4
(514) 286-9281

475 Rue Richelieu
Quebec City, PQ G1R 1K2
(418) 523-2555

SASKATCHEWAN

1942 Hamilton St., Suite 3
Regina, SA S4P 2C4
(306) 352-7601

Future Technology
World Future Society
4916 St. Elmo Ave.
Washington, DC 20014
(301) 556-8274

This is a nonprofit, educational, and scientific organization interested in the future with some 40,000 members and local chapters in about 100 cities. Although their bimonthly magazine, *The Futurist*, covers health, medicine, and other issues in addition to technology, it is one of the few sources for this kind of prognostication founded in research and reality rather than astrology.

Business operation Membership is $20 per year. A limited number of books is available.

Local Community Planning and Development
Pratt Institute Center for Community and
Environmental Development
275 Washington Ave.

Brooklyn, NY 11205
(212) 622-5026

The Pratt Center offers technical assistance and what they call *advocacy planning-organization*. They work primarily with civic groups and grass roots community organizations, assisting low- and moderate-income neighborhoods within the five boroughs of New York City. Many colleges and institutions now participate in programs along these lines in their own communities, giving back some of the resources they have accumulated. The Pratt Center provides services free, acting as a bridge between the community and government agencies. Their activities include providing a team of environmental designers to help a local housing group recycle old buildings for use as neighborhood day care and senior citizen centers, studying land use, providing complete architectural plans, and more. The center also maintains a modest book list on related subjects. It will send a publications list free and will offer to include your name on their mailing list so that you can receive periodic mailings related to housing, neighborhood economic development, and other community issues.

Renewable Energy Information Service

Conservation and Renewable Energy
   Inquiry and Referral Service
PO Box 8900
Silver Spring, MD 20907
(800) 523-2929
(800) 462-4982 (Pennsylvania only)
(800) 523-4700 (Alaska and Hawaii
   only)

Unless you have found all your sources and made all your decisions about active and passive solar, photovoltaics, wood heat, small-scale hydroelectricity, bioconversion, alcohol fuels—in short, all the leading issues of renewable energy and conservation—you will find this service indispensable. It exists to further the spread of information on the topics mentioned above. You can get in touch with these people at no cost and obtain all kinds of brochures, fact sheets, excellent bibliographies on specific energy subjects, and individually tailored responses. They also provide referrals to trade associations, state and local groups working in the field, federal agencies, private consultants, professional associations, and other special interest groups that may be able to help you. And what's nice is that this service is operated by the Franklin Research Center for the U.S. Department of Energy (at least for now, while they have a budget), and, therefore, makes no product endorsements and has no axe to grind. As an example, their Solar Water Heating Bibliography lists about eight books (like the excellent *Handmade Hot Water Systems* listed in this *Sourcebook*), four research reports, a series of pamphlets, five groups that sell do-it-yourself plans, and about fifteen recent articles on the subject —not bad for the cost of a stamp, even better for a toll-free call. If you have any interest in these energy issues *do not* pass up this source. It's excellent, a gold mine.

Self-Help Group Support

National Self-Help Clearinghouse
University Center City University of
   New York
33 W. 42 St., Room 1227
New York, NY 10036
(212) 840-7606

The Clearinghouse has sponsored many consumer conferences and is generally in the business of spreading self-help information, particularly to organized groups. Its newsletter, *Self-Help Reporter*, keeps track of self-help activities across the country, focusing on issues such as neighborhood crime prevention, neighborhood resources, foreclosure, rent control, and more. The Clearinghouse will provide a list of publications on request and will handle book orders when prepaid. *The Self-Help Reporter* is available for $10 for one year (5 issues).

Self-Help Housing

The Northern Housing Committee
Faculty of Engineering, University of
   Manitoba
MN, Canada, R3T 2N2
(204) 474-9220

This source propides construction manuals, training, and a limited amount of direct assistance on projects, particularly rural construction. As Professor A. M. Lansdown writes, it offers several summer courses "that involve self-help housing, mainly for rather remote locations, and using low quality timber. It is a labor-intensive method, developed to attempt to provide a solution to high costs in terms of money."

Business operation Write the committee for information about its construction manual and the emphasis of the courses.

Standards

American National Standards Institute
(ANSI)
1430 Broadway
New York, NY 10018
(212) 354-3300

When your car owner's manual calls for a specific type of motor oil, it's helpful to know that, whether you get Mobil or Quaker State or another brand, you can get the right type by reading the SAE number. And when you get a roll of film, it's nice to know it will fit into your Nikon or your Canon. And when you buy A or AA or some other kind of battery, it's nice to know that they will fit into your flash or your portable radio. These standardizations, which make selection—at least a reasonable, comparative selection—possible for consumers are all examples of agreements, usually between many parties, to make compatible products. In many fields, computers for example, consumers don't get this break. IBM's software doesn't interface with Wang's hardware, and so on. ANSI, a federation of some 900 companies and 200 trade, technical, professional, labor, and consumer organizations, coordinates the voluntary development of national standards. Approved American National Standards (there are about 10,000 of them) cover virtually every field and discipline. In this regard, they run consumer education programs and offer a biweekly newsletter, entitled *ANSI Reporter*, and several guides (for instance, the *ANSI Standards for Health and Safety*, which covers consumer and educational products, security, construction, and more). This booklet in particular is a bibliography of their detailed standards on specific areas in each field and is available on request.

Vocational Training

American Association for Vocational
Instructional Materials (AAVIM)
Driftmier Engineering Center
Athens, GA 30602
(404) 542-2586

The AAVIM collects up-to-date information and teaching procedures from educators and industry, and puts the results into training programs that are designed for both classroom and individual use. The AAVIM '83 catalogue covers electric motors, residential water systems, wiring, shop practice, pesticide application, fencebuilding, construction and design of utility buildings, and a lot more. They will send you the catalog on request, or direct you to one of their twenty-five centers in the United States and Canada. Most programs include a basic manual, teacher guide, student workbook, and audiovisual or slide program. Publications may be ordered separately.

Wood/Soil/Agriculture Information

Cooperative Extension
U.S. Department of Agriculture
University of California
Berkeley, CA 94720

This is one of the most active extension services (check with the nearest branch of your state university) offering a wealth of information on many agricultural subjects but also covering topics such as forestry, including mechanical properties of Central Sierra Cedar and control of the Monterey pine tip moth; engineering, including farm building plans, fire alarm systems for homes, and woodstove installation safety; and soil and water, including ecology of compost and drip irrigation. Write for their publications catalog, which contains a limited number of free publications and charges modest prices for other literature that is generally thorough and worthwhile. You do not have to be a California resident to order from this cooperative extension. However, extension services in your state will have information on local issues, i.e., Santa Ana winds and fire protection in the West, gypsy moths and deciduous trees in the East.

Practical Training

Alternative Life-style/ Homesteading
The Homesteading Center
RD 2
Oxford, NY 13830

I have seen references to this establishment as the "Christian Homesteading Movement," and one of their course offerings is a week of "learning how to celebrate and put meaning into Christian life." However, they also have week-long courses on just about all phases of homesteading: carving week, herbalism week, trapping and hunting week—even advanced homesteading week. If you detect some note of reservation in my description, here's why. Even though they offer a practical 2-week course on log cabin building using native trees and hand tools, their literature contains certain phrases that send me back 15 years to the formative stages of flower power and alternative life-styles—phrases such as, "You are probably among the many people who want to return to more basic things in life—like trees and earth, fresh air and sunshine, love and peace." In addition to practical teaching, they are ready to "open your awareness to . . . wild foods, herbs, the moon and the

stars." I'm sure they are very earnest, but I feel that one of the more refreshing advances in the alternative life-style movement is that it has finally left the "drop-out, love and peace" platitudes behind and gotten on to nuts and bolts, appropriate technology, and the like. Anyway, you can write for their course descriptions (fifteen per class limit), and, if interested, in what their literature describes as "the Catholic Homesteading community we have at the Homesteading School."

Pricing $75 for a week of basic homesteading.

Appropriate Technology
The Integral Urban House
1516 Fifth St.
Berkeley, CA 94710
(415) 252-1150

One of two centers run by the nonprofit Farallones Institute (the other is the Rural Center)—see page 000 for address). The emphasis is on environmentally sound building, energy use and recycling, and the aim is to achieve the greatest benefit from the least amount of technological effort. The Integral Urban House is open for tours on Saturdays, and workshops are conducted on such subjects as wind power, solar space heating, photovoltaics, pest control, composting toilets, organic hydroponics, and more. At the Rural Center, the same emphasis is on rural applications. One-day workshops are available in such topics as blacksmithing, gardening for young people, and solar energy for young people. Several 2-day workshops are offered covering beekeeping, passive solar design, and more.

Business operation Write for brochures with course descriptions and enrollment details and also for a good, specialized, appropriate technology booklist. If you get in the area you can drop by, see how the workshops operate, and tour the solar greenhouses and other on-site projects. This is not classroom theory. It's hands-on learning.

The National Center for Appropriate
    Technology (NCAT)
PO Box 3838
Butte, MT 59702
(406) 494-4572

NCAT is a nonprofit organizaiton created by Congress in 1976. Its purpose is to research, develop, and transfer small-scale technology that will help solve the nation's energy problems. To do this NCAT concentrates on conservation and renewable energy technologies that can provide immediate help to individuals, organizations, and community groups. Its staff designs, builds, tests, and evaluates the full range of renewable energy devices in current use and publishes low-cost reports on its findings. And NCAT provides a limited amount of training (some five-hundred people annually, but it's a start), including students. They also award grants to local agencies and organizations. For example, in their National Technology Transfer Program for passive solar greenhouses, more than 3000 low-income people received training in 281 community workshops, which resulted in the construction of 101 solar greenhouses. Again, small but promising numbers, accurately reflecting the need for direct, one-to-one education and training in these fields, which don't bear much fruit working under normal bureaucratic constraints and with large, anonymous bureaucratic numbers.

Business operation Write for NCAT's list of publications, particularly their free, annotated listing of NCAT technical reports.

Volunteers in Technical Assistance
    (VITA)
Information Department

1815 N. Lynn St., Suite 200
Arlington, VA 22209
(703) 276-1800

VITA was created in 1959 by a group of scientists, engineers, and others to work on both short- and long-term development with local organizations around the world. They didn't call it appropriate technology then, but that is the name for many of the spin-offs: practical, sensible, small-scale ideas that work. For consumers interested in appropriate technology, VITA maintains a unique book list on subjects like designs for water wheels, freshwater fish ponds, Savonius rotor construction, homemade, chain link fence-making machines, and more. Also, you may be interested in *VITA News* (for a $15 annual donation), an up-to-date, informative quarterly on small-scale technology, renewable energy, and other issues.

Business operation Write for their booklist and subscription information, as well as a small brochure that describes VITA's work around the world. An interesting source that practices what it preaches.

Arcosanti

Cosanti Foundation
6433 Doubletree Rd.
Scottsdale, AZ 85253
(602) 948-6145

The Foundation and Arcosanti are creations of Paolo Soleri, a gifted and imaginative architect. The foundation helps to support itself by manufacturing wind bells ($12 and up), and a limited series of sculptures. But the heart of the operation and Soleri's ideas is Arcosanti. Some of the design ideas and construction technologies developed here are exceptional achievements. For instance, Soleri pioneered earth-formed shelters, which are domelike structures of concrete poured over earth forms, left to harden, and then excavated to form a half under and half over ground shelter. But as a whole, Arcosanti is a series of contradictions: a fascinating, busy place of architecture and planning that also is a bit like a concrete circus; a utopian colony that says it is not utopian. In their literature describing the many courses and seminars offered on "habitat and land use," even "habitat and theology," a message asks participants to pay attention to this statement: "In the past we have been tagged as utopian—which we are not, as escapists—which we are not, as dreamers— which we art not, and as a commune— which we are not. We are a capital starved undertaking . . . which can have the most far reaching impact on society." There are so many contradictions in that statement, and the sense of a martyr's quiet desperation too. Arcosanti is a modernistic anachronism in the Arizona desert that may be ahead of its time or may have missed the boat of practical, small-scale self-sufficiency and appropriate technology—broad based movements that do not attempt to integrate you into someone else's master plan—no matter how inventive it is.

Building Research
University of Illinois at Urbana-
   Champaign
One E. Saint Mary's Rd.
Champaign, IL 61820
(217) 333-1801

One of the resources at this university is the Small Homes Council–Building Research Council, a nonprofit but self-supporting agency established for research, education, and public service in the area of housing and homebuilding. The council conducts research under the sponsorship of government agencies, trade associations, and some

companies, specifically in the area of simplifying construction techniques—things like roof trusses instead of conventional rafters, wall panel systems instead of conventional, step by step studding, sheathing, and siding. Also they deal with kitchen design and energy subjects.

Business operation   The council has an extensive publications list available on request. Circulars, technical reports, and full research reports cover such subjects as financing, built-up roofing, treated pole construction, hydronic systems, attic ventilation, gusset plate construction, nail/glued truss design, and much more. Also, slide presentations and instruction sheets are available that provide detailed construction information for carpenters and others on the job.

Pricing   The council's publication list is free. Circulars and technical notes are 50¢ each; instruction sheets are $1; research reports are $5. A housing advisory service, set up to answer specific questions from homeowners and builders, may be contacted by mail or in person at the above address.

Community Design Center
East Tennessee Community Design
   Center
1522 Highland Ave.
Knoxville, TN 37916
(615) 525-9945

Serving sixteen countries in east Tennessee, this private, nonprofit organization can provide free design, planning, and related assistance to community clients who otherwise would not be able to afford these services. The Design Center's staff is largely volunteer, consisting of architects, planners, engineers, landscape architects, and other professionals who donate their time and expertise—over 4500 hours of it from 200 people last year. In addition, several workbooks are available to local groups, including an appropriate technology approach to greenhouse design and construction, earth-sheltered design, movable insulation, solar heating, and other subjects.

Construction Trades

Institute of Design and Construction
141 Willoughby St.
Brooklyn, NY 11201
(212) 855-3661

This is one of the larger vocational training institutions, approved by the Board of Regents of the University of the State of New York, and offering an associate degree in occupational studies. Work-study programs are available, evening programs, financial aid, and many of the features found at conventional colleges. Courses cover blueprints, design, material and methods of construction, surveying, mechanical trades, and more.

Business operation You can write for a free brochure that describes the program in detail, gives a synopsis of each course, and explains the several options in scheduling and course load.

Edible Landscapes

Living Tree Center for Community
  Self-Sufficiency
PO Box 797
Bolinas, CA 94924

I got such a nice letter from these people that I could not help including them. They provide workshops and seminars on creating edible landscapes, i.e., community orchards and gardens. To this end, they sell fruit tree

seedlings (currently $12 each) through the mail. Also, they can provide an interesting newsletter on planting, harvesting, and other subjects so you can eat what you look at.

Garden/Landscape

Brooklyn Botanic Garden
1000 Washington Ave.
Brooklyn, NY 11225
(212) 622-4433

Aside from being a beautiful place to visit, the Brooklyn Botanic Garden, like many of its sister institutions in other states, offers a wide array of information, from fact sheets and tours to slides and handbooks on gardening practices, indoor gardening, landscaping, trees and shrubs, and more. Important information in the planning stage of homebuying or building, and later on too. A complete listing is available free on request; their books are shipped worldwide.

Handicapped

Government Information Sources with
  TTY, TDD, and other special access
  to home how-to information

As you will see throughout the Sourcebook, the federal government can provide a vast amount of information on subjects ranging from simple instructions on how to deal with insects to elaborate, technical reports on the mechanical properties of log construction. Many of the government agencies providing this information, which includes sources on education and training, can be contacted through TDDs (Telecommunications Devices for the Deaf) and TTYs (teletypewriters). (For TDD/TTY Operator Services: (800) 855-1155 or 1 (800)

855-1155.) The Library of Congress has several services, notably a free reading program for blind and physically handicapped persons, and offers brailled and recorded books and the loan of special playback equipment and cassettes from about 160 cooperating libraries. The service is free. So is the postage. For details write: National Library Service for the Blind and Physically Handicapped, The Library of Congress, Washington, DC 20542.

Special access to information for the handicapped is also available through the Department of Education. Following are the department's regional branches where you can get the details on TTY, TDD, barrier compliance, technical assistance, and information on education programs.

REGION I

Office for Civil Rights
140 Federal St.
Boston, MA 02110
(617) 223-400

Technical Assistance Office
John F. Kennedy Federal
  Building
Room 2307
Boston, MA 02203
(617) 223-1111

REGION II

Office for Civil Rights
26 Federal Plaza
New York, NY 10007
(212) 264-9464
Rehabilitation Services
  Administration
(212) 264-4714

REGION III

Technical Assistance Office
Gateway Building
3535 Market St.
Philadelphia, PA 19104
(215) 596-6794
Rehabilitation Services
  Administration
(215) 596-0319

REGION IV

Office for Civil Rights
101 Marietta St.
Atlanta, GA 30323
(404) 221-2010
Rehabilitation Services
  Administration
(404) 221-2352

REGION V

Rehabilitation Services
  Administration
300 S. Wacker Dr.
Chicago, IL 60606
(312) 886-5372
Office for Civil Rights
(312) 353-5693

REGION VI

Office for Civil Rights
1200 Main Tower
Dallas, TX 75202
(214) 767-6599
Rehabilitation Services
  Administration
(214) 767-2968

REGION VII

Rehabilitation Services
  Administration
601 E. 12th St.
Kansas City, MO 64106

(816) 758-3895
Office for Civil Rights
(816) 374-5025

REGION VIII

Office for Civil Rights
19th and Stout Sts.
Denver, CO 80294
(303) 837-3417
Rehabilitation Services
  Administration
(303) 837-2137

REGION IX

Rehabilitation Services
  Administration
50 United Nations Plaza
San Francisco, CA 94102
(415) 556-7638

Office for Civil Rights
1275 Market St.
San Francisco, CA 94103
(415) 556-1933

REGION X

Rehabilitation Services
  Administration
1321 Second Ave.
Seattle, WA 98101
(206) 442-4442
Office for Civil Rights
(206) 442-4542

National Center for a Barrier Free
  Environment
1140 Connecticut Ave. NW, Suite 1006
Washington, DC 20036
(200) 466-6896

This is nonprofit organization sponsored by, among others, The American Institute of Architects, Disabled American Veterans, National Easter Seal Society, the American Society of Interior Designers, and many corporate contributors. Its purpose is to provide factual information and technical assistance (not advocacy) on how to create accessible facilities. Unfortunately, the center's toll-free telephone line has been discontinued due to budget cutbacks, so I'll try to run down their services. First, you can call or use TTY (teletypewriter module). You can request literature, ask about services, and get one-to-one telephone consultation with a design professional. All phone services are free (aside from the cost of the call). The center can supply code and standard information, data on specific products used in building or renovating facilities to make them accessible, a copy of the American National Standards Institute's Specifications (ANSI A117.1–1980), for $2. Also available for $15 directly from ANSI (see listing for address) is the center's bimonthly newsletter called *Report* and a variety of specific publications called *Access Information Bulletins* ($1 each) on such subjects as doors and entrances, kitchens, single-family housing retrofit, and much more. Some of this information is available on audio cassette. Also, the center maintains a Technical Assistance Network, over 1000 professionals nationwide such as contractors, designers, manufacturers, and others who are willing to provide on-site help by referral from the center.

Inner City Rehabilitation

Harlem Restoration Project, Inc. (HRP)
525 W. 125th St.
New York, NY 10027
(212) MO2-8186

This is one of the many, relatively new, fledgling, inner city, grass roots organizations that is making progress, albeit on a small scale, in rescuing and improving city housing. Started in 1977 by former assemblywoman Marie Runyon, HRP "works on the everyday, day-to-day problems of renovating, managing, and maintaining the good building stock that is an important part of Harlem's heritage and future." Most of the work, carried out by a small crew, is done on *in rem* housing, i.e., buildings that have been taken over by the city in tax foreclosures. This group provides help with the plaster and wiring but also with management, leases, and the business side. They are constantly looking for people who simply care enough about the neighborhood to help.

SWAP (Stop Wasting Abandoned
  Property)
439 Pine St.
Providence, RI 02907
(401) 272-0526

There are some 500 abandoned buildings in Providence, Rhode Island, today, and newly abandoned buildings are appearing at the alarming rate of 150 per year. This problem is not peculiar to Providence but has been seen in many cities with an inner core that has decayed as people moved out. SWAP was started in 1976 to reverse this process. It serves only Providence neighborhoods but could serve as a source of information on organization and procedures in your neighborhood. Specifically, SWAP has helped over 200 inner city homesteaders buy and renovate abandoned buildings using sweat equity instead of a lot of money. The numbers may not knock your socks off—200 buildings is a very small piece of a major city. But sweeping solutions, massive, government-backed projects, and the like have often created more problems than they have solved. Real solutions seem more and more to rely on small-scale, often one to one, practical assistance backed by training in practical skills as well as education.

Business operation SWAP has nonprofit status. The acting director, Francine R. Gerace, writes, "We will work with any new owner-occupant wanting to repair an abandoned building in Providence."

Local Materials Construction/ Cordwood Masonry
Indigenous Material Housing Institute
Box H, Upper Gagetown
NB, Canada E0G 3E0
(506) 488-2477

Cordwood masonry is one of the more interesting alternative construction systems. And this is one of the best places to learn all about it. Jack Henstridge, author of *Building the Cordwood Masonry Home*, runs a series of seminars on the subject in a vacation–learning setting that includes country-style suppers, hands-on workshops, and more. Jack writes, "Our prime focus is on the development of the cordwood technique, as it appears to have so many advantages over the other methods and materials, particularly for the first time builder."

Business operation Write for a free brochure describing the seminars and the more specialized course in cordwood building. Seminars are conducted in the summer and limited to twenty-five per session. Accommodations can be arranged locally, and you can even rent camping equipment (or bring your own) or arrange to stay in a private

home in the area. The cost for the Sunday through Friday seminar is $125, $175 per couple; cordwood only seminar Sunday through Wednesday is $75, $100 per couple.

Log Home/Blacksmith Instruction
Restorations
Drawer G
Free Union, VA 22940
(804) 973-4859

Charles McRaven, currently a consultant to the *Log Homes Guide*, the preeminent sourcebook periodical for log enthusiasts, offers two hands-on workshop courses: blacksmithing, which runs for 6 days (usually in early December) emphasizes this craft as a homesteading skill and covers making and repairing tools and hardware, tempering, forge welding, and more; and log house construction which runs for 5 days (usually in early November) and covers foundation work, felling, hewing, notching, raising, chinking, and all special skills needed beyond conventional carpentry.

Business operation In addition to the workshop courses, McRaven offers consulting services that must be arranged on a case by case basis; also a series of eight timber frame plans. You can write or call for course details.

Pricing Blacksmithing course is $200; $165 for the course on log construction; plans are $10 to $25.

Owner-Builder Education
The Owner Builder Center
1516 Fifth St.
Berkeley, CA 94710
(415) 526-9222, (800) 517-3995

The Owner Builder Center is a nonprofit educational organization that offers individual classes, full programs, books, a quarterly newsletter, and consulting services mainly to people with little or no experience in construction or remodeling. As Leslie Fox, director of local programs, writes, "We have summer residence programs in which people from all over the country come, live on site, and actually build a house. We also offer classes throughout the California Bay Area. Every weekend we offer hands-on classes on specific topics . . . plumbing, electrical, deck building, wall framing, concrete work, and tile setting." Their newsletter outlines all workshops, consulting services that include site and house inspection, plan evaluation, plan and design services, and something called *site visitation*, which is a package of 25 hours' worth of on-site supervision as you start up a project of some duration. *The Owner Builder Newsletter* includes classifieds, editorials, a booklist, and a few book reviews.

Operation Full details are available on request. Ask particularly for a recent issue of the newsletter.

Pricing Sixteen-session housebuilding and remodeling courses offered in the summer are about $300 ($450 for a couple), and are given in Berkeley, Palo Alto, Concord, San Jose, San Francisco, and possibly other locations as well. Special one-day seminars are about $50; $95 for 2 days; and include such topics as rammed earth construction and estimating costs of labor and materials.

The Owner Building Exchange
1824 4th St.
Berkeley, CA 94710
(415) 848-5950

This source is not a trade association for owner builder schools but is one of the best central sources on owner builder education. The exchange is the newsletter arm of the Owner Builder Center in Berkeley, and it regularly trains groups who start their own centers and reviews and lists new owner builder schools. So please do not expect typical trade association services from this source. Figure instead that any help you get here is at their pleasure and good will. Several of the schools in operation now are listed below. The first two were started by personnel who had completed training at the Owner Builder Center.

Chico Housing Improvement Program, Chico, CA; (916) 342-0012

Connecticut Housing Investment Fund, Hartford, CT; (203) 233-5165

Domestic Technology Institute, Evergreen, CO; (303) 674-1597

Earthwood Building School, West Chazy, NY; (518) 493-7744

Home Building Institute, Summit, IL; (312) 735-3343

Legendary Loh Home School, Sister, OR; (503) 549-7191

Minnesota Trailbound Log Building Program, Minneapolis, MN; (612) 822-5955

Northwest Building Institute, Portland, OR; (503) 244-8266

Original Log House Construction School, Monroe, WA; (206) 885-4972

Southwest Solaradobe School, Albuquerque, NM; (505) 842-0342

Windstar Foundation, Snowmass, CO; (303) 927-4777

Solar Greenhouses (SGA)

Solar Greenhouse Association
34 N. Gore
Webster Groves, MO 63110
(314) 962-4176

The SGA is a not for profit, member supported organization, not a trade association representing solar manufacturers. Their purpose is to educate, in depth, serious members of the organization in the skills of designing and building functional solar greenhouses and other solar installations. The emphasis, as you might expect, is on energy conservation, but they also include information on self-sufficiency, for instance, how to grow plants for food, even in the winter. Here are a few of their more interesting activities. Their technical staff regularly prepares programs, workshops (the hands-on variety), and even tours of solar greenhouses built by their members. Many of these activities are available only for those in the St. Louis area. SGA provides other services for members across the country, for instance, they have prepared code-approved building plans for sale, books, and a newsletter.

Business operation Membership dues in SGA are $10 per year to receive the newsletter and attend local meetings, $30 per year for their plan selection, book, and membership fees for those who cannot attend the workshops and tour.

Vocational Training

National Association of Trade and
 Technical Schools (NATTS)
2021 K St. NW
Washington, DC 20006
(202) 296-8892

NATTS is a membership organization open only to schools that have been accredited. The NATTS Accrediting Commission, which works independently of review by the association, examines all member schools. A complete listing of schools, arranged by subject and followed by state listings of all schools offering programs in the field, is compiled in the NATTS booklet, *Handbook of Trade and Technical Careers and Training*. For a free copy, write the publication department of NATTS at the above address. The association also publishes a definitive book on the subject called *Getting Skilled: A Guide to Private Trade and Technical Schools*. It is available from NATTS for $1.50—well worth the very modest price—with lists of state accrediting agencies, schools, and a lot of practical advice on selecting a school.

READING AND REFERENCE

Appropriate/Alternate Technology

Appropriate Technology Sourcebook
 (Volumes 1 and 2)
 Darrow, Keller, and Palm
 Volunteers in Asia, Box 4543
 Stanford, CA 94305

A bibliography of books and plans in all kinds of AT fields from energy production to water management to construction—you name it. A few short paragraphs describe each source in enough detail to allow you to make an informed judgment about following up or moving on. The book is used worldwide and does not cover conventional, modern construction as practiced widely in the United States. But if you want to see what's available on shallow wells, etc., this is a good source, and an excellent buy at about $15 for the two volumes, which total some 800 pages.

META Publications
PO Box 128
Marblemount, WA 98267
(206) 853-8807

META, which stands for Modern Energy & Technology Alternatives, is a retail mail-order clearinghouse for books on appropriate technology, alternative energy, house construction, and related topics. It gathers titles from domestic and foreign publishers and has an extensive, thoughtful selection. Its list covers planning; solar buildings; biofuels; sun, wind, and water systems; tools and machines; metalwork, water supply, food and health, land use, and more. Drop into the middle of any subject listing and you will find a nice combination of indispensable classics (like Ramsey & Sleeper's *Architectural Graphics* in planning) and lesser known references (like the ASHRAE's *Fundamentals Handbook*). Sarah Huntington, of META, sums up the ideas behind this list. "Although the government is dragging its bureaucratic heels in supporting such things as passive solar construction and superinsulated houses, the people on the street see the benefits to themselves as well, perhaps, as seeing the collective benefit to society and the conservation of energy. These people are eager to get information on what they can do and how to do it. These are the people we serve."

Business operation The publication list is free, although META would appreciate a SASE for return postage.

The National Center for Appropriate
  Technology (NCAT)
PO Box 3838
Butte, MT 59702
(406) 494-4572

NCAT is a nonprofit organization which has been operating since 1976 when Congress created it. Its purpose is to research, de-velop, and transfer small-scale technology that helps to solve the nation's energy problems. To do this NCAT concentrates on conservation and renewable energy technologies that can provide immediate help to individuals, organizations, and community groups. Their staff designs, builds, tests, and evaluates the full range of renewable energy devices in current use, and publishes low-cost reports on their findings. And NCAT provides a limited amount of training (some 500 people annually, but it's a start), including students. They also award grants to local agencies and organizations. For example, in their National Technology Transfer Program for passive solar greenhouses, more than 3000 low-income people received training in 281 community workshops, which resulted in the construction of 101 solar greenhouses. Again, small but promising numbers, that accurately reflect the need for direct, one-to-one education and training in these fields.

Business operation Write for NCAT's list of publications, perticularly their free, annotated listing of NCAT technical reports.

Rain Community Resource Center
2700 N.W. Irving
Portland, OR 97210
(503) 227-5110

Rain is a very active proponent and educator in the field of appropriate technology—in the broad sense of that beginning-to-be-overworked phrase. They publish a bimonthly magazine, respond to direct consumer inquiries, sell a variety of books, conduct research projects, assist in the development of community networks and coalitions, conduct workshops on renewable energy resources, fundraising and program planning, and more. They have some experience in administering projects in these areas as well. In 1981, for example, Rain Umbrella co-administered the DOE's Appropriate Technology Small Grants Program for the state of Oregon. If you are interested in community or individual self-reliance, particularly in areas of energy, using small-scale technology, and ecologically sound materials and methods, contact Rain. Bob Baird, of Rain, writes, "Rain Magazine and some of your publications deal with renewable and alternative energy (i.e. solar, wind power), and on gardening alterantives (i.e. organic, solar greenhouse). The resource center responds to written and phone info requests on these and other issues. A contribution to cover costs is appreciated." Rain is non-profit.

> Transnational Network for Appropriate/
>   Alternative Technologies (TRANET)
> PO Box 567
> Rangeley, ME 04970
> (207) 864-2252

TRANET's quarterly newsletter keeps track of appropriate and alternative technology programs around the world, including very small-scale, third world programs, i.e., peasants from Upper Volta and Senegal visiting peasants in India and Sri Lanka to learn efficient, nonmechanical methods of farming. Entries cover banking programs, "alternative" Nobel Prizes, futurist symposiums, ecological studies, reports on palm oil extraction in the Cameroon, a review of a 172-page guide on beekeeping, energy news tidbits such as Wisconsin Power & Light's spending $2.5 million for a majority interest in a wind generating company, and more. Paragraph entries are bite-sized and include information sources for followups. Several pages are devoted to the specialties and activities of TRANET members.

Business operation The TRANET quarterly (about 16 pages) is sent only to members. Individual memberships are $15—an inexpensive way of locating special interest AT sources, and getting a selective but unique global picture of AT trends and practices.

Architectural Variation
Shelter II, by Lloyd Kahn
Home Book Service
PO Box 650
Bolinas, CA 94924

This book will give you all kinds of ideas for building. It is an eclectic presentation of yurts, domes, barn buildings in Nova Scotia, Victorian preservation, Mississippi shacks, thatched roofs, foundations, vapor barriers, termite control, a bamboo sky-scraper—endless fun, great pictures, interesting text, full of how-to, designs, fireplace construction. A treat for $10.

Consumer Education
Cooperative Extension
Cornell University, USDA
Ithaca, NY 14853

Cooperative extension services are available in most states through the U.S. Department of Agriculture extension branch at a state university. In New York State the program is run from Cornell and includes consumer literature (free on request for most titles) on every conceivable subject—from gardens and canning to firewood and woodstoves. Request that your name be added to their mailing list to receive regular bulletins. In New York these bulletins are called Consumer Close-Ups. A typical mailing may cover a topic like home sharing: pilot projects, funding, where you can get consumer and legal advice on the matter, various state and local agencies interested in the subject, the effects on property taxes, homeowner's insurance, and many other details, with a list of references for further reading. Information from cooperative extension services tends to be broad-based and basic, but not always. Write your state branch of the U.S. Department of Agriculture for the address of the extension in your state, and ask for their publications list.

Design and Invention

The Art and Science of Inventing, by
   Gilbert Kivenson
Van Nostrand Reinhold, 1977

This would be an excellent book to read before rushing off to build your own power system, your own tools, your own water supply system—in short, before getting carried away with the idea of a new machine, of a new way to build. It is an understandable, practical look at the process of inventing, of working out your ideas in models and putting them to the test before sinking too much time or money into them. Some of the examples and analogies used to explain solutions to problems are simply wonderful, and instead of bogging down in formulas and technicalities, this book really does shed light on the ideas at work—ideas and processes that you can put to use in countless other situations. Fascinating and practical reading; 195 pages for about $14.

Environment

Environmental Action
Environmental Action Foundation,
   Room 731
1346 Connecticut Ave. NW
Washington, DC 20036

This monthly (actually 11 issues for a $15 subscription) is an excellent way to stay current on environmental issues from land, water, and forest management to chemical waste disposal and more, particularly as these issues are raised in state and federal agencies. Up-to-date coverage of legislative action is combined with local coverage.

High Country News
331 Main
Lander, WY 82520

High Country News is an excellent source of information on environmental affairs in the western United States, particularly in the Rockies, the Northwest, and up to Alaska. Watersheds, wildlife, homesteading, farming, and much more are covered firsthand and in detail. Subscriptions are $15 a year for 25 issues.

Fire Protection Standards

National Fire Protection Association
Batterymarch Park
Quincy, MA 02269

For a complete listing of association standards covering all phases of construction, machinery, motors, and more, ask for the revised edition of *Codes and Standards*. It lists all standards and includes a short synopsis of each. Prices for standard booklets are generally $5 or $6.

Handicapped

Accent on Living
Gillum Rd. and High Dr.
PO Box 700
Bloomington, IL 61701

This quarterly magazine is, as Editor and Publisher Raymond Cheever writes, "edited for disabled people and rehab professionals. We are in our twenty-seventh year of publication." In addition *Accent on Living* has a special publications division including books containing practical ideas and plans for making homes accessible, minimizing problems with cooking, and more, and offers a computer search service (for $12) to collect sources of information on specific topics. Mr. Cheever says the magazine "includes valuable how-to information provided by disabled people themselves over the years explaining how something can be done. For example: it is one thing to know where to buy hand drive controls for a car but how does an individual transfer from his wheelchair into a car and then what does he do with the wheelchair after he is inside?"

Business operation *Accent* on *Living*'s subscription rate is $5 per year. A publications list with prices is free for the asking and may be accompanied by samples from the magazine describing the accessibility of major league baseball stadiums, wheelchair driven garden tractors, and the like. Worth a look.

Home Design
Texas Agricultural Extension Service
Texas A&M University System
303 Scoates Hall
College Station, TX 77843

You see the word *agricultural* and you think of cows and fences and all. That's a mistake. Many extension services have a lot more to offer. This one, for example, has an extensive publications list—a few thousand titles—on many subjects, including home design and construction and other related areas. In particular, Bill Stewart, an agricultural engineering specialist with the service who was kind enough to provide thorough answers, writes that the service "provides a broad range of programs . . . primarily educational . . . aimed at making the homeowner more capable of selection, care, construction, and use of the home, as well as

home furnishings . . . and can provide a lot of house plans for potential rural homeowners or builders."

Business operation Aside from the publications list, you might be interested in three booklets (costs are modest to cover printing and handling only): *House Plans For Texas, Moderate Home Plans—1,000 to 1,300 Square Feet*, and *Small Modern Homes*. Meetings on a regular basis are available to local residents, and in some cases specific problems such as foundation settling, extraordinarily high energy costs, and so forth may be dealt with and answered individually.

Homesteading
The Smallholder
Argenta, BC
Canada V0G 1B0
(604) 366-4283

The Smallholder is a magazine written for, and to a large extent by, country people. Letters from readers make up most of the copy. These letters relate in some detail experiences with homebuilding, growing gardens, raising animals, and the rest of the chores that start to become a way of life rather than a series of hassles when you live on a homestead. Most of the magazine's subscribers are in the northwest United States and Canada, although subscribers come from all over. The subscription rate is $11 for 12 issues; single copies are $1.25 each.

Library By Mail
Earthbooks Lending Library
Rte. 1, Box 364
Mountainburg, AR 72946
1 (501) 369-2928

Earthbooks is one of the most practical ideas floating around in the do-it-yourself and self-sufficiency field. It rents books in a very sensible way. A general membership fee of $7.50 gets you lending privileges and catalogs as long as you remain a fairly active user. Any title can be rented for $1, which is a nice way to get hold of a $35 technical how-to book. After reading a book you have the option of returning or purchasing it at a discount according to the number of times it has been rented. The main catalog is extensive and includes books on energy, food and health, homesteading, practical skills, recreation, and shelter, and each title is given a short blurb about the quality and scope of the book. Local chapters of this group are forming in several states.

Log Homes
Log Home Guide for Builders and Buyers
Muir Publishing Company, Ltd.
Gardenvale, PQ
Canada H9X 1B0
(514) 457-2045

This is the source (yes, there are some others but this is *the* one) for information on log homes, whether you're interested in slick, pre-cut kits, latchkey companies, the latest technical information on R values and building permits, or log building schools, or more. Started in 1977, Doris Muir now has the Log Home Guide out quarterly, plus a directory issue that covers the field and includes names, addresses, prices, brief descriptions of the homes offered by different firms, and articles. These folks are pro log homes, in a big way. That means they often get put in the position of defending log building against critics who say things like it's going back in time and not taking advantage of modern, energy-efficient construction systems. Say something like that to Doris Muir, and she'll hit you over the head with a stack of reports from testing labs, and builders, and owners.

Also, Muir Publishing has done its own five year study on log home energy-efficiency, entitled, The Energy Economics and Thermal Performance of Log Houses. A condensed version of this report is available for about $5; with full technical data it's about $10. Muir Publishing is also a good source of books on the subject. An informed, worthwhile source.

Preservation

The Association for Preservation
  Technology (APT)
Box 2487, Station D
Ottawa, ON
Canada K1P 5W6

The APT is an excellent source for specialized information on architectural restoration and preservation. Membership ($35 per year) nets their quarterly publication and a bimonthly newsletter containing information on projects, publications, courses, and more. They offer a brief brochure that lists reasons for joining but doesn't say much of anything about the organization. Anyway, the APT, an organization of professional preservationists, restoration architects and others, was formed in 1968, to promote research, encourage the training of professionals and craftsmen, and to serve as a central source of information on preservation through book lists and a useful catalog, *Conservation & Architectural Restoration Supply Sources and Brief Bibliographies*. Brief it is, giving names and addresses of many firms, manufacturers and professionals in a variety of fields: adhesives, chemical suppliers, hardware reproduction, masonry conservation, and more. Unfortunately you get only the names—no comments, evaluations, or descriptions. But it's a starting place. The catalog currently costs $5.50.

Problems with New Homes

Federal Trade Commission (FTC)
Public Reference Branch, Room 130
Sixth St. and Pennsylvania Ave. NW
Washington, DC 20580
(202) 523-3598

This is one of several sources (see below) that provides reports on the experiences of new home buyers with their new homes. If you are willing to wade through some of the dry statistical data, a picture emerges that clearly shows the trouble spots of residential construction—including where you are most likely to incur repair and replacement expenses and even how much they are likely to cost. It's useful although depressing reading for do-it-yourselfers and those who want the best possible results from professional contractors. The report (published jointly by the FTC and HUD) found, for example, that one of five new homeowners had a serious disagreement with the builder, that one of fifteen consulted a lawyer on the matter, and that one in twenty-five hired one. The problem areas cost each homeowner, on average, 74 hours, $175 beyond the actual repair expenses, and one day from work to settle the dispute. The report, *A Survey of Homeowner Experience with New Residential Housing Construction*, may be tracked down through a service called HUD USER, PO Box 280, Germantown, MD 29767; telephone (301) 251-5154.

Rural Housing

Rural America
1346 Connecticut Ave. NW
Washington DC 20036
(202) 659-2800

Rural America is an advocacy organization for rural and small-town people. In addition to a lengthy booklist on a wide range of subjects such as energy development, house design, self-help, and cooperative building, Rural America publishes a bimonthly newsletter. It covers case studies of important rural activities, new models for community development, political developments in Washington and around the country, and material on culture, education, and religion as it applies to rural living. An interesting publication. Subscription for one year is $10.

Self-Help Information

CoEvolution Quarterly and *Whole Earth Catalogue*
Box 428
Sausalito, CA 94966

It is difficult to decide how to describe this combined source (*CoEvolution* is a kind of staging ground for much of the information that winds up the *Whole Earth Catalogue*) —in one word, *practical*, or in hundreds— just because it covers so much ground. The *Whole Earth Catalogue* is probably the best starting point if you are beginning to get interested in some of the fields I'll get to in a minute and want to see some of the things this sourcebook shows you, i.e., the companies in the field and the kind of magazines and books available on the subject. Leaving a lot out, some of the fields covered are alternative construction; solar, wind, and water power; construction equipment; tools for building; repairing; crafts of all descriptions; logging; self-sufficient living; and more, plus access to tools and information on waste systems, land management, musical instrument making, and computers—it really does cover a lot of ground. I use it a lot, and I love using it, even though it is spotty; some of the views and reviews are absorbing, full of telltale indicators, while others are quite brief and tell you no more than that the company or book or whatever exists. Sometimes that's enough. Generally, though, the product and book entries are considerably shorter than most of the entries in this book. Still a monumental research effort that is well-presented and worthwhile. If you bought this book you'd probably like it. (Costs $16 now.)

National Self-Help Clearinghouse.
University Center/CUNY
33 W. 42 St., Room 1206A
New York, NY 10036

The Clearinghouse has sponsored many conferences, and is generally in the business of spreading self-help information, particularly to organized groups. Their newsletter, *Self-Help Reporter*, keeps track of self-help activities across the country, focuses on issues such as neighborhood crime prevention, neighborhood resources, foreclosure, rent control, and more. The Clearinghouse will provide a list of publications on request, and will handle book orders when prepaid. The Self-Help Reporter is available for $10 for one year (5 issues).

Self-Sufficiency
Back to Basics, by Reader's Digest

Presented in the same format, for the same price (about $20), and with the same clear illustrations as the other two Digest manuals (one on do-it-yourself home repairs and improvements, the other on fix-it-yourself repairs), this book is more interesting in that it exists than in what it has to offer. While the format and treatment in the other two books—generally brief and generic coverage of many different subjects—works where the topics are bite-sized (replacing a washer on a faucet, for instance), it does not work here. A lot is covered: homebuying, homebuilding, spring-fed water systems, cooking, canning, gardening, and so forth. But the subjects here are really skills, and skills that take some time, study, and experience to develop. This is one reason why there are so many specialty books on everything from getting hot water production out of a woodstove to the design and construction of farm buildings for livestock. *Back to Basics* will give you only the basics—in fact, the bare essentials of the basics. You might find it useful as a primer to decide what looks interesting. The book does steer you on to other sources but doesn't characterize them for you with a few quotes or editorial comments. The existence of this book, on the heels of the repair and fix-it manuals, does signal that a sophisticated company with heads-up marketing and sales people sees self-sufficiency, appropriate technology, alternate energy (or whatever you want to call this second generation how-to movement) as an idea that has moved into the mainstream of American thinking—an idea that is here to stay and grow.

The Guide To Self-Sufficiency, by John Seymour
Arbor House

John Seymour's guide will not waste your time with endless proselytizing. After all, if you didn't believe in it you wouldn't be reading it. Instead, this practical book, whose 251 pages are loaded with detailed but nonmechanical drawings, covers the full line of homesteading skills: running greenhouses, laying out and caring for gardens, butter and cheese making, farming, livestock care and feeding, building, making repairs—a lot of topics, along with the skills and equipment that go with them. An interesting book—you'll learn how to make hops, for instance—well worth the $10. (No reason why the self-sufficient home should be without an occasional cold brew.)

Soil Analysis

Soil and Plant Analysis
A & L Agricultural Labs
1010 Carver Rd.
Modesto, CA 95350

A & L is a testing lab, and it may not have expected to make such a hit with its booklet (80 fact-filled pages for about $2). Its business is testing soil and plant samples, minerals, chemicals, you name it—eighty different tests for pesticides, among other things. The little technical treatise is a good starting point, covering all kinds of tests and procedures, sample taking, and more. Remember that a standard percolation test is just the beginning if you intend to plant, garden, and use your land as more than a place to plunk down a house.

Trees

*A Directory of Forest Tree Nurseries
in the United States*
USDA/American Association of
Nurserymen, 1981

American Association of Nurserymen
230 Southern Building, 15th and
H Sts. NW
Washington, DC 20005

Produced jointly by USDA and AAN, this directory (about $5) lists public and private nurseries from which you can buy trees. No, it's not true that the government will send you packages of seedlings for the postage. However, state foresters will supply landowners with forest tree seedlings at very modest cost, provided that the trees are used in certain ways—as windbreaks, for reforestation, and the like.

Knowing Your Trees
Collingwood and Brush, American
Forestry Association
1319 18th St. NW
Washington, DC 20036

In print for more than 30 years (trees look about the same now as they did then), this book provides all kinds of illustrations, photographs, descriptions, and characteristics of tree species in general, their leaves, seed pods, bark, and seasonal variations—more ammunition than you could possibly need. Of obvious value to homesteaders, log and timber frame builders, and a beautiful look at nature, this book is a real bargain at about $10 for close to 400 illustrated pages.

PART TWO

BUILDING MATERIALS

PRIVATE FIRMS

Structure and Frame

Masonry

Architectural Antiques—Salvage
Structural Antiques, Inc.
3006 Classen Blvd.
Oklahoma City, OK 73106
1 (405) 528-7734

This firm carries American architectural antiques salvaged from buildings being demolished; including doors, windows, posts, mantels, flooring, and light fixtures. In addition, it offers repair, refinishing, and installation services with everything sold. The principal, Nancy Fashik, writes, "We try to give design ideas as well as do-it-yourself tips. We will be glad to answer phone calls and letters about architecturals. If we don't have what someone needs, we try to locate it."

Business operation Structural Antiques will respond to inquiries with photographs of specific items requested. It crates and ships just about anything and services customers across the country.

Pricing Item by item.

Brick
Glen-Gery Corporation
 PO Box 1542
 Reading, PA 19603
 (215) 374-4011 (For technical services)
 Rte. 61, PO Box S
 Shoemakersville, PA 19555
 215) 562-3076 (Sales and general
  information)

Glen-Gery is the third largest brick manufacturer in the United States and a subsidiary company of one of the largest brick makers in England. It makes bricks in 350 different sizes, colors, shapes, and textures, including extruded, machine-moulded, and handmade brick and also a wide range of paving brick.

Business operation Although most sales are not retail, the company will answer questions from consumers at their design/technical service center (see first address and phone above), and aside from dealing through authorized dealers and distributors (primarily in the midwest and northeast), consumers can buy bricks at substantial discounts at the company's two service yards in Reading, Pennsylvania, and Manassas, Virginia. Extensive product literature and detailed spec sheets are sent on request if not available locally.

Demolition and Salvage
Pelnik Wrecking Company, Inc.
1749 Erie Blvd. East
Syracuse, NY 13210
(315) 472-1031
Branch: PO Box 210
Yorkville, NY 13595
(Utica area)

Buildings may be taken down for a variety of reasons but generally not because all the materials and fixtures in and on them have gone bad. Pelnik has been in the building demolition business for four generations and has over 50 years of experience. It salvages much of what it takes down. Thomas Pelnik, Jr., writes, "We salvage old bricks, timbers, lumber, structural steel, artifacts in stone, wood, or cast iron, plumbing fixtures, radiators, entries—anything the public will buy that we can salvage at a profit." A refreshingly direct statement, indicating that the weird piece you're looking for might turn up in Pelnik's yard.

Business operation Pelnik has no literature to send you, and the majority of its business is retail. However, it will send photos and price quotes on request for major, select items.

Glass Block

Pittsburgh Corning Corporation
800 Presque Isle Dr.
Pittsburgh, PA 15239
(412) 327-6100

Glass block is a unique building material that combines the structural applications of masonry block with the glazing applications of transparent and translucent glass. It is not a material for inexperienced do-it-yourselfers, as great care is needed with mortaring, placement of reinforcing wire, and expansion joint details at jambs and heads. Nevertheless, no other material carries the characteristics of glass block: it is secure, weathertight, and reasonably energy efficient and light transmitting. Pittsburgh Corning supplies many different styles, including clear block, patterned block in many surface textures, solid glass block that looks like a piece of clear ice, even solar reflective block.

Business operation Write for two catalogs: GB–164, *Glass Block for the 80's*, which shows many applications and design possibilities, and GB–159, *Glass Block Installation Specifications*, which covers detailed specs and artwork of typical treatments at sills, jambs, and headers.

Stone

Delaware Quarries, Inc.
Lumberville, PA 18933
(215) 297-5496

This company sells almost all its products within 150 miles of eastern Pennsylvania because they sell stone, and that's about the last thing you want to pay shipping on. Delaware cuts sandstone, face stone, river jacks (split from granite boulders), golden vein fieldstone, and other varieties. Many sizes are stocked (their office and "showroom" is right in the quarry), and the company will produce sizable orders to custom specs.

Business operation R. H. Sargent, vice-president of sales, writes, "Our goal is to unselfishly furnish, free of charge, any help, pricing, literature, contractor references or other service that will expand our customer list, close the sale, and enhance our reputation." No nonsense there. Delaware's catalogs give full-color views of their stone varieties and many possible combinations and design patterns.

Wood

Antique Flooring/Timber Framing

The House Carpenters
N. Leverett Rd.
Montague, MA 01351
(413) 367-2673

The House Carpenters build custom, timber frames homes. They can supply the frame only or the frame with complete material packages for finishing inside and out, including windows and doors, and siding. Their timber frames are built traditionally with techniques that include mortise and tenon, dovetailing, oak peg construction, hand-planing, and chamfering. The materials are local red oak and white pine. The House Carpenters also recover old growth yellow pine from textile and shoe mills in New England that close down and mill it into the highest quality antique flooring. The last stands of these trees were cut by the beginning of this century and used primarily for shipbuilding and mill construction. The House Carpenters mill these massive timbers into three grades of flooring from 5- to 12-in widths, 12 to 20 ft long, all tongue and grooved, $1\frac{3}{16}$-in thick, planed both sides. Grade 1 is heartwood; Grade 2 has tight knots and some defects; Grade 3, cut from the outer edges of the timbers, has nail hole patterns.

Business operation A unique service worth investigating. All custom frame work is quoted on a case by case basis. Wood flooring samples are available. Write or call for brochures of suggested house plans and more details on antique flooring.

Architectural Columns

Hartmann-Sanders Company
4340 Bankers Circle
Atlanta, GA 30360
(404) 449-1561

Doric, Ionic, Corinthian, Tuscan, and plain columns have been made to custom and stock specifications at Hartmann-Sanders for over seventy years. They use clear heart redwood—a dense, sap-free, rot resistant, fire resistant wood species also used, for example, as rafter ridge poles in fire-risk areas of southern California. Interior columns and pilasters are clear poplar. The hollow columns complement a selection of fiberglass caps, bases, and plinths for most of their 16-in and larger diameter sizes. Estimates can be furnished based on architect's drawings for special columns, cornices, and colonial entrances. Columns in halves are available to surround existing structural supports, although the load-bearing capacity of an 18-in diameter, 14-ft high column made of 2-in thick staves is about 10,000 lb.

Business operation Sells wholesale and retail, generally to woodwork concerns.

Pricing Write or call for catalog and custom quotes.

Cut Nails

Tremont Nail Company
8 Elm St.
PO Box 111
Wareham, MA 02571
(617) 295-0038

There's got to be something special about a company that has already celebrated its 150th (yes, that's one-five-zero) anniversary. Lorenzo Wood, of Tremont, writes, "We are strictly a cut nail manufacturer—one of three in this country—and the nation's oldest nail manufacturer." They offer twenty different patterns in various sizes and ship them wholesale, retail, and via mail order nationally and overseas. Described in one article as a "living museum," most of the nail-making machines in Tremont's building are over 100 years old, and they fit right in with the resurgence of restoration; that is, authentic restoration. For the uninitiated, cut nails got the name because they were and continue to be cut from sheets of high carbon steel, rolled, and tempered to prevent bending. They have good holding power with four surfaces (instead of the conventional round shape).

Business operation Tremont will send along a catalog covering all the product details (it includes a nail machine poster and a few other extras like metal stencils) on request. They are in business to make nails, not to give tours, but if you get to Wareham and you would like a look give them a call Monday through Saturday 10:00 to 5:00.

Hand-Hewn Structural Beams
The Broad-Axe Company, Inc.
RD 2, Box 181–E
Brattleboro, VT 05301
(802) 257-0064

Broad-Axe is a small family company supplying hand-hewn white pine, structural beams for restoration, and new construction of timber frame homes and barns. Roughly 7 in square, the pine is air-dried approximately 6 months, scored with a felling axe, then hewn square with a broad axe—the way it used to be done. These are boxheart beams (the annular rings radiate from the center of the butt ends), weighing 10 to 12 lb per linear ft, available in 8-, 12-, 14-, and 16-ft lengths. Broad Axe makes three types of beams: hewn four sides for exposed beams and freestanding posts; sawn one side for three-side exposure of beams and joists; and half beams (a structural beam sawn in half along its length). Verify your structural requirements with the company's specs for white pine, which does not have the strength (fiber stress in bending or modulus of elasticity) of the rock-hard oak or chestnut still seen in place (weathered but structurally sound) on some England buildings 200 years after felling.

Business operation Custom hewing in white pine or red oak will be quoted if you send drawings and specs. This wood is sold green. Beams are batted and strapped for

protection in shipping. Ask for quotes, which get steep for long hauls.

Pricing Approximately $5 per linear ft for 7- to 8-in square beams at the factory.

Lumber/Paneling/Decking
Weyerhaeuser Company
Box B
Tacoma, WA 98401
(206) 924-2345

Weyerhauser makes a large selection of wood building products, including dimensional timber in many grades and something they call Handy Lumber; kiln-dried (to 19 percent moisture content), dressed, dimensional lumber in covered bundles. They also make paneling, siding, pressure-treated lumber, and a new building panel (used instead of plywood sheathing and decking) called Structurwood. Available in sheets up to 8 × 24 ft, in thicknesses from ¼ to 1⅛ in, the material is a composite flakeboard made by combining long, thin wood chips with liquid phenolic resin and hot wax. T & G edges are machined into panels used as decking.

Business operation The company sells through retail building supply dealers and home centers across the country. They provide literature on all products, information on warranties, performance specifications, and installations, all free, either from dealers or the headquarters in Washington.

Lumber—Old and New
John A. Wigen Construction, Inc.
RD 1, Box 281
Cobleskill, NY 12043'
(518) 234-7946

In a direct, hand-sketched, hand-lettered flyer, Mr. Wigen states, "If you plan to use any old beams or any old house parts in your next new home, remodeling, or commercial job, let me quote you. You will find my prices are fair and trucking can be arranged. If you plan to use new wood, I can supply you in wide widths and long lengths." Mr. Wigen stocks, among other things, hand-hewn barn beams, wide pine flooring, old doors and mantels, even complete old barn frames. In new woods, he carries pine, hemlock, and oak in widths up to 24 in and lengths to 18 ft, rough sawn.

Business operation Write for price quotes.

Redwood
The Pacific Lumber Company
500 Washington St.
San Francisco, CA 94111
(415) 771-4700

Pacific carries garden grade (rough) redwood, a full line of paneling and beveled redwood siding, kiln-dried and finger-jointed planking, all shipped nationally to local dealers. Frequently, lumber dealers at the local level will simply not tell you about shapes and sizes and finishes they do not have in stock—as though they do not exist. Pacific's catalogs show the variety of available structural redwood.

Restoration Lumber
Vintage Lumber & Construction
    Company, Inc.
Rte. 1, Box 194
Frederick, MD 21701
(301) 898-7859

Vintage specializes in the salvage and reclamation of old barns and log houses. In this work they accumulate heart pine flooring, weathered barn siding of all descriptions, complete log houses, and post and beam frames, chestnut, oak, poplar, and other woods used in cabinetry, flooring, and paneling, and a stock of large, plain and decorative structural beams.

Business operation Vintage will be happy to show you what they have by appointment only. Write for a limited brochure that tells no more than you've already learned but includes a complete, updated price list.

Pricing Sample prices are approximately $3.25/board ft for 4/4 (full thickness) heart pine flooring in 3- to 8-in random widths; beams from 4 in $\times$ 4 in to 9 in $\times$ 9 in, hewn four sides, up to 15-ft lengths in oak, poplar, pine and chestnut, $5 linear ft; chestnut lumber ¾-in thick in random widths from 3- to 12-in tongue and groove, $3.25/board ft. Complete log homes and pegged timber frames start at $3000. You must call for current availability.

Spiral Stairs
Curvoflite
205 Spencer Ave.
Chelsea, MA 02150 (plant)
(617) 889-0007
Branch: RFD 2, Box 145 SC
Kingston, NH 03848
(603) 642-3425

Curvoflite has been producing custom interior woodwork for fifty years, and although they are open to special projects built to your specs, they concentrate on Colonial circular stairs, kitchen cabinets, paneling, and moulding. On their stairs, three-piece tread members are dadoed into a center post —a nice touch, as tread support brackets carry a curvature that eliminates the choppy design of straight pieces in a round shape. Stairs are assembled in shop, then knocked down for shipment, and arrive ready for do-it-yourself assembly and installation. A color catalog contains complete technical specifications and design options.

Business operation Contact Curvoflite for a list of their requirements. Send them along, and Curvoflite will respond with shop drawings, recommendations, and a price quote for your custom job.

Pricing For units up to 9 ft high (floor to floor) prices range from about $1700 for 3-ft 6-in diameters, to about $3000 for 6-ft diameters. Terms are 50 percent down, and the remainder on pick up, FOB at the Massachusetts factory. Shipping is by common carrier nationwide.

Midwest Spiral Stair Company
2153 W. Division St.
Chicago, IL 60622
(800) 621-3887
(312) 227-8461 (in Illinois)

Midwest manufactures spiral stairs in red oak, with chamfered, Colonial, or Mediterranean balusters, in diameters from 4 to 7½ ft. Their budget, steel spiral stair (3-ft 6 in to 4-ft 6 in) is shipped knocked down for do-it-yourself assembly. Probably their most innovative design, the Floating Sequoia has a gentle, S-shaped center column that pierces the ends of tread planks that appear to float—like branches from a wavy tree trunk. It's a unique design, available in 4-ft 6-in to 6-ft diameters.

Business operation Midwest sells retail locally and nationally via mail order. Write for shipping quotes, and illustrated brochures. Use the toll-free line for price quotes.

York Spiral Stair
North Vassalboro, ME 04960
(207) 872-5558

The cover picture on York's catalog appears to have something missing—and it does. Their spiral stairs are made without center posts. The sculptural form that results is a double helix, mirroring the famous model of the DNA molecule. This striking effect is achieved with dual, laminated stringers and handrails wrapping $1\frac{7}{16}$-in oak treads that are recessed into the stringers and bolted with concealed fasteners. An attractive color brochure gives details on their 5-ft and 8-ft 6-in diameter units in red oak. The unique structural design captures your attention.

Business operation York provides a planning sheet, catalog, and price list on request. Ask for quotes on shipping or custom, floor to floor heights.

Pricing 5-ft diameter, 8-ft floor to floor, with eleven risers is under $2500. At an 8-ft 6-in diameter, a twelve riser stair is about $3000, all FOB at the Maine plant.

Structural Hardware
KC Metal Products, Inc.
1960 Hartog Dr.
San Jose, CA 95131
(408) 988-4754

KC makes a wide range of structural wood fasteners and connectors to join or strengthen virtually any wood frame joint: anchors that tie wood posts to concrete slabs and foundations, post beam caps, adjustable anchors, joist hangers, metal bridging, tie straps, and nailing plates. A wise alternative for do-it-yourselfers who can handle a circular saw but tend to chop up structural timbers when nailing and particularly when toenailing (driving nails through one timber into another at a steep angle). Also useful for resisting damage to framing from sudden or unexpected loads like heavy wet snow or exceptionally strong wind and to eliminate common areas of deterioration where deck posts, for instance, rest directly on or in the ground.

Business operation Sells nationwide at retail outlets. Answers consumer inquiries to the plant with illustrated and detailed product brochures. Ask for a suggested retail price list.

Simpson Company
1450 Doolittle Dr.
PO Box 1568
San Leandro, CA 94577
(415) 562-7775

Simpson manufactures a really complete line of wood-to-wood and wood-to-concrete structural connectors. Sizes and shapes are made to fit virtually any framing detail, and some, like post anchors that raise wood end grain off concrete, create their own details that are superior to conventional framing. A few of their most useful products include elevated post bases, mudsill anchors that eliminate the need to exactly align sills with anchor bolts, adjustable caps for girder post supports, and protective plates for plumbing and wiring notched into wall studs.

Business operation Simpson's products are covered in two catalogs: 82H1, *Strong-Tie Connectors*, and RDC, *Build the Expert Way*. Both should be available from local dealers.

Teco Products and Testing Corporation
5530 Wisconsin Ave.
Chevy Chase, MD 20815
(301) 654-8288

Teco manufactures a full line of structural wood fasteners including nail-on truss plates for special detail roof framing, metal bridging, and backup clips that are laid on top of the uppermost wall plate to act as bridging for wallboard or other ceiling material. These clips do not provide continuous support but can eliminate the need for nailers.

Business operation Teco sells worldwide through distributors to lumber dealers, hardware stores, and home centers, many of which have on hand Teco's information booklets, which include a remodeling guide for storage space, deck design guides, attaching additions to existing structures, and more.

Wood Columns and Capitals

Somerset Door & Column Company
PO Box 328
Somerset, PA 15501
(814) 445-9608

Somerset manufactures a full line of wood columns and capitals and is set up to manufacture almost any wooden architectural component except items requiring hand carving. Custom work to clients' specs is quoted case by case. They can handle columns up to 40 in in diameter, 40 ft in length. The mammoth lathe that handles this can move fast enough to eliminate the need for sanding. Tongue and groove joints are used between individual staves. Aviation-type casein glue is used for bonding of clear Idaho white pine, clear heart redwood, sterling white pine, and poplar. Columns are primed at the factory, and 12-in or better diameters are waterproofed inside with an asphalt compound. Correct column entasis is maintained without altering the column wall thickness.

Business operation Write for catalog and price list of stock items. Ships nationally.

Metal

Aluminus Cupolas/Columns/ Cornices

Campbellsville Industries, Inc.
Taylor Blvd., PO Box 278
Campbellsville, KY 42718
(502) 465-8135

Campbellsville manufactures cupolas, columns, shutters, vent grills, and full architectural cornices, all in aluminum with paint finish. Snap-together construction of a variety of columns, bases, and caps is easily within the capability of do-it-yourselfers. The company will provide complete drawings and anchoring details for all products. They also do custom design and fabrication.

Business operation Illustrated catalogs are sent on request. Items may be purchased from the plant or through local representatives.

Aluminum Decorative Columns

Moultrie Manufacturing Company
PO Box 1179
Moultrie, GA 31768
1 (800) 841-8674

Moultrie manufactures fluted structural columns with a snap-together locking system for joining individual aluminum staves. All have a factory-applied primer finish, or if you want baked-on finish paint. Moultrie also makes a variety of bases and capitals. The aluminum, in both round and fluted square styles, has surprising structural strength: an 8-in diameter column in 8-, 9-, 10-, 12-, and 16-ft lengthes is rated to carry a 29,000-lb load.

Business operation Moultrie will respond to consumer inquiries with a brochure that shows a typical do-it-yourself installation and answers basic questions about the product—like what do you do if you don't want to see the joints where the aluminum staves join? (Answer: caulk them.) For $1 they will send their 32-page catalog of ornamental iron furniture, which seems to be a kind of sideline to their column business.

Pricing Including standard cap and base, a 6-in diameter column, 8 ft high, is about $40 with a prime finish, 10 percent more with baked-on factory paint. A 12-in diameter column with the same specs is about $120 primed.

Exterior

Walls

Chain Link Fencing

Anchor Fence, Inc.
6500 Eastern Ave.
Baltimore, MD 21224
(301) 633-6500

Anchor designs and manufactures chain link fencing and swing, cantilever, and vertical lift gates. The product they sell most for residential applications is vinyl-coated chain link. They call it Permafused. And when a green vinyl is added to chain link it does soften the stark utilitarian "security fence" effect.

Business operation Anchor sells only through authorized distributors, generally east of the Mississippi. Inquiries are answered with product brochures and the name of an authorized fence installer in your area. About the only problem for do-it-yourselfers is getting the chain link tight during installation. If you would like to take a crack at it, call or write the company. They offer to respond to any and all questions.

Insulation Board

Homasote Company
Box 7240
West Trenton, NJ 08628
(609) 883-3300
(800) 257-9491 (toll-free)

Homasote, in business for seventy-five years, makes structural insulating board, in a variety of configurations for many different applications. Notably, their products are made from 100 percent recycled materials, which they note, "contributes to the conservation of 1,370,000 timber trees each year, and the annual elimination of more than 150 million pounds of solid waste as well." Well done, Homasote! Yes, wood is a renewable resource, but there are limits, and it's nice to see this drop staying in the bucket. As vice-president of sales P. Daniel Petrino writes, "Every Homasote product originates from all wood fiber structural insulating board that is moisture resistant, termite, rot, and fungi protected, persistently durable and completely weather resistant." For example, by combining their roof panels and Thermasote panels, you get a structural base for finish roofing and an R-27 rating. This type of product is the only way to insulate post and beam, t & g decked frames without covering up the simple but elegant structure on the inside.

Business operation Homasote sells nationwide through independent local lumber dealers. It suggests you try that local source first, and if you want additional product information write to the headquarters at the address above or use the toll-free line. Homasote has extensive product literature, including applications guides and performance specs.

Insulation/Siding/Roofing

CertainTeed Corporation
PO Box 860
Valley Forge, PA 19482
(215) 568-3771

CertainTeed manufactures fiber glass insulation, blowing insulation (sold only to contractors at this point), asphalt and fiber glass roofing shingles, solid vinyl siding, and vinyl replacement windows. Their products are sold through lumber yards, home centers, and such nationwide.

Business operation Write to the address above for information on any of their products (specific requests will net extensive product brochures and installation manuals), and, in particular, a recently completed brochure called *What You Should Know About Insulation, Roofing, Siding and Windows Before You Build or Remodel.*

Lumber

Georgia-Pacific Corporation
133 Peachtree St. NE
Atlanta, GA 30303

This is one of the very large lumber suppliers. It has tremendous timber holdings and facilities producing paneling, siding, dimensional timber, structural board, and other construction product lines, including gypsum products, roofing, insulation, and fasteners.

Business operation The company is quite responsive to consumer inquiries and can provide extensive product and installation information. You can write for free brochures. Ask particularly for GP's *Building Products Catalogue*, and *The Paneling Book*, which is a thorough and well-illustrated guide to installation. GP sells nationwide.

Mineral Fiber Siding/Roofing
Supradur Manufacturing Company
122 E. 42 St.
New York, NY 10168
(212) 697-1160

Mineral fiber roofing and siding is the name given to fiber reinforced concrete shingles. As the product literature states, these materials are fireproof and will not buckle, shrink, or expand. They are heavy-duty products ideal for applications where extreme wear or exposure is anticipated.

Business operation Supradur will send illustrated product information, available sizes and shapes, installation details, and technical specs on request. To work with these materials you must use an asbestos shingle cutter for cutting, hole punching, and notching. The company does not recommend the use of a saw or other abrasive tools.

Moulded Millwork
Fypon, Inc.
PO Box 365
Stewardtstown, PA 17363
(717) 993-2593

Fypon manufactures a wide range of millwork, all made of high-density polyurethane. As they say, it will not warp or rot or serve as a home to termites, or do any of the other bad things wood may do. Of course, it doesn't look like wood either. But Fypon's materials are well detailed, including such esoteric items as acorn door pediments, roof mantels (prefinished with copper paint), knee brackets, dental blocks, and more. If the simulation doesn't bother you, the maintenance characteristics of these products do offer advantages.

Business operation Write to Fypon for a free, well-illustrated catalog giving complete size variety but not prices. It sells nationally through building supply dealers.

Request a price list with serious inquiries. Also, plead for a sample—even a small one.

Post and Beam Outbuildings/ Lumber
Native Wood Products, Inc.
Drawer Box 469
Brooklyn, CT 06234
(203) 774-7700

Native Wood designs and manufactures post and beam outbuildings, including storage sheds, garages, and large barns. They sell blueprints of these buildings, complete lumber packages, and can provide custom buildings to your specs. Also, they carry a line of hand-forged building hardware, and finished pine lumber, including planking in many sizes that is kiln dried, planed, and milled to tongue and groove, shiplap, bead edge, and beaded clapboard patterns.

Business operation A modest package of illustrations and building layouts, with prices, is sent on request at no charge. (They appreciate a SASE.) Currently, the company sells along the eastern seaboard only. You should be able to get a look at their buildings in *Yankee, Country Journal*, and *Colonial Homes*, in which they regularly advertise.

Victorian Decorative Woodwork
Cumberland Woodcraft Company, Inc.
2500 Walnut Bottom Rd.
Carlisle, PA 17013
(717) 243-0063

Cumberland began as a custom wood shop, grew to take on repairing and duplicating Victorian millwork, and now specializes in intricate exterior and exterior decorative woodwork. All items are premium grade, solid, kiln-dried oak or poplar hardwood, manufactured by hand and machine and shipped machine sanded, ready for hand sanding and finishing. The impressive array (predominantly in 5/4-in stock, 1⅛-in thick) includes carved corbels, mantels and shelves, turnings and posts, and many sizes of lacy brackets, spandrels, grills, and fretwork—enough to make Queen Victoria seem like part of the family. Other items offered in Cumberland's detailed and color illustrated catalog are millwork medalions, balustrades and railings, mortise and tenon wainscoting, and full-height panels, all of which are designed to fit as modular pieces in any millwork pattern you care to design.

Business operation Order from current catalog and price list, allowing 6 to 8 weeks for delivery via Parcel Post or United Parcel for small orders (they'll sell you one little wooden knob if you want), or by common carrier freight collect for an unlimited number of 6-ft × 16-in open scroll partitions. Custom work in more exotic hardwoods and complete finishing at the shop can be arranged.

Pricing Items range from about $7 for a small knob turning to about $50 per linear ft for large, elaborate fretwork panels. Other details: minimum order is $75; 7 percent for shipping on small orders, an extra 25 percent for clear lacquer finish, 35 percent for stain; 5 percent is discounted on orders of twelve or more identical items.

Windows and Doors

Awning Machinery/Fabric
The Astrup Company
2937 W. 25th St.
Cleveland, OH 44113
(216) 696-2800

Astrup manufactures mechanical awning equipment and a limited line of awning fab-

ric. The hardware can be ratcheted from inside or out. Their Solair line is available in projections from 5-ft 7-in up to 10-ft 2-in. Standard widths are 10 through 50 ft in 1-ft increments, although special sizes will be quoted. Geared electric motors installed out of view in the awning tube, a sun sensing control, and even a high wind sensor, that triggers automatic operation can be included. Standard awning materials are an acrylic-painted army duck, vinyl-coated duck, vinyl-laminated polyester(all of these are flame resistant), and 100 percent acrylic woven fabric with mirror image patterns on both sides.

Business operation Astrup products are available nationally through local awning fabricators. For product information, fabric samples, and most importantly a recommendation of a qualified fabricator in your area, write the company.

Doors/Fanlights/Palladian Windows
The Woodstone Company
Patch Rd., PO Box 223
Westminster, VT 05158
(802) 722-4784

Woodstone produces architectural woodwork that includes several unique items. For instance, they manufacture fanlights and full palladian windows, weatherstripped in brass and bronze, all double glazed, surrounding pegged mortise and tenon frame doors with a foam core. It is a real mix of old-style craftsmanship and new energy-efficient design. But the nice part is you don't see the energy features. In mahogany or pine, Woodstone's doors range from 2-ft 6-in by 6-ft 8-in to 3-ft 2-in by 7 ft, all 1¾-in thick. (Costs range between $230 and $370.) The company does not have a set price list as much of their work is altered one way or another to suit client's needs. Woodstone also makes reproductions of period staircases, entrances, mantels, cabinetry, hundreds of moulding patterns, and turnings.

Business operation Woodstone will send a modest package of brochures with representative prices on some of their stock items, plus several photographs so you can get a look at the quality work. They sell retail regionally and will ship via mail order.

Etched Glass

Pocahontas Hardware & Glass
Box 127
Pocahontas, IL 62275
(618) 669-2880

This firm makes a selection of elaborately etched glass panels that can be set into doors, windows, transoms, and cabinets. The designs include urn and floral patterns and animal and wildlife scenes, and they are delicately rendered.

Business operation You buy the door (check the open panel size with the company first), then order the glass to fit. Or, if you like, you can order the door from the company—a five panel, oval, or three panel style in 1¾ or 1⅜-in thickness, all done in solid sugar pine.

Pricing Sizes up to and including 24 in × 36 in (6 sq ft) in any of the available patterns (write for a free brochure picturing them), cost about $200, including custom cutting to size, crating, and all shipping and handling charges. Delivery time averages 2 to 4 weeks after the order is placed. The company will respond to any questions by mail or over the phone. Get their literature and price list first.

Glass and Mirror

Shadovitz Bros., Inc.
1565 Bergen St.
Brooklyn, NY 11213
(212) 774-9100

Shadovitz supplies a wide range of glass, plastics, mirrors, and glazing hardware through a network of local glass dealers and by mail order. Of particular interest in its extensive catalog are plastic interior storm windows mounted with magnetic tape (their hottest seller during the winter), insulated glass replacements with "Heat Mirror" insulation, and a good range of polycarbonates such as Lexan and Tuffak.

Business operation Shadovitz offers considerable do-it-yourself literature at no charge. Appropriately, the president of the company is named Glazer.

Greenhouse Materials

Gro-Tek
RFD 1, Box 518A
South Berwick, ME 03908
(207) 676-2209

Gro-Tek is a full service supply house of quality tools, supplies, and information for greenhouses. It carries a full line of fans, glazing materials that include an interesting woven plastic, thermal storage units, thermostats, books, and blueprints. It also offers consultation services and design/construction services.

Business operation Gro-Tek's products are available nationally via mail order. Their new, expanded catalog is available for 50¢. See if you can get hold of a sample of their woven polyethylene glazing material (9.5 mils thick; tested to avoid cold cracking down to −110 degrees F), and their reflective fabric called Foylon—a heat reflector and moisture barrier, available in 54-in widths with an R value of 2.2.

Insulated Glass
Winsulite, Division Economy Glass
   Corporation
315 Columbus Ave.
Boston, MA 02116
(617) 536-2100
1 (800) 225-7928 (Toll-free out of
   state)

Winsulite is the oldest manufacturer of insulating glass in New England. They make both double- and triple-glazed units. Exterior glass can be clear, tinted gray, tinted bronze, or reflective. U values in night winter temperatures are approximately .58 for 3mm glass and .49 for 6mm thickness. Triple-glazed units have U values of approximately .40.

Business operation Winsulite's catalog with full specs and detailed weatherization data is sent on request.

Leaded Stained Glass
J & R Lamb Studios
30 Joyce Dr.
Spring Valley, NY 10977
(914) 352-3777

An established company (since 1857), this firm makes leaded stained glass windows of all descriptions. About 90 percent of its jobs call for custom design. It has designed approximately 10,000 windows for buildings in all parts of North America. Also, it provides complete restoration work and has worked for The Metropolitan Museum of Art in New York. It is approved for restoration work by the National Trust for Historic Preservation. The firm creates everything from small medallion insets to giant murals in stained glass.

Business operation Lamb's will send you its new stained glass window brochure at no charge. Also, ask for its information sheet detailing its restoration and preservation services. The minimum order is $150. Lamb's has business representatives locally in the following cities: Houston, New Orleans, Charlottesville, Detroit, Miami, and Springfield, Massachusetts. Its color brochure is a stunner.

Overhead Doors
Raynor Manufacturing Company
East River Rd.
PO Box 448
Dixon, IL 61021
(815) 288-1431

Raynor makes overhead doors (garage doors) for residential, commercial, and industrial installations. You could write them for a catalog, but I'm not sure they would send you one. I asked them some of the questions you probably would—about the different products they make, how they're made, etc.—and got a strange response: "We hesitate to give information such as you might publish in your book because of possible legal implications should personal injury occur as a result of our recommendations." Uh oh, I thought. They must make one mean garage door. On the other hand, maybe this extreme caution is a positive sign. Maybe they are just very, very careful. I glanced down to find that this letter was from a vice-president of sales. Hmmm. I always thought salespeople were supposed to push their product, get you interested in it. So I read on. "A garage door can be a dangerous device if not serviced by experts." Well!

Business operation I can suggest only that you write and see what happens.

Roof Windows

Velux-America, Inc.
74 Cummings Park
Woburn, MA 01801
(618) 935-7390

Although Velux calls their units roof windows, they are simply skylights. They do open, as many skylights do, but instead of lifting up from the top edge of the unit, they rotate on a pivot part way down the side of the unit. Hardware is typically Scandinavian (sleek and efficient), and sizes range from a small 21-in × 27-in unit up to a huge 52-in × 55-in model that will really open up an attic roof. As with most quality skylights (and this is certainly one of them) the key to a dry installation that stays dry lies in very careful flashing, liberal amounts of roof cement, and very selective nailing.

Business operation   Full details of Velux units are supplied in a 24-page brochure that is sent on request. A western area branch of the company is located at 4725 Nautilus Court South, Boulder, CO 80301; (303) 530-1698.

Screen Doors—Hardwood

Creative Openings
PO Box 2566
Bellingham, WA 98227
(206) 671-7435

Creative Openings manufactures twenty-one styles of hardwood screen doors, some with filigree and fretwork particularly well suited to restoration work. A few double doors are included, with single doors designed with asymmetrical hoopwork, lattice weaves, and fretwork combinations, all quite pleasing. Door frames are mortise and tenon, available in white oak, white ash, and Honduras mahogany.

Business operation   Doors will be made to your measurements (check them several times to be sure you were right the first time) to swing in or out with left- or right-handed hinges.

Pricing   Costs range from about $250 to $500. All doors are supplied with brass hardware and screening. Crated doors weight about 100 lb.

Screen Doors—Wood

JMR Products
PO Box 442
St. Helena, CA 94574
(707) 963-2077

JMR makes four different styles of wooden framed screen doors, all with one pattern or another of fretwork or decorative bracing inside the frame panel. All are made of solid, Number 1, kiln-dried redwood, a full 1⅛-in thick. The decorative elements are hardwood. The four styles are available in all stock sizes, from 30- to 36-in widths. They are unfinished and do not include either screening or hinge and handle hardware.

Business operation   JMR sells retail and wholesale. They will send you an illustrated brochure, free, showing the four styles.

Pricing   All doors (less screen and hardware) are about $175 retail. Shipping is additional.

Skylights

Ventarama Skylight Corporation
140 Cantiague Rock Rd.
Hicksville, NY 11801
(516) 931-0202

Ventarama designed the first opening and closing residential skylights. Its operator units come in many sizes (it also makes fixed units), with integral sunshades, a screen or acrylic panel to make the unit triple glazed, and controls for hand, pole, or motorized operation. I have installed several of these units and can report that they are absolutely first-rate in design and construction, due largely to the fact that the owner, Paul E. Bechtold, has not farmed out bits and pieces but manufactures all hardware, curbs, and flashing in house. Ventarama is one of the few companies using copper flashing (16-gauge all around) and makes its double Plexiglas domes with full-draped, 2-in sides.

Business operation Ventarama, which has eight stocking distributors in the United States, ships to dealers, professionals, and retail direct. They are very responsive to consumer inquiries and will likely send you a reprint of an article I wrote about the products nearly 10 years ago along with product brochures and specs. I liked the design and construction then and still do.

Solar Products
Solar Components Corporation
PO Box 237
Manchester, NH 03105
(603) 668-8186

The Solar Components catalog (available for $3) covers the spectrum of solar products in some 75 pages, including collectors, installation accessories, absorber plates, fixed and movable insulation, air and liquid circulators, storage containers, hardware and electrical equipment—a lot to look at. It covers products from many manufacturers, Sun-Lite storage tubes and unique air storage pods, Grumman heat exchangers, etc. The company claims their store in Manches-

ter is the nation's largest solar retail outlet.

Business operation You can order the catalog at the address above; place orders toll-free at 1 (800) 258-3072.

Stained Glass
Ed Hoy's Stained Glass Distributors
999 E. Chicago Ave.
Naperville, IL 60540

Although Ed Hoy wrote that his company is wholesale only and does not contact consumers directly, I have included them as a major source of all kinds of stained glass materials just in case your contractor, decorator, or whatever has trouble coming up with material. Inquiries on anything but a construction-related letterhead will likely go unanswered.

Ventilation
Lomanco, Inc.
2102 W. Main St.
PO Box 519
Jacksonville, AR 72076
(501) 982-6511

Lomanco manufactures a full line of ventilating products, from basic foundation grill vents to whole-house fans. They have wind-driven turbine ventilators (the type you are used to seeing on top of diners), under-eave vents, aluminum window shutters, and more.

Business operation Lomanco's products are sold through retail outlets like lumber yards and home centers. You can find out exactly where by calling the company toll-free at 1 (800) 643-5596 or by writing to the address above. Brenda Johnson of the

Customer Service Department writes that in response to the costs of air conditioning, Lomanco, "is manufacturing two direct drive, infinite speed, whole-house fans . . . with 3800 cu ft per minute of air displacement . . . and 5700 cfm . . . specifically designed with the do-it-yourselfer in mind by eliminating the need to cut the ceiling joist." Also, I got hold of an interesting report (it looks as though it was Xeroxed from someone's notebook) called simply *Ventilation*. It offers practical and understandable explanations of attic venting, gives requirements for vent areas, and more. There is no number or author, but see what you get by asking for the notebook copied report.

Wood Doors

E. A. Nord Company
PO Box 1187
Everett, WA 98206
(206) 259-9292

E. A. Nord is one of two high-quality wooden door manufacturers I dealt with in the building business. (Morgan Door is the other one.) As in any trade, as you get some experience, certain names keep surfacing and seem to enjoy a widespread reputation of quality. Nord has been in business since 1924 and manufactures all kinds of stile and rail doors, plus columns, architectural spindles, porch posts, bifold doors, and stair parts. Their 53-acre manufacturing site in Everett supplies products to distributors and on to lumber and building supply outlets and a very few home centers. There is little you could want in a door, from stained glass insets to laser-cut filigree reliefs, that you will not find in the elegant and comprehensive Nord catalog.

Business operation Although the standard price is $5, Nord will charge only $2.50 for initial requests for their 70-page, full-color catalog. Many other product sheets are available at no cost. Although it may sound a little hackneyed, Robert A. Virkelyst, Nord's advertising manager, has got it exactly right: "Nothing beats the warmth and beauty of real wood." A quality company with solid literature.

Roofing

Drainage Systems

Advanced Drainage Systems, Inc.
3300 Riverside Dr.
PO Box 21307
Columbus, OH 43221
(614) 457-3051

Advanced Drainage makes a full selection of corrugated polyethylene drainage pipe, tubing, fittings, and accessories. They can be used to extend roof drainage systems beyond foundation walls, to drain window wells and slabs, for leaching fields, and so on. The corrugated material is lightweight and moderately flexible, which makes excavation requirements considerably less rigid. Generally this kind of material is an economical replacement (in terms of cost and labor time) for corrugated steel culvert or either concrete or clay drain tile.

Business operation Advanced Drainage sells through a nationwide chain of distributors and dealers, in home centers, hardware stores, and other retail outlets. They have twenty-one manufacturing locations. Write for Catalog L–3010, and L–1040; the latter explains the product construction and application in detail.

Roofing/Insulation

Manville Corporation
Ken-Caryl Ranch
Denver, CO 80217
(303) 978-2000

Manville is a manufacturer of many different building materials including fiber glass insulation, shingles, builtup roofing systems, paneling—a huge number of products divided into five product groups. For information on products you can't find locally (and it will be hard not to) try specific requests to the company at the above address, which is the executive headquarters.

Slate

Hilltop Slate Corporation
Middle Granville, NY 12849
(518) 642-2270

Hilltop has quarries in Wells and North Poultry, Vermont, and Truthville, New York. (Wonder how that town got its name.) They ship direct throughout the country virtually all varieties of slate, including crazy quilt, multicolor Vermont slate patterns, sea green roofing slate in rough and smooth grades, and graduated-thickness roofing running from $\frac{3}{16}$ to $\frac{1}{2}$ in.
Business operation   Product literature is available from Hilltop at the above address.

Rising & Nelson Slate Company, Inc.
West Pawlet, VT 05775
(802) 645-0150

Rising & Nelson quarries Vermont Grade A roofing slate, and can supply black from Pennsylvania or Buckingham, Virginia. Specifically, they supply sea green (officially semiweathering green and gray that mutes slightly with weather exposure), Vermont black and gray black, unfading purple, varie-gated purple, unfading mottled gray green, unfading green, and red slate. It provides roofing in 10- to 24-in lengths in 2-in increments and random widths. Available thicknesses range from $\frac{3}{16}$- to $\frac{1}{4}$-in commercial smooth grade to rough texture quarry run from $\frac{3}{16}$- to 1-in.
Business operation   Rising & Nelson can provide architectural consultation on all aspects of slate selection, installation, maintenance, and so forth. James M. Mertz writes, "We are prepared to cut any kind of special butt—pointed, fishscale, clipped corner, etc. Just send us a template. Provide us with information and you will get a prompt reply." Write for their brochure, which supplies complete technical specs, sizes, and basic how-to information. The company sells predominantly to roofing contractors.

Vermont Structural Slate Company, Inc.
Box 98
Fair Haven, VT 05743
(800) 343-1900 (Toll-free)

One of the premier slate firms, this company takes its materials from a quarry 2 miles from its main offices. It makes exterior roof shingles, copings, sills, and paving slabs; interior flooring, treads, and risers; and a variety of slate specialties such as vanity tops, fireplace hearths, and more. The material for roofs is Grade A, unfading Vermont slate quarried from their Eureka Vein in the southwestern part of the state. Shingles are mottled green and purple, all gray green, or all purple. Standard thickness is $\frac{3}{16}$ to $\frac{1}{4}$-in. Vermont Structure also makes graduated-thickness slate with up to 1-in thickness for installation at eaves. Standard lengths are 12-, 14-, 16-, 18-, and 20-in in random widths. Special orders can be made for lengths up to 24-in. Vermont also cuts and tests assembles "ready-fit" slate flooring in random ashlar patterns.
Business operation   The company sells

worldwide to owners, general contractors, and particularly to specialty roofing subcontractors. You'll find its ad on an ongoing basis in the magazine *Architectural Record*. William Markcrow writes, "We provide an awful lot of information to consumers once they contact us. We reprinted a book on slate roofing which is an absolute bible on the subject. We will provide advice concerning installation, maintenance, and will visit historic jobs." Their literature is first rate.

Slate/Slater's Tools

Evergreen Slate Company
Box 248
Granville, NY 12832
(518) 642-2530

Evergreen has furnished roofing slate for some impressive clients, like the Boston Museum of Fine Arts, and the White House (Evergreen provided slate for the North Portico). They quarry and sell a variety of slate: semiweathering gray green, unfading mottled green and purple, blue black, unfading green, Vermont black, mottled gray, red, and more. Also, they sell quality slater's tools, specifically a slate zipper (with a long flat and toothed arm for cutting nails and removing broken slate; slate hooks (for securing new slate without ripping up the roof or using tar); a slate hammer (leather handled); and a slate cutter (made by ESCO) that is only 8 lb and has a nail puncher at the handle end. Evergreen supplies lengths from 10 to 24-in, ¼- to ¾-in thicknesses in standard smooth and rough quarry run.

Business Operation Write for product spec booklets that include color photographs of slate tones and a very informative brochure entitled *Hip and Ridge Application*, which covers some of the fine points for do-it-yourselfers.

Terne Roofing

Follansbee Steel Corporation
Follansbee, WV 26037
(304) 527-1260

Follansbee manufactures terne and TCS (terne-coated stainless steel) roofing. Although working with metal takes more time than working with asphalt, the resulting interlocked system of folded seams, flashing, and counterflashing is extremely weatherproof and durable. In fact, Follansbee's literature includes a wonderful reprint from *Ripley's Believe It or Not!* with a drawing of a terne roof house and this caption: "The roof of the Yale Faculty Club in New Haven, Conn. made of lead, tin and sheet steel has endured without a single repair for nearly 200 years." This item appeared next to "The Stone Sheep," an anthopomorphic rock formation in Gurley, Nebraska. So much for Madison Avenue advertising.

Business operation Follansbee makes precut flashing and many terne-related supplies. They provide a toll-free number for product information, requests for product spec sheets, and referral to local distributors: 1 (800) 624-6906.

Ornamentation

Architectural Ironwork

Architectural Iron Company
Box 674
Milford, PA 18337
(717) 296-7722
(212) 243-2664 (New York phone
     number)

This company does not have a lot of stock, cutesy iron railings. It does custom casting, fabrication of ornamental iron work, and restoration of ironwork. Donald G. Quick, the manager of the company's design and restoration services, has prepared a very informative letter explaining in detail the kind of work it does, the differences between wrought iron, cast iron, combination work, and so on. You can write for it. At its shops and foundry in Pennsylvania, Architectural Iron is equipped to duplicate a small casting weighing only a few ounces (from a photograph) and to restore (and rebuild to period detail where necessary) heavy cast fences where a single post may weigh a 1000 lb.

Business operation Write or call for restoration details. The company's philosophy is interesting. Mr. Quick writes, "There is a reward in meeting people interested in preserving the past. We like to think our work has permanence, and we intend to remain small enough to deal with each project on an individual basis."

Paint
Allentown Paint Manufacturing
   Company, Inc.
Graham and E. Allen Sts.
Allentown, PA 18105
(215) 433-4273

Allentown is the oldest ready-mixed paint manufacturing firm in the United States, founded in Philadelphia in 1855. They make an extensive line of paints including many specialties such as zinc chromate primer, fire retardant coatings, and more.

Business operation Allentown distributes regionally on the eastern seaboard through paint stores, hardware stores, and lumber yards, although they do a small amount of mail-order business with hard to find items. They will supply color cards and specific catalog pages on products. Their complete catalog, called *Quality Coatings*, includes color chips, full specs on architectural coatings, and a surface preparation guide.

Stain/Preservatives
McCloskey Varnish Company
7600 State Rd.
Philadelphia, PA 19136
(215) 624-4400

McCloskey manufatcures a wide range of interior and exterior stains, wood preservatives, polyurethanes, varnishes, and marine-grade spar varnishes. Its products are widely available and covered in an extensive catalog that is available only from the headquarters. It includes several specialty items: a cabinet rubbing varnish that dries dust free in one hour and hard in 12 hours; flatting oil, which is used as a vehicle for interior oil paint and enamel to produce a flat, washable finish and also as an undercoating; and seat and pew varnish, which dries in about an hour and does not soften under body heat. (Just right for a quick varnishing between Sunday services.)

Wood Stain
Samuel Cabot, Inc.
One Union St.
Boston, MA 02108
(617) 723-7740

Cabot's, established in 1877, is one of the oldest, most respected names in wood stains. It manufactures and distributes nationally and internationally some eighty-seven different shades of grain accenting, wood preserving, water repellent, and mildew resistant stain in semitransparent, semisolid, solid color, and decking mixtures. Cabot's advertisements run regularly in consumer and trade magazines and have increased of late along with what its advertising manager calls, "A definite trend to stains over paints—especially exterior." I see the same trend, which seems due to consumer's distaste for repainting every few years, particularly in older homes with no vapor barriers, and their acceptance of penetrating wood stain that colors but does not hide the wood underneath.

Business operation Cabot's will answer all specific questions on the use of its products and will send you color cards and technical specifications on request. If you want more information than you can get at a local dealer, write the national headquarters.

Interior

Structural Surfaces

Architectural Antiques

Evelyn Croton–Architectural Antiques
51 Eastwood La.
Valley Stream, NY 11581
(516) 791-4703

There are few sources of old parts for old houses. This firm handles hand-carved acanthus-leaf wood corbels, pilasters, door surroundings and door carvings, mantels, fretwork, terra-cotta keystones, iron and brass ornate grill registers, and similar specialities. Each piece is sold "as is," in the condition in which it was found on or in an old building. Carved corbels (brackets for roof overhangs) are the specialty.

Business operation No catalogs are available, but very specific inquiries will be answered with photos of stock that might fill the bill. The firm sells wholesale to dealers and retail via mail order.

Pricing Item by item basis.

Cabinets

Quaker Maid, Division Tappan
Rte. 61
Leesport, PA 19533
(215) 926-3011

Quaker Maid has been in the custom cabinet business for over thirty years. It makes kitchen cabinets, vanities, and a relatively new line of custom furniture. Many styles and sizes are available but the distinguishing characteristic of Quaker Maid is the ingenious storage systems behind the cabinet doors. They have corner revolving trays, pull-out storage bins and work surfaces, storage shelves that have storage shelves behind them that swivel, and a lot more space-saving hardware.

Business operation Quaker Maid sells direct from the factory through over 700 distributors nationwide. They advertise through the Yellow Pages, or you can write or call Leesport for the dealer nearest you. The company will send you several pieces of literature on request, but for planning purposes, get at least two of them: *Cabinet Specication & Accessory Guide* and *Convenience & Decorator Features*. Their booklet *Fact Tag* lists construction specs: 45-degree interlocked miter at corners, ⅝-in thick shelving, hand-rubbed finish, and other goodies.

Cast Iron Victorian Spiral Stairs

Steptoe & Wife Antiques, Ltd.
3625 Victoria Park Ave.
Willowdale, ON M2H 3B2
(416) 497-2989

The Steptoe spiral staircase is a Victorian reproduction built and shipped in modular form. Each package includes an extended top tread, sufficient handrail to match the tread number and final height, all requisite balusters, black-baked enamel finish, and all connecting hardware. The treads are cast in a vine tracery pattern. Currently this staircase is made in 4- and 6-ft diameters. New products include a 5-ft diameter spiral and a 3-ft wide straight staircase.

Business operation   Steptoe has approximately twenty-five dealers in the United States and Canada but will sell direct to consumers where it is not represented. (In some cases I think it is a distinct advantage to deal with companies who have distribution networks almost anywhere except where you live. You're going to pay for shipping one way or the other.) In any case, Steptoe will supply product literature (the reproduction staircase is well worth a look) and advice. This firm handles Hi-Art metal ceilings as well and continues to work on new restoration products, particularly modular, self-assembly designs.

Ceramic Tile
· Wenczel Tile Company
 Klag Ave.
 PO Box 5308
 Trenton, NJ 08638
 (609) 599-4503

Wenczel manufactures an extensive product line of ceramic wall tile and light duty residential floor tile, and it also imports Italian, Japanese, and Korean floor tile. Its products include all kinds of shapes, sizes, and finishes and are sold through about 150 distributors west of the Rockies.

Business operation   Wenczel will supply product literature on request that covers standard varieties plus veined, embossed, and decorative tile. Information is available also from its second main branch: Wenczel Tile Company of Florida, 6608 S. Westshore Blvd., Tampa, FL 33616; (813) 839-5301.

Ceramic Tile—Hand-made
Country Floors
300 E. 61st
New York, NY 10021
(212) 758-7414

If you go for this kind of thing you will go crazy when you see the Country Floors catalog. It's a knockout. They have a huge selection (a giant warehouse full of crates from all over the world) and stock mostly imported, hand-made, hand-painted ceramic tile from Holland, Portugal, France, Spain, Italy, Mexico, and Peru. Full-color catalog sheets show sensational color combinations and patterns: interlocking patterns, tableaux done in twelve-tile combinations, baskets of fruit, room-size tableaux from Italy (seventy-two tiles) of a landscape and single flowering tree, about thirty patterns of terra-cotta tile, and more.

Business operation   Write for color catalogs. The company ships anywhere and takes great pains with packing. For tile samples send the price of tile plus $3.

Pricing   Some modest designs like plain terra-cotta 11½-in squares are about $2.50 per sq ft. Some more exotic tiles are $30 per sq ft.

Drywall
United States Gypsum Company
101 S. Wacker Dr.
Chicago, IL 60606

U.S. Gypsum is a very large company that makes all kinds of construction-related products. Its paneling catalog seems to go on forever, describing different tones and textures and colors. But in particular this is one of the largest drywall manufacturers. The company, and a lot of people in the trade, calls its product Sheetrock, even though that is a trademark. U.S. Gypsum makes all kinds of wallboard (that's the generic name): vinyl wrapped, fire rated, and moisture rated, with butt joints and feathered edges. It used to make wallboard with resistance wiring built in for radiant heating on walls and ceilings. (A big U.S. Gypsum plant I was in a few years ago had several pieces of this "wave of the future" material that never caught on lying in a dusty corner.) The manufacturing process is nonstop, from boatloads of gypsum, to conveyors, to mixing, to a continuous sandwiching between paper coverings, to baking ovens, to cutters, to stackers, and finally onto the trucks for delivery. Impressive.

Business operation U.S. Gypsum products are sold nationwide. The company provides voluminous literature at retail outlets, but if you have inquiries about specific products you can write to the company; Attention: Marketing Services, Department 122. They have several idea and project booklets and a good, if brief, brochure on rigid styrene insulating board, which has endless applications in new and existing construction. Also, ask about U.S. Gypsum's 300-page paperback book, *Drywall Construction Handbook*. It will probably cost at least a few dollars by now, but it is the definitive book on drywall, profusely illustrated, completely practical, with full technical specs, application guides, for layman and professional alike—a gem.

Hardwood Floors

Harris Manufacturing Company
321 E. Maple St.
Johnson City, TN 37601
(615) 928-3122

Harris manufactures oak and maple flooring in many configurations: nine different styles of parquet from hardwood tiles the size of sugar cubes to diagonal picket squares; prefinished, rib-backed planking in 3-, 5-, and 7-in widths, random planking, and more. Most of their flooring is sold unfinished and is conventionally installed, sanded, and finished by professionals, although several prefinished products are available.

Business operation Harris sells only through distributors. The company will send a beautifully illustrated brochure of its products, including full specs on grades and finishes and a state by state listing of its dealers.

Kentucky Wood Floors, Inc.
4200 Reservoir Ave.
Louisville, KY 40213
(502) 451-6024

It is a treat to look through a catalog like the one from Kentucky Wood Floors. The color pages of different product lines are each introduced by a color picture of one of Kentucky's small crew that produces the flooring. It may sound like a clichéd presentation, but it's not. Of particular interest is the seven-man crew that produces Kentucky's Custom Floors line. Their work in unfinished and prefinished hardwoods is installed in the Metropolitan Museum of Art, the East Room of the White House, the Smithsonian Institution, and, as the literature states coyly, in "a Former President's Office: Atlanta, Georgia." These exceptional patterns in plain and quartered oak, ash, walnut, and cherry are made with a variety of finishes, beveled edges, mixed species designs, and more. Several other lines include all endgrain flooring, parquet, and planking; elegant, quality work.

Business operation The catalog covers all floor types, pattern selection, ordering information. Call the number listed above for distributor name and number.

Insulation

Owens-Corning Fiberglas Corporation
Fiberglas Tower
Toledo, OH 43659
(419) 248-8000

One of the largest insulation manufacturers, Owens-Corning has quite naturally pushed more insulation as the be-all and end-all, *the* way to save energy dollars. I think they, and the other big companies, have gone too far. Maybe it's a case of the other options not being publicized enough. In any case, not everyone needs more insulation. If you live in a northern climate and have in the neighborhood of 6 in of insulation in the attic but no storm windows, more insulation is probably not the cost-effective answer. Remember, the first inch of insulation saves more energy than the second, which saves more than the third, and so on; the law of diminishing returns is in effect here, as every inch costs the same. Within this commonsense framework, adding some insulation when you have none or only a little is essential. Owens-Corning's extensive literature tells you how. Their basic product line is as follows: batts in 48- and 98-in lengths and 16- and 24-in widths, thick enough to give up to an R-38 rating; polyisocyanurate foam sheathing (no formaldehyde here); pouring wool; blowing wool (usually reserved for contractor installations); pipe wrap; grid ceiling systems; flexible ducting; and fiber glass mat roofing shingles (all have a Class A fire rating).

Business operation Owens-Corning materials are sold through most lumber yards and building supply outlets. You can find them almost everywhere, along with exten-sive, generally high-quality consumer information, or you can write for free booklets and brochures from the headquarters if not available locally.

Marble

New York Marble Works, Inc.
1399 Park Ave.
New York, NY 10029
(212) LE4-2242

New York Marble is one of the premier marble firms on the East Coast. In business since 1900, it sells marble in many different shapes and sizes and offers both stock pieces and custom work in approximately 120 different color tones. It also repairs and restores marble furnishings and has done work for Sotheby Parke Bernet and the Metropolitan Museum of Art in New York. Items commonly requested include ¾-in thick counter tops (about $20 per square foot and up), and natural tiles (about $4.25 and up for 12-in squares). As to their repair and restoration services, you can bring in your piece (call first), or send a photograph or two illustrating exactly what the problem is, and New York Marble will quote a rough price on the spot. Its retail store (you should be able to find one in Los Angeles soon) shows much of what it carries.

Business operation Repair and restoration work should be arranged by appointment. New York Marble will arrange shipping. The work generally takes about 2 weeks. It welcomes inquiries from architects, contractors, and consumers. Write for brief product descriptions and an interesting, short, but thorough piece on marble cleaning and care. The company carries marble cleaners and adhesives.

Metal Ceilings

Hi-Art East
6 N. Rhodes Center NW
Atlanta, GA 30309
(404) 876-4740

This firm is the East Coast outlet for the W. F. Norman Sheet Metal Manufacturing Company. It sells an array of tin, brass, and copper ceilings, including stamped tiles, cornice, center medallions, girder finishes, and frieze plates.

Business operation   Hi-Art will send you an illustrated catalog containing about 120 original patterns for $3. Its retail showroom displays much of what it sells.

Pricing   Generally the material runs between $1.50 and $2.50 per square foot. Installation can be handled by competent do-it-yourselfers.

Metal Ceilings/Walls

Shanker Steel Corporation
70–32 83rd St.
Glendale, NY 11385
(212) 326-1100

Shanker uses huge power presses (18 ft high weighing 65 tons) to impress metal ceiling patterns with 800 tons of pressure per blow. As the company says, "This assures accuracy and sharpness of design." They have been making metal ceilings since 1912, and "sell direct to anyone, anywhere."

Business operation   Shanker's catalog offers twenty-two different patterns in 2-ft × 8-ft sheets (with subdivided design squares), plus several cornice moulding patterns that match and accent the ceilings.

Pricing   Keeping things simple, the price per sheet with a volume under 100 is $26.85; over 100, $22.20 (it pays to order 101 instead of 99); over 200, $20.75.

Millwork

Mendocino Millwork
Box 669
Mendocino, CA 95460
(707) 937-4410

Working also under the name of Hallelujah Redwood Products (quite a combination), this firm manufactures mouldings, corbels, porch railings, appliqué, sash, shingles, and doors. It produces several stock components (shown in its catalog) and special designs to order. The style is generally Victorian, and the firm can match pieces from detailed drawings of components in your home that must be replaced. Some of its products are available in soft- and hardwoods as well as redwood.

Business operation   The catalog is sent on request.

Pricing   Corbels range from $15 to over $70 for elaborate detailing; window sash ranges from $1 to about $7 per foot. Discounts of 15 and 20 percent (depending on quantities) are offered to builders and contractors.

Mouldings

Driwood Moulding Company
PO Box 1729
Folrence, SC 29503
(803) 669-2478

Driwood manufactures ornamental wood mouldings in air- and kiln-dried poplar, or, on special order, in maple, walnut, oak, and mahogany supplied in lengths from 6 to 16 ft. Its catalogs display stairs and handrails, panelwork, window casings, ceiling cornices, picture mouldings, plate rails, and more.

Business operation   Two Driwood color catalogs are available, each for $3. For restoration work ask for Volume 1, *Period*

Mouldings and for other applications, Volume 2, *Ornamental Wood Moulding & Millwork.*

Mouldings—Period
Focal Point, Inc.
2005 Marietta Rd. NW
Atlanta, GA 30318
(404) 351-0820

While companies in the business of reproducing or recreating period building materials stress authenticity—old time woods, old time tools, old time skills, Focal Point stresses its combination of modern technology and Victorian millwork. The process is detailed in one of their brochures (*The American 19th Century Collection*), and documents cases where the company takes clay impressions of mouldings at historic sites and painstakingly recreates the design in a flexible, rubberized production mould, which is used to cast its mouldings. While the detail is impressive and the company lists all sorts of endorsements and affiliations with restoration and design authorities, the final product is something called Endure-all. I assume it is plastic of some kind and that company policy is to avoid any use of that word. The Victorians, after all, even though they had a fascination for the new wave of machine-made products, did not use Endure-all and therefore, no matter how authentic the design of the reproduction, it can never be considered truly authentic. And I searched through the company's literature for a straightforward explanation of Endure-all—what it is—but found only advertising superlatives. Nevertheless, the company offers a collection of deeply etched and intricate mouldings, particularly cornices, and also center medallions and domes.
Business operation Write or call the company for information on product availability. It is an interesting alternative as

the material comes factory primed; can be painted and stained; and is weather resistant.

Ornamental Supply
The Decorators Supply Corporation
3610–3612 S. Morgan St.
Chicago, IL 60609
(312) 847-6300

In three elaborate catalogs, this firm displays a staggering range of architectural and ornamental fixtures including composition carvings, plaster ornaments, special cabinet woodwork, mantels, column caps, you name it. If you need to match existing work and have trouble locating a piece to suit, this firm may well have what you need. The company has been in business since 1892 and has just started to advertise nationally. It is open to questions and inquiries from consumers on restoration problems, in which it has some experience. All of its material is hand cast or moulded from original pieces designed in the nineteenth century. And all of the materials used (except for the wood products) are flame retardant and meet local fire codes.
Business operation The master catalog, with over 350 pages illustrating some 13,000 patterns and compositions, costs $15. Specialty catalogs on such things as ornamental plaster are $2 to $3.

Paints/Acrylics
E. L. Du Pont de Nemours & Company, Inc.
Marketing Communications Department
Du Pont Company
Wilmington, DE 19898

A mammoth company producing, among an endless line of varied product lines, all forms of house paint under the brand name of Lucite; the brushes, rollers, and other tools to apply them; and a line of solid acrylic laminates under the brand name of Corian. Lucite products and literature can be found in countless paint stores and other retail outlets. Corian, an interesting alternative to Formica (almost a generic name by now), available in white, several light shades, and slightly marbelized finishes, is used for some shaped products like basins and bar tops and also comes in ¼-, ½-, and ¾-in thicknesses for counter surfaces. If information is not available locally, product details will be sent on request from the address above.

Parquet Flooring
Hartco, Inc.
Oneida, TN 37841
(615) 569-8526

Hartco makes solid oak parquet flooring in many tones and finishes and the materials needed to install and maintain it. Specifically, its 12-in × 12-in tiles (showing 4 6-in × 6-in tiles on the surface), are Appalachian oak, much of it quartersawn for better wear. The floor tiles are not structural. (They must be installed over a structural underlayment—the smoother and stronger the better). They are tongue and grooved with a modified V-shape to the joint that makes installation a little easier. The prefinished tiles are available with plain backs (installed with adhesive); self-sticking backs (press to install, but make sure the surface is very clean); and foam backs (installed with Hartco latex adhesive to provide a more resilient surface, some sound deadening, and a vapor barrier facsimile.

Available finishes range from a two-coat polyurethane with a wax surface application to acrylic impregnated tile for heavy traffic areas.

Business operation Hartco sells nationally in retail outlets. It will respond to inquiries with color brochures showing the range of tones and finishes and will provide technical information. That's the only point that bothered me. In with all the tongue and groove and other details should have been a basic piece of information: how thick is the wood? But it wasn't there. Made me a tad cautious.

Plaster Ornaments
Dovetail, Inc.
PO Box 1569
Lowell, MA 01853
(617) 454-2944

Plaster ornamentation, in all shapes and sizes and in all locations—in center of ceilings, at the edges, on porches—used to be moulded as the ceiling and walls were plastered. In many homes in which some of this fine detail work has decayed, repair and restoration can be time consuming and quite costly. And in homes where complete replacements or completely new designs are wanted, much of the work is being replaced with moulded plastic simulations. However, Dovetail has a reasonable, interesting answer between these two extremes. Working with U.S. Gypsum, it developed a fiber glass reinforced cement plaster that acts like plaster in a mould but is stronger and lighter. Also, it does not sustain combustion and will not, as most plastic will, add toxic fumes to a fire. Using this material, Dovetail makes moulds and hand casts some seventy items, ranging from elaborate center medallions and corner blocks to complete ceiling patterns. Installation is accomplished by laying contact cement on the back of the piece and securing it with screws through a thin flange attached to the sculpture. When all pieces are in place, a final skim coat of plaster is added to the ceiling, covering the flange. It is a system that combines improvements in technology without sacrificing detail and craftsmanship.

Business operation Dovetail sells via mail order and does custom work and repair. Write for its illustrated catalog, free on request.

Salvaged Materials

Salvage One
1524 S. Peoria St.
Chicago, IL 60608

Salvage One has been in business only a few years. Walter Ratner, the owner, once ran a used brick business. But as contractors and others starting bringing him mantels, stair railings, and other items out of old buildings, and as the demand for restoration products increased, he expanded. Salvage One now occupies seven floors of a 360,000 sq ft building. The stock includes some 2500 fireplace mantels (from $200 to $8000), 18,000 doors in over 700 different sizes ($40 to $4000), about 60,000 stair balusters, 16,000 engraved door knobs, and more. Their hottest items? Old, fancy doors. Mr. Ratner says, "People love a fancy front door and they usually put them on the front of a new home."

Business operation Write for details of mail order service, or, if you're going to be near Chicago, leave the better part of a day free and bring a specific shopping list.

Siding/Paneling/Roofing

Masonite Corporation
Marketing Services Department
29 N. Wacker Dr.
Chicago, IL 60606
(312) 372-5642

One of the giants, Masonite is probably best known for an array of interior panels in umpteen colors, patterns, and textures, but they also manufacture exterior siding and roofing products, including a new product called *Woodruf*, an "engineered wood fiber" roofing panel that simulates thick cedar shakes.

Business operation By directing inquiries to the address above, you can receive voluminous information on products and applications as well as information on local availability.

Slate

Vermont Structural Slate Company, Inc.
Box 98
Fair Haven, VT 05743
(800) 343-1900 (Toll-free)

This is one of the premier slate firms, taking their materials from a quarry two miles from their main offices. They make exterior roof shingles, copings, sills, and paving slabs; interior flooring, treads and risers, and a variety of slate specialties such as vanity tops, fireplace hearths, and more. The material for roofs is Grade A, unfading Vermont slate quarried from their Eureka Vein in southwestern part of the state. Vermont also cuts and test assembles "readyfit" slate flooring in random ashlar patterns.

Business operation The company sells worldwide to owners, general contractors. You'll find their ad on an ongoing basis in *Architectural Record* magazine. William Markcrow writes, "We provide an awful lot of information to consumers once they contact us. We reprinted a book on slate roofing which is an absolute bible on the subject. We will provide advice concerning installation, maintenance, and will visit historic jobs." Their literature is first rate. Write for it.

Spiral Stair Kits

Mylen Industries, Inc.
650 Washington St.
Box 350
Peekskill, NY 10566
(800) 431-2155
(914) 739-8486 (New York only)

Mylen spiral stairs are prepared in kit form. After measuring and ordering (a planning kit is included in the company's catalog), installation consists of sliding the sleeves welded to the strair treads onto the center pole, attaching the top platform to the second story frame, and screwing on the threaded balusters and handrails. No welding or special tools are required. All hardware is included, plus step by step instructions. Stair diameters range from 3-ft 6-in to 8-ft. Among several options are select red oak handrails, and either checkered safety plate, smooth plate, or predrilled plate treads to which any surface wood is easily added.

Business operation Product literature covering basic and elaborate models is sent on request. The budget spiral stairs come painted with a zinc-chromate primer.

Stair Components

Mansion Industries, Inc.
14711 E. Clark
Industry, CA 91745
(213) 968-9501

Mansion tries to work around the problem that each stairway installation is a little different from all others by providing a line of stair component parts, including a wide selection of turned posts and spindles, railings, finials, balusters, and a series of shelf and room divider components. The flexibility of this system is based on a clever idea. Top and bottom rails (the balusters in Mansion's many systems do not attach to stair treads) are set parallel to each other within posts. Under normal circumstances balusters would have to be cut at angles, carefully, at both ends, to get a good fit. But Mansion's balusters end in a small horizontal cylinder—like a dowel set at right angles to the upright baluster—which slides in, sideways, to corresponding holes in the railings. Since the dowels and holes are round the angle between baluster and rail is not a problem.

Business operation Stair components in clear, kiln-dried hemlock, are sold in small component groups at home centers and other building material retailers. The company will provide descriptive product literature on request. Their installation manuals are quite thorough and well illustrated.

Stairs—Kit and Custom

Woodbridge Ornamental Iron Company
2715 N. Clybourn Ave.
Chicago, IL 60614
(312) 935-1500

Woodbridge makes many types of spiral stairs with rectangular, tapered, or legged frame treads or with closed risers. Also, they manufacture custom stairways, including full shop drawings to suit your site conditions, even for one-of-a-kind circular stairways that are shop built, and then knocked down for shipping. At the economy end of its line is a do-it-yourself spiral stair kit ($5000 FOB Chicago), that includes twelve treads (all 16-gauge steel), platform, handrail, balusters, all bolting hardware (that's all you need), and center post—a complete package for a 4-ft diameter stair. Options include ¾-in particleboard treads ($65), or 1-in oak treads and platform ($275). They will deduct $75 if you supply your own center column pipe.

Business operation Write the company for product specs and illustrations.

Steel Stairs

American General Products
1735 Holmes Rd.
Ypsilanti, MI 48197
(313) 483-1833

American General manufactures a series of basic steel spiral stairs that are relatively easy for do-it-yourselfers to install and require no welding or special tools. The eleven-tread twelve-riser packages (9 ft 6 in floor to floor) are handled through distributors in some parts of the country, but the firm will sell direct.

Pricing Costs FOB factory are $532 for 4-ft diameters and $630 for 5-ft diameters. The firm will send complete catalogs, prices, and a dealer list on request.

Tin Ceilings

Chelsea Decorative Metal Company
6115 Cheena
Houston, TX 77096
(713) 721-9200

Metal ceilings were introduced in the 1860s as an expedient replacement for costly ornamental plasterwork. Many building materials introduced this way, as a cheaper coverup, continue to blight homes inside and out. Not so with metal ceilings. They remain elegant, rugged, and easy to maintain. Chelsea reproduces some twenty-two patterns, in some cases using original dies dating back as far as the Civil War. Styles range from Greek Revival and Rococo to Art Deco, in 2-ft × 8-ft sheets with a silvery tin finish that can be painted if desired. The 26-gauge tin is lightweight, easy to handle, and can be applied over plywood without furring strips. Also, Chelsea offers ten cornice patterns and various fillers and edge trim in 4-ft lengths.

Business operation The interesting brochure includes photographs and prices. The company provides labor and material locally, sells retail through the mail.

W. F. Norman Corporation
214–32 N. Cedar St.
PO Box 323
Nevado, MO 64772
(800) 641-4038
(417) 667-5552 (Missouri residents call collect)

Norman is one of the prime sources for metal ceiling, siding, and roofing materials. It has been producing its many patterns since 1908 and offers several lines now that it offered then. This makes them an ideal source for restorers. And this is really different than going to a company that has gone to great pains to recapture authentic designs. Norman's catalog is 70 pages of authentic designs. The W. F. Norman catalog costs $3, covers installation methods, single squares, large panels, center medallions, corner miters, mouldings, and cornices, all in floral (almost florid) Victorian designs. Also, Norman makes several varieties of metal shingles, some simulating Spanish tile, mission tile, plus decorative trimmings.

Business operation Mark S. Quito of Norman writes, "At any stage of pattern selection, design layout, or installation, we will gladly help anyone with their questions." The company sells nationwide. Call for referrals to retail outlets or order direct.

Wide Board Lumber Supply/Bed Reproductions

The Country Bed Shop
Box 222
Groton, MA 01450
(617) 448-6336

This shop produces seventeenth- and eighteenth-century reproductions of beds, chairs, tables, and case furniture. The proprietor, Charles E. Thibeau, one of the few Americans elected to The Guild of Master Craftsmen in London, produces work on commission but does offer a sampling of work in the Bed Shop catalog. Other operations of this firm include the production of hand-made, old-fashioned milk paint for restoration work and the milling of wide board flooring and paneling, in oak from 4 to 16 in wide, and in pine from 12 to 24 in wide.

Business operation The Country Bed Shop catalog is available for $3. Small brochures on milk paint products and wide board lumber are sent for 60¢ in stamps to cover postage.

Pricing A Hepplewhite Field bed with headboard and gracefully raised ogee canopy frame is about $1600 with cherry, maple, or mahogany posts. Less elaborate chairs and tables range from $375 (for the bow-back Windsor) to about $600.

Wide Board Pine

Carlisle Restoration Lumber
Rte. 123
Stoddard, NH 03464
(603) 446-3937

Maybe you too will receive a wonderful little color snapshot of a wide board pine floor bathed in sunlight along with your stock and price sheet. Carlisle mills pine up to 22 in across, oak to 12 in, and pine ship lap and featheredge clapboards—simple, primary Colonial materials. Stock is cut 1⅛-in thick to finish at 1 or ⅞ in, as opposed to most available stock that is ¾ in or a shade less. This makes Carlisle's lumber compatible with old boards in renovation and restoration projects. The company guarantees complete coverage, as Dale Carlisle writes, "with no percentage of waste, and can do this because of our quality grading before our lumber is cured." Lengths come from 8 to 16 ft.

Business operation Carlise ships nationwide at reasonable rates via St. Johnsbury Trucking in Bellows Falls, Vermont, and its sister companies.

Pricing Lumber prices generally can be volatile so write for current rates. Currently, 16- to 22-in pine is over $2 per board foot (note that one board foot is 12-in × 12-in × 1-in; 12- to 16-in pine is about 20 percent less. Oak in 6- to 12-in widths is also about $2.25 per board foot.

Decorating and Finishing

Building Supplies

Renovation Concepts, Inc.
PO Box 3720
Minneapolis, MN 55403
(612) 377-9526

New kinds of firms are generally a good indicator of the level of new consumer interests. This firm, which is just into its fifth year, indicates a kind of second generation interest in renovating (not remodeling) and restoring old homes. Obviously, some of this interest has been forced on owners of older homes by the economy and the costs of new homes (also their durability compared with some of those rock-solid Victorian monsters with 2 × 4's in the wall that actually measure 2 in × 4 in). Renovation Concepts represents themselves and forty other manufacturers who make period lighting fixtures, moulding, brass rail, metal ceilings, wood columns, plumbing fixtures, beveled glass, and more. Many of these firms are listed in this sourcebook, but not all of them. The idea is to have a single source of supply for all the different materials you might need to restore or faithfully renovate an older house.

Business operation Renovation Concepts will provide its professional, three ring–type catalog for $10 and a condensed, consumer retail catalog for $5. Many of the pages may be obtained direct from the manufacturers of course, some at no charge. But this firm also offers free consultation service and has an architect and a renovation contractor on staff to answer your questions about products and their applications. It will send a small brochure free. Catalog costs are refundable with your first order.

Cedar Closet Panels
Giles & Kendall, Inc.
PO Box 188
Huntsville, AL 35804
(205) 776-2979

The response you get from an inquiry to Giles & Kendall is likely to be different from other letters because it smells, quite pleasantly, of 100 percent pure Tennessee aromatic red cedar. The company turns the material into thin facing panels, used particularly for lining clothes closets. The panels are made by debarking logs, flaking the wood, and spraying it with adhesive and

wax to stabilize the pieces as they are steam pressed into 4-ft × 8-ft panels. Aside from the wonderful fragrance, cedar gives some protection against moths and mildew. The full ¼-in panels can be cut by conventional plywood circular saw blades, or finishing saws, then nailed or glued over studding (relatively few building codes permit this) or over wallboard. With a Class C fire rating, ⅝-in fire code wallboard would make a sensible backup panel. No finishing is required or productive. The company wants 50¢ for a short pamphlet of four closet plans, which show only rough, overall dimensions without any construction details but come with a sample of the product. Try a SASE for a sample of cedar and look elsewhere for useful, complete plans. This product is similar to pressboard and flakeboard, with random flake sizes and whitish to reddish color tones.

Business operation Sells retail nationwide. Write for the name and address of the dealer nearest you.

Decorative Moulding
Bendix Mouldings, Inc.
235 Pegasus Ave.
Northvale, NJ 07647
(201) 767-8888

Bendix imports an extensive collection of mouldings, made of both hard- and softwoods and both embossed (stamped and not quite as clear-cut as you'd like) and carved (by machine and extremely well detailed). It offers a wide selection of styles, ranging from very basic to very ornate. Also, it carries a line of picture frame mouldings including modern, snap-together packages) and elaborate wood frames with fabric-covered liner pieces.

Business operation Bendix makes a substantial effort to help consumers use their products by offering a collection of how-to booklets covering the tools, skills, materials, and methods of picture framing, building wainscoting and chair rails, turning very basic, unpainted furniture into highly detailed and individualized pieces, and more. Many of these booklets are substantial and contain detailed drawings. There may be a small charge if you write the plant for these project booklets. Product catalogs showing sizes and silhouettes are available free. The company sells through a distribution network to home centers, lumber dealers and other retail outlets across the country. Write for product information and the name and address of the Bendix dealer nearest you.

Decorator Hardward/Fixtures
W. J. Weaver and Sons, Inc.
1208 Wisconsin Ave. NW
Washington, DC 20007
(202) 333-4200

A decorator supply house with an extensive catalog of locks, door knockers, light fixtures, all kinds of hardware, mouldings, signs, weathervanes, porcelain lavatory bowls, and a lot more.

Business operation W. J. Weaver features a selection of moulded styrene ceiling ornaments—such as very detailed shell and sunburst patterns in which, for example, you might center a chandelier. A catalog illustrates these mouldings and center medallions. They are applied with contact cement.

Pricing Ceiling medallion prices range from about $7 for small (2 in $\times$ 4 in) designs and up to approximately $15 for intricate 34-in diameter designs. The catalog, 60 pages of pictures and descriptions to ooh and aah at, is available with complete price list for $2.50. This firm has been in business since 1889 and ships nationwide.

Hand-Crafted Tiles
Delft Blue
PO Box 103
Ellicott City, MD 21043

Delft Blue is a source for hand-painted earthenware tiles. The company will send catalogs and product literature on request and sells wholesale, retail, and via mail order.

Hand-Painted Tile
Dutch Products & Supply Company
14 S. Main St.
Yardley, PA 19067
(215) 493-4873

I had never seen hand-painted, dutch tile motifs used in place of several typically metal components of chandeliers, but this company has done just that and also offers a collection of tiles. The chandeliers are a little peculiar looking, I think, but the tiles are something else. Dutch Products has small tiles with floral patterns, series of six or eight tiles that form a mural, a vertical stack of anywhere from six to twelve tiles in blue on white that form an intertwined column of peacocks; a fourteen-tile pattern forming the stations of the cross; and tiles with windmills, boats, baskets of flowers—quite a selection.

Business operation Dutch Products will send an illustrated brochure of chandeliers and one of tiles (called Westraven) on request. It also carries hand-made weathervanes.

Pricing Two-tile tableaux in blue are about $30 wholesale, $37 in multicolor; four-tile tableaux are about $60 in monochrome and twelve tiles about $225. A price list is sent with the brochures.

Masonry Fabric

Flexi-Wall Systems
101 Carolina Ave.
PO Box 88
Liberty, SC 29657
(803) 855-0500

This unique product is a patented, flexible, gypsum-impregnated, jute fabric wallcovering, i.e., like thick, open-weave wallpaper with a masonry base. It can be used in a one-step application over concrete or block foundation walls in a basement, over drywall, over chipped and deteriorating plaster, even directly over old paneling. The material has passed rigid fire and toxicity tests required by the New York City Buildings Department (just about the most rigid codes going) and has a Class A flame-spread rating under ASTM. The material is applied with special Flexi-Wall adhesive and generally follows procedures similar to the application of conventiona wallcovering. Many color tones are available.

Business operation Flexi-Wall is sold through national distributors such as Sherwin-Williams (you should be able to get product information at their dealers), and retail direct. The company will send catalogs and a price list to consumers at no charge.

Pricing Flexi-Wall is sold in 40 sq yd rolls, in three different jute weaves, for about $5.30 per sq yd. Shipping weight is 55 lbs per roll.

Paint

The O'Brien Corporation
450 E. Grand Ave.
South San Francisco, CA 94080
(415) 761-2300

O'Brien manufactures paints for consumers, professionals, plus industrial marine and automotive finishes, all sold through a network of about 3600 independent retail outlets across the country. Fuller-O'Brien paints and stains are sold in up to 1000 custom colors.

Business operation The company in its infancy worked on automotive finishes because the original owner, Patrick O'Brien, was a finishing superintendent at the South Bend Studebaker plant. Product literature, color charts, and more are available at local dealers and from O'Brien's five regional headquarters. The main headquarters is listed above.

Paint/Stain/Caulk

Glidden Coatings & Resins
900 Union Commerce Building
Cleveland, OH 44115
(216) 344-8140

Selling paint, stain, wallcoverings, and related products nationwide, Glidden also manufactures Macco adhesives, available at home centers, paint or hardware stores.

Business operation Several interesting pieces of literature are available from Glidden, including a pamphlet called Paint Pointers, which is a guide to all Glidden products and their applicaitons; Booklet No. 01525 on stains with excellent samples of solid latex and semitransparent stain tones; and an informative booklet on one of its new products called Insul-aid, a moisture resistant paint. (Nothing is moisture proof except impermeable, perfectly sealed foil.) Glidden reports on independent tests show the vapor barrier paint keeps up to nine times more moisture out of the wall cavity compared with latex paint, and provides a 20 percent decrease in heat loss. Feel free to write for details if this number strikes you the way it struck me—maybe a tad optimistic.

Resilient Flooring/Ceilings/Carpeting

Armstrong World Industries, Inc.
PO Box 3001
Lancaster, PA 17604
(717) 397-0611
(800) 233-3823 (Except Pennsylvania)
(800) 732-0048 (Pennsylvania only)

Armstrong makes a very large selection of resilient sheet flooring and tile, residential ceilings and accessories for tile and track or lay-in systems, and carpeting. It distributes nationally through wholesalers to a network of independently owned dealers, including many national chains. The selection seems limitless, so to help you out Armstrong offers, free on request, product brochures. Of particular interest are *Guide to Armstrong Floors, A Shopper's Guide to Carpet Quality*, and *How to Core for Your Carpet.*

Business operation   Armstrong maintains a Consumer Response Center at the Lancaster headquarters to handle requests for literature, general and specific product inquiries, and complaints.

Sculptured Ceiling Tile

Ceilings, Walls, & More, Inc.
PO Box 494, 124 Walnut St.
Jefferson, TX 75657
(214) 665-2221

"The gaslight era recreated" is the tag line for this relatively new company with limited literature and a small but expanding line of ceiling panels that simulate decorative plaster detailing. Three patterns—a lattice with border, a rosette box, and a raised egg and dart moulding square—are reproduced in die-cut, .035-in thick, high-impact polymer material, and, if needed, a self-extinguishing vinyl to meet strict fire codes.

The surface patterns are bold and precise but are, after all, plastic, not plaster. The higher the ceiling the less this matters. The 2-ft sq panels (and a 2-ft $\times$ 4-ft chain pattern filler) may be cut by scoring and snapping—the way glass is cut. Butt seams can be covered with moulding, concealed with Dap filler, or left exposed. The tile surface can be painted (spraying is recommended) only with oil base enamel. Instruction literature includes recommendations for direct adhesive application to a plaster or wallboard surface. Also, the panels will fit many grid suspension systems, although this mix of style and technology conjures up pictures of Shaker rockers in high polished chrome.

Business operation   This company ships nationwide. For a preview, it offers a $6 sample kit of available panels and filler strip. Write for the dealer nearest you.

Pricing   Tiles and fillers are about $2 per square foot; self-extinguishing vinyl prices are quoted case by case. Orders direct from the factory in Texas are discounted 20 percent.

Veneers

Homecraft Veneer
901 West Way
Latrobe, PA 15650
(412) 537-8435

Homecraft stocks domestic and imported veneers in $\frac{1}{28}$- to $\frac{1}{40}$-in thickness and widths from 4 to 18 in, all generally supplied in 3-ft lengths, with custom lengths up to 8 ft available on request. Virtually every type of species is covered: five types of cherry, bubinga, ebony, six types of mahogany, rosewood, teak, walnut, you name it. Homecraft also carries veneer supplies such as contact cement, glues, solvents, cutting and repair tools, and the like.

Business operation   Homecraft ships nationally via mail order. Its minimum order is $10. Write for a free supplies list with prices.

Wood Finishing
The Flecto Company, Inc.
PO Box 12955
Oakland, CA 94606
(415) 655-2470

Flecto makes a reasonably standard selection of wood stains, various clear sealers, and a product called Varathane Plastic. It is available clear or in colors (pigmented versions of the clear material). I have used the white pigmented material many times, and it is a strange combination of paint and polyurethane—at least that's the way it behaves going down. A coat thinned 20 percent or so over raw plywood, followed by a light sanding, and a full-strength finish coat produces an extremely hard and durable finish with exceptionally uniform color and satin finish.

Business operation Varathane sells only through distributors. However, you can write or call the company to locate a retailer near you who handles its products. Additionally, it will send, at no cost, product information that covers in great detail application, coverage, and more.

Wood Sealing/Finishing
Watco-Dennis Corporation
1756 22nd St.
Santa Monica, CA 90404
(213) 829-2226

Dennis Enterprises, established in 1904, became Watco-Dennis and has been manufacturing penetrating Danish oil finishes since 1957. It sells twelve different wood finishes, eighteen stains, and three sealers and hardeners for masonry in 35,000 retail outlets. Watco oils are popular for the one-step application that seals and solidifies the surface of, say, a wood floor, as opposed to multistage applications like wax or polyurethane that sit on the surface. Different Watco oils are made for interior hard and soft woods, tropical hardwoods, redwood and cedar, exterior timbers, marine teak and mahogany, and a variety of masonry. The clear oils produce a low luster, slightly yellowed, grain-enhancing finish on fine-sanded raw wood. Average coverage is 200 to 300 sq ft per gallon.

Business operation Watco responds to consumer inquiries with a letter, a list of distributors, and an informative, 12-page brochure containing complete product descriptions and application instructions. Watco Danish Oil and Teak Oil (very nice over birch veneer plywood), are nontoxic when polymerized (hardened) and used by many school districts, parks, and recreation departments. Products are sold in 8-oz to 55-gallon containers in all states, and fifty-four countries overseas.

Pricing Varies at retail outlet.

Wood Veneers
Wood Shed
1807 Elmwood Ave.
Buffalo, NY 14207
(716) 876-4720

Wood Shed sells an extensive line of veneers, and some exotic hardwoods as well. Their catalog starts with blistered birch in 18- by 106-in sheets and continues through plum pudding mahogany, padauk, fiddleback maple, ash burl, mahogany crotch in 20-in $\times$ 40-in sheets (must have been some huge tree), butternut, cherry, hickory, and more. They have crossbanding veneers, $\frac{1}{16}$-

and ⅛-inch special thickness veneers, and sample packs for wood shops and woodworkers.

Business operation Wood Shed sells by the square foot. Prices vary drastically according to material. The catalog, which unfortunately is not illustrated, is sent on request.

Woodwork/Hardware Supplies

The Woodworker's Store
21801 Industrial Blvd.
Rogers, MN 55374
(612) 428-4101

This is one of the best, if not the best presentation of tools, materials, and supplies in this field; 112 pages of large, crystal clear, color photographs, color artwork with cut-away views showing hardware details and operation—a beauty, and a bargain for $1. Woodworker's sells the opposite of what you find in Rickles. Not to knock Rickles (at least not to knock it too hard), but The Woodworker's Store catalog doesn't carry tools and materials of undistinguished quality. (Was that tactful enough?) General coverage includes veneers, inlays, hardwood lumber, carved mouldings, cabinet and specialty hardware, all kinds of hand tools, finishing materials, kits, and books. Here are a few goodies: concealed, self-closing hinges; thirteen different kinds of lid and drop-leaf supports; magnetic touch catches (you really ought to try one of these); Tite Joint furniture fasteners; platform rocker springs; and Ulmia hardwood planes. The latter are carried in several mail-order catalogs but indicate the general quality of the selection here.

Business operation Retail stores are located in Minneapolis, Denver, Seattle, and Boston. The company has been in business for 30 years and sends mail orders nationwide. It has a mailing list of 125,000. A dollar well spent for the catalog.

TRADE ASSOCIATIONS

Asphalt (Blacktop) Properties

Asphalt Institute
Asphalt Institute Building
College Park, MD 20740
(301) 927-0422

The institute conducts research and education programs related to asphalt products and will respond to consumer inquiries with a list of model job specifications so that you can match up the facts and figures on an estimate with a theoretical standard. Write for a list of publications, including booklets, engineering manuals, and construction specifications.

Brick Work

Brick Institute of America
1750 Old Meadow Rd.
McLean, VA 22102
(703) 893-4010

The Brick Institute (yes, there's an institute on just about everything) represents manufacturers of brick and other clay products like flue tile. It produces voluminous materials on the manufacture and use of brick, both for professionals and do-it-yourselfers.

Business operation The institute will send a complete publications list on request and offers to answer questions, "regarding the use of brick, problems concerning brick or brick structures, availability of specific types, etc." It maintains twelve regional offices (write the address above for local names and addresses).

Concrete Data

American Concrete Institute
Box 19150 Redford Station
Detroit, MI 48219
(313) 532-2600

A technical society of engineers, architects, and contractors, ACI sponsors over eighty technical committees that evaluate and produce data on all phases of concrete manufacturing and use, including code compliance in all types of building conditions.

Insulation Standards/Contractors

Insulation Contractors Association of
America (ICAA)
905 16th St. NW
Washington, DC 20006
(202) 347-2791

ICAA can provide referrals of contractors in your area and publishes a code of conduct applying to advertising as well as installation. For instance, it recommends that all product performance claims be made in writing; that any limitations on performance such as settling or shrinking be disclosed; and that insulation thickness or density be explained to consumers only at R values. In the forest of energy-saving claims, ICAA provisions can help you find a clear path.

Lumber

Southern Forest Products Association
(SFPA)
PO Box 52468
New Orleans, LA 70152
(504) 443-4464

SFPA represents lumber mills that produce southern pine. However, like many lumber associations, it does a lot more than hawk wood. For instance, it produces voluminous amounts of technical data on wood strengths, applications, durability and maintenance, and more. SFPA regularly develops new publications and audio visual materials, staying current with new construction systems and particularly with the trend toward "economical" framing. Many of the new minimal systems require careful calculations and construction, as they do not have the structural buffer of the older, somewhat overbuilt house frames. In fact, C. G. Gehring, vice-president of marketing for SFPA, reports, "We constantly monitor the market to identify changes, trends, and new products. The two newest trends have been the growth of the treating industry [wood preservative treating] and the use of flat wood floor trusses in residential construction."

Business operation Write SFPA for its publications list for a starter. West of the Rockies, you may catch them at a local home-related trade show. Elsewhere you may be able to get very thorough, very specific technical support for your building project from a local field representative. The headquarters office will tell you who and where the field reps are. Generally all information is free.

Masonry Properties and Uses

International Masonry Institute
823 15th St. NW, Suite 1001
Washington, DC 20005
(202) 783-3908

A source for general information on products and performance, for example, brick grading (different types for different conditions), variations of slate, sandstone, limestone, bluestone, and other materials covering hardness, porosity, and other characteristics.

Portland Cement Association (PCA)
5420 Old Orchard Rd.
Skokie, IL 60077

Write for Portland's publications list, which includes extensive technical data on cement products and their installation, including a general guide, *Your Guide to Cement and Concrete.* It also publishes a well-illustrated brochure on block walls. A note of caution: of the hundreds of trade associations I have dealt with, groups that exist to further the interests of their members by dispensing endless brochures, reports, and the like, PCA is the only one that has provided me with material, and then, weeks later and without any warning, sent along a substantial bill—definitely dirty pool. Check the publications list for costs carefully. One book worth noting is the *Concrete Masonry Handbook,* with over 200 pages of illustrated data and installations.

Plywood Design/Specifications/Grading

American Plywood Association (APA)
7011 S. 19th St.
PO Box 11700
Tacoma, WA 98411
(206) 565-6600

The APA is a nonprofit trade association that is the most abundant and one of the best informed sources on design, performance, and installation of plywood products. They represent mills that produce about 80 percent of all structural wood panel products manufactured in the United States. They have an extensive amount of information available to consumers, some of it very basic, some quite technical. Among the APA's most important functions is the development of industry-wide guidelines for product specs and performance, including stringent grading rules. APA maintains eight quality testing labs and a research center in Tacoma to this end. Other functions and services include: conducting regional seminars on design and performance, publishing an extensive list of books and brochures, sponsoring an annual design competition for architects, builders, students, *and* do-it-yourselfers. They also have a limited number of home plans using plywood products.

Business operation First, write for the APA Publications Index. Most of the titles listed are available at the rate of five different titles for $1 to cover postage and handling. Of particular interest to builders and do-it-yourselfers is booklet No. C20D, "Grades & Specifications," that fully explains the variety of structural panels, their markings, performance, sizes, uses, and more; booklet No. F405, "Performance-Rated Panels," on the variations of plywood and composite board; and booklet No. X505J, "Panel Handbook & Grade Glossary," a 40-page handbook with illustrations.

Redwood Lumber
California Redwood Association
One Lombard St.
San Francisco, CA 94111
(415) 392-7880

This active trade association provides information, technical specs, and many project plans using redwood lumber products. Specifically, it has over 100 different pieces of literature available to consumers, generally for a modest charge of 25¢ or 50¢ to cover mailing, and can provide help with questions on applications and finishes by phone or mail. Write or call California Redwood's Technical Services Department. Pat Young, the promotion manager, helps to produce quality literature that is helpful and detailed.

PROFESSIONAL SOCIETIES

Asphalt Contractors
National Asphalt Pavement Association
(NAPA)
6811 Kenilworth Ave.
Riverside, MD 20840
(301) 779-4880

Over 1000 members include paving contractors, equipment manufacturers, engineering consultants, and others. NAPA maintains committees on product research and application, and environmental control and will provide referrals to local contractors and an informative booklet, *Consumer's Fact Sheet for Hot-Mix Asphalt Driveways,* particularly valuable for novices.

GOVERNMENT AGENCIES

Construction Data/Reports
Center for Building Technology
National Bureau of Standards,
    Department of Commerce
BR Room B266
Washington, DC 20234
(301) 921-3106

This section of NBS keeps track of developments in structural engineering, fire research, all kinds of building materials, building standards and code compliance, housing technology in general, and other subjects. It will either answer inquiries or refer to appropriate government agencies. Plan ahead. Write first for a publications list to see if NBS has the information you need.

Engineering Research Reports
Construction Engineering Research
    Laboratory
Department of the Army
PO Box 4005
Champaign, IL 61820
(217) 352-6511

Boasting some 3000 books and 7000 technical reports, this source specializes in fibrous concrete, the waterproofing of concrete and masonry, construction design and economy, and other somewhat particular fields of interest. It answers inquiries, makes referrals, and permits on-site use of its information resources. Technical reports are available through NTIS (National Technical Information Service).

Fire Characteristics
Fire Information Reference Services
National Bureau of Standards
Washington, DC 20234
(301) 921-3246

If you are near Gaithersburg, Maryland, and need information on the fire safety of building materials you can get access to NBS's collection of some 8000 documents, journals, technical reports, films, and more on fire research and safety, including fabric flammability. Write for a list of publications.

Housing Technology
Office of the Assistant Secretary for
    Research and Technology
U.S. Department of Housing and
    Urban Development
451 Seventh St. NW
Washington, DC 20410
(202) 755-5634

This research division of HUD covers housing technology in general, housing quality and costs, standards for manufactured housing, and more. It answers inquiries and makes referrals to other HUD divisions.

Product Safety Standards
Consumer Product Safety Commission
    (CPSC)
Washington, DC 20207
(800) 638-8326 (Toll-free continental
    United States)
(800) 638-8333 (Toll-free Alaska,
    Hawaii, Puerto Rico, and Virgin
    Islands)
(800) 492-8363 (Toll-free Maryland
    only)

Stated simply, the purpose of CPSC is to protect the public against unreasonable risk of injury associated with consumer products used in and around the home, schools, and recreation areas. *Unreasonable* is the operative word. CPSC can set safety standards for lawn mowers and chain saws, get warning labels applied by the manufacturers, and more. But it can't make you buy the safest model or use it safely once you have it. Granted, CPSC may be somewhat behind public opinion and behind local and state governments as well. For example, after fears about urea formaldehyde foam insulation were well documented in scientific studies, some local communities moved to ban its use. Later some states did the same. Then, finally, so did CPSC. But that seems to be about par for the federal government. Some of CPSC's areas with the highest priority now are chain saws, where "kickback" was found responsible for 23 percent of some 125,000 injuries in a 1980 study; house wiring and circuit breakers; wood- and coal- burning heating equipment; and upholstered furniture relating to fire hazards.

Business operation CPSC will provide publication lists from which you can order reports (many are free) on a wide variety of materials and products.

Toxic Materials
Technical Services Division
Office of Pesticide Programs
Environmental Protection Agency
4770 Buford Hwy.
Chamblee, GA 30341
(404) 633-3311

This is a good source if you have questions about the content of building materials and chemical contamination. The office maintains some 25,000 index cards on pesticide literature, has an extensive library on the subject, answers inquiries, provides literature search services, makes referrals, and permits on-site use of materials.

Wood and Frame Research
USDA Forest Service, Forest Products
  Laboratory
PO Box 5130
Madison, WI 53705
(608) 264-5600

The Forest Service is one of the best sources of information on wood use and performance in structures. It maintains a gigantic testing facility and offers literally piles of reports on all aspects of wood use. Of particular interest is their Form 81–020, *List of Publications of Interest to Architects, Builders, Engineers, and Retail Lumbermen.* No, you don't have to be one of the above to get the list. But the title does tell you that this is not basic how-to advice. It is a source of generally technical reports on such subjects as wood diaphragm materials and racking strength of wood frame walls. It includes absolutely fascinating reports (obviously, not fascinating to everyone) on subjects like long-time performance of trussed rafters, strength of log bridge stringers after several years' use in southeast Alaska, and much more. The list is free, and better yet, single copies of the reports are free—but only if you get the list first and make limited, specific requests.

READING AND REFERENCE

Adobe
Adobe (Build It Yourself),
  by Paul Graham
University of Arizona Press

This practical book covers the complete adobe process, from brick making to bond beam, finishing, and roofing. Several adobe styles are covered with enough technical and on the job background to be really useful. A good book to start with; 160 pages; $9.

Making the Adobe Brick,
  by Eugene H. Boudreau
Random House

Even though home-grown books like this one are generally short on technical data and a little narrow on design applications, I find them exhilarating because they are plain-language, personal accounts of the endless decisions, plans, dreams, and problems of construction and are not so technical on the spot solutions found only in a case history

story. This couple made over 100 tons of adobe brick (oh, for a Cinva-Ram press), experimented with mixtures, sifting, batching, and virtually all the little pieces of work that are the backbone of building a home. About 90 pages; $5.

Bricks
Bricklaying Simplified,
   by Donald R. Brann
Easi-Bild
PO Box 215
Briarcliff Manor, NY 10510

This modest book is geared more to outdoor projects like backyard barbecues and patios than to the structural use of brick in home-building but still manages to cover the basics of the materials, tools, and mortars. Part of the Easi-Bild series of books, this one is thorough enough to be useful. Some titles in the series are sketchy.

Codes and Regulations
Building Regulations, by Edmund Vitale
Charles Scribner's Sons

A good book to use in addition to *The Owner-Builder and the Code*, this one concentrates on reading and understanding code language and how to present the case for unorthodox materials and methods of construction in order to obtain a building permit.

The Owner-Builder and the Code,
   by Ken Kern, et al.
Owner-Builder Publications
PO Box 817
North Fork, CA 93643

Building codes vary from region to region, even from town to town. This causes a prob-

lem for any book that tries to cover the subject in enough detail to have value for a project in Westchester as well as in the woods of Oregon. But the many case histories presented here offer owner-builders insights into what to expect, particularly if they are working with other than conventional materials and standard, stick-built construction; 180 pages; about $5.

Concrete
Concrete Manual
U.S. Department of the Interior, 1979

This tome is 600 pages of everything you could possibly want to know about concrete. Significant portions are devoted to large-scale projects—dams, for instance—but even there the information and photographs are educational. Not a book for do-it-yourselfers, unless they have a lot of time on their hands.

Do-It-Yourself Materials
The Handbook of Do-It-Yourself
   Materials, by Max Alth
Crown Publishers, 1982

Sort of a poor man's Sweet's catalog (that's the bookshelf of volumes covering every conceivable building product used by architecture firms, planning departments, etc.), this handbook covers a lot of territory from roofing and siding to locks and wiring. The information is strictly limited to what exists and what shapes and sizes and colors it comes in, with a smattering of how-to stuff tacked on. Published in 1982 and reasonably current, it tries to serve as a giant catalog for builders, remodelers, and so forth, although all the details it contains and more are certainly available direct from manufacturers and others. Try the library; about $19; some 300 pages.

Estimating

Estimating for the General Contractor,
by Paul J. Cook
R. S. Means Company, 1982

This book offers complete coverage of labor and material estimating with many sample projects worked up, estimate summary forms, and special issues such as adjusting prices according to complexity or simplicity of a project. Over 200 pages of detailed explanations; the cost is about $28.

National Construction Estimator
Craftsman Book Company
542 Stevens Ave.
Solana Beach, CA 92075

Updated every year, this book is one of the few that is usable and practical for do-it-yourselfers. Also, the cost is reasonable at about $11. The tables are organized according to work category, such as flooring and glazing. Under each heading the different components of each job, both labor and materials, are broken down and priced. Cost adjustment factors are given for different parts of the country. You need not price your project strictly by the book, but it will certainly help you catch all the little details it is easy to overlook in the excitement of planning a project.

Formwork

*Construction Manual: Concrete and
Formwork,* by T. W. Love
Craftsman Book Company, 1973

Concrete footings, the part of any structure that gets buried, often get neglected even though all the time and effort and money you put into the rest of the building is literally riding on what you do down at the bottom. This book covers a moderate amount of technical information on con-

crete but is particularly helpful for builders who do not have much experience with building forms. Published in 1973, the book specifies 1-in $\times$ 6-in form construction, which is generally less economical than plywood, although you do wind up with nice horizontal striations. Text and illustrations also opt for homemade wire ties instead of commercial spreaders and nuts. About 175 pages; $6.50.

Hardwoods

Fine Hardwoods Selectorama
American Walnut Association
666 North Lake Shore Dr.
Chicago, IL 60611

Yes, there is a trade association for just about every kind of material and skill, including walnut trees. However, this 60-page book ($6) covers bubinga, East Indian satinwood, and other exotic hardwood varieties as well as black American walnut, alder, and other domestic species. More than a simple wood selector, this book gives you a lot of information (like hardness, shrinkage characteristics, specific gravity, and other technicalities) in addition to the pretty pictures.

Insulation

*Optimum Insulation Thickness in
Wood-Framed Homes*
USDA Forest Service Report No.
001–001–00394–8
Superintendent of Documents, U.S.
Government Printing Office
Washington, DC 20402

This small (37 pages), inexpensive (85¢) booklet will help you resist the heavily advertised advice to add more and more insulation to your home. It contains no-nonsense graphic displays of cost per inch and resulting thermal efficiency and will enable you to find the point of diminishing return in your home. If you want to go past that point it's up to you. But at least you'll know that you'll be spending a lot of money for a little improvement in efficiency. The booklet covers insulation in roofing, walls, and floors, with regional weather taken into account.

Insulation Advertising Standards
Council of Better Business Bureaus
1150 17th St. NW
Washington, DC 20036

One of BBB's most informative brochures, the *Standards for Home Insulation Materials; Advertising and Selling* (Publication 24–138) is an understandable, readable look at what salespeople and contractors should be telling you before you buy. This nonbinding industry code specifies, among other things, that any time R value, price, or thickness is quoted, several pieces of information must appear as well in a "clear and conspicuous manner": a warning about shrinkage and settling, specifics of the type, form, thickness of insulation, and much more. Interesting before you buy.

Materials Index
Sweet's Architectural Catalog File
Sweet's Construction Division
McGraw-Hill Information Systems
Company

This is one of the best resources for contractors, homeowners, designers, do-it-yourselfers, and remodelers—just about anyone interested in architecture and construction, both residential and commercial. Unfortu-

nately, you can't buy it, and unless you live near a city you may not even be able to use it. Sweet's is on the shelf in every major architectural firm in the country (technically, the 10,000 most active firms) but only in libraries in cities with a population of 250,000 or more. The twelve volumes cover commercial construction, building products, residential construction, interiors —everything you could possibly need for a building. The 20,000 pages amount to a giant compilation of company catalogs. Many firms produce special product sheets only for this presentation, making the case for their company mainly to architects who will be leafing through the *Catalog* while writing specifications. You can't own it yourself, and if you live in a small town your best bet is to park on the doorstep of the local building department or local architectural firm and plead for their old edition. The entire *Catalog* is updated annually so a one-year old copy is still accurate and valuable. This is one of the best ways to see what is available in any given field. Your local hardware store may have several models of one brand of lockset. Sweet's will show you hundreds.

Thomas Register of American Manufacturers
Thomas Register
310 E. 44 St.
New York NY 10017

You can imagine that this must be a big book. In fact it is a 16-volume series, eating up about 6 ft of shelf space. The inexpensive paper and mass printing nets a price for the entire set of about $140, although the price seems to rise on a regular basis. The *Register* includes some 140,000 product classifications, including manufactured products and the parts of the products; the machines and equipment used to make the products and the parts; the machines that make the machines; and more. You get the idea. The price is steep for anyone who does not use the *Register* regularly, but unlike Sweet's catalog, which is available only to town planning departments, major architectural firms, and the like, you can buy this monster if you want to. But almost all libraries have a current or recent edition. Since the *Register* is updated annually, there are a lot of one-year-old copies floating around, and you won't miss much in one year. The system includes an alphabetized listing of products and services, a list of companies, a subject index, an index of trade and brand names, which together give you several ways to find what you want. Also, there are countless ads, many of them illustrated. Short entries describe the products and services without positive or negative recommendations. Sorting out the good guys and the bad guys is still up to you. I have a 1977 edition that I bought and an 1982 edition that I got from my local library, and I use them regularly. Phone numbers and addresses in current editions are generally reliable—quite a feat of research for over 25,000 pages of fine print.

Materials Safety
The Household Pollutants Guide,
    by Albert J. Fritsch
Doubleday & Company

Maybe a little more thorough than you really need and a bit overcautious too (but not hysterical), this book is a guide to the materials commonly used in home construction and repair, and all the bad things they may (that's the key word) do to you. Produced by the Center for Science in the Public Interest, this book is well documented, a little scary, and worthwhile; $3.50 for about 300 pages of solid information.

Materials Use in Architecture
Architecture without Architects, by
    Bernard Rudofsky
Doubleday & Co.

Before you limit your thinking to 2 $\times$ 4's, and plywood sheathing, and three-tab asphalt shingles, you should read this book. It is an eye-opener and a classic. It's almost 20 years since the first edition, and the book is just as valuable, showing what people (not necessarily highly trained architects, engineers, or builders) do with the materials available to them. The text is consistently interesting, examining not only building materials but methods of construction and building use, particularly those that are passed over as too primitive but, with a closer, more ingenious look, show an uncanny blending of climate, use, maintenance, durability, and more. About 160 pages, with a lot of photographs covering all kinds of materials and construction around the world; about $6.

Plywood
Plywood Publications Index
American Plywood Association
PO Box 11700
Tacoma, WA 98411

APA publishes extensive reports, specification guides, and booklets on how to use plywood efficiently in house construction, and more. Start with the publications index, which is free.

Skylights
The Skylight Book, by Al Burns
The Running Press

Skylights are increasingly popular because they transform a room with a minimum amount of effort in a limited work area that does not turn half the house into a temporary workshop. This book is very specific, covers all types of units, and shows detailed sequences of installation. Skylights do require holes in the roof, after all, and they tend to leak unless you are very thorough and very cautious with flashing. A good look at the subject; 110 pages; about $6.

Slate

Slate Roofs
National Slate Association
Vermont Structural Slate Company
PO Box 98
Fair Haven, VT 05743

Now somewhat of an exotic building material, slate is still the Rolls Royce of roofing. As it deteriorates, which does take a while under normal conditions, the cost of decent repair or replacement makes it tempting to many homeowners to opt instead for asphalt shingles. This book, prepared by the trade association in the field, is filled with details about flashing, installation, care, and repair and just may help you keep the best roof you can get. The book is reprinted from the original 1926 edition—back when there was time and money enough to do things carefully and solidly.

Soil Cement

Soil-Cement (Its Use in Building)
United Nations Publications
Room A-3315
New York, NY 10017

The idea is simple: to stabilize certain types of earth with cement additive so that building block can be made almost exclusively of local, extremely low-cost materials. This is the book to use in conjunction with the Cinva-Ram, the $350 or so, hand-operated press machine that turns the ground on your building site into your house. Intended primarily for underdeveloped countries, this system of construction will certainly meet resistance with building departments. This book lays out the building process and design applications; extremely interesting appropriate technology; $7.

Stone

Building Stone Walls, by John Vivian
Garden Way Publishing

Presented with the same thoroughness you'll find in Mr. Vivian's books on wood heat (and the newer one on homesteading), this book covers the practical, how-to details on the different types of stone, the tools you need to split it, move it, and lay it in place, and the variety of effects possible depending on available materials. The one thing no book can show you is the time and muscle needed for this work—even for a modest garden wall. Spend 3 or 4 hours a day building a stone wall and after a month, when you get out of the shower and look in the mirror, you will look quite different.

The Forgotten Art of Building a Stone Wall, by Curtis P. Fields
Yankee Books
Depot Square, Peterborough, NH 03458

Published by a Yankee for a New England audience (that's where most of the stone in this book will be found), this book concentrates on flat stone walls laid up without mortar, including tips on moving and positioning the larger slabs without killing yourself, on how to split granite, and repair and maintain older, existing walls so they do not go back to the earth. Scratchy illustrations get the point across; 65 pages; about $5.

Structural Materials

Homebuilding, A Comprehensive Guide to Footings, Foundations, and Framing Systems, by Mike McClintock
Scribners, 1982

Not too proud to plug my own book, I do it because it contains pages of tables on wood framing members and their strengths, allowable spans, and design characteristics. The same type of information is provided for concrete and masonry block construction. For moderately advanced do-it-yourselfers; cost is about $20.

Wood

The Encyclopedia of Wood
Forest Products Laboratory
U.S. Department of Agriculture
Sterling Publishing Company
Two Park Ave.
New York, NY, 10016

One of the excellent Forest Service publications, this book covers all types of wood and their characteristics—the kinds of loads they can take, the spans they can make, what sizes and shapes different woods are milled to, proper nailing schedules, and a lot more. Updated in 1980; 375 authoritative pages; well illustrated; about $13.

TOOLS
AND
EQUIPMENT

PRIVATE FIRMS

Hand Tools

Adhesives/Tools

Roberts Consolidated Industries
(Weldwood)
600 N. Baldwin Park Blvd.
PO Box 1250
City of Industry, CA 91749
(213) 338-7311

Weldwood makes an extensive line of adhesives and tools used in laying floors, carpets, tile, and more; also Penta-brand preservatives and Woodlife-brand water repellent preservatives. Adhesives include contact cements; epoxy glues; and woodworkers' glue for home and hobby use; contact cements and solvents for laminates; flooring adhesives; construction adhesives for ceramic; plastic and metal tile, drywall, wood subfloor and general structural applications.

Business operation Weldwood products are widely available. For a complete look at tools and materials write for catalog RFC/WC, Roberts Weldwood Flooring Specialties. Several specialized tools may be difficult to find elsewhere; for instance, electric carpet cutters and complete carpet tool kits.

Antique Tools

Iron Horse Antiques, Inc.
The Fine Tool Journal
RD 2
Poultney, VT 05764
(802) 287-4050

Iron Horse offers a selection of antique tools for sale via mail order. You can stop in to look over the impressive stock or get an idea of what they do there by subscribing to the *Fine Tool Journal*. Both enterprises are run by Vernon A. Ward, who writes that he has plans to turn the ten-times-a-year newsletter for collectors and craftsmen into a full-fledged magazine. Currently, subscriptions are $10 per year. You can write and ask for a sample issue and also for the book list. The newsletter is well-illustrated, full of information and book reviews, runs a regular "Whatsit" feature (you think you know what the tool in the picture is for but you're probably wrong), and is generally a total treat for those interested in antique tools. I remember buying hardwood moulding planes for $5 and even less at barn sales in Vermont and New Hampshire. It was a lot of money because I didn't have much money, but I didn't buy them for an investment—just because they were, and are, stunning. Try an issue. Have some fun looking, even if the prices have gone up.

Chimney Cleaners

Neuman Chimney Cleaners
Rte. 2
Ogema, WI 54459
(715) 767-3586

Neuman makes a unique tool for cleaning chimneys, eliminating the need for hiring professional chimney sweeps, and along with them an expensive selection of wire brushes, cables, and extensions. This system is expandable—simply a rigid wire basket with curled ends that can be lowered into the chimney, then expanded against the flue walls with a second rope. If the wire basket gets stuck, which happens particularly in older, irregular flues and flues with heavy creosote buildup, releasing the tension collapses the basket so it can be removed. Obviously this system will not do the type of finish cleaning that a fine steel brush can do. But creosote can be stubborn and just may need a heavy-duty scraping before it breaks loose. The basket wires are a lightweight, rustproof alloy. The company estimates you'll need five to ten pulls up and down to do the job.

Business operation   You can write to the factory at the above address for a simple brochure explaining how the system works, with illustrations and directions for chimney cleaning. Write the company for the retail outlet nearest you.

Woodmart
Box 202
Janesville, WI 53545
(608) 752-2816

Woodmart makes chimney brushes, both round and square, in a variety of sizes to fit flue tile, raw flue block, and most other flue configurations. The brushes are made of wire twisted in a heavy four-wire spindle with a ⅜-in threaded nipple on one end and a ¾-in wire loop on the other end. The idea is to attach flexible extension rods to the threaded end and a rope to the loop end and work the brush up and down the flue to clear away dirt, soot, and creosote buildup. Square sizes range from 6 in × 6 in up to 14 in × 14 in, including some rectangular shapes along the way. Round brushes range from 4¾-in diameter up to 14-in diameter.

Business operation   Woodmart sells wholesale and through the mails. It will be happy to send you a one-page, illustrated brochure showing its products, prices, and various connectors and extensions, but only if you send them a SASE.

Pricing   The 4¾-in diameter brush is

about $12; the 14-in version about $21. Extensions in 6-ft sections are $7.

Clamps

Adjustable Clamp Company
  (Jorgensen/Pony)
417 N. Ashland Ave.
Chicago, IL 60622
(312) 666-0640

This company makes two classic woodworking and construction clamps (and a lot of others too): Jorgensen hand screws and Pony pipe clamps. The handscrews are simple blocks of hardwood joined with two threaded rods that can be adjusted to apply pressure along part or all of the block bearing surface. Sizes range from a model with 4-in jaws and 2-in opening capacity to a monster clamp with 24-in jaws and 17-in clamping capacity. There are imitations, but these are the best and most durable I've ever used. Another standard, used more for construction, is the Pony pipe clamp. It consists of two sections: one has a cam action so the unit can slide to any point along a standard black iron pipe; the other end is threaded to the pipe and has an adjusting screw like a vise. The nice part is that all you need to buy is the fittings—two or four sets, for instance—and then as many pieces of pipe in as many different lengths as you need. But this company makes many other clamps as well, for practically any possible situation in construction, furniture building, and more.

Business operation   Catalog 20 is the one to get. It illustrates all products, gives all sizes, and shows several applications. Write the company if you cannot get product literature locally. These clamps are sold in most quality mail-order catalogs that carry woodwork equipment and tools.

Clock Kits/Tools/Case Hardware
Mason & Sullivan Company
586 Higgins Crowell Rd.
West Yarmouth, MA 02673
(617) 778-1056

Mason & Sullivan makes a really fine line
of kit clocks, from extremely elaborate and
detailed grandfather clocks complete with
solid brass reproduction hardware, to small,
simple, mantel clocks. In addition to an extensive selection of kits and movements
(grandfather movements are guaranteed for
three years, which is unusually long), the
company carries skeleton kits (you assemble
the movements), a good selection of brass
case hardware, including hinges, lock hardware, pulls, and handles, and a modest collection of beautiful, professional clockmaker's tools imported from Switzerland.

Business operation   Mason & Sullivan's
excellent, 30-page, full color catalog is sent
on request.

Drywall
United States Gypsum Company
101 S. Wacker Dr.
Chicago, IL 60606
(312) 321-3865

U.S. Gypsum is a large company that makes
all kinds of construction-related products.
Their paneling catalog seems to go on forever with different tones and textures and
colors. But in particular they are one of the
largest drywall manufactures. The company,
and a lot of people in the trade, call it Sheetrock, even though that is a trademark.

Business operation   U.S. Gypsum products are sold nationwide. The company provides voluminous literature at retail outlets,
but if you have inquiries about specific products or drywall tools and equipment you can

write to the company; Attention: Marketing
Services, Dept. 122. They have several idea
and project booklets and a good, if brief,
brochure on rigid styrene insulating board,
which has endless applications in new and
existing construction. Also ask about U.S.
Gypsum's 300-page paperback book, *Drywall Construction Handbook*. It will probably cost at least a few dollars by now, but it
is the definitive book on drywall, profusely
illustrated, completely practical, with full
technical specs, application guides including
the types and uses of conventional and specialty equipment, for layman and professional—a gem.

Glass Cutters
Pro Glass Cutter Company, Inc.
PO Box 651
Farmington, MI 48024
(313) 471-3452

What caught my attention was the simple
addition to the basic design of a hand glass
cutter. This one has a hole in it—rather,
a ring of metal, mounted dead center in the
cutter stem so you can stick your index
finger through the hole for added support
and control when you cut. It's the kind of
idea that presents itself after you've ruined
the umpteenth piece of glass because the
cutter wobbled or your fingers got tired. It
makes sense because the first scoring line
on glass is the most important. If it's
crooked, lacks consistent pressure, or has
other imperfections, your break may not be
clean. This small firm also is adding a replaceable wheel cutter—good if you do a
lot of stained glass work or professional
glazing.

Business operation   The designer of the
Magewick Comfort Grip glass cutter,
Aloysius F. Magewick, writes that he is

turning out a revised product brochure. The item is sold via mail order. Hats off to a modest idea that does what it's supposed to.

Hammers/Sledges/Mauls

Marion Tool Corporation
PO Box 365
Marion, IN 46952
(317) 664-7324

Marion manufacturers and distributes (only through hardware distributors who sell, in turn, to retailers) an extensive line of drop-forged hammers, utility anvils, fire axes, hatchets, camp axes, picks, mattocks, wedges, mauls, and sledges. They also offer a limited line of masonry trowels.

Business operation   The Marion catalog is available on request and includes specs of several specialty tools such as cobbler's hammers, magnetic tack hammers, and what the company calls "ladies" hammers (5- and 8-oz models).

Hand and Power Tools—General

Sears, Roebuck and Company
Sears Tower
Chicago, IL 60684

If there is one firm in this book that could be listed in almost every section it is Sears. Mike Mangan of the marketing department writes quite accurately that 'Sears carries everything for the entire house, be it replacement windows, to heating and cooling appliances, portable and bench power tools, all the elements one needs to tackle most DIY projects." Most of the thousands of products offered for sale (not manufactured) by Sears are covered in the shop-at-home catalog, but your best bet is to write Sears and tell them the specific area you

are interested in. Each area is now covered completely by what Sears calls *specialogs*. And they do have just about everything—from a $615 John Wayne commemorative Winchester carbine complete with John Wayne ammunition to tractor-powered post hole diggers. Three catalogs that include most of the areas covered in this sourcebook are F7410, *Home Improvement*; F7495, *Craftsman Power and Hand Tools*; and F7417, *Farm and Ranch*.

Business operation   Sears has more than 2100 selling outlets in the United States, some 865 retail stores, and what they describe as a "brigade" of catalog selling units. If you cannot get the information or products you want at a local store contact Sears at the above address, Attention: Department 703.

Hand Tools—Woodwork

The Fine Tool Shops
20–28 Backus Ave.
Danbury, CT 06810
(203) 797-0183

This firm runs two retail shops in Connecticut, one in Westport, one in Danbury. But their catalog is a kind of showroom—a Rolls Royce of fine tool presentations available for $5, which is steep even for 128 or so pages of color. The selection, however, is really stunning: hardwood tool chests, Henry Taylor chisels and gouges from Sheffield, England, Wilhelm Schmitt woodcarving tools (that's the firm with two red cherries on the label for those who remember pictures instead of names), Marples boxwood handle chisels, 24-in beech body Primus try planes, Record planes (the Multi-Plane is $350 here) plus Makita power tools—page after page of gems, everything beautifully photographed. If the names haven't got you oohing and aahing, just trust me. The principal, Mortimer V. Schwartz, talks about "significant quality," and although he admits you can carry a no-compromise attitude too far, this is what happened on one of his recent visits to Japan. "I discovered . . . a father, his two sons, and four helpers who hand produce about 1000 plane irons per year. The father personally makes—from start to finish—120 to 150 irons. The process requires fusing hundred-year-old anchor chain and high-carbon alloy steel. One third of the father's production must be set aside for the building of temples." Mr. Schwartz bought one month's production. You may well find better prices elsewhere but probably not a better selection.

Frog Tool Company, Ltd.
700 W. Jackson Blvd.
Chicago, IL 60606
(312) 648-1270

The new Frog catalog ($2.50 for a 2-year subscription) has nearly 100 pages of quality tools. They have a modest selection of Japanese tools, instrument kits, and an extensive book list, but their strength is in cutting tools, particularly carving and turning tools, and chisels. Three sizes of swan-neck chisels, sets of knob-ended, one-hand carving chisels, and exceptionally long and heavy-duty turning chisels imported from England. An excellent selection of heavy-duty hand tools.

Hand Tools

The Princeton Company, Inc.
PO Box 276
Princeton, MA 01541
(800) 343-6130 (For orders)

The Princeton catalog carries a good selection of high-quality tools, although there are some inconsistencies. On one hand they carry little work tables to which you can attach a router or saber saw to "convert" it into a table saw or shaper (which is the last thing you want to do if you are at all serious about getting quality results). On the other hand they carry the Zyliss vise, and both the Puukko skinner and folding knives—all distinctive tools of excellent quality and not readily available. It's an interesting mix with some questionable gadgets mixed in with the pearls.

Business operation The 80-page catalog is sent on request.

Robert Larson Company
1007 De Haro St.
San Francisco, CA 94107
(415) 821-1021

Larson is a major importer and wholesale distributor of high-quality woodworking tools made in Europe, Japan, and the United States. In response to consumer inquiries, they will provide names of local dealers and mail-order companies that carry their products.

Hobby Wood/Tools

Craftsman Wood Service Company
1735 W. Cortland Ct.
Addison, IL 60101
(312) 629-3100

Craftsman is a large mail-order house offering some 400 items in a compact catalog, including wood, veneers, glues, hand tools, small furniture and clock kits, small power tools, mouldings, cane, hardware, lamp parts, plans for large furniture pieces, and more.

Business operation At this point the catalog is available for $1.50. It is lavish, with 145 pages in full color that give a good look at what you're getting.

Japanese Tools

Tashiro's
618 S. Jackson St.
Seattle, WA 98104

An interesting company, Tashiro's is a family run operation, started in Japan in 1888 and in the United States since 1917. Tashiro's catalog, which is newly revised, is free for the asking, and covers a good selection of hand tools that have slowly earned a growing acceptance by Western craftsmen, hobbyists, and do-it-yourselfers. They are different. For one thing, Japanese saws cut backward, i.e., the teeth are set to do the cutting on the back stroke, the Western back stroke at least. Generally these tools are made of very high-quality steel that keeps a sharp edge. Japanese planes tend to be large, solid slabs of wood with wedge-set cutter blades—a bit tough to adjust for minor depth variations until you get used to them. Craftsmen who have the time to find out more than simply how to do it will be interested to know that Frank Tashiro, who is well versed in Japanese blacksmithing. He writes, "I am in a position to be of service by selecting Japanese tools based on performance and consumer benefit. Toward this end I am writing instructions for use and care of the tools in the catalog."

Woodline: The Japanese Woodworker
1731 Clement Ave.
Alameda, CA 94501
(415) 521-1810

Woodline has been in business about ten years. They specialize in Japanese tools and go about getting them in a special way. Proprietor Fred Damson writes, "We obtain our woodworking tools from small tool merchants. A number of these master toolmakers work alone or with only one or two apprentices." Also, Woodline has arranged with some of the Japanese toolmakers they have met over the years to produce their own brand name tools, which are generally lower priced than most of the imports. The Woodline catalog is comprehensive, with about the largest selection of Japanese chisels, planes, saws, and more I have found under one roof. And some of the items are quite special—a general-purpose kitchen knife (about $180) that is handcrafted with the same kind of attention and forging steps used to fabricate samurai sword blades. The catalog includes power tools, sculptor's and carver's tools, hammer heads, brushes— even a good book list.

Business operation   The Woodline catalog is available for $1.50; it's worth the price.

Landscape/Garden Tools

By Hand & Foot, Ltd.
PO Box 611
Brattleboro, VT 05301
(802) 254-2101

The products offered by this company include a two-wheeled hand cart (not unlike the well-advertised Garden Way cart), scythes and harvesting hand tools, and lumbering tools like peaveys and axes. Its products generally seem of high quality. My hesitation comes from a kind of earnest presentation of the old way as the best way. I don't know much about farming and cannot judge its tools or information in that category. But their woodsplitting brochure talks about splitting kindling with a froe and mallet (possible, surely, but time consuming and not nearly as efficient as a sharp axe would be) and makes much of the safety differences between conventional steel splitting wedges as opposed to their wood-headed wedges—particularly, that the head won't mushroom under constant use or chip away into dangerous projectiles. And there on the opposite page is a conventional steel wedge, drop-forged so it is "much less likely to chip upon impact." I am probably too critical, but I like a straightforward presentation of the facts and get queasy when positives and negatives are included so selectively. Here's a for-instance. The company offers an axe handle guard "for beginners and infrequent users to protect the handle from breaking." To me, that's a mistake, encouraging people to get in over their heads with a false sense of security. Anyway, I suggest you write for their three interesting brochures and their book list.

Masonry Tools
Marshalltown Trowel Company
PO Box 738
Marshalltown, IA 50158
(515) 754-6100

Marshalltown manufactures high-quality tools for cement finishing, bricklaying, plastering, and drywall work. In almost all retail outlets they are uniformly higher priced than similar tools made by other companies, but that is because the similarity is only skin deep. Weight, strength, and durability are the differences most apparent at a glance and at a heft. Also, Marshalltown makes an extraordinary selection of trowels: small and large, rounded pool trowels, flexed drywall trowels; plus mud pans, drywall saws, all kinds of jointers and runners, mason's lines and blocks, wood and rubber floats, etc. Finally, Marshalltown makes some of the best tool bags around, i.e., leather tool bags with all kinds of storage pouches that you wear on your hip while you work.

Business operation The company sells to wholesalers who in turn supply retailers such as hardware stores and lumber supply outlets. One of their information booklets, *Troweling Tips and Techniques*, is sent for $1. Their products catalog is sent free on

request. An established company (in business since 1890) making quality tools.

Paint and Surface Preparation Tools
Hyde Manufacturing Company
54 Eastford Rd.
Southbridge, MA 01550
(617) 764-4344

Hyde has been in business since 1875 and now makes over 300 different cutters, trimmers, scrapers, rollers, and more to handle most surface preparation jobs.

Business operation Write for their Catalog No. 269, *Surface Preparation and Maintenance Tools*, which, in addition to the spackle knives and other tools you can find in most hardware stores and home centers, has some very handy, hard-to-find items like corner trowels, 48-in wallboard T-squares, ceramic tile cutters and nippers, professional wallcovering trimmers, a guide wheel window scraper that takes off paint on the glass but leaves the paint on the putty, and ladder-hung paint can hooks. It also offers a how-to guide for $2 that I found extremely basic, although it covers a lot of ground (that's the problem). Better yet, ask for their small booklets called *How To Do It Right The First Time*, with individual, moderately basic coverage of painting (#82100), and wallpapering (#82200).

Plumbing Tools
The Ridge Tool Company
400 Clark St.
Elyria, OH 44036
(216) 323-5581

The name you may recognize is Rigid, the brand name applied to a wide variety of pipe threading, drain cleaning, and plumbing hand tools made by this company. Its catalog includes wide size variations in threaders, cutters, and more.

Business operation Rigid tools are manufactured in the United States, South America, Belgium, and Ireland. They are sold exclusively through a distributor network. There are some 6000 distributors in the United States. Local dealers should be prepared to get you the right tool for the job. However, if you want to know more, you can write the headquarters at the address above with your questions. Jim Lucas of Customer Service writes, "By contacting us we will be more than happy to answer any questions consumers may have and supply a list of distributors in their area."

Pricing Varies at local level.

Shop Heater/Splitting Maul
Sotz Corporation
13600 N. Station Rd.
Columbus Station, OH 44028

Those familiar with Sotz will recognize the peculiar combination of a shop heater and a splitting maul—the company's primary products. In business for twenty-six years, it has stuck to them, advertising nationally, and selling via mail order. Its shop heater comes in kit form and consists of all equipment necessary to turn a standard 55-gal drum into a reasonably efficient woodstove. This equipment includes door and frame, draft control, and hardware. Double stoves that use two drums can also be adapted. As the literature reads, "Before you spend $500 or $600 on a wood heater try the Sotz heater for under $60. If within one year you don't agree it outperforms any wood heater money can buy or (within 10 years) if the kit cracks, warps, or burns up, your money will be refunded, including shipping charges."

Talk about confidence in the product. Sotz's "Monster Maul" (about $25) is a V-shaped steel head and steel handle splitter that is similarly guaranteed.

Business operation For a complete and totally entertaining look at both products, ask for a copy of *The Sotz News*, a 12-page newsletter with all sorts of information on the products and testimonials. One, with picture, says, "One hundred twenty five cords of wood split last year with our monster maul. Average time of two hours per cord." Many of the testimonials are titled: "Men Folk Laugh!" (the woman wants to order two splitters), "Man, 73, Splits 7 Cords," and so on. There is simply no way not to admire a company that is so unabashed in its self-praise and so stuck on two very simple, useful items.

Slate/Slater's Tools
Evergreen Slate Company
Box 248
Granville, NY 12832
(518) 642-2530

Evergreen has furnished roofing slate for some impressive clients, like the Boston Museum of Fine Arts and The White House (Evergreen provided slate for the North Portico). It quarries and sells a variety of slate. Also, it sells quality slater's tools, specifically a slate ripper (with a long flat and toothed arm for cutting nails and removing broken slate, slate hooks (for securing new slate without ripping up the roof and using tar), a slate hammer (leather handled), and a slate cutter (made by ESCO) that is only 8 lb, and has a nail puncher at the handle end. Evergreen supplies lengths from 10 to 24 in, ¼- to ¾-in thicknesses in standard smooth and rough quarry run.

Business operation Write for product

spec booklets that include color photographs of slate tones, and a very informative brochure entitled "Hip and Ridge Application," which covers some of the fine points for do-it-yourselfers.

Specialty Tools

Garelick Manufacturing Company
St. Paul Park, MN 55071
(612) 459-9795

This company manufacturers two products of particular interest to homeowners because they help with jobs that are time consuming and, frankly, boring. First, is a log carrier/trash-bag dolly made of tubular aluminum. It weighs about 6 lb and can carry about 135 lb. Another unique item is Garelick's snow rake. Yes, it sounds silly —like a soup fork—but in northern climates these very lightweight (about 6 lb for the 21-ft-long model) rakes can make it easy to pull large snow loads off a roof. This may be desirable to avoid gutter backups and roof deterioration or to relieve excessive strains on framing systems. A 16-ft and 21-ft pole plus 5-ft extensions are offered.

Business operation   Write for a free illustrated brochure on either item, and the name of a local retail outlet that carries the products. Pricing varies at retail level.

Staplers

Swingline
3200 Skillman Ave.
Long Island City, NY 11101

Swingline carries a full line of stapling machines, from the common office variety through hand staplers used for fastening insulation batts, screening, and such, to electric versions that send the staple home at the touch of a button. They also make pop rivet tools—about the best way to install sectional metal gutters and make connections on any thin wall metal short of soldering or welding. Two tools in particular are valuable during construction: the Rivet Professional (an efficient, small-nosed model of their consumer model) and Swingline's hammer stapler. This is simply a conventional stapler that is swung like a hammer to drive the staple in. It is faster on jobs such as laying roofing felt and a little easier on your hand than conventional, hand-squeezed staplers.

Business operation   Swingline has clearly illustrated product brochures. If they are not available locally, write to the company: Attention: Customer Relations Department, at the above address. Catalog No. H2012 covers staplers and pop rivet tools.

Timber Framing Tools/ Construction

Fox-Maple Tools/Fox Maple Post
   & Beam
RR 1, Box 583
Snowville Rd.
West Brownfield, ME 04010
(207) 935-3720

Fox-Maple's tool business grew out of its post and beam building business. Steve Chappell, the president of Fox-Maple, writes, "We felt that a source for the highest quality tools presented in a simple straightforward catalogue at reasonable prices could be invaluable to the owner-builder and craftsman alike." The tool catalog is worth writing for, including Ashley Iles turning tools from England, large framing chisels, Stanley and Record planes, Makita sanders, many different bits and large augers, and even a timber framer's tool set.

Fox-Maple's post and beam building business produces what I know as timber frame homes, all made to order with oak pegs holding mortise and tenon or dovetail joints (no nails are used). Fox-Maple will set up the structure or build the house start to finish within the limits of travel time. However, they ship anywhere owner-builder packages, which include blueprints, materials for siding, roofing, insulation, flooring, and other supplies on request. Costs vary with each project. Fox-Maple Post & Beam will send illustrated material on several of their projects, including construction details and a picture of their most popular frame, a classic, center chimney saltbox with shed roof extension, complete with 9 over 6 lite windows, and what looks like 3 or 4 in to the weather clapboards—an absolute knock out.

Tools and Hardware—General

The Stanley Works
PO Box 1843
New Britain, CT 06050
(203) 225-5111

Stanley is one of the largest, best-known manufacturers of hand tools, including hammers, rulers, screwdrivers, planes, squares, you name it. Once it was premier (or close to it) in this field—Stanley block and bench planes were common choices for general contractors and homebuilders. But as Stanley has become the standard for do-it-yourselfers (good from their sales point of view), I keep hearing comments about its chisel steel not being what it used to be and similar criticisms about its planes. I have made the comments myself. But I think for do-it-yourself work Stanley quality is fine. Plus their selection is extensive with wide availability. And another strong point. Stanley is very responsive to consumer questions, offers good instruction and application liter-

ature, even a selection of thorough do-it-yourself construction plans for various home projects. Finally, Stanley is very strong in the hardware department. Try to get hold of their massive Catalog No. 130. It includes an extensive, single source selection of everything from fence hardware to brass drawer pulls.

Business operation Stanley sells only through wholesalers and retailers and has no mail order. Inquiries about products, plans, etc., should go to Stanley at Department PID, PO Box 1800, New Britain, CT 06050.

Tools/Builder's Hardware

Macklanburg Duncan Company
Box 25188
Oklahoma City, OK 73125

Macklanburg Duncan makes a line of builder's hardware, shelving systems, some hand tools, and several product lines in the field of weatherization: weatherstripping, caulking, sealants, and thresholds.

Business operation The company sells nationwide through hardware stores and home centers. You can write for a free copy of their booklet, "Anyone Can Do It Home Weatherproofer's Guide," which shows installations of weatherstripping, caulking, and thresholds.

Tool Supply/Sundries

Brookstone Company
669 Vose Farm Rd.
Peterborough, NH 03458
(603) 924-7181

"Sundries" hardly does justice to the selection in the Brookstone catalog, *Hard-to-*

Find Tools. The mail-order house supplies an 80-page, full-color catalog on request. A significant number of items are high-quality imported tools such as Japanese pruning shears, a Swedish pruner with levered cutting jaws (I've used it for years and it is incredibly strong), plus elegant wooden tool chests, watchmaker's tools, all kinds of home security gadgets, grommet sets, a complete tool kit in a briefcase, and battery cables—a catchall that is fascinating and fun.

Upholstery Tools

C. S. Osborne & Company
125 Jersey St.
Harrison, NJ 07029
(201) 483-3232

The Osborne catalog offers a comprehensive treatment of upholstery tools, particularly for the do-it-yourselfer. It has 3 pages of tack hammers; staple setters and lifters; webbing stretchers; endless specialty pliers, including spring clip pliers, and a plier designed only to pull antique nails. It also advertises several pieces of equipment suited more for commercial shops, like foam rubber cutters. The selection is complete.

Business operation Osborne sells nationally through wholesale distributors who supply retailers, although the company writes that it does sell some by mail order. Its policy is to respond to inquiries with a complete catalog and a referral to local retail sources.

Pricing Tools are reasonably priced, for instance, $13.60 for a canvas plier (Osborne has a patent pending) that can pull canvas tightly around wooden frames. Catalog 17 is the one to ask for.

Wall Pattern Printers

Rollerwall, Inc.
PO Box 757
Silver Spring, MD 20901
(301) 649-4422

Rollerwall tools provide an interesting alternative to painting and wallpapering. In essence, the system works just like a commercial wallpaper printer; the pattern is raised on a metal roller that rests next to a feeder roller. As the raised portions of the metal roller (holding the pattern) contact the feeder, they pick up paint or other colorants and lay the pattern on the wall as they rotate.

Business operation Rollerwall has dozens of different patterns and will send you a free brochure illustrating the styles and the two different types of applicators. They sell nationally via mail order.

Pricing The basic, double roller applicator is about $15; the same configuration with an integral container for colorant (so you can stay on the wall longer without going back and forth to the supply) is about $30. Raised pattren rollers are $12 each.

Wood and Garden Tools

Smith & Hawken Tool Company
68 Homer
Palo Alto, CA 94301
(415) 324-1587

Smith & Hawken tools are manufactured by Bulldog Tools, Ltd., of Clarington Forge in England, which traces its business history back to 1779. In addition to imports and tools from other companies, the Smith & Hawken catalog covers all kinds of spades, forks and cultivating tools, Haws watering cans (expensive but incredible), all types of woodcutting tools including Hults Valley axes, sharpening stones, and more. Design and quality is generally very high. For example, spades are forged with a high proportion of manganese for extra hardness and flexibility and have a weldless solid socket and full length ash handles.

Business operation   Write for the Smith & Hawken catalog, which is sent, for now, free on request.

Pricing   Garden forks range from $39 to $42; spades about $35; Haws cans about $50; Hults axes $20 to $30.

Woodburning/Energy Saving/ Kitchen Goods

The Plow & Hearth, Inc.
PO Box 560
Madison, VA 22727
(703) 948-7010

This very nice catalog carries high-quality equipment in many areas: woodburning and wood handling, kitchen goods, gardening tools, bird feeders, energy-saving devices, general hand tools, and more. Plow & Hearth has a retail store in Madison (north central Virginia) and sells nationally via mail order. Generally a limited, thoughtful selection of interesting goods, including many nonstock items you will not see in most mail-order catalogs.

Business operation   Mail order by phone at (703) 948-6873 works Monday through Friday from 9:00 to 5:00. The catalog is available for $1.

Pricing   A few of the nifty items include a water heater setback timer, $42; a cast iron, table mount, meat grinder with five cutter plates, $65; lifelike inflatable predators (a 2-ft horned owl and a six-ft snake) for realistic garden "scarecrows," $7.50; cast iron woodstove kettles, $35 to $49; and a lot more.

Woodwork and Shop Tools/ Workbenches

Leichtung, Inc.
4944 Commerce Pkwy.
Cleveland, OH 44128
(800) 321-6840
(216) 831-6191 (Ohio only)

The Leichtung Catalog has a good selection of imported chisels and turning tools, Forstner bits, and many other hand and power tools that are common to several of the fine tool mail-order houses. Of special interest here are Lervad workbenches, not inexpensive by any means ($500 for a small, narrow, 5-ft-long woodworkers' bench; about $700 for a full-size bench with side and end vises) but very high quality, machined to tolerances of .2 mm (that's .008 in) and made of furniture grade Danish beech, kiln dried down to 5 percent humidity and assembled in a humidity controlled factory—beautiful pieces of work preserved when the top panel is emersed in linseed oil and lacquered.

Business operation   Leichtung will forward their 66-page color catalog at no charge.

Wrenches/Handtools/Tool Boxes

Utica Tool Company
Orangeburg, SC 29115
(803) 534-7010
(800) 845-2215 (Toll-free)

Utica makes an extensive line of hand tools, a really complete line of automotive-type tool boxes and storage systems, wrenches with a unique design for applying more turning force with less damage to fittings, and a few other high-quality specialty tools. Utica's Loc-Rite wrenches are designed to apply a tangential force on nuts and other fittings by distributing pressure on hex nut flats instead of their points. Another goodie is Utica's precision wire stripper, a system that is accurate enough to strip fiber optic cable. There are others, all covered in Utica's 136-page catalog.

Business operation Utica sells only through authorized distributors, although one of its marketing people wrote that "Our door is open to all users." This may not mean you can order factory direct, but the company has offered to send the impressive catalog and price list on request. The catalog is very interesting and contains hundreds of tools you rarely see: hand-held adjustable torque screwdrivers, brake shoe retaining tools, precision-ground, angle-set cutting pliers, all kinds of tool kits, and more.

Power Tools

Chain Saws/Generators
Homelite, Division Textron, Inc.
Columbia, SC 29260

Homelite chain saws range from tiny little 8-lb models with 10-in bars and 1.6 cu in engines up to 23-lb monsters with up to 43-in bars and 6.8 cu in engines. All their smaller consumer saws (but not the larger, commercial grade models) feature a safety device called the Safe-T-Tip, simply a small guard around the end of the bar to keep the operator from getting into a position where kickback is likely. It is certainly helpful but also reduces the effective cutting length of the bar. And I always worry about safety devices that may give users a false sense of security. Chain saw accidents are not the most common home how-to related

injuries, but when they do happen they tend to be severe, as you can imagine. In fact, chain saw and lawn mower accidents are right at the top of the Consumer Product Safety Commission's injury severity list, which measures the frequency and the consequences of home product injuries. Now Homelite is introducing a new chain design, called Tri-Raker, that works against kickback by reducing energy levels transferred to the bar (and maybe back into your body) when chain raker gauges penetrate the cut. Homelite also manufactures all kinds of yard equipment, and a line of portable generators, including an interesting package (HSB–50), which includes an emergency generator that can turn out 5000 watts, packaged in a weatherproof outdoor box (there is room for fuel, etc.), that can be hooked up to your home electrical system. It can take over during blackouts.

Business operation Homelite has voluminous product literature available at sales and service centers across the country.

Chain Saws—Line Trimmers
Baird-Poulan, Division Emerson
    Electric Company
5020 Flournoy-Lucas Rd.
Shreveport, LA 71129
(318) 687-0100

Baird-Poulan makes a consumer line of trimmers, called Weed Eaters, and a complete line of chain saws, ranging from backyard models with 10-in blades and 1.8-cu-in engines up to 5.2-cu-in models that can take 36-in bars, with antivibration mountings.

Business operation These tools are widely available. The company will provide product brochures if they are not available locally.

Drain Cleaning Tools
General Wire Spring Company
1101 Thompson Ave.
McKees Rocks, PA 15136
(412) 771-6300

General Wire manufactures drain cleaning augers, both hand and power operated. It sells through plumbing supply houses in the United States and Canada, mostly to contractors and other professionals. Most of the equipment is a lot more than you need for an occasional job on the kitchen sink. But its hand augers and the smallest of their power units will suit the task. (Some have wonderful names like Sewermatic and Sewerooter Senior.) If you do have recurring drainage problems, however, you might look into its water ram. It is a small cylinder that is pressurized by a hand pump (pressure is metered), then discharged through a nozzle that is surrounded by a rubber stopper. Generally, you have to stop up overflow drains and any other air-vent outlets to get the effect of a hydraulic wave, really a shock wave of water triggered by the blast of compressed air. It's a very practical system (I have used a similar tool from another manufacturer) that does an excellent job without chemicals. The only drawback is that too much of a blast will tend to find the weak spots in your plumbing system say, one of the solder connection, and pop it open.

Business operation Write for General Wire's catalog HO–CC–80 or for full spec sheets on specific products.

Drills/Construction Tools
Milwaukee Electric Tool Corporation
13135 W. Lisbon Rd.
Brookfield, WI 53005
(414) 781-3600

Milwaukee is probably the premier manufacturer of drills. Some may argue with this contention, and it is true that this company does not bother with super cheap, super light, plastic, so-called do-it-yourself models. Way back when I started building and investigated every piece of equipment I bought with a frenzy of attention to detail, I bought, and still have, a Milwaukee, in-line, ⅜-in hole shooter—a triple-geared drill with incredible torque. But as I mention Milwaukee in Skil's entry, it is only fair to note that my feeling—Milwaukee for drills, Skil for saws—is reflected somewhat in the catalogs of these two companies, i.e., Skil lists its saws first; Milwaukee lists its drills first. Anyway, Milwaukee does make an impressive array of drills for general and very specialized use. Also, they make an exceptionally fine Sawzall (a power reciprocating saw).

Business operation Milwaukee has major branch offices and service centers in seventeen states, and two or more authorized service stations in nearly every state as well. You can write for the current catalog, which is free. Also, Milwaukee has a 237-page, large-format, profusely illustrated book called their *Training Manual*—a first-class job with parts illustrations, accessories and their uses, safety, lubrication, applications, procedures, and more. The manual costs $15, but if you use quality power tools a lot you'll find this manual worth every penny. Write or call for more information on the book.

Lumber Maker
Haddon Tools
4719 W. Rte. 120
McHenry, IL 60050
(815) 344-2915

Haddon makes a simple, inexpensive attachment for chain saws that converts them for use as lumber making tools. It has been on the market for about 10 years and has been used to make squared beams and log walls for cabins, fencing, commercial buildings, and more. In a nutshell, the device is a piece of steel in a wide, flattened U shape, built to hug and ride along a 2 × 6 guide board. You nail this board, which you supply, to, say, the top of your log, then bolt your chain saw to the U-shape with a pivoting bolt (part of the tool) that lets you control the angle of cut as you work down the log. The only time consuming part is resetting the guide board to establish a new plane for each cut. The tool is only about 4 lb.

Business operation   Haddon sells nationwide through a dealer network and via mail order. They will provide basic information describing and illustrating the tool free on request. A complete owner's manual is available for $1. This is the way to go if you have questions. I wish more companies made the same offer.

Pricing   Tools are slightly under $50 including shipping and handling.

Masonry Tools and Equipment
Goldblatt Tool Company
511 Osage
PO Box 2334
Kansas City, KS 66110
(913) 621-3010

This is one of my favorite companies. It makes an extensive line of high-quality masonry tools and equipment, and that accounts for some of my feeling. But I also feel this way because for most of the 10 years I was building houses full time I used a large Goldblatt tool bag, which I still have. In the current catalog the 14-in × 22-in canvas bag with leather bottom, handles, and straps is still only $33.50. I forget exactly what I paid, but I surely beat the hell

out of it on the job, and got my money's worth. I had the opportunity to come across a new one recently, which seems just as rugged. So much for that. Goldblatt carries every conceivable type of trowel, float, and screed, levels and transits, brick tongs, water saws, and drywall stilts—a complete line of tools, equipment, and even clothing for all trowel trades.

Business operation   Goldblatt products are widely available. Write for their catalog, one of the clearest, best-illustrated tool catalogs around, and, if you have trouble finding products locally, for the name of a retail outlet in your area where you can find what you need.

Portable Saw Mill
Sperber Tool Works, Inc.
Box 1224
West Caldwell, NJ 07006
(201) 744-6110

When you can't get the wood you want from a lumber yard or a mill, or when you can't get the trees you have to a mill to become lumber, the answer is to take a portable mill to the source. Sperber makes one- and two-man mills in several sizes. They are essentially chain saws sold with or without engines to handle logs from 15- to 48-in diameters. The portable mills use an aluminum channel slabbing rail to get the first square surface and a system of horizontal and vertical guide rollers for remaining cuts. The thickness of your cuts is adjustable. Complete mills come with Stihl 076AVE or Stihl 090 engines—not cheap but unbeatable for power and dependability.

Business operation   Inquiries net an illustrated brochure and price list, including accessories like an electric chain saw sharpener (battery powered for on-site use), metal detectors for work on fenceline or yard trees (one old nail can kill a new chain), and even moisture meters to keep track of your fresh lumber as it dries. Responsive to questions by phone or mail, Sperber sends a 30-page operation manual for $3 (free with each mill bought).

Pricing   The one-man mill with a 6.7-cu-in engine is about $1000, roughly half that without the engine. The two-man, 34-in capacity mill with two Stihl 076's is about $1700, roughly one third without the engines. Shipping is UPS for smaller mills, by truck freight collect for larger mills and long slabbing rail.

Power Tools—General

Robert Bosch Power Tool Corporation
PO Box 2217
Hwy. 55 West
New Bern, NC 28560
(919) 633-4133

One of the premier manufacturers of heavy-duty power tools used largely in commercial and industrial applications, Bosch offers an extensive selection of drills and hammers, grinders and polishers, routers, sanders, saws, and other construction equipment like portable alternators, tampers, wet/dry vacuums, and more. *Heavy-duty* is a word that gets thrown around too easily, and I've used it here because Bosch makes tools such as a 2-in rotary hammer pulling 1100 watts that can handle 2-in solid masonry holes and 5 in core bits.

Business operation   Bosch sells through a network of authorized dealers nationwide. The company will provide the name and address of the dealer nearest you. This equipment is not inexpensive and is suited for production work.

Rockwell International, Power Tool
   Division
400 N. Lexington Ave.
Pittsburgh, PA 15208
(412) 247-3593

Rockwell is quite a large manufacturer, into all sorts of product lines, among them the power tool division, which makes portable and stationary power tools for do-it-yourselfers, contractors, and commercial shops. As with most large tool manufacturers, you have to be very selective with the "homeowner" line of tools. Over the years, these products have in general lost quality and durability in order to keep prices down to a point where you might actually on impulse "pick up" one of the quarter-inch drills beside the cash register in the home center. If you intend to use power tools more than occasionally, and certainly if you have any heavy-duty or production applications in mind, stick with the contractor-or-better products. One Rockwell tool (in the catalog marked AD–4300, *Rockwell Machinery for Building Trades and Home Shops*), called a sawbuck, is particularly interesting. It is a bar-mounted circular saw suspended above a rotating miter table, all of which is attached to a platform grid with fold-down legs, and even a set of wheels so you can easily cart the thing around with you. It is like a light-duty version of the large, vertical pull cut-off saws used in many lumber yards. The other catalog worth writing for is AD–4100, *Rockwell Industries Machinery*, which includes band saws, drill presses, grinders, planers, lathes, radial saws, shapers—the works, and all for serious or professional woodworkers.

Business operation   Rockwell sells nationally through local distributors. Write or call the office listed above if you have any trouble locating a branch in your area.

Thor Power Tool, Division
   Stewart-Warner Corporation
175 N. State St.
Aurora, IL 60505

Thor makes a line of heavy-duty power tools it describes as "for industry only." However, if you are a contractor or use tools as a contractor would, write for their catalog and look for Thor tools at contractor supply houses (as opposed to home centers).

Saws/Drills/Sanders/Routers
Skil Corporation
4801 W. Peterson Ave.
Chicago, IL 60646
(312) 286-7330

If you get enough carpenters and general contractors together in one group and ask them about the tools they would pick for work, you would get the names of most major tool manufacturers. However, some names would pop up more than others. My feeling is pretty straightforward and, I think, reflects the general concensus: Milwaukee for drills; Skil for saws. I know it's not too tactful to put a competitor's name in here, but these folks know each other. In fact, *Skilsaw* is nearly a generic word for *circular saw*. Again, speaking for myself, after several years of carpentry apprenticing and starting to work on my own jobs, I finally settled on a Skilsaw 6½ in circular saw for all around cutting, particularly for cuts where the saw weight must be carried, i.e., cutting rafter tails in place or plywood sheathing openings on the frame. My second

saw was and still is (it seems indestructible) what I consider the ultimate—a Skil 7¼ in, worm drive saw—a saw with an in-line handle perfect for production cutting that develops an incredible 25-ft lb of torque with the worm gearing.

Business operation Skil tools are sold through hardware stores, home centers, and contractor supply houses. Parts, service, advice, catalogs, specs, and more are available from a network of eighty service centers across the country. You can write for the Skil catalog, which is sent free, and includes do-it-yourself, tradesman, and professional quality tools. And Skil drills are very fine products, even though its extensive line of saws is tops.

Stationary Power Tools
Toolkraft Corporation
250 South Rd.
Enfield, CT 06082
(203) 741-2261

Toolkraft manufactures a full line of stationary power tools for professional carpenters and do-it-yourselfers, including table saws, radial arm saws, drill presses, jointers, lathes, and such.

Business operation The company sells nationally through mail-order houses and retail dealers and will sell direct to consumers who write to the factory. J. David Leichtung of its consumer department notes, "Many manufacturers are experimenting with lines of smaller model bench top tools that can hold the price line by sacrificing size and/or special features." Toolkraft responds to inquiries with full product catalogs and names and address of local dealers, and answers how-to questions.

Stationary Tools—General

DeWalt, Division, Black & Decker, Inc.
715 Fountain Ave.
Lancaster, PA 17601
(717) 393-5831

DeWalt offers radial arm saws, table saws, and miter saws (generally referred to as cut-off saws), with many accessories. Their "consumer" catalog carries radial arm models (and that's what it has experience with) up to 12 in, which is probably more than enough for home shops. But if you ever get the chance to check out the radial arm saw in some old lumber yard that deals with 8-in $\times$ 8-in posts and such, you may just find an old, exceptionally heavy-duty De-Walt radial up to 18-in diameter or more. Again, you have to be careful with "home-owner" tools. Decide what kind of work you will be doing, and if it might make sense to move up a step to the contractor or commercial line of products for more capacity and durability.

Business operation DeWalt sells nationally through home centers, hardware chains, and so forth. Most outlets offer two books on saw use that were done for Black & Decker.

Tools and Hardware Supply

U.S. General
100 Commercial St.
Plainview, NY 11803

This large catalog (over 6000 items) is free for the asking and carries a tremendous selection of many name brand tools at reasonable prices. For instance, the last catalog I saw had Milwaukee's Sawzall (the two-speed model plus case and blades) for $137 —a pretty good price for a construction classic. U.S. General's drill section also covers B & D, Skil, Makita, and Rockwell;

it lists hoists, machine tools, four kinds of bolt cutters, shop vacs, fire extinguishers, furniture casters—tons of stuff. Write for the catalog, order small to start to make sure you're happy with quality, shipping, and so forth. Mailing is reliable and prompt.

Construction Equipment

Adhesives

Franklin Chemical Industries, Inc.
2020 Bruck St.
PO Box 07802
Columbus, OH 43207
(614) 443-0241

Franklin is a major supplier of adhesives to the woodworking and furniture industry. Also, it makes a wide selection of adhesives for consumers, concentrating in four areas: wood glues, caulking and sealants, flooring adhesives, and construction adhesives. The latter are often overlooked by consumers who do not realize the great holding power that panel adhesive, for instance, can have when used in addition to conventional nailing. Including adhesive for securing panels to metal frames, contact cement for laminates, tile adhesive, and more, Franklin offers a sub-floor and plywood adhesive approved by the APA (American Plywood Association), a nonflammable, water-based mastic used with polystyrene foam insulating panels, and a general purpose construction adhesive that exceeds APA Specification AFG–01 and FHA/HUD Use of Materials Bulletin No. 60.

Business operation Franklin can supply a great many product booklets. For economical new construction you might be particularly interested in Booklet CA25–82 on construction adhesives that discusses the APA glued floor system. The company sells nationally through wholesalers into building material chains, hardware stores, and lumberyards. Write for a product listing and technical data.

Cinva-Ram Block Press
Schrader Bellows, Division Scovill
200 W. Exchange St.
Akron, OH 44302
(216) 375-5202

The Cinva-Ram is a hand-operated press used for making many different kinds of building blocks and tiles. It is a proven piece of appropriate technology used particularly in developing countries but surprisingly little in the United States. The Ram is manufactured by a company in Bogota, Colombia (Metalibec S.A.) and handled only by Schrader in this country. And it is strange to see this machine discussed on stationery bearing the Scovill name, a company known for fairly flash and reasonably decadent Western appliances. But to its credit, it encompasses this firm as well. Anyway, Schrader sells only 100 to 150 units a year. Kathy Easterling of Schrader was quite forthright about this and said that a stock of approximately 50 machines is kept on hand. The Ram is simply a small, boxlike container on which a lever is mounted that can be operated by hand (no power) to apply incredible pressure on soil alone or in combination with other materials like cement to produce semihollow blocks, channel blocks, floor tiles, and more. The Ram comes with wooden inserts that act as dies to produce the different configurations. Net weight is 140 lb; size, 3.5 cu ft. The trick to using the Ram is in selecting the right soil or soil combination to put into it. Generally, local soil can be tested (the Ram booklet contains instructions for basic, on-site tests), then screened, and depending on the use intended, combined with 5 or 10 percent cement, then moisturized, and pressed. On average, Ram-built block costs about one-twentieth of conventional masonry. Schrader will send information on request. The final block are uniform, sound, and durable.

Climbing/Safety Equipment
Klein Tools, Inc.
7200 McCormick Blvd.
Chicago, IL 60645
(312) 677-9500

Although Klein sells tools that are designed specifically for professional "climbers," i.e., construction workers who go up scaffolding, utility poles, transmission towers, and steel framing, you may have need for such equipment, particularly if you decide to tackle jobs like setting your own roof trusses, setting up your own windmill towers, and the like.

Business operation Write for a catalog showing a full array of climbing and safety gear, sent on request to professionals and most likely to all seriously interested parties.

Excavating/Farm Equipment
J. I. Case
700 State St.
Racine, WI 53404
(414) 636-6011

This company, in business since 1842, makes backhoes, bucket loaders, tractors, and all kinds of construction, farming, and excavating equipment in heavy-duty versions for industry and surprisingly small and compact versions for homesteaders, small farmers, homeowners, and others.

Business operation   Case machines have the reputation of quality and durability. They sell worldwide, with about 2000 outlets in North America alone. The company can provide complete product information. Two manuals are of particular interest: No. A45182B, covering tractors and Case's extremely compact and versatile Uni-Loader (35 in wide, 6-ft 4½ in high including the steel roll cage, with a 700-lb lift that turns tight circles—really incredible and fun to run); and No. TPG80, a planning guide covering yard and garden tractors, and the many attachments available for tilling, discing, load hauling, and more. The company has recently moved its headquarters to Atlanta.

Folding Ladders
Little Giant Industries, Inc.
2241 S. Larson Pkwy.
Provo, UT 84601
(800) 547-5995

The folks from Little Giant have shown up at several of the homebuilding trade shows I attend. Their demonstrator whips Little Giant's 22-ft ladder through its six operating positions, freezing bypassers with the clattering magic show. He puts the 22-ft system through these paces: folded up into a 5-, 6-, 7-, 8-, or 9-ft step ladder; separated into two, independent 5-ft trestles for scaffolding; hinged off-center with unequal leg lengths for stairs; unfolded partially as a lean-to ladder; unfolded completely through telescoping rails to a 22-ft extension ladder; folded for storage to 5 ft 7 in high by 8 in wide. It is nifty. Little Giant also makes 13- and 17-ft models, plus several accessories such as work platforms.

Business operation   Write the company for information on cost and availability.

Gauges/Test Instruments
Dwyer Instruments, Inc.
PO Box 373
Michigan City, IN 46360
(219) 872-9141

I first came across Dwyer by using its small, very lightweight wind gauge out of curiosity, when I was wilderness camping in Canada, in September, and wanted to know what conditions I was exposed to as I was sleeping only semiprotected under a tarp tent. The little gadget was quite inexpensive, disarmingly simple, and accurate—an unusual combination. As it turns out, Dwyer makes high-quality gauges and controls for all kinds of measurements and operations. Its catalog is voluminous and contains product descriptions and specs on the following: dial gauges, manometers, air filter gauges, pressure switches, flowmeters, air velocity instruments, and several complete kits—for instance, a combustion test kit, carbon dioxide indicators, and more.

Business operation   Dwyer has several sales offices across the country. The headquarters can supply the names and addresses, and they are listed in the catalog.

Imported Tools and Equipment
JET Equipment & Tools
PO Box 1477
Tacoma, WA 98401
(206) 572-5000

JET currently carries some 600 items that are sold through about 6000 distributors and dealers. Its products (about 90 percent are imported) range from tiny screwdriver sets for jewelers to 24,000-lb engine lathes.

Business operation   Some of JET's products may be found in hardware stores. However, by writing the company you can receive literature on specific products and the name and address of local sales reps and retailers.

Lawn/Garden/Snow Equipment
Atlas Tool & Manufacturing Company
7100 S. Grand Ave.
St. Louis, MO 63111
(314) 353-7800

Although this firm makes a relatively standard selection of lawn mowers, snow blowers, and the like (under the Atlas label), it is always interesting to discover one of the firms that makes things for stores that sell things. Atlas does what's called private label work for J. C. Penney, True Value Hardware, Greenbrier, and others. Naturally, most of its sales are wholesale (the chains have the volume). Atlas also has an astonishing network of authorized service centers —thousands of them—nationwide.

Business operation Connect JET by mail or by dialing its toll-free line ([800] 325-3800, except Missouri). Atlas will help with product manuals, price, and parts information.

The Toro Company
8111 Lyndale Ave. South
Minneapolis, MN 55420
(612) 887-8810

Toro is a major manufacturer of lawn mowers, tractors, snow blowers, and other yard and garden equipment. Machinery is made for small to very large plots and sold through authorized sales and sales/service centers across the country.

Business operation Connect JET by a very active consumer information program. Barbara Scamehorn of the public relations department writes, "The Toro Company welcomes questions/comments of all kinds . . . brochures/literature, operating manuals, photos, service information, and regional dealer listings may be obtained by writing to the public relations department."

Logging Supplies
Bailey's, Inc.
PO Box 550
Laytonville, CA 95454
(707) 984-6133

If you are looking for almost any tool or piece of equipment or accessory that has to do with logging, Bailey's catalog is likely to carry it—along with some items you should know about if you're serious about this kind of work. For example, Bailey's carries a full selection of Alaskan Mills (portable slabbing mills), chain saws, replacement bars and chains, sharpening tools, bumper-mount winches and come-alongs, good boots, first aid kits, and a lot more.

Business operation Selling nationally via mail order, Bailey's catalog is updated five times a year. Write for it. Good equipment at moderate prices.

Rolling and Step Ladders
Putnam Rolling Ladder Company
32 Howard St.
New York, NY 10013
(212) CA6-5147

Putnam makes high-quality, durable ladders in many varieties, including aluminum extension ladders, scaffolding, ladder jacks, roof hooks, and the like. But the gems are its wooden rolling ladders, complete with brass hardware—absolute beauties. Putnam can even manufacture and install ladders that can track through curved corners completely around a room. Standard ladder material is oak, although Putnam will use any suitable wood you want. Also, it now offers hardware that is silver painted, black, or brass plated and polished.

Business operation   Even if you do not have a high wall library, rolling ladders can serve as access to lofts and balconies. The Putnam catalog shows many applications and gives complete details in a clear straightforward presentation. The catalog with price list is available on request. And you will probably get a reprint of Putnam's rating in Consumer Reports. Gregg P. Monsees of Putnam's writes, "In the New York area we take measurements for the customer and/or install the track and ladder if desired, although installation of our track and ladders is not difficult, and most of our customers install the track and ladders themselves." The firm sells wholesale, retail, and via mail order.

Roofing Equipment
Roofmaster Products Company
750 Monterey Pass Rd.
Monterey Park, CA 91754
(213) 261-5122

Roofmaster makes equipment, tools, and accessories used to lay roofing, including hot asphalt kettles, all types of ladders, vents, hand tools, saws, spray system parts, vents, and more.

Business operation   This specialty company is not able to provide any how-to advice but will send along a brochure on its products. If unable to find its products at roofing and building supply outlets you can order direct or ask for the name and address of a local dealer. This company is one of the largest distributors of roofing-related tools and equipment.

Sawhorse Hardware
Fas-Set Manufacturing, Inc.
252 Airport Blvd.
Santa Rosa, CA 95401
(707) 544-1404

Fas-Set makes a series of sawhorse hardware that is designed to get more out of a few 2 × 4's than a standard, slightly rickety, A-frame horse. For instance, it manufactures a bracket (used in pairs) with telescoping legs so you can get a level work surface even where the ground isn't level. The bracket has a U-shaped welded piece on top that accepts 2 × 4's on edge; logholders that clamp onto this 2 × 4 and hold logs in a Y-shaped, toothed opening; a reversible top bracket so the 2 × 4 can lie on the flat as well as on edge; platform converters that clip onto 2 × 4 horses and provide a pocket for 2 × 4's at right angles (a simple way to make a sturdy work platform supported on all four sides); plus camper legs (for trailers, boats, etc.); and other such goodies.

Business operation   Fas-Set sells through several mail-order outlets, including Sears, and the Brookstone catalog. Write or call the company about ordering direct from the factory. These are simple, practical items worth investigating.

Stone Working Tools
Trow and Holden Company, Inc.
45–57 S. Main St.
Barre, VT 05641
(802) 476-7221

This firm offers power tools, hand tools, and construction equipment like pneumatic hammers, portable crane surfacers, and rock bits—generally tools and equipment for professionals or serious amateurs.

Business operation   Write for Catalog 12, *Stone Cutting Tools*, or call toll-free 1 (800) 451-4349. Those in the business will recognize the brand names Barre and Trowco in the catalog.

Tool Belts

Occidental Leather
PO Box 483
Occidental, CA 95465
(707) 874-3650

Occidental makes heavy-duty, leather tool belts, aprons, and accessories. All are hand made of Number 1 grade leather, and many include attachments and holders for hand tools—your ruler, tri-square, and so forth. Not for the occasional do-it-yourselfer, these items are mandatory for efficiency in the construction trades. So, if you do a lot of carpentry work and wind up going back to the nail box again and again, or have a larger project in mind, like an addition to your home, consider time-saving equipment like this.

Business operation Occidental offers at no charge a small brochure outlining its products. Also, it has a custom design service for special needs.

Well Drilling

DeepRock Manufacturing Company
2200 Anderson Rd.
Opelika, AL 36802
1 (800) 633-8774
(205) 749-3377 (Call collect from Alabama, Alaska, Hawaii, and Canada)

DeepRock sends one of the most distinctive packages of product information you are likely to see from any company. It concerns their well-drilling machinery, which is a small-scale, one-man machine. A Tecumseh motor provides the power and can be hand-held or mounted on the company's "power mast" frame. An 18 to 1 gearbox turned by the 3 HP engine generates 200 rpm. Pipe sections are threaded together as needed while a drilling pump (DeepRock's or yours) supplies water to the line. With the weight of the engine behind the pipe, you can stand back and watch until it is time for another pipe length. The company sells pilot and reamer bits, screen and casing, pipe lengths with threaded couplings, a swivel attachment for your garden hose that keeps the water flowing and the hose stationary as the drill rotates, plus other accessories.

Business operation The Hydra-Drill information kit is simply wonderful: blow-by-blow photographs from packages of parts to flowing water; a full-color brochure showing all parts and explaining how to order the right package for your site; an informative brochure on water sources, quality, supply, and more; and the kicker, a flexible, 33⅓ LP record of case history interviews, conducted over the phone, so that the people interviewed come across as neighbors, as people down the street. It's great.

Pricing The engine, power mast rigging system (with pulley system for lifting the motor and attaching new pipe sections), and power swivel connection for garden hose is sold as a kit for about $500. Bits are about $35; what appears to be PVC casing is $35 for ten 5-ft sections. Call toll-free for information.

Shop Equipment

Abrasive Cords and Tapes

E. C. Mitchell Company, Inc.
88–90 Boston St.
Middleton, MA 01949
(617) 774-1191

Mitchell manufactures flexible abrasives—like sandpaper on a string—in endless different coatings, grains, and grits that are ideal for burring holes; grinding or polishing hard-to-reach places; and cleaning V-grooves and slots in any curved surface from a spring clip groove on a power tool to a curved section of wooden sculpture. Supplied on 25-yd spools, abrasive cords are available from .012-in to .150-in diameters; tapes are $\frac{1}{16}$-in to ¼-in wide.

Business operation   For $1, Mitchell will send a sample card of aluminum oxide cords and tapes in thirteen different sizes, with order instructions, and a complete listing of available grits and sizes. The samples are, unfortunately, too short (about 2 in long) to give you a good chance to use them. An introductory home-shop special (for $12) includes three sample spools. If you do much metal work or highly detailed woodwork, you will have need for these items somewhere along the line.

Adhesives
Wood & Stone, Inc.
7567 Gary Rd.
Manassas, VA 22110
(703) 369-1236

Akemi adhesives (distributed by Wood & Stone) are used by professionals who work with building stone, monuments, and ceramics. Several varieties are offered, including white flowing for horizontal surface filling or mending; transparent flowing, which accepts iron oxide color to match the surrounding stone and polishes to a high gloss; limestone patch; and more, plus coloring pastes and polishing fluid.

Pricing   Half pints range from $4.50 to about $6.

Ceramic Equipment
Eagle Ceramics
12266 Wilkins Ave.
Rockville, MD 20852
(301) 881-2253

Eagle carries a full line of ceramic tools, supplies, and equipment, including all types of clay, brushes, rollers, and other hand tools and also heavy-duty gas and electric kilns. Its catalog includes a good, 4-page book list and educational materials and is sent on request.

Clamps
Universal Clamp Corporation
6905 Cedros Ave.
Van Nuys, CA 91405
(213) 780-1015

Universal is a very distinctive company. The limited line of tools it makes, particularly its clamps, are unlike those found at other manufacturers. Overall, they have a simple, utilitarian quality, as though some fellow who did a lot of shopwork and built a lot of furniture bumped into the limitations of the tools he had and designed new versions. First, its clamps: they are short clamps for long work. Customarily, wide spans must be clamped with long and heavy pipe clamps—a plate at one end, a threaded pressure plate at the other—holding the work together. One end of the universal clamp is threaded (and operated by a large, comfortable, butterfly nut), but the other end, which is only a few inches away, is a cam action bar that can grip the stock anywhere along its length. Another goodie: Universal's salvage pry bar—perfect for popping up roof sheathing boards and such. Write for more information on both these products. (The pry bar is disarmingly simple.)

Business operation   Universal distributes nationwide to tool dealers and sells via mail order direct to woodworkers. It is responsive to all types of questions about its products, shop practice, and the like. Write for illustrated brochures and price list.

Pricing   The basic half cam half screw clamp is $13.50. A wide variety of mounts and fixtures is available. The pry bar is about $30.

Economy Stationary Power Tools

American Machine & Tool Company Inc.
of Pennsylvania
Fourth Ave. and Spring St.
PO Box 70
Royersford, PA 19468
(215) 948-0400

AMT equipment is low priced. For instance, a drill press costs $90, a belt and disc sander combination costs $70, a table saw costs about $55, all without motor, as is the case with most manufacturers. So the question is, Does the cheap price mean you get a cheap tool—one that won't cut straight, that whines and groans and then breaks? That question is impossible to answer definitively. You have to use the tools to be sure for yourself. But I can give you an idea by covering the specs on AMT's deluxe power saw ($63.50). Without the motor, the 8-in model has a 10½-in × 13-in table, (side extensions are available as options), a ⅝-in spindle, 2¼-in depth of cut upright, 1⅞-in at a 45 degree pitch, a front locking knob for blade tilt, a cam lock for blade height, a miter gauge in ⅜-in × ¾-in milled table groove. It weighs about 25 lb.

Business operation   AMT sells nationally via mail order. It will send you free, extensive product literature and spec sheets for specific tools, including jointer-planers, lathes, spindle-shapers, and a selection of vises. It also sells a 10-in contractor's table saw ($462) and other commercial-duty tools. Write for all the details you want. Be straightforward. Tell AMT the low prices make you wonder. By now it has to used to this reaction.

Electronic and Appliance Testers

Amprobe Instrument
630 Merrick Rd.
PO Box 329
Lynbrook, NY 11563
(516) 593-5600

Amprobe makes a variety of test instruments, such as probes for testing furnace ignition transformers, appliance leakage testers, temperature probes, and more. Its primary market is commercial users, not home consumers. However, it will respond to inquiries with detailed product literature at no cost. Joe Perz, their advertising manager, writes that Amprobe has several articles that provide information on the use of its instruments as well. Write for them.

Electronic Test Equipment

Triplett Corporation
Bluffton, OH 45817
(419) 358-5015

Triplett manufactures electronic test equipment such as ammeters, general purpose and laboratory accurate V-O-Ms, digital multimeters, logic probes, telephone testers, and a temperature probe useful in furnace tuning and efficiency calculations. It also makes a full line of panel instruments for shop applications.

Business operation Triplett will send product specs on request. It sells nationally through distributors who supply, in turn, Allied Radio and Newark Electronics, two of the firms that sell Triplett's products via mail order.

Equipment Surplus/Security Equipment

Burden Sales Company
1000–1015 W. O St.
PO Box 82209
Lincoln, NB 68501
(402) 435-4366

Burden operates two separate businesses under one huge roof. The Surplus Center sells retail and via mail order. It stocks all kinds of tools and equipment, hydraulic parts and machines, motors, pumps, tarps, wind generators—100 catalog pages. Burden's other company is Burdex Security, which sells security products, complete systems, provides installation information and advice on selection.

Business operation Catalogs for both companies are sent on request.

Glass Tools and Materials

Whittemore-Durgin Glass Company
PO Box 2065
Hanover, MA 02339
(617) 871-1743

Whittemore and Durgin is an excellent source for all kinds of glass, stained glass, kits, supplies, spare parts, tools, and more. Its catalog goes on and on for 70 pages and includes precut stained glass kits; complete tool kits for stained glass craftspeople;

project sheets with pieces laid out to scale; endless styrene lampshade forms on which leaded framing is laid out; and an extensive selection of tools, including cutters, etching equipment and patterns, lamp stems and hardware, and beveled glass supplies—really a complete selection at moderate prices.

Business operation Whittemore-Durgin has two retail stores: one in Rockland, Massachusetts (825 Market St.; [617] 871-1743) and one in Middlesex, NJ (436 Lincoln Blvd.; [201] 469-5350). A full catalog with price list is sent on request. It describes the contents as "the choicest and most elegant materials for the perpetrating of STAINED GLASS ARTISTRY . . . CERTAIN PATENTED DEVICES . . . for every variety of GOODS and PATTERNS for the production of QUALITY LEADED GLASS WORK."

Instruments

Abbeon California, Inc.
123–107A Gray Ave.
Santa Barbara, CA 93101
(805) 963-7545

This interesting mail-order firm sells many different precision measuring instruments and a few unrelated items as well. Its emphasis, however, is on items such as hygrometers, Fahrenheit and Celsius thermometers, humidity indicators, pipe thermometers, freezer alarms, sound level meters, and more.

Business operation Abbeon will send you its catalog on request. It sells via mail order nationally.

Pricing A certified, solid brass casing, hygrometer with 5-in dial (certified accurate plus or minus 3 percent) is about $80; freezer alarm with 9-volt battery is about $60.

Kits/Tools/Supplies

Wikkmann House
Box 501
Chatsworth, CA 91311
(213) 349-5148

Wikkmann's catalog, for $2, offers quite a wide range of furniture kits and a limited selection of tools and hardware; also an extensive selection of full-size plans and blueprints for grandfather clocks, models of all sizes and descriptions, toys, chests, and more. They carry the "Careful Wrecker's Friend" salvage pry bar (one of my favorites because it is so simple and does its job so efficiently), Duplimaster lathe attachments, full plans for home workbenches, etc. Generally the styles are decorative, maybe even a tad gadgety as opposed to sleek and efficient, although you should probably look for yourself as capsule descriptions of style can only hint at what you'll find.

Business operation Wikkmann sells nationally via mail order, and will sometimes locate a source for you if they cannot fill your needs. Their large-scale plans are exceptionally clear and uncomplicated, probably just right for a near novice.

Pricing Plans range from under $2 for small projects to $7 and $8 for larger ones.

Lathe Accessories

Toolmark Company
6840 Shingle Creek Pkwy.
Minneapolis, MN 55430
(612) 561-4210

Toolmark carries several interesting lathe accessories including centers, safety shields, and a duplicating machine. It consists of a slide table assembly, a set of pattern holder brackets, and a hand-held duplicator body with cutters.

Business operation The model 520B duplicator is approximately $270. Catalogs with illustrations demonstrating operation are sent on request.

Lathe Duplicators

Turn-O-Carve Company
PO Box 8315
Tampa, FL 33674

A pantograph for lathes, the duplicator made by Turn-O-Carve is a heavy-duty version of something you might think up and make on your own. Say you had a table leg or had designed and made one that you wanted to duplicate. Setting up a piece of stock in your lathe and cutting it exactly like another piece requires constant checking, back and forth, between original and copy. The Turn-O-Carve system solves this by rigging the original on angle irons bolted to a platform and suspending it directly above the new stock. Then a feeler arm and a cutting tool are mounted in vertical alignment on a tree that is held perpendicular to the work surface on a metal bed. Like a contour gauge used to measure moulding, the imprint of the original acts as a guide—and through the feeler arm a stop—for the cutting tool. The supplier makes two types of duplicators, and an interesting, ball-bearing steady rest that bolts to a lathe bed to reduce vibration, particularly on thin turnings.

Business operation The company supplies several illustrations and descriptions of products that do everything but give you reassurance about their strength. Some Rube Goldberg tools work well in principle but don't have the solidity to do the job—or rely on you to provide it with reinforced mounting, etc. Try the basic literature first, then go back again for more details.

Pricing The large duplicator is about $140, plus shipping.

Machine Tools/Metalwork/ Models

Cowells, Inc.
PO Box 245
Cadillac, MI 49601
(616) 775-6296

This company provides a catalog for serious metalworkers. It features top-quality equipment imported from England: beautifully machined vertical milling guides; engraving kits; all types of cutters; and many lathes, including the Myford Super 7B, 3½-in × 19-in lathe (about $5800) that performs as beautifully as any Rolls Royce. Plus this firm carries a wonderful line of scale models by Stuart Turner: vertical steam engines (5 in × 7 in), mill engines, and more, all in kit form. It is page after page of oohs and aahs for metalworkers: a hardwood boxed set of twenty-one taps and seven dies for model engineers (about $140), an extensive book list, miniature overhead drilling machines (13 in total).

Business operation Cowell's catalog is, at this point, sent on request—a steal. Prices are good, although the United States–British rate of exchange can change prices at any time. Another good point: Cowells now has any of the plans listed in *Model and Allied Publications Handbook* Volumes 1 through 5 (MAP plans) and has been appointed subscription agent in the United States and Canada for *Model Engineer*.

Miniature Power Tools

Blackstone Industries, Inc. (Foredom)
Bethel, CT 06801
(203) 792-8622

Well known by the trade name Foredom, this is the other manufacturer of bite-size power tools. (The other company in the field is Dremel.) Foredom tools, writes Ellen Fahrenholz of Blackstone, "are used primarily by industry and the professional. However, an ever-increasing number have found their way into home workshops to people who pursue the hobby of decoy carving, making miniature furniture and doll houses, the lapidary, the antiques restorer, and many others." Foredom tools work off a flexible driveshaft connected to a motor— a simple disconnection of power supply and power output. Endless attachments and accessories are available: cutters, grinders, polishers, little drills, brushes, sanding drums, hammer handpieces, and more. Also, the power system can be operated with a foot switch (a nice touch for two hands on the work). Another point: Blackstone also handles the Cutawl Machine, a proven, mini– band saw with a blade that swivels 360 degrees.

Business operation Write Foredom for product information sheets, particularly Model 4272 Projects Kit and Catalog 280 B, which also includes things like dental engines (boo, hiss). Blackstone also handles Olson band saw blades.

Dremel Division Emerson Electric
    Company
4915 21st St.
Racine, WI 53406
(414) 544-1390

Dremel makes the kinds of tools that you know, if only you had them, you could use to turn out all kinds of nifty models and pipes and little wooden sculptures and on and on. Dremel calls them compact, and that they are. Most are hand-sized power tools, some with variable speed, that can be bought in kit form with an array of tiny sanding drums, grinders, burrs, drills, and more. It also makes speed control attachments, vises, and mini–drill presses, one with a flexible shaft, and compact shop tools like table saws (a 4-in tilt arbor design with a ¾-in depth of cut limit at 45 degrees). Its illustrated catalog and price list also covers chain saw sharpening tools and small soldering irons. I can't help it: when I think of Dremel I picture a shop full of little people turning this stuff out and eating little sandwiches for lunch. But Dremel tools are really exciting for imaginative hobby and craft people. (Yes, it is all right to use an electric tool and still call what you do a craft.) With the right accessories there is little you can't cut, trim, sculpt, shave, or polish.

Business operation   One of two companies offering a solid line of compact power tools (the other is Foredom), Dremel products are widely available through hobby and hardware stores and carried in many tool and craft catalogs. Write for the Compact Power Tools Price List (fully illustrated). A real treat to have power and versatility at this small scale.

Shop and Antique Tools
Conover Woodcraft Specialties, Inc.
18125 Madison Rd.
Parkman, OH 44080
(216) 548-3481

Conover's catalog is a disarming combination of antique and modern tools. The company carries threadboxes and tap sets so you can make your own screw clamps or tool handles, hardwood moulding planes, spoke shaves, spoon bits, and also $8000 commercial metal lathes. Its power equipment is professional grade—for production shops, although some of the lower end models are suitable for high-quality home shops.

Business operation   Conover's retail store shows its wares. The catalog is sent on request. There is no minimum order.

Stationary Power Tool Kits
Gilliom Manufacturing, Inc.
1700 Scherer Pkwy.
St. Charles, MS 63301
(314) 724-1812

This company supplies all machined parts and plans for a variety of stationary shop tools. You supply the labor (and materials) for cabinet construction and assembly. Naturally, this saves you a lot of money. For instance, buying direct from the factory (Gilliom does not use dealers), you could order kits for a circular saw, sander, and bandsaw for about $250, total. When you get done, these machines will not look like brand name tools. They will look homemade. So if part of the appeal in shop tools is the slick, aircraft cockpit type of appearance, look elsewhere. But if you don't plan to give tours of your shop, this should interest you. These kits have been sold for almost 40 years. All the machined parts, like belt drive wheels, spindles, rip fence bar, table tilt hardware, blade guards, and more come in the kit.

Business operation   Gilliom will send you an illustrated brochure introducing its products with sample specs of a wood shaper, table saw, and three different band saws.

Pricing   Complete building plans cost about $4. Costs for various kits are $113 for a 12-in bandsaw, about $180 for an 18-in band saw, $70 for a tilting arbor saw, $70 for a wood shaper. Write for a complete, illustrated price list.

Storage/Organizers
Akro-Mils
1293 S. Main St.
Akron, OH 44301
(216) 253-5593

Akro-Mils manufactures plastic and metal storage organizers, including metal cabinet, plastic drawer units for all kinds of small shop hardware (like sixty-drawer cabinets), and all kinds of larger, bulk storage systems, multiple plastic bins on wheels, and more. Many of the applications are commercial and industrial, but many of the moulded plastic items (like extremely compact swing bins) are ideal for recapturing some dead kitchen cabinet space.

Business operation The company offers to respond to inquiries by phone or mail and will send illustrated product literature with prices on request. David Moreland of Akro-Mils writes, "With smaller homes and more people living in apartments than ever before, their space is more valuable and they need to be able to store things economically and efficiently, which Akro-Mils offers the consumer." Pricing is quite reasonable, and it is almost certain that you will find a good use for one of the storage systems in the catalog.

Surplus Tools/Equipment/ Machinery

Airborne Sales Company, Inc.
8501 Stellar Dr.
PO Box 2727
Culver City, CA 90230
(213) 870-4687

Airborne started as a government surplus mail-order house over thirty years ago. Their 90-page catalog includes a lot of hydraulic equipment, parts, motors, actuators, cylinders, and the like, but also a typically crazy quilt surplus selection: aircraft instruments, compressors, engines, fans, filters, fire extinguishers, hose, levels, log splitters, pulleys, hand tools, welding supplies, winches. Some stock is new surplus, some used.

Business operation Airborne's illustrated catalog is sent on request.

Thickness Planer/Moulder

Williams & Hussey Machine Company
Milford, NH 03055
(603) 673-3446

This company makes an interesting thickness planer that, because of its unique design, works well as a moulder, edger, and jointer. It is a strong possibility for home shops that have the basic stationary power tools but don't have the machinery to make the last step up to really good furniture construction. To do that you have to be able to run your lumber to your own specs and to absolutely uniform dimensions. And even though it is supposed to come that way from the lumberyard, an accurate thickness planer and edger will usually turn up discrepancies. The Williams & Hussey machine has one free side, riding up and down on two posts that are both on one side of the machine. This permits running lumber 14-in wide by reversing the material and making two passes. Some forty-one sets of knives are available for the machine, allowing a wide variety of custom moulding and edging.

Business operation Write for product specs. The company sells nationally via mail order and provides a toll-free line for inquiries: 1 (800) 258-1380.

Pricing The moulder planer with hand feed is about $430, $585 with power infeed; power infeed and outfeed is about $675.

Tools—General

General Hardware Manufacturing
   Company, Inc.
80 White St.
Department CL
New York, NY 10013
(212) 431-6100

One of the really good tool catalogs offering generally inexpensive, quality tools.

But as Tom McGannon, a vice-president at General, writes, "Note that we do not make the hammers, saws, pliers type of basic hand tools available from many other manufacturers, but do do specialize in plumbers, carpenters, machinists, electronic technician and hobbyists specialized hand tools. We also feature a top quality line of precision measuring tools including dial indicators, micrometers, calipers, and stainless steel rules." Catalog No. 82 A is the one you want. General will send it on for $1. New products in the catalog include a variable angle drill guide (attaches to your power drill)—ask for tear sheet DG–82—and a set of three shave hooks with different contours for scraping moulding and furniture—ask for tear sheet TDS-582.

Business operation General sells nationally via mail order and has been doing so for sixty years. Unless you're stuck on a particular brand name (and you really shouldn't be, at least not for all hand tools), spring for the dollar and take a look.

Pricing As a rule, prices are extremely competitive: a 10-in, wood handled spiral ratchet screwdriver for $8.60; a Number 1 to 60 metal drill case for $15.18; an eight-piece, dowel centering punch kit for $2.36. Prices may go up, but comparatively they're starting pretty low at this source.

Vacuums
Royal Appliance Manufacturing
  Company
650 Alpha Dr.
Cleveland, OH 44143
(216) 449-6150

Royal manufactures a line of household and commercial vacuum cleaners. The one I'm thinking about is a small, all metal, hand-held model, with suction and brushes just like a big vacuum, that would make a nice addition to a going shop. Royal will

send you product brochures, the name and address of the dealer nearest you, and suggested retail prices.

Wiring/Cords
Belden Corporation
2000 S. Batavia Ave.
Geneva, IL 60134
(312) 232-8900

Belden is a major manufacturer of extension cords, droplights, booster cables, wire and battery cable sets, and some automotive test and tune up equipment. Its complete catalog (No. 781P, for $3) includes connectors, cables, terminals, and more for most cars, trucks, and heavy machinery, including farm and excavation equipment.

Business operation Belden sells to original equipment manufacturers, automotive stores through National Automotive Parts Association (NAPA).

Wood Sanding
Kuster Woodworkers
Box 34
Skillman, NJ 08558
(201) 359-4680

Kuster sanding equipment is a tad elaborate for basic home shops, although high-quality finish sanding can make the difference between mediocre and exceptional final appearances. Trademarked and advertised as Dynasand, Kuster manufactures three basic products. First is a thickness sander in three sizes: 12-, 18-, and 24-in width capacities, all in modified kit form. Everything but the motor is included—the metal sanding drum, pillow block arbor bearings, drive pulleys, thickness adjuster, and assembly hardware for the support platform. This machine has a 1-in drum shaft and interchangeable 6- and 12-in diameter sanding drums machined to a .005-in tolerance. Second are Kuster airsanders, made to work off your portable drill, lathe, or other drive source. They are soft drums, inflated with a bicycle pump, that give enough to conform to sculpted and other irregular contours. Eleven different lengths and diameters are sold. Third is an electrically heated splicing press so you can manufacture your own sanding belts to your own specifications; 75- and 150-ft rolls of sandpaper are available from 60 to 180 grit. All are aluminum oxide resin bondcloth.

Business operation Kuster sells nationally via mail order. Write for the well-illustrated brochure.

Pricing Thickness sander kits are about $200 for the 12-in model, $250 for the 18-in model, and $300 for the 24-in model. Plans, free with the kits, are sold separately for $10.

Woodworking Machinery
PAL Industries, Inc.
11090 S. Alameda St.
Lynwood, CA 90262
(213) 636-0621

PAL manufactures Davis & Wells Woodworking Machinery, and Apex Disc Sander/Granders. This is industrial equipment, available to anyone but required only by the most serious and accomplished craftsman, whether professional or amateur. For example, here are some of the specs on their 16-in tilting arbor table saw: 24-in × 33½-in cabinet base, 35 in high with sawdust cleanout front and rear; 32-in × 40-in table with one 32-in × 52-in extension, 1-in diameter arbor; heavy-duty hand wheels for tilt and depth of cut with direct reading gauges; 5¾-in depth of cut; 24½-in maximum rip without extensions; rip fence on machined, graduated rail; motor mounts to carry up to 10 hp, 3 phase type, and more. They make jointers, boring machines, shapers, band saws, bench and pedestal sanders and grinders, and more.

Business operation PAL will supply product sheets with specifications and the name and address of one of its 250 dealers nearest you. Bob Olsen, PAL sales manager, writes, "We provide free information or advice about maintenance, service, and availability. When requested, we will also provide literature and parts drawings on all of our equipment."

GOVERNMENT AGENCIES

Consumer Information
Consumer Information Center
Pueblo, CO 81009

Consumer Information Center
General Services Administration
Washington, DC 20405

Two of the most accessible sources for many different kinds of consumer information, it makes sense to start by asking for the *Consumer Information Catalogue*, which introduces hundreds of publications available from the government on insulation, residential framing, fire safety, tools and equipment, do-it-yourself projects—you name it. The catalog is updated quarterly.

Product Safety Standards

Consumer Product Safety Commission
(CPSC)
(800) 638-8326 (Toll-free continental
United States)
(800) 638-8333 (Toll-free Alaska,
Hawaii, Puerto Rico, and Virgin
Islands)
(800) 492-8363 (Toll-free Maryland
only)

Stated simply, the purpose of the CPSC is to protect the public against unreasonable risks of injury associated with consumer products used in and around the home, schools, and recreation areas. Unreasonable is the operative word. The CPSC can set safety standards for lawnmowers and chain-saws, they can get warning labels applied by the manufacturers, and more. But they can't make you buy the safest model, or use it safely once you have it. Some of their areas with the highest priority now are: chain saws, where "kickback" was found responsible for 23 percent of some 125,000 injuries in a 1980 study; house wiring and circuit breakers; wood- and coal-burning heating equipment, and upholstered furniture relating to fire hazards.

Business operation The CPSC will provide publication lists from which you can order reports (many are free) on a wide variety of materials and products.

READING AND REFERENCE

Antique Tools

Ancient Carpenter's Tools, by Henry C.
Mercer
Bucks County Historical Society/
Horizon Press, 1975

This book has been through many editions—not that the material would ever become dated. It is a well-illustrated book working through each group of tools; where they came from, what the first ones were like, how they evolved, and how and why they were refined for specialized tasks. A scholarly treatment; fascinating tidbits throughout.

Country Craft Tools, by Percy W.
Blandford
Harper & Row
10 E. 53 St.
New York, NY 10022

This book will give you a tour of all the fine old tools you can hardly find anymore.

Pictures of several types of ice saws (the preelectric ice cube maker on a grand scale) brought to mind an ice saw I bought for $6 about 15 years ago at a barn sale in Canaan, New Hampshire—an incredible hunk of metal, about 6 ft long. Saws like this are hard to locate now at any price. The book is a bit short on tool use but very direct and interesting; about $8.

Iron Horse Antiques, Inc.
The Fine Tool Journal
RD 2, Poultney, VT 05764
(802) 287-4050

Iron Horse offers a selection of antique tools for sale via mail order. You can stop in to look over the impressive stock or get an idea of what they do there by subscribing to *The Fine Tool Journal*. Both enterprises are run by Vernon A. Ward, who writes that he has plans to turn the ten times a year newsletter for collectors and craftsmen into a full-fledged magazine. Currently, subscriptions are $10 per year. You can write and ask for a sample issue and for their book list. The newsletter is well illustrated, full of information, book reviews, runs a regular "Whatsit" feature (you think you know what the tool in the picture is for but you're probably wrong), and is generally a total treat for those interested in antique tools.

Blacksmithing

The Modern Blacksmith, by Alexander G.
    Weygers
Van Nostrand Reinhold Company
7625 Empire Dr.
Florence, KY 41042

Building on the skills and experiences covered in Weygers' more basic book, *The Making of Tools*, this book covers more traditional blacksmithing products: hinges and hardware plus large-scale tools such as an anvil made from a piece of railroad rail. Thorough illustrations help, but this is a book for experienced and resourceful fabricators.

Blasting

ABA Publishing Company
406 W. 32 St.
Wilmington, DE 19802
(302) 762-3928

Even though Joe Dannenberg, the publisher of ABA, which produces books on blasting, has warned that blasting materials are hazardous and belong only in the hands of highly trained professionals, and almost but not quite asked that I not list his company

as a source, it is here simply for your information. As with all the sources in this book, it is up to you to use your good judgment about inquiring, buying, using, and maintaining any products you discover on these pages. It's not up to me. I assume that if you are homesteading and need to clear stumps or ledgerock, you may not decide this is another run of the mill do-it-yourself job, and you should give it a try. If your judgment was in fact that bad, I believe you would have a difficult time acquiring any form of explosives in any case. But it may be necessary to do some investigating, to read up on what a blasting contractor is telling you about your options. So if you want information, generally technical information at that, you can write ABA for its book list. It includes *Stumping with Explosives, Blasting Rocks, Boulders, and Ledges*, and more. ABA's *Explosives Training Manual* is offered by mail order for $10.

Casting

Foundrywork for the Amateur, by
    B. Terry Aspin
Model and Allied Publications—Argus
    Books
14 St. James Rd.
Watford, Herts WD1 5PN England

Foundrywork is generally perceived to be completely outside the range of how-to work, but it is a simple process that can be handled on a small scale. This book bridges the gap between perception and reality very nicely, introducing melting, moulding, and casting—even projects that can be done using a kitchen stove. It also shows how to build a small furnace if you want more, and you probably will. Don't start with plans to cast your own woodstove, but learning this trade will enable you to cast a good replacement for a cracked grate, a broken hinge, and small parts for things that have disappeared from store shelves. If you have woodworking skills, this book will help you translate that talent into another medium, cast metal; about $5.

Early American Tools
A Museum of Early American Tools, by
    Eric Sloane
Funk & Wagnalls, 1964

A typically warm, conversational Sloane sketchbook devoted solely to tools, from timber framing to blacksmithing. The inexpensive Ballantine paperback may still be available. A nice guide for antique tool hunters who can't drive by a "Tools for Sale" sign.

Garden and Landscape Tools
Crockett's Tool Shed, by James
    Underwood Crockett
Little, Brown & Company

This is Mr. Crockett of "Crockett's Victory Garden," a nice, informative, and informal garden-type program shown on public television channels. The book is a catalog of Crockett's picks. With a 1979 copyright, the tool prices are no longer useful (although comparatively they will hold up). But the 250-page paperback is an excellent presentation of available equipment—big, clean photos, and a few paragraphs on each entry. While gardening tools dominate, the book includes all kinds of greenhouse fixtures and supplies, sharpening stones, gloves, ladders, and more.

Japanese Tools
The Care and Use of Japanese Tools, by
    Kip Mesirow and Ron Herman
Woodcraft Supply
313 Montvale Ave.
Woburn, MA 01888

About 1975 or so, Japanese tools started to appear in the catalogs of Woodcraft and several other firms. Tool users were taken by their simplicity and clean design—the promise of ideal form and function. This book (about $9, 100 pages) covers the different styles of tools and provides sequence illustrations of their use. Still, it is hard to discover the problems until you use the tools first hand: most of the planes are blocks of wood with simple cutter blades, which makes it difficult (for me anyway, and I've used them for many years off and on) to get strong, even power behind the shaving stroke. Another point; the saws cut backward (backward for Westerners) on the return stroke. I've never been able to get used to it. Generally the plane and chisel steel is of exceptional quality. An interesting introduction to the subject.

Jigs and Shopwork
Jigs & Fixtures for Limited Production,
    by Harold Sedlik
Society of Manufacturing Engineers
PO Box 930, One SME Dr.
Dearborn, MI 48128

Jigs are devices used in the shop (in this case a metal shop) to help make fabrication uniform, for example, when you need to make four special hinges, connectors for dimensional timber used in domes, or multiples of almost any part where uniformity is important. One approach is to limit yourself and your designs to items that can be fabricated with stock parts. The other approach is to use a book like this to help with your own jigs, which can be used with a drill press or lathe, for instance, to turn out identical parts. Jigs can be time consuming to set up and require some ingenuity. And that's the strength of this book—converting all kinds of common shop items and parts to jigs and showing you how to use them. About $14.

Machining

The Home Shop Machinist
PO Box 1810
Traverse City, MI 49684
(616) 941-7160

This magazine is a consumer publication directed to amateur machinists who operate a home shop for fun and also to small commercial machine shop operators. Hobby projects presented in some detail run regularly along with do-it-yourself add-on projects for lathes, mills, drill presses, etc. Regular columns appear on welding, sheet metal, shop safety, shop math, and "shop of the month."

Business operation The small editorial staff cannot respond to all letters and inquiries, although they will research questions that apply to their general readership. Rates for the bimonthly are $17.50 for 1983 in the United States and $20 in Canada. Subscription requests on credit card numbers may be phoned in toll-free: (800) 824-7888. Generally it is wise policy to get a

back issue to make sure the content is interesting and worthwhile and not too complicated or too simple for your level of interest.

Power Tools

The Homeowner's Handbook of Power Tools, by Len Buckwalter
Funk & Wagnalls

Homeowner's is the key word here. A very basic book that tells what's available, what it does, and not a whole lot about how to use it. For fine points of tool use and shop practice look elsewhere, but a good starter for new homeowners and other beginners.

Power Tool Use

De Cristoforo's Complete Book of Power Tools, by R. J. De Cristoforo
Harper & Row

A complete book covering almost 450 pages, plus hundreds of illustrations (about $19). De Cristoforo is an experienced shop man, has written extensively for most of the how-to magazines and keeps the information in layman's language. Think of it as a service manual for the skills needed along with the tools, including information on all kinds of jigs and other time-savers, how to make most of your own moulding (with a variety of tools, not just an expensive shaper), and 1001 things that can be done with a radial arm saw. De Cristoforo's other book, *Housebuilding Illustrated*, is a pale comparison to this one, with weak, single-line artwork puffed up to fill space needlessly. Shops and shop projects are his real strength. A worthwhile book you may keep in the shop for years.

Practical Tool Information

CoEvolution Quarterly and *Whole Earth Catalog*
Box 428
Sausalito, CA 94966

It is difficult to describe this combined source (CoEvolution is a kind of staging ground for much of the information that winds up the Whole Earth Catalog) in just one word, *practical*, or in hundreds, because it covers so much ground. The *Whole Earth Catalog* is probably the best starting point if you are beginning to be interested in some of the fields I'll get to in a minute and want to see some of the things this source book shows you, such as what are some of the companies in the field and kinds of magazines and books are available on the subject. Leaving a lot out, some of the fields covered are: alternative construction, solar, wind, and water power; construction equipment; tools for building and repairing; crafts of all descriptions; logging; self-sufficient living, and more, plus access to tools and information on waste systems, land management, musical instrument making, computers —a lot of ground. If you bought this book you'll probably like it (costs $16 now).

Sharpening

Home and Workshop Guide to Sharpening, by Harry Walton
Popular Science Books, Harper & Row

One of the Popular Science Skill Books, this one has some 160 pages devoted to a very specialized subject. Axes, spade point shovels, knives, chisels, and more are covered in detail, along with all the different sharpening stones, belts, and power equipment. The book is well illustrated but lacks sequence illustrations that would show the really practical details of how you move a chisel over a stone to get an edge and other "hands on" information.

Tool and Equipment Repair Manuals

Technical Publications Division
Intertec Publishing Corporation
PO Box 12901
Overland Park, KS 66212

Have you ever given up on a chain saw or a lawn mower or another piece of equipment because it was past its prime and you couldn't figure out how to fix it yourself? Many repair shops will simply tell you to buy a new one if you bring them something out of the ordinary. This source offers a free catalog of publications, which includes service and repair manuals for all kinds of equipment: chain saws, tractors, mowers of all types and sizes, outboard motors, and more. Prices vary, generally $5 to $10 for manuals that are profusely illustrated and may run as long as 300 pages. This won't always work, but in many cases a little accurate information enables you to add a few years on to the life of a piece of machinery others advise you to bury.

Tool Making

The Making of Tools, by Alexander G. Weygers
Van Nostrand Reinhold Company

One of the momentous steps in evolution is the point at which man (and some animals) began to use tools to make things and do things—even if it was a rock to crack open a shell. So it is with do-it-yourselfers who use tools—a giant leap to using tools to make tools. But this well-illustrated book does a reasonable job, with careful, realistic illustrations and reasonable explanations. Yet much is assumed. Tool making is an art. I recall making a set of kitchen knives from unsharpened blanks, adding teak handles with brass rivets. They came out okay, but that's about all. Be prepared to work at this craft, to get mediocre results for a while, even with the aid of this book. (A good buy at about $7.)

Welding
Electric and Gas Welding, by E. F.
     Lindsley
Popular Science, Harper & Row

This is a fine little book on welding, brazing, and soldering with carbon-arc, oxyacetylene, and MAPP gas equipment. All the tools and materials are well illustrated, and the book is thankfully short on projects. You can think of your own, right? Though there are chapters on TIG welding and even the delicate process of working aluminum with oxyacetylene, practice is the final answer. A good basic book for those who want to learn and want to do more than solder a few copper pipes once in a while.

Woodworking
Complete Book of Woodworking,
     by Rosario Capotosto
Popular Science, Harper & Row

A thorough look at wood, hand and power tools, tool techniques, all kinds of cabinet making techniques, covering some 400 pages with first-rate photographs—clear and full of people and hands doing things, generally in sequence, so you get a sense of how the process works. Also, Capotosto is excellent on jigs, multiple setups, and many other shop practices that come only with a lot of time on the job. The text is almost secondary, pretty cut and dried. But with fourteen-picture sequences of a simple process like making bent frames with laminations, this book is unbeatable.

HOMEBUILDING

PRIVATE FIRMS

Factory Built

Greenhouses
Lord & Burnham
Box 255
Irvington, NY 10533
(914) 591-8800

Still probably the Rolls-Royce of greenhouses, Lord & Burnham has small and large, plain and simple greenhouses to offer. Its catalog reveals an array of options and accessories: automatic venting and shading, automatic watering systems, heaters, vents, blowers—the works. It's a knockout.

Business operation The latest catalog should be available from the headquarters address above or from one of the four other regional sales offices (including one in St. Catharines, Ontario). Also request the catalog *Greenhouse, Equipment, & Accessories*. Relatively expensive products at, or at least near, the top of the line.

Manufactured Homes
Champion Home Builders Company
5573 North St.
Dryden, MI 48428
(313) 796-2211

Champion builds mobile/manufactured homes. That's the transition phrase in use now, bridging the not-so-pleasant connotations of *mobile*, and the more modern, if not a bit antiseptic, overtones of *manufactured*. Anyway, Champion is *the* company in this growing field. It got there early (1953) and produced close to 20,000 homes last year in twenty-two plants across the country and

sold them through a network of some 1500 retailers. It's a big company (you hear its name on the stock reports on a regular basis), and it is also big on consumer information. For instance, if you have trouble locating a dealer in your area, you can write the headquarters for a complete listing; also request brochures that show floor plans and elevations and the booklet that uses illustrations to lay out step by step how the homes are constructed, *From Foundation to Furnishings*. It covers some of the standard features: gypsum walls and ceilings, code compliance (or exceeding codes) for insulation and fire safety, 2-in $\times$ 4-in wood studwalls, 2-in $\times$ 6-in floor joists over steel frame, copper branch wiring, and more.

Manufactured Post and Beam
Deck House, Inc.
930 Main St.
Acton, MA 01720
(617) 259-9450
(800) 225-5755 (Toll-free for consumer information)

Deck House houses are not what would normally spring into your mind when you think of manufactured housing. That phrase has come to imply cheap, mass produced construction where shop labor bears no direct responsibility for field installation—for ironing out all the inevitable rough spots and structural monkey wrenches—which, I think, is the main drawback of this economical system. Anyway, Deck House homes are elegant. The basic structural system is post and beam, using laminated 4 $\times$ 12's and better, heavy-duty beam hangers, wood t & g decking—the nice, simple but elegant post and beam system. However, these folks

161

include things like cedar decking, solid mahogany trim throughout, insulated glass that incorporates the most innovative improvement in this field, called Heat Mirror, a transparent, heat reflective shield mounted inside the dead air chamber of double glazed units. Plus, many of their fifty-seven standard designs (all of which may be customized) include integral passive solar features, not slapped on "energy savers." In business since 1960, this firm turns out quality houses.

Business operation Deck House sells total house envelopes. You provide the land and the builder. Sizes range from 1500 to over 4000 sq ft. Costs range from about $31 to $41 per square foot. You can write the main office (or call toll-free) or one of their eleven sales offices across the country. Its catalog of plans is $12, free at its model homes.

Manufactured Traditional/ Colonial
Scholz Homes
3103 Executive Pkwy.
Toledo, OH 43606
(419) 531-1601

Scholz makes what are called *panelized homes*. Components are made in the shop, then shipped to the site to be put together. Part of the idea is to offer the appeal of a custom home by having hundreds of designs ready for assembly while still maintaining the cost efficiency possible when homes are shop built. The style here is best described as traditional, which includes Colonial, Tudor, Georgian, or what home buyers have come to expect when they hear these names. They are wealthy suburb type homes. Scholz shop-built components are made of kiln-dried stock, windows are double insulated, and exterior doors are metal clad and foam filled.

Business operation These homes are sold and built nationwide. Write for construction details and fully illustrated plan books.

Panelized Homes
Homecraft Corporation
PO Box 359
South Hill, VA 23970
(804) 447-3186

Homecraft sells panelized homes. Pieces of the predesigned homes are made up in its shops and transported to the site for assembly. It offers over 300 models, presented in a plan book (available for $4) showing small views and floor plans including single-family, vacation homes, duplexes, townhouses, condominiums, and some light commercial structures. It distributes these homes on the East Coast from Florida to Massachusetts and assists builders in finding clients. Of course, you can do this the other way around: write Homecraft and get your own builder.

Business operation Homecraft will send you a free brochure and is prepared to answer your questions by phone or letter. Styles are generally traditional and include what I call *development houses*—better known as ranches, high ranches, etc. I don't use that phrase because the word *ranch* still makes me think of horses. Anyway—one small point in the brochure bothered me, although I have a feeling it was only a semantic mistake on Homecraft's part: ". . . designs with a quality control that cuts every piece of lumber to $\frac{1}{16}$-in tolerance." Of course, if every piece of lumber in a house was $\frac{1}{16}$-in off, they would have to be off in a complementary way (one short and one long) or all off the same way, to make the house anything but lopsided and loose as a goose.

Pedestal Base Homes
Topsider Homes
PO Box 849
Yadkinville, NC 27055
(919) 679-8846

Topsider makes very unique, pedestal base, largely prefabricated homes. Their Model 101 is a complete two bedroom, two full bathroom house, with about 900 sq ft. One hundred feet is in the pedestal base that serves as a utility and storage area. Looking a little like a saucer from outer space (with shake siding) this tree house is shipped with a complete kitchen, including cabinets, double-basin stainless steel sink and eating bar, plus double glazed, safety glass windows, two fiber glass modular bathrooms that are preplumbed and prewired. Topsider's Model 102 has an additional 100 sq ft in the pedestal to serve as an entry, with a spiral stair up to the main level.

Business operation The company's literature is very specific. It lists exactly what you do and do not get, which is refreshing, as some companies really bury this information. Also they tell you what the owner-builder is responsible for in detail. Illustrations and floor plans are included.

Pricing Wholesale prices range from about $26,000 for the standard equipped Model 101 to about $28,000 for Model 102. A completely unique design.

Precut Homes
Curtis Homes
Department 5 B
2201 Florida Ave.
South Minneapolis, MN 55426
(612) 542-4300

Curtis has taken the idea of panelized or component homes a step further. It calls its homes "precut, complete-it-yourself, affordable construction," and supplies the materials and instructions to do the job yourself. As you might imagine, homebuilding is not a trade that you can pick up either quickly or by reading a 45-page book of instructions. As a matter of fact, homebuilding is a trade that very few people know. There are good carpenters, electricians, plumbers, and masons, but good general contractors who know how all the pieces fit together rarely know how to do all the jobs that specialty subcontractors can do. In any case, if you have some experience (you'll have to decide how much is necessary after looking at Curtis's plans and instructions) this is a way to save a lot of money. Curtis also provides financing.

Business operation This is one of the few companies selling precut homes with financing, and some are extremely modest and inexpensive. It's worth investigating, remembering that on many do-it-yourself projects, big or small, the first time around you tend to make the mistakes and learn from the experience so that the second time around you do a pretty decent job. The company is responsive to calls and letters requesting information.

Prefab Greenhouses
Sun System Prefabricated Solar
   Greenhouses
60 Vanderbilt Motor Pkwy.
Commack, NY 11725
(516) 543-7766

You want more room. You have some building experience but don't want to get into endless details of planning and design and construction. Maybe you can afford to expand a little but not if you have to buy a larger capacity furnace. In these situations and many others, a reasonable alternative is to prepare the footing and slab yourself (or have a contractor do it), and enclose the space with a greenhouse kit. Sun System greenhouses are available in a wide variety of shapes and sizes, all double glazed, with the flexibility of extra doors, windows, automatic venting systems, and other options. The aluminum frame is what the company calls "100 percent thermally broken," i.e., at no point does the aluminum exposed to cold winter air outside come in contact with the aluminum on the inside. On many inferior replacement windows, even those that are double glazed, the lack of such a thermal barrier causes sweating on the metal frames.

Business operation   Sun System will send you a complete, well-illustrated catalog on request, which includes all possible shapes and dimensions and provides a toll-free line for any further questions: 1 (800) 645-4506.

Kits

Basic Shelter
Shelter-Kit, Inc.
22 Mill St.
PO Box 1
Tilton, NH 03176
(603) 934-4327

Shelter-Kit produces two types of products. Its Unit One is a simple, slope-roof box with a double glass door front. In combination with 9-ft × 12-ft porch platforms, roofed or unroofed, these modules can be joined to form many layouts. The kits are inexpensive (about $3800 with deck) and extremely easy to assemble. The company now offers a similar idea in a different form, called Lofthouses, which have steeply peaked roofs. These designs are already a significant step away from the Unit One toward more conventional building and design. Unit One can be assembled in about three or four days by two people with *no* building skills. The kit contains all materials, all precut and predrilled. And the materials are bundled together in 100-lb packages so you can carry your house to your site if need be. No power tools are needed for building with this post and beam framing system.

Business operation   This is an excellent solution to problems with remote sites, or a piece of land that you can't afford to put a building on (at least not a conventional building), but there is a hang-up. Roy Newsome of Shelter-Kit writes that catalogs will be sent only when a $6 fee is sent with the request, and frankly, that's steep and very surprising considering the kind of thought and viewpoint embodied in the Unit One. The modest Unit One catalog presentation is informative, shows sample layouts, some drawings, and a few photographs—but no blueprints and no assembly manual. Everything about Unit One is worth investigating, everything except the hatchet job up front. Too bad.

Cedar Homes
Justus Homes
PO Box 98300
Tacoma, WA 98499
(206) 582-3404

Justus manufactures solid Western Red Cedar homes, precut to one of 300 suggested designs or to your specifications. Wall timbers in these homes are solid, 4-in × 8-in cedar with double tongue and groove joints. Corners are dovetailed. Doors and windows are framed, trimmed, and pre-hung.

Business operation Justus offers complete design services, and an elegant, 68-page color portfolio for $4. Home packages include all structural components and roofing, routed stair assemblies, closet shelves, hardware, mouldings, etc. The company reports that many units are sold to owner-builders who do the job themselves. Local dealers are prepared to give advice and guidance with these jobs, or recommend a contractor in your area. Justus homes are shipped nationwide.

Dome Hardware/Kits

Timberline Geodesics
2015 Blake St.
Berkeley, CA 94704
(415) 849-4481

Timberline manufactures complete dome kits (from 8- to 45-ft diameters), connector systems only, and plans, plus some individual components such as skylights that are suited for geodesic panel roofing. Unless you live nearby, it really does not make sense to buy any lumber. Timberline's connectors (and those of most companies in the field) can be used with dimensional timbers straight from the lumberyard, i.e., you don't have to do any complicated angle cutting.

Business operation Timberline provides a comprehensive catalog on request and also sells plans for cutting lumber efficiently (in this case, plywood, which is produced in rectangular sheets that work against geodesic layouts). The firm has a limited number of

distributors, clustered in the Southwest and West.

Domes

Monterey Domes
1760 Chicago Ave.
Box 5621–AA
Riverside, CA 92517
(714) 684-2601 (California residents call collect)
1 (800) 854-9977 (Toll-free except California)

Monterey makes geodesic dome kits that are, as Robert Gunther, the principal at Monterey, writes, "designed for the first time builder with no previous building experience. These [kits] are completely pre-cut, predrilled, color-coded, ready to assemble using only a hamer and two wrenches (included with the kit). The heaviest piece is 35 lb." The kits are available in sizes from under 1000 to over 4000 sq ft. The heart of the system is a patented, five-point, color-coded, welded steel, star connector. Depending on the dome size, 2 × 4 or 2 × 6 framing is used in the triangular frames that are joined to make the geodesic dome shell. All lumber, fasteners, plywood, star hubs are included in the kit. Lumber is kiln-dried Douglas fir. In addition, Monterey offers many options, such as framed skylight kits, a foam-filled plastic, simulated wood shake roofing system, insulating panels, extensions, dormers, and more. You have to provide the site, utilities and foundation.

Business operation Monterey will send you a modest amount of literature free, including the name and address of its major branch nearest you. For $8 they send a series of catalogs with over 100 pages of photographs, plans, and details. Its *Basic Construction Handbook*, the thing you have to rely on, is very well organized, and even includes pages of drywall cutting patterns to minimize waste.

Pricing Ranges from about $4000 to almost $14,000.

Double-Wall Greenhouses

Vegetable Factory, Solar Structures
   Division
100 Court St.
Copiague, NY 11726
(516) 842-9300

All Vegetable Factory greenhouses have two shatterproof glazing panels sandwiching a ½-in dead air space, supported in a bronze finish aluminum framework. The panels of acrylic fiber glass are separated from aluminum uprights by a PVC foam strip to make a thermal break. This helps the structure retain heat and resist sweating, which is not likely to form on the window areas because the double glazing gives them a U value of .55—220 percent more effective insulation than single thickness glass. Several styles offered include standard height and high-rise, 45-degree slant, and bay window models.

Business operation The company's detailed and informative brochure is sent for $2; it covers all models feature by feature, energy-saving data, plus a full line of accessories.

Gazebo Blueprints

A.S.L. Associates—Architects
PO Box 6296
San Mateo, CA 94403
(415) 344-5044

Anthony S. Lalli offers a single product via mail order: a set of blueprints for a charming, six-sided, 8-ft diameter gazebo. Plans call for a raised deck, lattice work railings, and a cedar shake roof. The plans themselves are full-size blueprints with a perspective view, full plan and elevations, plus another page of construction details. They are clear, highly detailed (even to nailing specs), and presented in a way that will actually help you build the design. I know that sounds elementary, but many blueprints come through half fuzzed over with fine print specs that only experienced blueprint readers can make out. A complete materials list is included.

Business operation The three 17-in $\times$ 22-in drawings plus materials list is sent for $10. Nice work.

Log Homes

Alta Industries, Ltd.
PO Box 88
Halcottsville, NY 12438
(914) 586-3336

Alta manufactures thirty standard models of log homes. Its specialized construction system (locking systems and corner construction and the like are what separate one manufacturer from another, in most cases) consists of solid white pine logs with Lincoln Log-type locking corners, horizontal locking grooves at the top and bottom edges, and splined joints at butt seams. Twelve-inch spikes are used for assembly.

Business operation Alta will sell you materials, complete packages, or latchkey service(it hands you keys to the front door when all work is done). Write for a brief color brochure showing its locking system and a few of its floor plans. For $5 it will send you a catalog of its thirty standard models with perspective views and floor plans. Alta currently has dealers in Maine, Maryland, New Hampshire, New York, New Jersey, and most eastern seaboard states up to Ohio and Illinois. It'll send you a list. Alta is a member of the Log Homes Council/NAHB.

Green Mountain Log Homes
Box 190
Chester, VT 05143
(802) 875-2163

Green Mountain's twist on packaged, machined log homes is a single spline grooved into a series of arrow shapes for positive locking between logs. However, what really distinguishes Green Mountain is the pains it takes to help you design your own log home. One of its booklets displays several of its stock plans but is straightforward enough to say, "We know these designs are not for everyone. People who want log homes are individuals with their own ideas." To this end Green Mountain provides an elaborate design kit (for $4.50), complete with graph paper, furniture patterns to scale, and instructions on how to select only the parts you need from its catalog. It reads, "Finally, we show you how to price each item from our price list. You can then compare our prices with other suppliers. As an example, people frequently purchase their roofs locally." Hats off for some sensible, practical copywriting.

Business operation Green Mountain will send a comprehensive little booklet on request. It ships nationally, which, being very straight, it again qualifies saying it has shipped as far as Florida, Nebraska, and northern Wisconsin. The company president, Alan Wilder, is also president of the Log Homes Council.

Green River Trading Company
Boston Corners Rd.
Millerton, NY 12546
(518) 789-3311

Green River manufactures basic log home packages (all delivered in a single truck load) with complete blueprints and materials. Blueprints for the home designs in its free brochure are available for $65 per set, and its complete catalog can be had for $5. For doubters, Green River can also provide a brief of tests done on log homes versus conventional structures, comparing energy efficiency. The test rated a conventional FHA stud wall at 1151 BTU/hour, and a horizontal, 5½-in thick log wall at 852 BTU/hour thermal transmission. Green River offers a choice between hand-peeled or rough-sawn timbers, supervision and technical assistance, and custom plans. Its modest plans range from approximately $7645 (748 sq ft) to $11,300 (1244 sq ft saltbox).

Business operation The blueprint purchase price is applied to kit purchase. The kits include all structural elements but not windows, doors, etc., which must be bought locally.

Hearthstone Builders, Inc.
Rte. 2, Box 434
Dandridge, TN 37725
(615) 397-7523

Hearthstone makes hand-hewn, dovetail-notched log homes. That means the inside and outside walls are relatively flat, and the strong horizontal lines of logs and chinking do, to me at least, have a Kentucky–Tennessee kind of flavor, even though this type of log construction has many Germanic and Scandinavian antecedents. Randy Giles of Hearthstone writes, "We build them like they really were—not some assembly line precision milled stack of poles that most companies offer." I love it; the way he won't even call them logs when they are machined. And he does have a solid point. Many packaged log homes have wonderful construction details, insulating systems, and more, but because of the log uniformity they lose the quietly stunning effect of random logs brought together in a structure. The Hearthstone catalog has several pictures of old log homes, like the Belle Meade plantation in Nashville, which is about 200 years old (and the original logs are still structurally sound, by the way) and several pictures of Hearthstone's buildings, and there is not a whole lot of difference in appearance. A few specifics: beams are 4-in $\times$ 8-in; wall logs are 6-in $\times$ 12-in; between logs a 3½-in polyurethane box panel (foil-backed) is covered inside and out with hardboard splines notched slightly into the log on top and set slightly into a water table cut into the log on the bottom, then covered with a textured masonry chinking. The hardboard spline left uncoated is equally appealing.

Business operation   Hearthstone will ship anywhere in the United States. Prices range from $3000 to about $14,000; many designs, or your own. Free brochures on request; excellent, informative catalog is $6.

Lincoln Logs, Ltd.
Gristmill Rd.
Chestertown, NY 12817
(518) 494-2426
1 (800) 833-2461 (Toll-free outside
    New York)

The components of Lincoln Log homes are not like the wonderful toys of the same name—the dark-stained dowels with half notches at each end. These logs are debarked and milled with flat interior surfaces, uniformly rounded exterior surfaces, and flat bearing surfaces milled with a double tongue and groove system. Lincoln Log makes twenty-two do-it-yourself packages and will provide custom packages. Customizing is easier for Lincoln than for most firms because Lincoln Log does not precut its logs to length. Some firms make a point of numbering components so there is nothing left to the imagination. Lincoln Log makes a point of not doing this. Packages include Adirondack white pine logs, roofing, win-

dows and doors, nails, caulking, insulating strips, and spikes—all components of a weather-tight shell, plus blueprints. In an industry that Lincoln predicts will do about a million and a half dollars in sales next year, there seems to be room for many variations on this basic building system. The only obvious drawback to its machined method is overlapping corners with double tongues and grooves hanging out there in mid air.

Business operation   Lincoln Log sells through sixty distributors in twenty-five states. Representatives are able to provide on-site instruction. A complete portfolio is sent for $4.

Pricing   Basic packages range from about $9000 to over $30,000.

New England Log House
2301 State St.
PO Box 5056
Hamden, CT 06518
(203) 562-9981

Some forty different designs are offered by New England Log Homes in complete and closed in, frame only packages, in three different types of logs. Its hand-peeled log is full width (7- to 11-in diameter) with bearing surfaces cut to leave a tongue and groove locking system. Its Panellog is machine trimmed on all four sides. Its Duolog is trimmed on three sides, leaving a flat, clean interior but a rounded, hand-peeled exterior. All pine logs are premilled and precut and sealed with an open-cell elastomeric foam sealant during construction. Complete log packages include the following: all precut logs, posts, girders, and structural members (all log material is dip-treated in what the firm says is an "EPA-approved preservative" (I assume that means it has an EPA Registration Number), plus hardboard end splines, doors, windows, all casings, wood combination storm doors with screens, second floor decking, and a complete roof—the works. Its basic package includes all structural materials, and a roofing and insulation system that is not as elaborate or as energy efficient as the one supplied with the complete package.

Business operation   Full details are available in the company's product manual. Complete blueprints for individual models are sold separately for $25, as is the step by step construction guide for each model.

Pricing   Total packages range from about $8000 up to expansive log homes at about $55,000.

Southland Log Homes, Inc.
Rte. 2, Box 5-B
Irmo, SC 29063
(803) 781-5100

Southland logs are planed top and bottom only and sealed with rubberized gasket strips and acrylic sealant. Its log home package includes all 8-in $\times$ 6-in logs, joists, ship lap log siding for gable ends, all windows and doors, caulk and sealant, log penetrating sealer—a complete shell. Its catalog includes a planning kit.

Business operation   Southland ships mainly on the East Coast.

Pricing   Costs range from about $10,000 to over $40,000.

Timber Log Homes
Auston Dr.
Marlborough, CT 06447
(203) 295-9529

Timber Log makes an unusual presentation of its product because in addition to the full specs and design portfolios that you expect to see, it includes Scott Publications' consumer's manual for buying a log home and also a copy of its construction manual so you can see what you're getting into. Its homes are made of precut, uniform logs that are notched and numbered to correspond to detailed blueprints—something like painting by the numbers—so it is difficult to make a mistake. The northern white pine kits include all structural timbers, splines, spikes, Geocel sealant, and joist hangers and are available in several styles, including capes, ranches, and lodges from a 500 sq ft cabin to a 2300 sq ft, four bedroom Colonial model. Timber Log also manufactures custom designs and has cut log structures that are used for such things as school dormitories and airplane hangars. The logs are all 8 in wide and 6 in high, machine flat top and bottom with grooves for splines.

Business operation   Write Timber Log for a product information kit.

Pricing   Kit prices range from about $8000 to $25,000, which does not include windows, doors, and some lumber that must be purchased locally.

Ward Cabin Company
PO Box 72
Houlton, ME 04730
(207) 532-6531

Ward has been making log cabins for over fifty years. There are several unique characteristics about its procedures. First is the material used—solid, northern white cedar, a dense, durable wood. Second is the way the logs are made up. Many new companies in this growing field have devised ingenious systems employing special interlocking beams, ways to incorporate insulating panels, and other improvements. Trouble is, the more improved everything gets the less it gets like a log home. Ward does do some machining on its cedar logs, but only some. Specifically, they leave the exterior face of the log rounded and intact. On the bearing edges they machine a flat with tongue and groove and also cut the interior face flat. This last step seems unnecessary to me, but at least you wind up with something that still looks and acts like what it is—and not dressed timbers shaped a little like a log. There are other details, and Ward will send you brochures outlining the full construction process, the help you can get during construction, and more. That information is free. If you would like to look through its extensive plan book that covers many different models, send $6.

Pricing Costs in solid cedar with standard equipment like Andersen Perma-Shield windows, Morgan solid core doors inside and out, and Schlage heavy-duty locksets (all top of the line materials) range from about $17,000 to $40,000.

Wilderness Log Homes
RR 2
Plymouth, WI 53073
(414) 893-9416
(800) 558-5881 (Toll-free)

Wilderness makes precut log homes. It has over fifty different stock designs in northern white cedar or pine and offers custom design service and a special, energy-efficient type of construction called Insul-Log. Here are some of the Insul-Log kit specs: wall R value of 30.7 (impressive); three sets of construction blueprints; solid, 9 lite, 1¾-in exterior doors; double glazing throughout; No. 260, Class A, fiber glass roof shingles; all nails, spikes, and hardware; ridge and soffit vents, and more. Its logs are hand peeled, air dried for up to a year, and milled flat for wide bearing surfaces on walls, with V-cut corner mortises all precut.

Business operation Wilderness sells through over 100 dealers nationwide. You can use its toll-free number for requests of information and brochures. Its plan book, showing the different models in some detail, costs $6. Lou Bule from Wilderness writes, "Log homes are energy efficient. They can be heated with one wood stove, are aestheti-cally pleasing and they appeal to do-it-yourselfers who want the adventure of building their own home."

Pricing Ranges from about $8000 for a basic, one-large-room type of cabin, to about $42,000 (both Insul-Log). Full, 10-in diameter pine log kits in the same home sizes as above are about $9000 (for the one-roomer), and $58,000 for its nearly 1500 sq-ft "Williamsburg" model.

Passive Solar Homes

Green Mountain Homes
Royalton, VT 05068
(802) 763-8384

Green Mountain makes twenty-five models of passive solar design homes. All are factory panelized construction that use design principles rather than mechanical equipment to save energy and incorporate features such as air entrance locks and superinsulated walls and ceilings into classic New England barn shapes. Its model home, which is used as a test house, was monitored by Dartmouth's Thayer School of Engineering personnel, who came to these conclusions: heating costs in the 1300-sq-ft home were $248.68 for the winter of 1976–1977 and $211.91 for the winter of 1977–1978 which included fossil fuel and the small amount of electricity needed to run the system.

Business operation Green Mountain sells nationally direct to buyers. Its design brochure costs $5, and each design shown is delivered with a photo illustrated construction manual. Also, the company provides personalized design service to insure proper solar orientation on site. Information on the company's solar greenhouse, designed for its own buildings and as add-ons for other existing homes, is sent on request.

Pricing Estimated total costs excluding land, septic, water supply, and other site improvements, range from about $18,000 to about $70,000. The firm estimates that an owner-built kit will be 40 percent of the kit plus contractor costs.

Post and Beam Outbuildings/ Lumber
Native Wood Products, Inc.
Drawer Box 469
Brooklyn, CT 06234
(203) 774-7700

Native Wood designs and manufactures post and beam outbuildings, including storage sheds, garages, and large barns. It sells blueprints of these buildings and complete lumber packages, and it can provide custom buildings to your specs. Also, it carries a line of hand-forged building hardware and finished pine lumber, including planking in many sizes that is kiln dried, planed, and milled to tongue and groove, shiplap, bead edge, and beaded clapboard patterns.

Business operation A modest package of illustrations and building layouts, with prices, is sent on request at no charge. (An SASE is appreciated.) Currently, the company sells along the eastern seaboard only. You should be able to get a look at its buildings in *Yankee, Country Journal*, and *Colonial Homes*, in which it regularly advertises.

Post and Beam Packages
Solar Northern
Box 64
Mansfield, PA 16933
(717) 549-6232

Solar Northern post and beam packages include the frame only, or frame with insulating panels, windows, doors, roofing, siding, and trim. Ten basic plans are offered. All are built of rough-sawn Pennsylvania white pine with hand-cut, mortise and tenon and lap joints that are pinned with wood pegs. Composite insulating panels include ½-in interior wallboards, 3¼-in of urethane or polyisocyanurate foam, and $7/16$-in exterior sheathing that give a total R value of 27.0.

Business operation The company rarely handles construction, but the principal, Stephen Keller, reports, "We provide what we call a hand holding service of helping our customers through the designing and building process." Write or call for a portfolio of floor plans and elevation views with price list.

Pricing A 756 sq ft modified A-frame with contemporary glazing is about $16,000 complete. A 1752 sq ft gambrel design is roughly twice as much. Frame only prices are quoted on request. Shipping is additional.

Precut Cedar Homes
Lindal Cedar Homes
4300 S. 104th Pl.
Seattle, WA 98178
(206) 725-0900

Lindal sells precut cedar homes in some sixty standard plans, although several of the plans are inventive, and distinctive in the best sense of the word. Basically, since cedar is a relatively expensive building material, these are homes for severe climates, particularly tropical or extremely wet sites. The construction is post and beam using twin, 2-in × 10-in floor joists at 5-ft 4-in centers, on which a 24-in center, 2-in × 6-in floor joist system is laid. Verticals are 4-in × 4-in posts, in some cases much larger. Exterior walls are precut, a full 2 in, double tongue and groove cedar planking applied over ½-in plywood sheathing and felt paper. Lindal designs net a standard R value for walls of 21.14 (with a vapor barrier), and Lindal offers an optional "polar" wall system with an R value of 29.14. All windows are double glazed. Roofing is No. 1 hand-split and resawn 24-in cedar shakes over a roof with standard 2-in × 12-in rafters and insulation for a R value of 33.3. Options go up to roofing with an R value of 63.3. None of this tells you that while many of the more conventional designs (homes with names like Executive Series) seem to be a contradiction of design and materials, several are knockouts, and they are concentrated in one of Lindal's exceptionally well-photographed and presented catalogs called *Hawaii Planbook*. It costs $1.50 and includes precuts from about $13,000 to $20,000. Exceptional.

Business operation Write Lindal for complete prices and literature. Its full plan book is $4.

Precut Laminate Timber
Pre-Cut International Homes
PO Box 97
Woodinville, WA 98072
(206) 668-8511

This firm manufactures completely precut shells, most of which are relatively modern in design due to the large amount of glass and the appearance of the exterior walls, which look like standard 2-in × 6-in, t & g decking. Pre-Cut's wall system is like a log wall system; the material stands on its own. But instead of solid logs they use five different kinds of laminated timbers: a 2¼-in × 7-in tropical cedar made of three pieces with the center board offset to create a tongue and groove with the other two; the same shape in pine; a double tongue and groove assembly measuring 3⁹⁄₁₆-in × 7-in; a single tongue and groove with the same oversize

dimensions; and a 4⅜-in × 7-in lamination with a foam core for added insulating value.

Business operation Pre-Cut offers well-illustrated product brochures of its house plans, which range from a very basic one-roomer to elaborate homes close to 3000 sq ft. Also, you can write for its detailed technical report (SE 1613), prepared by the Pittsburgh Testing Laboratory, which covers compressive load tests, wind tests, racking load tests, and more. If you're really serious, ask for its construction guide, which details all the steps, tools, and skills required for assembly.

Pricing Pre-Cut's smallest model (272 sq ft) is about $7500 in pine, $10,500 in cedar foam core. Its largest model (2718 sq ft) is about $63,000 in pine, $80,000 in foam core.

Solar Design
Soltice Designs
Box 2043
Evergreen, CO 80439
(303) 674-1597

Soltice provides custom design services for residential and commercial applications (using AIA standard contract and agreement documents, a nice sign in this sometimes fly-by-night field where the word *expert* is often used prematurely), also long- and short-term consulting, site analysis to help owners and builders determine what kind of solar systems or designs, if any, will work for them, and performance evaluation, i.e., monitoring thermal and economic performance of solar systems. In addition, Soltice offers several do-it-yourself plans for attached greenhouses, domestic hot water systems, solar forced-air heating systems, all for a very reasonable amount (about $20 each on average). For serious folks, Soltice has complete solar house plans, information on small-scale ethanol fuel plants, and other appropriate technology goodies.

Business operation A comprehensive brochure is available on request, covers the plans in detail with illustrations, and lists a series of slide packages on subjects such as the construction and operation of solar food dryers, an economic analysis of five basic types of solar greenhouses, and more. Soltice has interesting, thorough material. Worth a look.

Timber Frame Packages

Timberpeg
PO Box 1500
Claremont, NH 03743
(603) 542-7762

Timberpeg designs and manufactures precut timber frames, including all materials required for a complete weather-tight shell. Main framing members are massive 8-in $\times$ 12-in's, 6-in $\times$ 8-in's, and 6-in $\times$ 6in's. Collar ties and angle braces are 6-in $\times$ 6-in and 4-in $\times$ 4-in, all assembled into a frame with mortise and tenon, wood pegged joints. The firm has several stock designs and is ready to make alterations so your ideas and needs can be incorporated in the plan.

Business operation Timberpeg frames and complete shells are sold by local representatives who are prepared to help with planning, design, how to approach banks for a loan, and how to select the right builder if you do not wish to assemble the building yourself. The company's complete design catalog is sold for $10, a bit steep.

Pricing Timberpeg frames and shells run from $10,000 to $15,000 for its basic Cluster Shed designs to $35,000 and up to about $60,000 for larger models.

Timber Frame/Solar

Dovetail, Ltd.
PO Box 1496
Boulder, CO 80306
(303) 449-2681

Dovetail makes precut timber frame homes, available as frame only, frame with prefabricated insulating panels, and other packages. It also offers a solar home, architectural services, and blueprints all geared toward energy-efficient, modest, owner-built housing. Dovetail also offers workshops and seminars on energy-efficient design, a small selection of books written by the principal of the firm, Stewart Elliot. Its blueprints are expensive ($1500 for a set of six) but run 36 pages.

Business operation Dovetail will provide brochures on its Prence kit (an $8000 frame enclosing 1664 sq ft), its Solar Starr house, and information on its educational programs and books. The solar house frame costs $19,000 (1938 sq ft). An interesting company; worth your inquiry, although much of its literature is a little strong on selling and light on nuts and bolts.

Alternative Design

Barn Frames Restored

The Barn People
PO Box 4
South Woodstock, VT 05071
(802) 457-3214

These folks started taking down old barns for the siding and beams but now concentrate on the skeleton instead of the skin. First, they photograph and measure the structure, then sketch and mark all components before dismantling. At their mill, each beam is checked for soundness, and all defective or missing parts are replaced. The structure is test assembled, wire brushed, bundled, and shipped to your site. The Barn People off-load, assemble, and erect the frame. You are responsible for the site and foundation. A unique derivation of the post and beam firms providing new versions of old frames (frequently going to great pains to duplicate milling, joinery, and hand skills used by Colonial craftsmen), the Barn People have the real thing, which they describe, "with their well-seasoned and mellowed timbers, possessed a traditional beauty that could not be duplicated. They were one-of-a-kind and were built by hands working in an era when people took the time to do things right."

Business operation A brief, illustrated brochure is free; $10 nets a detailed portfolio of their barn inventory, including photographs and measured drawings.

Pricing Ranges from $4500 to about $15,000; includes photographs, blueprints, a scale model, full restoration, and assembly. Shipping costs vary, but the company estimates $2 to $4 per loaded mile from its mill in Windsor, Vermont.

Cedar Gazebos

Cedar Gazebos, Inc.
10432 Lyndale Ave.
Melrose Park, IL 60164
(312) 893-1200

Many of Cedar Gazebos' designs are simple enough to build on your own. But this firm does all the cutting and ships complete gazebos, hot tub and spa skirts (small decks), and lattice work in kit form ready to assemble. It makes eight different models, all in western red cedar and unfloored, that

should take about three hours to assemble.

Business operation The company has an illustrated brochure (for $1), that it will send if you cannot locate a dealer near you.

Pricing A 7½ ft hexagon is about $800; 12-ft decagons are about $1500.

Cinva-Ram Block Press Construction

Schrader Bellows, Division Scovill
200 W. Exchange St.
Akron, OH 44302
(216) 375-5202

The Cinva-Ram is a hand-operated press used for making many different kinds of building block and tile. It is a proven piece of appropriate technology, used particularly in developing countries but surprisingly little in the United States. The Ram is manufactured by a company in Bogota, Colombia (Metalibec S.A.), and handled by Schrader in this country. Schrader sells only 100 to 150 units a year. Kathy Easterling of Schrader was quite forthright about this and said that a stock of approximately 50 machines is kept on hand. The Ram is simply a small, boxlike container on which a lever is mounted that can be operated by hand (no power) to apply incredible pressure on various combinations of earth, earth and cement, etc. to produce semihollow block, channel block, floor tile, and more. The Ram comes with wooden inserts that act as dies to produce the different configurations. Net weight is 140 pounds; size, 3.5 cu ft. The trick to using the Ram is in selecting the right sail or soil combination to put into it. Generally, local soil can be tested (the Ram booklet contains instructions for basic, on-site tests), then screened and, depending on the use intended, combined with 5 or 10 percent cement, then moisturized and pressed. On average, Ram-built block costs about ¹⁄₂₀th of conventional masonry. Schrader will send information on request. The final block products are uniform, sound, and durable.

Earth-Sheltered Homes
Earth Shelter Corporation of America
Rte. 2, Box 97B
Berlin, WI 54923
(414) 361-2266

By itself and through a system of franchises, this firm has been designing and building earth-sheltered homes since 1976. The designs originate with its in house architecture and engineering staff and come with a 20-year limited warranty on waterproofing and many of the other advantages of this type of housing.

Business operation The company will send along a brochure on request, which is devoted largely to telling about the advantages of earth-sheltered design. Attached is a questionnaire offering more information for builders, buyers, developers, and those interested in a franchise. Its "design packet" of floor plans and renderings of some twelve designs is available for $12—a little stiff for a look-see.

Timber Construction/Framing Tools
Fox-Maple Post & Beam/Fox-Maple Tools
RR1, Box 583
Snowville Rd.
W. Brownfield, ME 04010
(207) 935-3720

Fox-Maples' post-and-beam-building part of the business produces what I know as timber-frame homes, all made to order with oak pegs holding mortise and tenon or dovetail joints (no nails are used). Fox-Maple will set up the structure, or build the house start to finish within the limits of travel time from West Brownfield. However, they ship owner-builder packages anywhere that include blueprints, materials for siding, roofing, insulation, flooring, and other supplies on request. Costs vary with each project. Fox-Maple Post & Beam(at the same address above as the tool company) will send illustrated material or several of their projects, including construction details, and a picture of their most popular frame, a classic, center-chimney saltbox with shed roof extension, complete with 9 over 6 lite windows and what looks like 3 or 4 in to the weather clapboards; an absolute knockout. Take a look.

Underground Housing
Terra-Dome Corporation
14 Oak Hill Cluster
Independence, MO 64050
(816) 229-6000

Terra-Dome is one of the relatively new companies in the field of underground housing. Its construction system consists of a continuous pour of reinforced concrete forming exterior and interior walls and the ceiling. The walls are vertical. The ceiling is dome shaped, roughly 4 ft higher in the center of the dome, making an arch in the 24-ft dome module. Twenty-eight and 40-ft modules are also available. The load bearing capacity of the roof is billed to hold 6 to 8 ft of earth. Working through a network of dealers who offer plans and construction services, Terra-Dome also has a road crew that will travel to your site. In addition, the company can provide information on a proprietary rubberized sealer, floor plans, and its seminars on underground housing.

Business operation You can write for illustrated brochures showing typical floor plans, how the modules may be combined, and a limited amount of structural specifications. Currently, it has dealers in sixteen states. It will send you a complete list with its product information.

TRADE ASSOCIATIONS

Homebuilding Information and Contractors

National Association of Home Builders (NAHB)
15th and M Sts. NW
Washington, DC 20005
(202) 452-0404

This is the major homebuilding trade association in the United States, encompassing some 130,000 members in 700 local groups, including home, condominium, and apartment builders. NAHB will provide referral services for member builders in your area, information about its Homeowner's Warranty Program)called HOW) for new construction, illustrated brochures on efficient modular building systems, energy-efficient construction, and more. Ask for its catalog covering the annual NAHB convention, which includes a survey of new products, manufacturers, contractors, government regulations, and other subjects. There may be a charge for this as it is extensive. Also, ask NAHB for its schedule of seminars and conferences held regionally on such special issues as land use, construction costs, mortgage credit, remodeling, and other topics. Most local NAHB groups can provide arbitration of serious disputes. Generally, there is a modest fee (about $25) for this service. Complaints against member builders also get attention from the Director of Consumer Affairs at the national headquarters.

Logbuilding

Canadian Log Builder's Association
PO Box 403
Prince George, BC
Canada V2L 4S2

Founded in 1974 at the Mackie School of Log Building, this association keeps members up to date with a newsletter six times a year. The newsletter also carries information and ads on log builders and log homes for sale. The association has also completed the first written performance standards for the industry. Copies are available at the above address for $2. Membership is $10 per year. The annual three-day meeting is open to all interested parties.

Manufactured Housing (Mobile Homes)

Manufactured Housing Institute (MHI)
1745 Jefferson Davis Hwy.
Arlington, VA 22202
(703) 979-6620

Today, particularly when mortgage money is relatively expensive, mobile homes are the only reasonable options for many families who want some equity in the place where they live but can't afford to get into fixed-site housing, though many of these units look as fixed and permanent as any development house. Often, mobile homes are sold fully equipped with all major appliances, lamps, carpeting, and more. Furthermore, all mobile/manufactured homes produced after June 15, 1976, have been built to the guidelines of the National Manufactured Home Construction and Safety Standards Act of 1974, established and enforced by HUD. Now there are some 10,000 mobile/manufactured home retailers in the United States, almost 25,000 mobile/manufactured home communities, and 1.8 million sites. For information on construction and safety standards and which units have or do not have urea formaldehyde foam insulation in the walls, write MHI for their brochure "Quick Facts." (Send a SASE.) They can direct you to your state association as well. It pays to work at the state level with people who have familiarity with dealers in your area.

Redwood Lumber
California Redwood Association
One Lombard St.
San Francisco, CA 94111
(415) 392-7880

This active trade association provides information, technical specs, and many project plans using redwood lumber products. Specifically, they have over 100 different pieces of literature available to consumers, generally for a modest charge of 25¢ or 50¢ to cover mailing, and can provide help with questions on applications and finishes by phone or mail. Write or call California Redwood's Technical Services Department. Pat Young, the promotion manager, helps to produce quality literature that is helpful, detailed, and beautifully photographed.

GOVERNMENT AGENCIES

Consumer Information
Federal Trade Commission
Bureau of Consumer Protection
Sixth and Pennsylvania NW
Washington, DC 20580
(202) 523-3667

The FTC's List of Publications contains an extensive listing of booklets and brochures, many at no charge, on such subjects as woodstoves, home siding, R values, warranties, sun-reflective film, and other aspects of homebuilding. The list is free and a good place to start looking for specific information sources. The FTC also publishes a Consumer's Resource Handbook (also available from the Consumer Information Center, Pueblo, CO 81009), which is a 90-page listing of government agencies (state by state and even county by county), including services for the handicapped, state utility commissions, Better Business Bureaus, state and local consumer protection agencies, and more.

Handicapped
Accent on Information
PO Box 700
Bloomington, IL 61701
(309) 378-2961

An excellent primary source on products and special devices that can make homes barrier free for handicapped persons. This organization operates a data bank of products, including furniture and appliances either specially adapted or made specifically for handicapped persons. For more help on this subject contact the Clearinghouse on the Handicapped, Office of Special Education and Rehabilitation Services, U.S. Department of Education, 400 Maryland Ave. SW, Washington, DC 20202; (202) 245-0080.

Home Design

Texas Agricultural Extension Service
Texas A & M University System
303 Scoates Hall
College Station, TX 77843

You see the word *agricultural* and you think of cows and fences and all. That's a mistake. Many extension services have a lot more to offer. This one, for example, has an extensive publications list—like a few thousand titles—on many subjects, including home design and construction and other related areas. In particular, Bill Stewart, an agricultural engineering specialist with the service who was kind enough to provide thorough answers, writes that the service "provides a broad range of programs . . . primarily educational . . . aimed at making the home owner more capable of selection, care, construction, and use of the home, as well as home furnishings . . . and can provide a lot of house plans for potential rural home owners or builders."

Business operation Aside from the publications list, you might be interested in three booklets (costs are modest to cover printing and handling only): "House Plans for Texas," "Moderate Home Plans—1,000 to 1,300 Square Fee," and "Small Modern Homes." Meetings on a regular basis are available to local residents, and in some cases specific problems with foundation settling, extraordinarily high energy costs, etc. may be dealt with and answered individually.

Problem Contractors

Federal Housing Administration (FHA)
Printing Office
451 Seventh St. SW
Washington, DC 20410

One special service of this giant agency, which is concerned with so many aspects of your home, is maintaining what is called the DSI list, an updated listing of some 1500 major building contractors who work predominantly on multifamily housing like condominiums and are declared debarred, suspended, and ineligible contractors. Contractors make the infamous list for cute tricks such as price gouging, fraud, deceptive advertising, and major violations of building codes. Some mortgage loan officers at local banks may have a copy of the list. If not, write FHA. The current list is available to consumers on request.

Standards

National Center for Standards and
    Certification Information (NCSCI)
National Bureau of Standards
Department of Commerce
Technology Building, Room B166
Washington, DC 20234
(301) 921-2587

The NCSCI maintains a reference collection of engineering and related standards, including some 240,000 specific standards, specifications, test methods, codes, and recommended practices. The agency responds to over 5,000 individual inquiries every year, providing the source for standards on the specific subjects you inquire about. That's the key—being specific. For example, if you ask about residential housing you won't get anywhere. You will get a meaningful response if you ask for wood frame construction, or concrete masonry foundations. The agency can also send you information on their computer-produced keyword context (KWIC) so that you can use punch cards to track down standards on electric toasters, the properties of fireclay brick, and more.

Wood and Frame Research

USDA Forest Service, Forest Products
   Laboratory
PO Box 5130
Madison, WI 53705
(608) 264-5600

The Forest Service is one of the best sources of information on wood use and performance in structures. They maintain a gigan-

tic testing facility and offer literally piles of reports on all aspects of wood use. Of particular interest is their form 81-020, "List of Publications of Interest to Architects, Builders, Engineers, and Retail Lumbermen." You don't have to be one of the above to get the list, but the title does tell you that this is not basic how-to advice. It is a source to generally technical reports on such subjects as wood diaphragm materials, racking strength of wood frame walls. It includes absolutely fascinating reports (obviously, not fascinating to everyone) on subjects like long-time performance of trussed rafters, strength of log bridge stringers after several years' use in southeast Alaska, and much more. The list is free and, better yet, single copies of the reports are free—only if you get the list first, and make limited, specific requests.

CONSUMER EDUCATION

Information and Services

Appropriate Technology for Building and Water Use

Intermediate Technology Development
   Group (ITDG) of North America, Inc.
777 United Nations Plaza
New York, NY 10017
(212) 972-9877

ITDG was established in 1979. Its work, generally in the field of appropriate technology, centers in four areas: distributing AT information, initiating small-scale en-

terprises, trying to include AT training in the technical training programs of colleges, and hooking up its AT effort with other groups worldwide. It holds detailed workshops periodically in different parts of the country on such subjects as low-cost solar hot water heaters.

Business operation Write for its publications list, which includes manuals for small building construction using locally available materials, biogas manuals, and titles on cookstove technology, water supply, and waste systems.

Waterlines is its journal of appropriate water supply and sanitation ($14 per year for 4 issues). Write for subscription information to ITDG Publications Office, PO Box 337, Croton-on-Hudson, NY 10520.

Arbitration

American Arbitration Association
140 W. 51 St.
New York, NY 10020
(212) 484-4000

In a letter of agreement, or a more formal and detailed construction contract or contract for design services or remodeling, etc., all possibilities are supposed to be covered. But that's not the way it works. In some cases, whether problems start because of personalities or timing or money or quality, some form of mediation is necessary. Smart consumers provide for this contingency in their contracts. One way to do it is to write to the American Arbitration Association for guidelines, even specific contract language that will get you and your contractor, for example, into arbitration as a last resort before using the courts. Costs for this service are moderate, charged on a sliding scale according to the value of your job. The association has branches and facilities in most major cities and has experienced volunteer arbitrators, many of whom are established engineers and architects. Write for their literature before you go to contract.

Building Research

University of Illinois at Champaign–
   Urbana
One E. Saint Mary's Rd.
Champaign, IL 61820
(217) 333-1801

One of the resources at this university is the Small Homes Council—Building Research Council, a nonprofit, self-supporting agency established for research, education, and public service in the area of housing and homebuilding. The council conducts research under the sponsorship of government agencies, trade associations, and some companies specifically in the area of simplifying construction techniques: how to use roof trusses instead of conventional rafters, wall panel systems instead of conventional, step by step studding, sheathing and siding. They also deal with kitchen design and energy subjects.

Business operation   The council has an extensive publications list available on request. Circulars, technical reports, and full research reports cover such subjects as financing, built-up roofing, treated pole construction, hydronic systems, attic ventilation, gusset-plate construction, nailed/glued truss design, and much more. Also, slide presentations and instruction sheets are available that provide detailed construction information for carpenters and others on the job.

Pricing   The council's publications list is free. Circulars and technical notes are 50¢ each, instruction sheets $1, research reports $5. A housing advisory service, set up to answer specific questions from homeowners and builders, may be contacted by mail or in person at the above address.

Construction Trades

Institute of Design and Construction
141 Willoughby St.
Brooklyn, NY 11201
(212) 855-3661

This is one of the larger vocational training institutions, approved by the Board of Regents of the University of the State of New York and offering an associate degree in occupational studies. Work-study programs, evening programs, financial aid, and many of the features found at conventional colleges are available. Courses cover blueprints, design, material and methods of construction, surveying, mechanical trades, and more.

Business operation You can write for a free brochure that describes the program in detail, gives a synopsis of each course, and explains the several options in scheduling and course load.

Deck Construction Details

U.S. Department of Agriculture, Forest
   Service
12th and Independence Ave. SW
Washington, DC 20250
(202) 447-6665

One of the Department of Agriculture's handbooks, *Construction Guides for Exposed Wood Decks* (Handbook No. 432), contains well-illustrated details. The text is thorough and straightforward, missing only some of the modern, frame-connecting hard-ware. Published first in 1972, the thrust of the designs is somewhat conventional. The structural information is solid.

Education/Training
State Approval and Licensing Agencies

In every state there are hundreds of vocational schools and other programs of education and training in virtually all fields of homebuilding, including repair and maintenance. Many of these educational sources are listed in the appropriate sections of the Sourcebook. Before you part with a down payment or sign any type of enrollment form, check with the state agency responsible for approving and/or licensing the institution. These agencies, listed state by state, follow.

ALABAMA

State Department of Education
Division of Vocational
   Education
845 State Office Building
Montgomery, AL 36104

ALASKA

Vocational & Adult Education
Department of Education
Pouch "F"
Juneau, AK 99801

ARIZONA

Arizona State Board of Private
   Technical & Business Schools
1812 W. Monroe
Phoenix, AZ 85007

Arizona Veterans Service
   Commission
PO Box 6123
Phoenix, AZ 85005

ARKANSAS

State Approving Agency for
   Veterans

Department of Education
Arch Ford Building
Little Rock, AR 72201

CALIFORNIA

State Department of Education
217 W. First St.
Los Angeles, CA 90012

Bureau of School Approvals
721 Capitol Mall
Sacramento, CA 95814

COLORADO

Proprietary Schools & Veterans
   Education
State Board of Community
   Colleges & Occupational
   Education
503 State Service Building
1525 Sherman St.
Denver, CO 80203

CONNECTICUT

Consultant for Private Schools
State Department of Education

PO Box 2219
Hartford, CT 06115

Veterans Education & Services
State Department of Education
PO Box 2219
Hartford, CT 06115

DELAWARE

Director of Vocational
   Education
Department of Public
   Instruction
Dover, DE 19901

DISTRICT OF COLUMBIA

License Branch
Department of Economic
   Development
614 H St. NW, Room 308
Washington, DC 20001

Services to Veterans
415 12th St. NW
Room 1001
Washington, DC 20004

FLORIDA

State Board of Independent
  Postsecondary Vocational,
  Technical, Trade & Business
  Schools
490 Barnett Bank Building
Tallahassee, FL 32304

State Approving Agency for
  Veterans Training
1720 S. Gadsden St.
Tallahassee, FL 32304

GEORGIA

Department of Veterans Service
One Hunter St. SW
Atlanta, GA 30334

State Department of Education
312 State Office Building
Atlanta, GA 30334

HAWAII

Accreditation & Private School
  Licensing
Department of Education
1270 Queen Emma St.
Honolulu, HI 96813

IDAHO

State Approving Agency
Department of Education
State Office Building
Boise, ID 83707

ILLINOIS

State Approving Agency
Illinois Veterans' Commission
1229 S. Michigan Ave.
Chicago, IL 60605

Private Business & Vocational
  Schools
316 S. Second St.
Springfield, IL 62706

INDIANA

Indiana Private School
  Accrediting Commission
ISTA Building, Suite 810
150 W. Market St.
Indianapolis, IN 46204

Department of Veterans' Affairs
707 State Office Building
100 N. Senate Ave.
Indianapolis, IN 46204

IOWA

Veterans Education & Training
Department of Public
  Instruction
Grimes State Office Building
Des Moines, IA 50319

KANSAS

Kansas Veterans' Commission
701 Jackson St.
Topeka, KS 66603

Proprietary Schools
State Department of Education
120 E. 10th St.
Topeka, KS 66612

KENTUCKY

Veterans Education
State Department of Education
Capitol Plaza Tower, 22nd Floor
Frankfort, KY 40601

Proprietary School Licensing
  Unit
Bureau of Vocational Education
Department of Education
Frankfurt, KY 40601

LOUISIANA

Proprietary School Commission
State Department of Education
Baton Rouge, LA 70804

Veterans Education & Training
Department of Education
PO Box 44064
Baton Rouge, LA 70804

MAINE

Bureau of Vocational Education
Department of Educational &
  Cultural Services
29 Chapel St.
Augusta, ME 04330

MARYLAND

Business, Trade, & Technical
  Schools

Baltimore-Washington
  International Airport
PO Box 8717
Baltimore, MD 21240

MASSACHUSETTS

Agent for Veterans Affairs
Board of Higher Education
Department of Education
182 Tremont St.
Boston, MA 02111

Office of Private Schools
Division of Occupational
  Education
Department of Education
182 Tremont St.
Boston, MA 02111

MICHIGAN

Private Trade Schools
Department of Education
PO Box 420
Lansing, MI 48902

MINNESOTA

Veterans Education Unit
Department of Education
Capitol Square Building
St. Paul, MN 55101

Private Vocational School Unit
Special Programs & Services
  Section
Vocational-Technical Division
Department of Education
Capitol Square Building
St. Paul, MN 55101

MISSISSIPPI

Veterans Affairs Board
120 N. State St.
War Memorial Bldg.
Jackson, MS 39205

Mississippi School & College
  Registration Commission
PO Box 771
Jackson, MS 39205

MISSOURI

Veterans Education
State Department of Education
PO Box 480
Jefferson City, MO 65101

MONTANA

Veterans' Education & Training
Department of Public
  Instruction
State Capitol Building
Helena, MT 59601

NEBRASKA

Private Vocational Schools
  & Veterans Education
State Department of Education
233 S. 10th St.
Lincoln, NE 68505

NEVADA

Professional Standards Branch
State Department of Education
Carson City, NV 89701

NEW HAMPSHIRE

Veterans Educational Services
Department of Education
Division of Postsecondary
  Education
163 Loudon Rd.
Concord, NH 03301

NEW JERSEY

Bureau of Area Vocational
  Technical & Private Schools
Division of Vocational
  Education
State Department of Education
225 W. State St., PO Box 2019
Trenton, NJ 08625

NEW MEXICO

Governor's Approval Committee
  for Veterans' Training
State Capitol Building
Santa Fe, NM 87501

Private & Postsecondary Schools
Department of Education
Capitol Building
Santa Fe, NM 87501

NEW YORK

Bureau of Occupational School
  Supervisions
State Education Department
Albany, NY 12224

Bureau of Two-Year Colleges
State Education Department
Albany, NY 12224

NORTH CAROLINA

Veterans Education
Department of Public
  Instruction
Heart of Raleigh Building
Raleigh, NC 27601

NORTH DAKOTA

Private Vocational Schools
State Board of Vocational
  Education
900 E. Blvd.
Bismarck, ND 58501

OHIO

State Board of School & College
  Registration, Room 3646
30 E. Broad St.
Columbus, OH 43215

State Approving Agency for
  Veterans' Training
240 Parson Ave., Room 207
Columbus, OH 43215

OKLAHOMA

State Accrediting Agency
PO Box 53067, Capitol Station
Oklahoma City, OK 73105

OREGON

Vocational & Private School
  Licensing
State Department of Education
942 Lancaster Drive NE
Salem, OR 97310

PENNSYLVANIA

Bureau of Private Schools &
  Vocational Education
Department of Education
Harrisburg, PA 17124

RHODE ISLAND

Veterans Education
State Department of Education
Roger Williams Building
Providence, RI 02903

SOUTH CAROLINA

Division of Veterans Education
1429 Senate St.
Columbia, SC 29201

SOUTH DAKOTA

Consultant in Guidance &
  Counseling
Human Resources Development
  Division
Department of Public
  Instruction
State Capitol Building
Pierre, SD 57501

TENNESSEE

Division of Veterans Education
State Department of Education
111 "E" Cordell Hull Building
Nashville, TN 37219

TEXAS

Proprietary Schools & Veterans
Texas Education Agency
201 E. 11th St.
Austin, TX 78701

UTAH

Veterans & Vocational Technical
  Affairs
Utah System of Higher
  Education
1201 University Club Building
Salt Lake City, UT 84111

VERMONT

Educational Field Services
Department of Education
Montpelier, VT 05602

VIRGINIA

Proprietary School Service
State Department of Education
PO Box 6–Q
Richmond, VA 23216

Committee on Veterans
  Education
State Department of Education
PO Box 6–Q
Richmond, VA 23216

WASHINGTON

Veterans Education & Training
Coordinating Council of
   Occupational Education
216 Old Capitol Building
Olympia, WA 98304

WEST VIRGINIA

Supervisor of Private Schools
Department of Education

1900 Washington St. East
Charleston, WV 25305

Veterans Education & Training
Department of Education
1900 Washington St. East
Charleston, WV 25305

WISCONSIN

Educational Approval Council
Department of Public
   Instruction

4802 Sheboygan Ave.
Madison, WI 53702

WYOMING

Licensing & Certification
   Services Unit
State Department of Education
Capitol Building
Cheyenne, WY 82001

Veterans Education
Capitol Building, Room 317
Cheyenne, WY 82001

State Vocational and Training School Associations

In every state there are hundreds of vocational schools and other training and education institutions covering virtually all fields of homebuilding, improvement, and repair.

Many are listed in the appropriate section of this book. But you can check on curriculums, costs, accrediting agencies, and more before you enroll in any course with the statewide associations representing these schools. Such associations exist in most states, as follows.

Arizona Private School
   Association
PO Box 2668
Mesa, AZ 85204

California Association for
   Private Education
926 J St.
Sacramento, CA 95814

Santa Clara County Association
   of Private Schools
1414 N. Winchester Blvd.
San Jose, CA 95128

Colorado Private School
   Association
3501 E. First Ave., Suite One
Denver, CO 80206

Connecticut Association of
   Private Schools
2279 Mount Vernon Rd.
Southington, CT 06489

Chesapeake & Potomac
   Association of Private Schools
720 Providence Rd.
Towson, MD 21204

Florida State Association of
   Private Schools

1005 E. Jackson St.
Tampa, FL 33602

Georgia Private School
   Association
PO Box 7174
Atlanta, GA 30309

Illinois Federation of
   Independent Private Schools
1135 W. Fullerton Ave.
Coyne American Building,
   Room 600
Chicago, IL 60614

Indiana Association of Private
   Schools
PO Box 1665
Indianapolis, IN 46202

Iowa Private Specialized
   Schools Association
2500 Fleur Dr.
Des Moines, IA 50321

Kansas Association of Private
   Career Schools
6211 Beach
Wichita, KS 67208

Massachusetts Association of
   Private Schools

Hanscom Field, Box 426
Lexington, MA 02173

Michigan Association of Private
   Schools
1625 E. Grand Blvd.
Detroit, MI 48211 -

Minnesota Association of Private
   Vocational Schools
160 W. Ninth St.
St. Paul, MN 55102

Missouri Association of Trade
   and Technical Schools
722 Walnut
Kansas City, MO 64106

Nebraska Council of Private
   Vocational Schools
1660 N. Grant
Fremont, NE 68025

Nevada Association of Private
   Schools
2635 N. Decatur Blvd.
Las Vegas, NV 89108

Private Career School
   Association of New Jersey
PO Box 6832
Journal Square Station, NJ
   07306

New Mexico Association of
  Private Schools
225 San Pedro NE
Albuquerque, NM 87108

Private Vocational Schools
  Association
88 W. Broadway
New York, NY 10007

Ohio Council of Private
  Colleges & Schools
1441 N. Cable Rd.
Lima, OH 45805

Oklahoma Private School
  Association
8820 E. Pine
Tulsa, OK 74151

Oregon Association of
  Accredited Independent
  Vocational Schools
2416 N. Marine Dr.
Portland, OR 97217

Oregon Private School
  Association
PO Box 2721
Portland, OR 97208

Pennsylvania Association of
  Private School Administrators
Box 21036
Philadelphia, PA 19114

Tennessee Association of
  Proprietary Schools
4711 Old Kingston Pike
Knoxville, TN 37919

Texas Association of Proprietary
  Schools
8585 North Stemmons,
  Suite 201
Dallas, TX 75247

Utah Private School Association
805 E. 3300 South
Salt Lake City, UT 84106

Washington Federation of
  Private Vocational Schools
1923 Fifth Ave.
Seattle, WA 98101

Wisconsin Council of
  Independent Education
174 W. Wisconsin Ave.
Milwaukee, WI 53203

Frame Construction Details

U.S. Department of Agriculture,
  Forest Service
12th and Independence Ave. SW
Washington, DC 20250
(202) 447-6665

This agency puts out many consumer guides. *Wood Frame House Construction* (Handbook No. 73, Catalog No. 0–572–135) is a thorough, profusely illustrated manual of conventional stick construction from foundation to finishing. An updated version is in the works. The current edition is dated in some respects, particularly concerning insulation, vapor barriers, and modular framing systems. It's still worth the modest charge, practical, and easy even for inexperienced do-it-yourselfers to follow.

Home Study

National Home Study Council (NHSC)
1601 18th St. NW
Washington, DC 20009
(202) 234-5100

NHSC is the umbrella accrediting agency for some ninety home study schools that offer over 500 different academic and vocational courses by mail. It may be a slightly dry way to learn hands-on skills like carpentry and plumbing, but it is a viable option.

Business operation The NHSC *Directory of Accredited Home Study Schools* is available free on request and includes schools offering courses in building construction, building contracting, interior design, drafting, heating and ventilation, interior decorating, masonry, plastering, solar heating, upholstery, and more. Check with NHSC before signing up for vocational training.

Vocational Training

American Association for Vocational
Instructional Materials (AAVIM)
Driftmier Engineering Center
Athens, GA 30602
(404) 542-2586

AAVIM collects up-to-date information and teaching procedures from educators and industry and puts the results into training programs that are designed for both classroom and individual use. The AAVIM 1983 catalog covers electric motors, residential water systems, wiring, shop practice, pesticide application, fencebuilding, construction and design of utility buildings, and a lot more. It will send you the catalog on request or direct you to one of its twenty-five centers in the United States and Canada. Most programs include a basic manual, teacher guide, student workbook, and audiovisual or slide program. Publications may be ordered separately.

Wood/Soil/Agriculture Information

Cooperative Extension
U.S. Department of Agriculture
University of California at Berkeley,
CA 94720

This is one of the most active extension services (check with the nearest branch of your state university) offering a wealth of information on many agricultural subjects, but it also includes topics such as forestry (the mechanical properties of central Sierra Cedar, control of the Monterey Pine tip moth), engineering (farm building plans, fire alarm systems for homes, woodstove installation safety), soil and water (ecology of compost, drip irrigation). Write for their publications catalog, which contains a limited number of free publications and charges

modest prices for literature that is generally thorough and worthwhile. You do not have to be a California resident to order from this cooperative extension. However, extension services in your state will have information on local issues, such as Santa Ana winds and fire protection in the west, gypsy moths and deciduous trees in the east.

Practical Training

Alternative Lifestyle/ Homesteading

The Homesteading Center
RD 2
Oxford, NY 13830

The Center has a week's course on just about all phases of homesteading: carving one week, herbalism another, trapping and hunting later, even advanced homesteading week.

Also, they offer a 2-week course on log cabin building, using native trees and hand tools. Their literature contains certain phrases that send me back fifteen years to the formative stages of flower power and alternative lifestyles, like, "You are probably among the many people who want to return to the more basic things in life—like trees and earth, fresh air and sunshine, love and peace." In addition to practical teaching, they are ready to "open your awareness to . . . wild foods, herbs, the moon and the stars."

Anyway, you can write for their course descriptions (15 per class limit), and, if interested, for information about what their literature describes as "the Catholic Homesteading community we have at the Homesteading School."

Pricing For a week of basic homesteading, $75.

Appropriate Technology
Mother Earth News
PO Box 70
Hendersonville, NC 28791

One of the bibles of alternative energy and appropriate technology and a full-fledged money-making venture at the same time, *Mother Earth News* has taken a step few organizations do; it has established an open testing ground for the ideas and final, practical applications of its self-sufficiency doctrines. It is called Mother's Eco-Village and occupies 622 acres in the mountains near Hendersonville, North Carolina. It is a showplace for both elaborate and simple projects for do-it-yourselfers, all of which have appeared in the magazine. Eco-Village runs an ongoing series of "show-how" demonstrations covering earth-sheltered housing, wind power, log construction, cordwood construction, and a lot more.

Business operation   One year of 6 issues of *Mother Earth News* is $18. Daily admission to Eco-Village is $6 for adults, $4 for children 12 to 20. (There are quite a few 20 year olds who won't like that description.) Admission is free for ages 11 and under. Information including illustrated brochures of village activities and demonstrations is sent on request. This is the only place I have found where you can get a close look at so many different self-sufficiency disciplines. Worth investigating.

Construction Home Study
NRI Building Construction School
McGraw-Hill Continuing Education
   Center
3939 Wisconsin Ave.
Washington, DC 20016
(202) 244-1600

NRI offers a comprehensive home study construction course. It covers seventy sep-

arate lessons in site selection, working drawings, building materials, foundation concrete, stairways, heating systems, wiring, estimating, and more. NRI is accredited by the National Home Study Council and offers a sophisticated brochure, covering all kinds of back up and consulting services for graduates.

Business operation   The NRI brochure is sent on request. Of course, the obvious question is how much can you really learn from a home study course, even one that includes book work and practical projects. Successful building depends so much on experience, in learning all the accommodations and adjustments that are part of quality construction. In any case, NRI does offer a comprehensive approach to this extremely complicated subject that may be a starting place for owner-builders or fledgling professionals.

Local Materials Construction/ Cordwood Masonry
Indigenous Material Housing Institute
Box H
Upper Gagetown, NB
Canada EOG 3EO
(506) 488-2477

Cordwood masonry is one of the more interesting alternative construction systems, and this is one of the best places to learn about it. Jack Henstridge, author of *Building the Cordwood Masonry Home*, runs a series of seminars on the subject in a vacation learning setting that includes country-style suppers, hands-on workshops, and more. Jack writes, "Our prime focus is on the development of the cordwood technique, as it appears to have so many advantages over the other methods and materials, particularly for the first-time builder."

Business operation   Write for a free brochure describing the seminars and the more specialized course in cordwood building. Seminars are conducted in the summer, limited to twenty-five per session. Accommodations can be arranged locally, and you can even rent camping equipment (or bring your own) or arrange to stay in a private home in the area. The cost for the Sunday through Friday seminar is $125, $175 per couple; the cordwood-only seminar (Sunday through Wednesday) is $75, $100 per couple.

Log Building
B. Allan Mackie School of Logbuilding
PO Box 1205
Prince George, BC
Canada V2L 4V3
(604) 964-4515

One of the most complete sources of information and practical training in this field, the Mackie School offers regular sessions from 1-day seminars to 6-week building courses. Tuition ranges from $35 for the seminar to about $750 for the general building session. Graduate sessions are available as well for people who have completed at least two log homes and are interested in the fine points as well as teacher training in this growing field. The school has no phone, no door to door mail delivery, and no grocery store. Campsites and small cottages are on-site, and the school charges what it calls a "caution" fee of $50 for each site, which is refunded if you leave it as clean as you found it. That small point says a lot about the school. Allan Mackie is a respected teacher in this field, an author, and principal force behind the Canadian Log Builder's Association, which has its permanent home at the school.

Business operation A brochure describing the school, courses, fees, and more is sent free on request. The school is somewhat of a wilderness workshop about 24 miles west of Prince George, British Columbia.

Log Home/Blacksmith Instruction
Restorations
Drawer G
Free Union, VA 22940
(804) 973-4859

Charles McRaven, currently a consultant to the Log Homes Guide, the preeminent sourcebook periodical for log enthusiasts, offers two hands-on workshop courses: blacksmithing, for 6 days (usually in early December) emphasizes this craft as a homesteading skill and covers making and repairing tools and hardware, also tempering, forge welding, and more; log-house construction, for 5 days (usually in early November) covers foundation work, felling, hewing, notching, raising, chinking, and all special skills needed beyond conventional carpentry.

Business operation In addition to the workshop courses, McRaven offers consulting services that must be arranged on a case-by-case basis; as well as a series of eight timber-frame plans. You can write or call for course details.

Pricing The blacksmithing course is $200; the course on log construction $165; plans are $10 to $25.

Owner-Builder Training
The Owner Builder Center
1516 Fifth St.
Berkeley, CA 94710
(415) 526-9222

The Owner Builder Center is a nonprofit educational organization that offers individual classes, full programs, books, a quarterly newsletter, and consulting services, mainly to people with little or no experience in construction or remodeling. As Leslie Fox, director of local programs, writes, "We have summer residence programs in which people from all over the country come, live on site, and actually build a house. We also offer classes throughout the California Bay Area. Every weekend we offer hands-on classes on specific topics: plumbing, electrical, deck building, wall framing, concrete work, and tile setting." Their newsletter outlines all workshops, consulting services that include site and house inspection, plan evaluation, plan and design services, and something called site visitation, which is a package of twenty-five hours' worth of on-site supervision as you start up a project of some duration. The *Owner Builder Newsletter* includes classifieds, editorials, a booklist, and a few book reviews.

Business operation   Full details are available on request. Ask particularly for a recent issue of the newsletter.

Pricing   Sixteen-session housebuilding and remodeling courses offered in the summer are about $300 ($450 for a couple), given in Berkeley, Palo Alto, Concord, San Jose, San Francisco, and possibly other locations as well. Special 1-day seminars are about $50; $95 for 2 days, and include such topics as rammed-earth construction and estimating costs of labor and materials.

The Owner Builder Exchange
1824 Fourth St.
Berkeley, CA 94710
(415) 848-5950

This source is not a trade association for owner-builder schools but is one of the best central sources on owner-builder education. The Exchange, the newsletter arm of the Owner Builder Center in Berkeley, regularly trains groups who start their own centers and reviews and lists new owner-builder schools. So please do not expect typical trade association services from this source. Figure instead that any help you get here is at their pleasure and good will. Several of the schools in operation now are listed below.

The first two were started by personnel who completed their training at the Owner Builder Center.

Chico Housing Improvement Program, Chico, CA; (916) 342-0012

Connecticut Housing Investment Fund, Hartford, CT; (203) 233-5165

Domestic Technology Institute, Evergreen, CO; (303) 674-1597

Earthwood Building School, West Chazy, NY; (518) 493-7744

Home Building Institute, Summit, IL; (312) 735-3343

Legendary Loh Home School, Sister, OR; (503) 549-7191

Minnesota Trailbound Log Building Program, Minneapolis, MN; (612) 822-5955

Northwest Building Institute, Portland, OR; (503) 244-8266

Original Log House Construction School, Monroe, WA; (206) 885-4972

Southwest Solaradobe School, Albuquerque, NM; (505) 842-0342

Windstar Foundation, Snowmass, CO; (303) 927-4777

Yestermorrow
Warren, VT 05674
(802) 496-5545

This owner-builder school in Vermont offers seven different 2-week courses: four sessions on basic designing and building, one on renovation and remodeling, and two that separate the basic course and dwell on design and building respectively. The design course is directed to people who have some construction experience, and the construction course is for design professionals and architecture students who want hands-on experience. (Oddly, few U.S. schools supply this training, even to students specializing in residential design.) The Yestermorrow staff is comprised of professional architects, builders, engineers, and woodworkers. Class size is limited to fifteen students. And after graduation, students are invited to return, without tuition costs, to follow up with subsequent courses—an unusual offer. The organization also offers follow-up consultation services (on an hourly fee basis) for questions that can't be handled in a phone call.

Business operation   The school will send complete course descriptions on request, including information on accommodations, special supplies needed, suggested reading before you show up, and more.

Pricing   Tuition is currently $375, which includes materials, instruction, insurance, and alumni privileges. Room for 13 nights plus board for 12 days is $300.

Rural Appropriate Technology

The Rural Center
15290 Coleman Valley Rd.
Occidental, CA 95465

One of two centers run by the nonprofit Farallones Institute (the other is the Integral Urban House—see *Part 1: CONSUMER INFORMATION, Practical Training, Appropriate Technology*). The emphasis is on environmentally sound building, energy use, recycling, and generally achieving the greatest benefit from the least amount of technological effort. At the Rural Center, emphasis is placed on the applications of these principles to the rural setting. One-day workshops are available in blacksmithing, gardening for young people, solar energy for young people, and more. Several 2-day workshops are offered covering beekeeping, passive solar design, and more.

Business operation   Write for brochures with course descriptions and enrollment details and also for a good, specialized, appropriate technology book list. If you get in

the area you can drop by, see how the workshops operate, and tour the solar greenhouses and other on-site projects. This is not classroom theory. It's hands-on learning.

Solar Owner-Builder Services

Cornerstones Energy Group, Inc.
54 Cumberland St.
Brunswick, ME 04011
(207) 729-5103

Cornerstones was founded in 1976 as an owner-builder school. And as interest in solar design increased, Cornerstones added more courses and more services, including special courses for solar design and retrofit professionals, an extensive bookstore (all titles are sold by mail order as well), design and consulting services, complete building plans, energy audit software, and training programs.

Business operation   For complete course descriptions (some last only a few days, some several weeks) write Cornerstones. Students have built many energy-efficient homes and solar greenhouses during their training. Cornerstones Journal covers topical energy news, a few projects in great detail, and carries updated information on course schedules.

Stone Construction

Stonehouse Publications
Sweet, ID 83670

Among several books on building, using logs, earth, passive solar design, and other alternative technologies, the mainstay here is a book called *How to Build a Low Cost House of Stone*. The book was written (and the house shown inside was built) by Lewis and Sharon Watson. They are not professional builders or architects or engineers, and it shows. And although that is a kind of criticism, I learned a while ago not to be a technology snob, to appreciate trial and error and even finishing techniques and small construction details that may lack a sense of style or efficiency. This book has primitive artwork but a lot of photographs, and it is a documentary of a learning experience, laid out step by step, that covers real concerns instead of textbook problems. It deals with real solutions that account for site conditions, limited budgets, and limited engineering expertise. The method can be summed up as slip-form construction, a way of stepping up forms as the walls grow, providing suitable strength while using far less material than conventional forms. There are many books on this kind of building. This one may leave out some of the theory and some of the math, but I would spring for the $6 to get a realistic idea of what's involved.

Business operation The Watsons will send along several flyers describing their books on request. The stone building book seems to do what the flyer says it will:

"Shows how an average family can gather free rocks and build a full-sized, three-bedroom rural stone house in one summer, working totally alone, at the cost of $2000." Really quite an accomplishment. Hats off.

Trade School
The Williamson School
Media, PA 19063
(215) 566-1776

Although this school offers full, 3-year programs covering the wide range of building skills and is not for occasional do-it-yourselfers, I've included it to let you know that there are options to conventional education. The school is accredited by the National Association of Trade and Technical Schools and approved to grant associate degrees in specialized technologies by the Commonwealth of Pennsylvania. A brochure describing classes, tuition (many scholarships are available) is available on request.

READING AND REFERENCE

Architectural Engineering
Why Buildings Stand Up,
by Mario Salvadori
McGraw-Hill, 1980

This is one of the most enjoyable technical books I've read. But *technical* is really the wrong word because while you do wind up with a reasonably technical understanding of basic engineering you don't get it by struggling over equations. There are chapters on the Eiffel Tower, Brooklyn Bridge, Hagia Sophia, tents and balloons, prehistoric houses, and pyramids. Try to find this one;

an inexpensive paperback that, with a careful reading, can give you more than most vocational or college courses.

Cabins and A-Frames
How to Build Country Homes,
by Paul Corey
Funk & Wagnalls, 1975

I don't mind a book showing construction details that may not be code approved in some areas, books that miss some things while they are busy providing real help somewhere else. It is surprising that you can still come across how-to books dispensing absolutely incorrect information—things like using green wood in construction frames even though that will create all kinds of havoc as the wood dries, and little tips like laying tight flooring by assembling the last few pieces too tightly, so they buckle up, then stomping on them even though they will buckle up again in damp weather. This books is thin in spots, and a little dated in design (updated in 1975), but it doesn't steer you wrong, and for every falling there is a practical tidbit that comes only from someone who went through the process—things like the number of nails per pound, owner-built panelized construction, and more. An interesting tour of A-frames, cabins, and what can be characterized as sixties-style vacation homes. It's the kind of book I've almost donated to the library a few times but haven't because it's still useful.

Cordwood Masonry
*Cordwood Masonry Houses: A
   Practical Guide for the Owner-Builder,*
by Robert L. Roy
Sterling Publishing
Two Park Ave.
New York, NY 10016

Cordwood masonry is a very specialized type of construction. The finished product produces a very specialized appearance. Although cordwood construction can be used independently (once you have a proper footing and foundation), it is commonly used as a filler for post-and-beam framing. This book is the only one I know of that provides a thorough treatment of the subject from selecting and preparing the wood to very thorough, hands-on explanations of building techniques. Much of the artwork is primitive. Nevertheless, the mortaring in-

formation is just what you need to do the job yourself. And surprisingly, thick cordwood with insulation and mortar bound between logs offers a strong, energy-efficient, long-lasting wall; unique; worthwhile.

Excavation
Moving the Earth,
by Herbert L. Nichols, Jr.
North Castle Books
212 Bedford Rd.
Greenwich, CT 06830

One of the most thorough books you will find on any subject, not cheap (about $40), but close to 1,800 pages and endless illustrations leave (sorry about this one but I can't resist) no stone unturned. Everything from trenching to stump clearing to cutting access roads to moving boulders is presented in commonsense detail that covers all options, equipment needed, how to use it, what you can use instead if you can't get hold of the ideal machine for the job or if the job just doesn't seem to fit the textbook solution. Unfortunately, I have not found this book in the several libraries I use regularly, and it is a bit expensive and specialized for low-budget, nonmetropolitan libraries. But try anyway. I hate to send people after $40 books that may be used only a few times.

Farm and Utility Buildings
The Wheeling Farm Building Book,
by W. A. Bell et al
Popular Library

Although the blurb inside my edition says this selection "represents titles by the world's greatest authors"—well, maybe good authors—this strange little paperback is an example of specialty titles put out by manufacturers and trade associations. And it's pretty good, covering farm layout, different types of utility buildings, heat, passive solar design, concrete mixes, venting, and, of course, a heavy section on corrugated steel roofing—the company's product. Try the company (Wheeling Corrugating Company) first. The illustrations are a bit scratchy but still communicate the purely practical framing, siding, and roofing details.

Frame Construction
Wood-frame House Construction,
by L. O. Anderson
Craftsman Book Company
542 Stevens Ave.
Solana Beach, CA 92075

From a publisher that turns out consistently thorough, no-nonsense how-to books (long on information and short on tips and tricks), this 235-page, heavily illustrated, large-format book shows and details all aspects of wood frame construction—the conventional variety. Basic carpentry skills are assumed here so that when you see how the valley rafter is caught by the roof header, jack rafter, and doubled full rafter, you have to know about the compound miters required. You don't get a 10-picture how-to sequence on how to set up your circular saw. An excellent buy at around $5.

Handcrafted Construction
The Craftsman Builder,
by Art Boericke and Barry Shapiro
Simon & Schuster

With no how-to details and practically no text, this picture book is still full of information. Crystal-clear, beautifully lit color photographs show overall views and details of personal and imaginative pieces of building, from adobe and masonry to log and pole—incredible doors of log faces swimming together with intermingled knots and

grain, stone with tile and mosaics built into a rock cliff. It's a visual treat with a lot of ideas; you'll ooh and aah; about $8.

Homebuilding
Residential Carpentry,
by Mortimer P. Reed
John Wiley & Sons

This 700-page monster is one of the more complete residential building manuals with good clean artwork and a fair number of photographs. Although the forward specifies that the book "is not written exclusively for those studying carpentry in school," it does have a textbook flavor, breaking every job down into steps, with a little quiz at the end of each section. But the information is practical. For example, a few short paragraphs on cantilevered decks includes tips on how to deal with finished floor discrepancies from inside to outside, mentions the two-thirds supported, one-third extended structural principle, and warns about vibration at this limit of practical design. But some nitty gritty how-to details are overlooked. Try the library first.

Log Building
The Craft of Log Building,
by Hermann Phelps
Lee Valley Tools, Ltd.
2680 Queensview Dr.
Ottawa, ON
Canada K2B 8J9

This excellent book is not so much a practical guide as an investigation into all the components of log structures. I've singled it out here (there are many new books on log construction) because it is a distinctly European view. Much of the detailing is German, Norwegian, and Swedish, and you will be surprised to see notching and other techniques that somehow were not transposed to American, or at least western, log construction. Profusely illustrated; many photographs appear to be from the early 1900s, which only adds to the unique perspective offered by this book; about $30 from Lee Valley.

Hand-Hewn, by William C. Leitch
Chronicle Books
870 Market St.
San Francisco, CA 94102

This is a friendly, concise, well-illustrated, and practical book that may not go into every detail but is an excellent tour of what you will be up against if you decide to build your own cabin. It includes information on design, tools and equipment, foundations, and so forth, with heavy use of pictures to show design and construction possibilities—elegant door designs, incredible wedged and toothed log corner notches, and more. A compact 122 pages; about $5.

Log House Publishing Company, Ltd.
PO Box 1205
Prince George, BC
Canada V2L 4V3

A good source for varied and detailed information on logbuilding, offering many books covering general log building, notching, log span table books, log tools, and more. Write the address above for a publication list with brief descriptions and prices.

Log Homes
Buying a Log Home, by F. Wood
Scott Publications
Box 817
Westbrook, CT 06498

This 16-page guide to buying log homes covers many of the basics, poses many sample questions you might ask a dealer, but does not refer to specific manufacturers or models. Cost is $3, possibly a bit stiff for basic, generic advice.

Log Home Guide for Builders and Buyers,
   Muir Publishing Company, Ltd.
Gardenvale, Quebec
Canada H9X 1B0
(514) 457-2045

This is the source (yes, there are some others but this is *the* one) for information on log homes, whether you're interested in slick, precut kits, latchkey companies, the latest technical information on R-values and building permits, log-building schools, or more. Started in 1977, The *Long Home Guide*, edited by Doris Muir, is now out quarterly, plus a directory issue that covers the field and includes names, addresses, prices, brief descriptions of the homes offered by different firms, and articles.

Also, Muir Publishing has done its own five-year study on log-home energy efficiency entitled *The Energy Economics and Thermal Performance of Log Houses*. A condensed version of this report is available for about $5; with full technical date it's about $10. Muir Publishing is also a good source of books on the subject. An informed, worthwhile source.

Owner-Built Homes
Handmade Houses,
   by Art Boericke and Barry Shapiro
A & W Publishers

Subtitled *A Guide to the Woodbutcher's Art*, this small and extremely beautiful book (the color photography and printing really make a difference), may sell itself a little short in the subtitle. The homes illustrated are unique, imaginative, and often border on the weird. But the pictures alone can get a lot of your wheels turning. About $8; worth a look.

The Owner-Built Home, by Ken Kern
Charles Scribner's Sons

Although this book takes some work, with 375 pages of details and drawings (not the clearest art in the world) it is laced with solid, practical tips on all kinds of efficient and inexpensive construction, from esoteric third-world imports to somewhat more useful pole-frame building. If you are used to conventional stick building, this is a good book to use to break the bond, to see some of the leaner alternatives.

Pole Building
Low-Cost Pole Building Construction,
by Doug Merrilees and Evelyn Loveday
Garden Way Publishing

This large-format, well-illustrated, and inexpensive ($5) book is a good introduction to the subject, including pole treatment (even home applied preservative, which is something you want to think twice about), several pole buildings in pictures and plan drawings, and a modest how-to section that shows the basics, although it is short on the nitty gritty how-to details and techniques. Still, a worthwhile look at the subject for the price.

The Owner-Built Pole Frame House,
by Barbara and Ken Kern
Charles Scribner's Sons

Of Kern's several books, this one seems to be the most familiar ground for him. While the book is severely limited by scribbly and cluttered drawings, many of which are quite hard to decipher because of messy, hand-printed notes, dimensions, and arrows pointing all over the place, its information core is very solid and very practical; so much so that you should look for the book if you are serious about building with poles. While many owner-builder books are not for owners at all, this one is. It regularly provides practical points on figuring material needs and generally opts for low-cost, common-sense solutions to field problems. For example, while most books detail the theoretical, this book takes the time to explain how to use a water level, a simple, incredibly inexpensive, and absolutely accurate tool that is just right for muddy, bumpy, littered, construction sites. Try your library first as the small-format, 175-page book seems overpriced at over $18.

Stairs
Simplified Stair Building
A. F. J. Riechers
PO Box 405
Palo Alto, CA 94302

This small book (only 16 pages, $4) has large diagrams covering one of the most challanging processes of home construction. Stair layout would not be too complicated if you could simply start at the bottom, determine a comfortable riser height and tread width, and then build the second floor wherever you happened to finish the stairs. But with two predetermined points (the landings at first and second floors), cutting up the spaces between is too much for many builders as well as do-it-yourselfers. In most areas you can subcontract this work. But if you have special materials in mind and want to build your own, this book will really help.

Standards

Architectural Graphic Standards,
by Charles George Ramsey and
    Harold Reeve Sleeper
John Wiley and Sons

On the shelf in every architecture office (and in every library) this massive book (close to 800 pages, with thousands of illustrations) covers every aspect of design and construction. What it does best is show you what's available. It's not often that you need to know the average length and width of a kitchen eggbeater, but just in case you're building a set of drawer dividers and you need to know, Ramsey and Sleeper will show you. Generally, the drawings are so clean and complete that, for instance, you can see all the details of balloon framing as opposed to western framing—down to recommended nailing patterns. The book has excellent solar design information, good detailing of flashing and roofing systems, information on commercial as well as residential materials and practices, and more. Remember though, it is not a book with step by step photos and captions showing how to make the cuts and how to trim the edges. But you will find every kind of moulding, wood, stone, brick pattern, grout mixture, etc.

Building Construction Illustrated,
by Francis D. K. Ching
Van Nostrand Reinhold

Architectural Graphic Standards costs about $75; this book, about $12. It doesn't offer the kind of detail or notated drawings of the Ramsey and Sleeper classic, but it is affordable and practical on the job. Using three-quarter views (isometric and oblique drawings) instead of the largely plan views in *Architectural Graphic Standards*, this book aims to show you the different components of foundation, frame, roof, etc., along with mechanical systems, windows and doors,

gutters, and leaders. The drawings are clean but less formal (handprinted notes that require some work to read) than the super-clear Ramsey and Sleeper treatment. A good book for builders and remodelers with endless design options; also a good buy for over 300 illustrated pages.

Surveys and Layouts

Building Layout, by W. P. Jackson
Craftsman Book Company
542 Stevens Ave.
Solana Beach, CA 92075

Too often the jobs of surveying and laying out are left to the "professionals." This is understandable with surveying, although it pays to go over all the vectors and dimensions on any plot plan very carefully whether you are the builder or the owner. However, building layout is not a mysterious science beyond the scope of how-to information. This book covers it thoroughly (including surveying) as it relates directly to residential construction, i.e., regulating cut and fill ratios, squaring building lines, leveling foundations, establishing grades, and more. Another straightforward book from Craftsman requiring some familiarity with construction.

Timber Frame

Building the Timber Frame House,
by Tedd Benson and James Gruber
Charles Scribner's Sons

This is an interesting, well-illustrated tour of timber frame construction including a little history of tools and design and a sprinkling of on the job construction photos. Almost all of the how-to details, however, are relegated to scratchy, unprofessional drawings. And this reflects the text as well: a lot of time is spent showing what's possible and not so much time on the nitty-gritty details of how to do it. The strength of the book is the good coverage of the timber frame process. In the few sequence photos, you get directions like, "Drive corner chisel into corners" that tell you only what must be done. This book will show you that timber frame building approaches cabinetwork in a part of the house that is usually buried, and generally does not require work of appearance quality. This can slow you down. Attending one of the timber frame building schools would be in order before building your own.

The Timber Frame Planning Book,
by Stewart Elliot
Housesmiths Publishing
209 Canyon Blvd.
Boulder, CO 80302

This mamouth book (over 350 large-format pages, although a bit padded with empty pages for "notes") is unique. Instead of how-to details, it presents complete plans— but really complete—for nine houses and three barns down to the size of each timber, where the mortises are, how big they are,

and more . The historical blueprints are painstakingly accurate. You have to figure out where to get the wood, how to prepare the foundation, and all that other good stuff. A bargain at $15.

Utility Buildings
USDA Plans
Western Regional Agricultural
   Engineering Service
Agricultural Engineering Department
Oregon State University
Corvallis, OR 97331

The USDA (U.S. Department of Agriculture) cooperates with many state agricultural schools (this is but one of them) to make all kinds of valuable information available to homebuilders and particularly farmers. This western source will respond to inquiries with a list of plans, including many agricultural and utility buildings, most using pole construction. One of the most interesting publications is the Farmstead Planning Handbook (ISBN 0–89373–001–7), which covers site design building layout and construction, drainage, storage, and much more in great detail. It sells for $4.

RESTORATION AND REMODELING

PRIVATE FIRMS

Restoration

Whole House

Architectural Restoration
The Preservation Partnership
345 Union St.
New Bedford, MA 02740
(617) 996-3383

This group of architects and conservators provides full architectural restoration services relating to historic buildings, including inspection, writing specs for restoration work, and supervising jobs. Nationally, the group has taught homeowner seminars on the proper care of old houses and ways to make them energy efficient without disrupting their special, historic qualities.

Business operation Maximilian L. Ferro, managing partner of the group, writes, "There is no technical problem too difficult for us to solve, from the consolidation of crumbling plasterwork to the repair of damaged marble mantels. We can write contract documents for the most exacting restorations, design compatible additions . . . and document recreation of period interiors." A brochure describing the group, its services, and many completed projects is sent on request.

General Contracting
Wm. J. Warren & Son, Inc.
300 S. Howes St.
Fort Collins, CO 80521
(303) 482-1976

Warren & Son is a general contracting firm specializing in renovating old and historic structures. They also operate a home inspection service. Let one of their recent jobs speak for the firm. It took $4000 and many hours of research for Mr. Warren to uncover the original contract for a home in Fort Collins, drawn up by a noted Colorado architect, Montezuma Fuller, and the original design, published with full material specs in a 1902 edition of *Carpentry & Building Magazine*. Restoration began while applications were being filed to get historical landmark status for the building. Off came siding and all interior work except original bearing supports. New mechanical systems were installed and painstaking finishing work started, guided in part by a 1902 family photograph showing the original exterior detailing. On went some 200 corbels and 14 different exterior mouldings. The "before" and "after" pictures are remarkably similar—even down to finials and downspout locations.

Business operation Mr. Warren writes, "I will send a descriptive brochure about our inspection services free to anyone who requests it. I will also estimate any project, consult on any construction matters, and perform a variety of supervising and management jobs on an hourly basis. I will travel anywhere!" Incidentally, the landmark building cost $88,000. Warren put in $250,000 (all tax deductible due to the historical status). It is now rented as office space at a profit, although Warren has been offered as much as $600,000 for his finished product.

Historic Preservation/Restoration

James Thomas Wollon, Jr., A.I.A.,
    Architect
600 Craigs Corner Rd.
Havre de Grace, MD 21078
(301) 879-6748

This archtect specializes in historic structures. Their services include the traditional practices of preparing drawings and specifications, help with contractor selection, and inspection during construction. Unique services include consultation on architectural history, building condition, code compliance, and nomination to the National Register of Historic Places. The architect is registered to practice full services in Maryland, Virginia, Pennsylvania, Delaware, and North Carolina. Consulting services are possible in New Jersey and West Virginia as well. Mr. Wollon notes the growing interest in the continued use of old buildings, adding, "The Bicentennial gave this movement a great boost. New awareness of conservation in more recent years has further sustained the movement."

Paint Matching

Frank S. Welsh, Historic Paint Color
    Consultant
859 Lancaster Ave.
Bryn Mawr, PA 19010
(215) 525-3564

Mr. Welsh worked as an architectural technician with the National Park Service at Independence National Historical Park in Philadelphia and has worked on many private and public buildings, mainly in the South and Northeast. He is prepared to provide microscopic paint analysis, which can determine how many layers of paint are in place; the types of coatings (oil or water base, glazing, varnish, etc.); the original color, gloss, and texture; the approximate age of the coatings, and even details of graining and stenciling. But Mr. Welsh does not confine his operations to a lab. He offers a unique service called the Paintpamphlet. It lets you do the on-site investigation, explaining how and where to take paint samples, tools to use, and more. Then you can send the samples in for analysis.

Business operation The Paintpamphlet costs $5, shows some twenty locations, both inside and out, where you are most likely to get quality samples, explains what happens to your samples in the lab, and even gives you a glossary of paint terms so you and Mr. Walsh can talk the same language. Obviously, this is a service for those interested in restoration to very exacting standards. Short brochures are available that include a listing of Mr. Welsh's many projects.

Restoration Contracting

Historic Boulevard Services
1520 W. Jackson Blvd.
Chicago, IL 60607
(312) 829-5562

This is a relatively new restoration company that started on a decaying residential mansion and took it through a complete restoration back in 1974. Currently, it offers design and restoration services and employs craftsmen who specialize in some of the lost arts of working with marble, tin, stained glass, and more. As a kind of sideline it makes and sells several varieties of terra-cotta chimney pots.

Business operation You can write for a brochure describing the restoration services and recent projects (several of which have been written up in local Chicago papers), as well as specs and prices on the chimney pots.

Restoration Contracting/Training

Restoration Workshop
National Trust for Historic Preservation
635 S. Broadway
Tarrytown, NY 10591
(914) 631-6696

An interesting organization that, unfortunately, works regionally on a small scale. I say unfortunately because in addition to doing careful, documented restoration work, it is the only arm of the National Historic Trust (the only private, nonprofit organization chartered by Congress to encourage preservation of sites, buildings, and objects significant in American history), that provides full-time apprentice training in restoration crafts. To help support its organization, the workshop does a variety of restoration contracting—on buildings, churches, old waterwheels, and more—for a price, as private contractors would. It has done work for the National Park Service and National Trust member organizations from Massachusetts to South Carolina. It works predominantly for these groups and for private owners of landmark houses and registered properties, although under the constraints of a limited budget, it just may be able to find something historically interesting about your old house. It's worth a try, anyway. Be advised that it is not cheap. The crew currently consists of a workshop director, foreman, and seven apprentices. They expect to have more openings soon and accept people committed to restoration with at least one year in the building trades. Apprentices stay one to three years, receiving on-the-job training—education and a salary. The small shop also turns out a modest amount of millwork. Write for free brochures describing the workshop, and, if interested, details about the apprentice training program. A unique source.

Restoration Engineers

Skyline Engineers, Inc.
58 E. St.
Fitchburg, MA 01420
(617) 342-5333
(800) 343-8847 (Toll-free nationwide;
   call collect in Massachusetts)

Skyline provides full service restoration work, including carpentry, painting, masonry, sheet metal work, roofing, chemical cleaning, waterproofing, sandblasting, lightning protection, repainting, and goldleafing. You may not want the turret on your Victorian to stand out like a state capitol, but, as Daniel Quinn, the president of Skyline points out, "Skyline is the only firm to gold-leaf five state capitol domes: Atlanta, Denver, Concord, Montpelier, and Boston." They have impressive credentials including restoration projects such as Faneuil Hall and the Old North Church in Boston. Mr. Quinn reports, "Skyline was founded in 1947 by my father. For over 35 years we have specialized in the restoration of churches, historic houses, steeples, and buildings all over the United States."

Business operation Detailed consultation is required prior to job estimates. Arrange preliminaries through Skyline's toll-free line, or write.

Restoration—General

Restorations Unlimited, Inc.
24 W. Main St.
Elizabethville, PA 17023
(717) 362-3477

This company maintains small crews who specialize in restoration—not remodeling or home improvements. Beth Facinelli writes, "There is no doubt that it [restoration] can be expensive, but one must realize the reason for the costs. Older houses were generally much better constructed than the new, and had finer appointments and handwork in them. Cheap, modern products on the market which are produced to 'take the place of' or 'look-alikes' just don't make it in a restored house. Solid, good quality products and hand-work craftsmanship (unhurried!) cost more than cheap paneling and production carpenters." In accordance with this serious attitude toward restoration, this firm offers start-to-finish services, including reconstruction of original floor plans, period design and procurement of architectural antiques, a wide range of traditional crafts such as slate roofing, embossed steel ceiling work, and stenciling, in addition to carpentry. The crews will travel far afield if lodging can be arranged.

Business operation The firm works predominantly in Pennsylvania, northern Maryland, and eastern New York. Write for a brief brochure outlining its services, then follow up with a phone call or letter to make specific inquiries. With most serious restoration work, extensive consultation is required before any work begins.

Restoration Materials
Renovation Products
5302 Junius
Dallas, TX 75214
(214) 827-5111

In the mail-order business since 1981, this firm manufactures its own Victorian "gingerbread" and has started to make turned posts, doors, and a variety of mouldings. Other items included in its catalog are corbels, switchplates, fence pickets, ceiling medallions, Hi-Art steel ceilings, and Victorian park benches.

Business operation The company offers design services for clients who need advice on renovating Victorian homes and will

quote on custom woodwork jobs. The catalog, with updated inserts, is available for $2.

Restoration/Preservation Consultants
Preservation Resource Group, Inc. (PRG)
5619 Southampton Dr.
Springfield, VA 22151
(703) 323-1407

PRG is comprised of professionals in several housing and preservation fields, including structural engineers, historic architects, planners, and even chemists and education specialists. Together, they provide comprehensive restoration and preservation services on a consulting basis to individual homeowners, communities, schools, historical societies, and others. PRG began as an outlet for education on the subject and offers an extensive list of books, as well as several specialized tools, like three moisture meters ranging from $125 to $270.

Business operation Consultants in the group work nationally and internationally. One recently returned from a project in Peru, in fact. Write for PRG's interesting and select book list, its products bulletin, and information on services.

Structural Components

Architectural Antiques
The Architectural Antique Warehouse
PO Box 3065, Station D
Ottawa, ON
Canada K1P 6H6
(613) 562-1818

"All sorts of bits and pieces out of old houses," they say. Like what? Like stove pipe collars, shutters, gates, hinges, letter-slots, railings, mechanical bells, everything from a door knob to an entire house. The company will work with you, your architect, or your designer to meet restoration requirements. In addition, it can act as a consultant on renovation projects, supplying blueprints and job supervision.

Business operation   The Warehouse deals in house parts via mail order throughout Canada and the United States. Answers general inquiries with a one-page flyer.

Pricing   Item by item basis.

Evelyn Croton—Architectural Antiques
51 Eastwood La.
Valley Stream, NY 11581
(516) 791-4703

There are not many sources of old parts for old houses. This firm handles hand-carved acanthus leaf wood corbels, pilasters, door surroundings, door and door carvings, mantels, fretwork, terra-cotta keystones, iron and brass ornate register grills, and similar specialties. Each piece is sold as is, in the condition in which it was found on or in an old building. Carved corbels (brackets for roof overhangs) are the specialty.

Business operation   No catalogs are available, but very specific inquiries will be answered with photos of stock that might fill the bill. The firm sells wholesale to dealers, and retail via mail order.

Pricing   Item by item basis.

Olde Theatre Architectural Salvage
   Company
1309 Westport Rd.
Kansas City, MO 64111
(816) 931-0987

This firm deals in recycled building parts, particularly those of midwest origin. The proprietor, Patricia Shaughnessy, writes, "These artifacts are chosen as decorator items and because of the quality materials and craftsmanship not readily available today. The prices of recycled parts are one-quarter to one-third what they would cost new, if available." The firm handles interior and exterior woodwork of all kinds, railings, columns, doors, hardware, light fixtures, stonework, glass, and some very exotic items like complete commercial door fronts and metal elevator cages.

Business operation   Olde Theatre sells retail locally and through the mail, and also to builders, designers, decorators, and architects direct.

Pricing   All item by item. Write for quotes of specific pieces you are looking for.

The Wrecking Bar of Atlanta, Inc.
292 Moreland Ave. NE
Atlanta, GA 30307
(404) 525-0468

The Wrecking Bar's mission is to "rescue the past from the future," and it was created "solely for the preservation and restoration of this rich, ornamental, and decorative heritage." The Wrecking Bar has 18,000 sq ft on three levels to hold their $2 million inventory of wood carvings, brass and copper lanterns, mantels, andirons, wood brackets and capitals, paintings, posts and spindles, beveled, etched and stained glass, hardware, even carousel horses.

Business operation   No catalog is provided, because of inventory turnover. However, if you send them detailed requirements including dimensions, style, period, and general price range, the firm will provide photographs of several possibilities. The Wrecking Bar sells nationally through the mail and retail locally.

Architectural Antiques/Barn Beams

Dennis C. Walker Company
PO Box 309
Tallmadge, OH 44278
(216) 633-1081

This firm sells a wide selection of architectural antiques—things like door fronts, stained glass, stairway parts, and fencing—and a good selection of barn beams that are hand hewn, weathered, and sawn. As a matter of fact, it has most of the things you would find in the structure of a nineteenth-century building, including cut nails, roof slate, hand-cut barn stone, up to 50-ft lengths (incredible, yes) of major beams in poplar, oak, and chestnut 6 × 6's, and even up to 12 × 12's.

Business operation   Walker sells nationally by mail order, including complete barn frames, which can ring up substantial shipping charges. He will send you a brochure outlining the wood species, sizes, and other products in stock.

Pricing   Item by item basis. Write or call for quotes.

Architectural Ironwork

Architectural Iron Company
Box 674
Milford, PA 18337
(717) 296-7722
(212) 243-2664 (New York telephone number)

This company does custom casting, fabrication of ornamental ironwork, and restoration of ironwork. Donald G. Quick, the manager of the company's design and restoration services, has prepared an informative letter explaining in detail the kind of work they do, the differences between wrought iron, cast iron, combination work,

and more. You can write for it. At their shops and foundry in Pennsylvania, Architectural Iron is equipped to duplicate a small casting weighing only a few ounces (from a photograph), and to restore, and rebuild, to period detail where necessary, heavy cast fences where a single post may weigh a thousand pounds.

Business operation   Write or call for restoration details. The company's philosophy is interesting. Mr. Quick writes, "There is a reward in meeting people interested in preserving the past. We like to think our work has permanence, and we intend to remain small enough to deal with each project on an individual basis."

Chimney Relining

Energy House
PO Box 4035
Manchester, NH 03108
(603) 669-5136

One of three enterprises of Clifford Martel, who puts out the *Woodstove Directory*, this firm produces Z-Flex Stainless Flexible Chimney Liner, useful for safety's sake on any flue and particularly for relining crooked flues in older homes where straight pipe sections just will not work. Z-Flex components include mounting collars for masonry flue-top connections, length connectors, and T-sections, fireplace adaptors, all tied together with flexible flue that can be bent even to 90 degrees while remaining structurally sound and airtight. Standard 25-ft lengths are definitely workable by do-it-yourselfers who are comfortable working on the roof. The liner is recommended for use with all fuels except coal. Temperature resistance has been measured in excess of 2100 degrees F.

Business operation   Write for a brochure to the address above, which covers product details. The company should also be able to steer you to a retailer who handles their products in your area.

Connecticut Valley Millwork Reproductions
Architectural Components
PO Box 246
Leverett, MA 01054
(413) 549-1094

Architectural Components reproduces eighteenth- and nineteenth-century millwork from measured drawings and actual samples, particularly patterns common in Connecticut Valley architecture. It manufactures interior and exterior doors, small pane window sashes (like 12 over 12), and plank window frames, all made with mortise and tenon joints secured with square pegs. In addition to a modest line of stock items, the company does custom millwork, including raised panel walls, semicircular and elliptical fanlight sashes, and more. All material is kiln-dried eastern white pine finished with a hand plane.

Business operation A straightforward brochure is sent on request that shows typical details of construction. Prices are very reasonable.

Decorative Iron Fencing
1890 Iron Fence Company
PO Box 467
Auburn, IN 46706
(219) 925-4264

The 1890 Iron Fence Company builds only one kind of fence. Briefly, it is a narrow gauge iron picket with two horizontal rails. Every fourth upright has a distinctive three-ringed floral head, while the uprights on each side of it are closed across the top of the design to form a protective hoop. The effect is light, airy, decorative, and definitely Victorian. Stephen Anders, the proprietor, states that "this design was carefully chosen from historic examples and original catalogs. You will find it compatible with homes of every style from Queen Ann to a 1920s bungalow." Two heights, 40- and 72-in, are available in 6-ft-long sections. Fence pickets are ⅜-in mild steel, rails are ½- × 1½-in channel steel. Gates and monograms are available.

Business operation The firm sells via mail order and locally and will provide installation directions, which, as they say, are geared to the handyman homeowner or the local contractor. You can write for an illustrated brochure, a price list, and a well-organized planning sheet on which you use the graph layout and symbols provided to mark out exactly the layout you want.

Pricing Six-foot fence sections, including connecting braces and bolts, are $12 per foot; 3-ft-wide gates are about $90; gate end corner posts about $70. Standard paint is semigloss black enamel.

Doors/Fanlights/Palladian Windows
The Woodstone Company
PO Box 223
Patch Rd.
Westminster, VT 05158
(802) 722-4784

Woodstone produces architectural woodwork that includes several unique items. For instance, they manufacture fanlights and full palladian windows, weatherstripped in brass and bronze, all double glazed, surrounding pegged, mortise and tenon frame doors with a foam core. It is a real mix of old style design and craftsmanship and new energy-efficient features. But the nice part is you don't see the energy features. In mahogany or pine, Woodstone's doors range from 2-ft 6-in by 6-ft 8-in to 3-ft 2-in by 7-ft, all 1¾-in thick. (Costs range between $230 and $370.) The company does not have a set price list as much of their work is altered one way or another to suit individual client's needs. Woodstone also makes reproductions of period staircases, entrances, mantels, cabinetry, hundreds of moulding patterns, and turnings.

Business operation   Woodstone will send a modest package of brochures with representative prices on some of their stock items, plus several photographs so you can get a look at the quality work. They sell retail regionally, and will ship via mail order.

Hardwood Screen Doors

Creative Openings
PO Box 2566
Bellingham, WA 98227
(206) 671-7435

Creative Openings manufactures 21 styles of hardwood screen doors, some with filigree and fretwork particularly well suited to restoration work. A few double doors are included, with single doors designed with asymmetrical hoopwork, lattice weaves, fretwork combinations—all quite pleasing. Door frames are mortise and tenon, available in white oak, white ash, Honduras mahogany.

Business operation   Doors will be made to your measurements (check them several times to be sure you were right the first time), to swing in or out with left- or right-handed hinges.

Pricing   Costs range from about $250 to $500. All doors are supplied with brass hardware and screening. Crated doors weigh about 100 lb.

Leaded Stained Glass

J & R Lamb Studios
30 Joyce Dr.
Spring Valley, NY 10977
(914) 352-3777

An established company (since 1857), this firm makes leaded stained glass windows of all descriptions. About 90 percent of their jobs call for custom design. They have designed approximately 10,000 windows for buildings in all parts of North America. Also, they provide complete restoration and have worked for The Metropolitan Museum of Art in New York. They are approved for restoration work by the National Trust for Historic Preservation. They can create small medallion insets or giant murals in stained glass.

Business operation   Lamb's will send you their new, stained-glass window brochure at no charge. Also, ask for their information sheet detailing their restoration and preservation services. Their minimum order is $150. They have business representatives locally, in Houston, New Orleans, Charlottesville, Detroit, Miami, and Springfield, Massachusetts. Their color brochure is a stunner.

Tin Ceilings

W. F. Norman Corporation
PO Box 323
214–32 N. Cedar St.
Nevada, MO 64772
(800) 641-4038
(417) 667-5552 (Missouri residents call collect)

Norman is one of the prime sources for metal ceiling, siding, and roofing materials. They have been producing their many patterns since 1908, and offer several lines now that they offered then. This makes them an ideal source for restorers. And this is really different than going to a company that has gone to great pains to recapture authentic designs. Norman's catalog is 70 pages of authentic designs. The W. F. Norman catalog costs $3, covers installation methods, single squares, large panels, center medallions, corner miters, mouldings, cornices, all in floral (almost florid) Victorian designs. Also, Norman makes several varieties of metal shingles, some simulating Spanish tile, mission tile, plus decorative trimmings.

Business operation Mark S. Quito of Norman writes, "At any stage of pattern selection, design layout, or installation, we will gladly help anyone with their questions." The company sells nationwide. Call for referrals to retail outlets or order direct.

Interior Specialties

Antique Lighting
St. Louis Antique Lighting Company
PO Box 8146
St. Louis, MO 63156
(314) 535-2770

The St. Louis Company manufactures solid brass reproductions of antique lighting fixtures, including chandeliers, table lamps, and wall sconces. They also restore antique light fixtures and do custom design work.

Business operation Their extensive catalog is available for $3, includes complete prices, and full-page black and whites of the fixtures that show exactly what you're getting. For restoration buffs, you may be interested in the daisy ruffle and diamond daisy glass shades, two sizes of snowflake shades, elegant satin floral and basket-weave shades, off-center, single-fixture chandeliers, and a few truly incredible designs such as a cast bronze "lily lamp," with the base of a water lily, complete with bronze stems climbing the lamp stem to end in small leaves. Their catalog is blunt about this remarkable product: "These lamps are individually cast, signed, and numbered. They are such a pain in the neck to make that we make as few as possible. Call or write for details." An amazing collection all around, expensive ($36 for a satin floral glass shade) with some fixtures like the more elaborate chandeliers running to $500 and above. Stunning nonetheless; worth a look, although the $3 will keep some people away, I'm afraid.

Architectural Plaster Ornaments
Dovetail, Inc.
PO Box 1569
Lowell, MA 01853
(617) 454-2944

Plaster ornamentation, in all shapes and sizes, in the center of ceilings, at the edges, on porches, used to be moulded as the ceilings and walls were plastered. In many homes in which some of this fine detail work has decayed, repair and restoration can be time consuming and quite costly. And in homes where complete replacements or completely new designs are wanted, much of the work is being replaced with moulded plastic simulations. However, Dovetail has a reasonable, interesting answer between these two extremes. Working with U.S. Gypsum, they developed a fiber-glassed reinforced cement plaster that acts like plaster in a mould but is stronger and lighter. Also, it does not sustain combustion and will not, as most plastic will, add toxic fumes to a fire. Using this material, Dovetail, makes moulds, and hand casts some seventy items, ranging from elaborate center medallions and corner blocks to complete ceiling patterns. Installation is accomplished by laying contact cement on the back of the piece and securing it with screws through a thin flange attached ot the sculpture. When all pieces are in place, a final skim coat of plaster is added to the ceiling, covering the flange. It is a system that combines improvements in technology without sacrificing detail and craftsmanship.

Business operation Sells via mail order and does custom work and repair. Write for illustrated catalog, free on request.

Colonial Hardware

Acorn Manufacturing Company, Inc.
PO Box 31
Mansfield, MA 02048
(617) 339-4500

Acorn forge has been producing Colonial builders hardware, decorative hardware, fireplace equipment, and similar items for about thirty-five years. Their wide selection that includes cabinet latches, door and drawer pulls, strap hinges, H and H-L hinges, thumb latches, and more, is generally available in four different finishes: hand-wrought black iron, pewter finish, antique copper, or antique brass. Most of their pieces can be purchased with plain or forged edges.

Business operation Robert M. DeLong, Acorn's president, writes, "If consumers are unable to purchase through a local retailer, they may order direct from the factory at the suggested retail." A complete catalog is available with a price list.

Colonial Joinery

Maurer & Shepherd Joyners, Inc.
122 Naubuc Ave.
Glastonbury, CT 06033
(203) 633-2383

This firm makes high quality, custom reproductions of Colonial millwork—items like raised panel doors that are clinch nailed to beaded batten boards; carved rosettes; complete raised panel walls; fireplace mantels, wainscoting, and more. All its woodwork is hand planed and joined with mortise and tenon construction pinned with square pegs. It has made complete door surrounds and elaborate corner cabinets with cockleshell and barrel-backed bolection moulding.

Business operation Write for a brief brochure. Send plans and specs for price quotes.

Colonial Rim Locks

Colonial Lock Company
172 Main St.
Terryville, CT 06786

Colonial makes a variety of rim locks, those flat-cased, rectangular locks still found on older buildings in New England. It has updated them somewhat and manufactures one rim lock with a hardened steel bolt throw, 1½-in wide and ½-in thick, with one inch of travel. The case measures 2⅝-in × 3¾-in × ⅞-in thick. It also makes essentially the same lock in a solid maple case.

Business operation Colonial will send you a flyer briefly describing these products and will include information on The Lock Museum of America, a modest building up the street from Colonial that houses a collection of rare and antique locks from many manufacturers. It offers membership in the museum for $5, or, for $15, membership plus a book (normally $12.50) called *Early Locks and Lockmakers of America.* If you are interested in lock collecting, auctions, etc., write to the president of Colonial, T. F. Hennessy, who is also the president and curator of the museum.

Pricing Colonials rim locks range from $20 to $25.

Color Quality
Munsell Color
2441 N. Calvert St.
Baltimore, MD 21218
(301) 243-2171

Munsell color books are used extensively by science and industry as a tool in color quality control and are also used by artists, decorators, and others because of their three-dimensional color wheel (really an ingenious way of expressing color chroma, hue, and value). Also, Munsel offers several special services, including the production of special colors, educational materials, and more. A unique way to color match virtually any shade of any color.

Custom Hardware
Steve Kayne Hand Forged Hardware
17 Harmon Place
Smithtown, NY 11787
(516) 724-3669

Steve Kayne does hand forging and fabrication of iron work to custom specifications and from photos or even rough sketches of original pieces. He will repair or restore pieces as well. He carries a stock line of custom forged builders hardware (house hardware) that includes kitchen and fireplace equipment.

Business operation Steve Kayne offers two different catalogs (each for $2 or $3.50 for both), one on Colonial hardware containing an amazing array of tin lanterns, candleholders, brass bells, door knockers, bolts, small animal sculptures, hinges, and more. The second catalog, *Hand Forged Hardware*, contains some door hardware and a full selection of fireplace tools and equipment. A short but entertaining and informative booklet on blacksmithing by Kayne, titled *Get It Hot and Hit It!* (also $2), might be a nice way to find out about the basics of the craft.

Pricing Item by item basis.

Early American Lighting Fixtures
The Saltbox
2229 Marietta Pike
Lancaster, PA 17603
(717) 392-5649

The Saltbox makes authentic reproductions of a variety of lighting fixtures, including post lanterns in antique brass, tin and brass chandeliers, and many different lanterns and wall sconces. Most chandeliers are available either electrified or ready for candles. In total it offers some 250 different styles, all handcrafted, from a 3½-in × 3½-in × 12-in lantern to an 18½-in × 18½-in × 40-in post light.

Business operation Its retail store in Lancaster is open from 10:00 until 4:30 Wednesday through Saturday, or by appointment. Write for an illustrated catalog showing a selection of items. Ask for a price list. Delivery is made approximately six weeks after an order is placed.

Firebacks and Hearth Accessories

A. E. S. Firebacks
334 Grindstone Hill Rd.
North Stonington, CT 06359
(203) 535-2253

A. E. S. offers a limited selection of cast iron firebacks, all reproductions of seventeenth- and eighteenth-century originals. Mr. Singer manufactures these firebacks the way they used to be made—by hand carving a hardwood pattern, pressing it into sand to form a mould, and pouring molten iron into the mould. Designs range from a perching rooster on Chippendale scrolls to very simple motifs such as a small, raised heart shape taken from a gravestone design. Sizes range from about 24-in × 20-in to 20-in × 17-in. Weight is between 40 and 55 lb per fireback, heavy enough to absorb significant amounts of heat, protect mortar and brick, and radiate heat into the room.

Business operation Write for the A. E. S. brochure, which includes photographs, notes on historic origin, shipping and price information.

Pricing Although many firebacks may be produced from a single pattern carving, I feel the prices are low, ranging from $70 to $85 at this writing. Considering the size and weight of each piece, it is remarkable that the price includes shipping and handling. A. E. S. does want an extra $10 for delivery west of the Mississippi.

Pennsylvania Firebacks, Inc.
1011 E. Washington La.
Philadelphia, PA 19138
(215) 843-6162

A fireback is a cast iron plate that is leaned against or fixed to the back wall of a fireplace. Introduced in Europe in the fifteenth century, the decorated plate preserves the masonry (particularly the mortar) from heat decay, and increases heat radiation from the fire. Pennsylvania Firebacks makes a stunning presentation of its products in a small package that is more like a lengthy, personalized invitation than an advertisement. Its president, Terry Polis, writes, "It is a collection of unique, hard-to-find products that reflect America's rich craft heritage. We have brought together, with a personal touch, the work of independent artisans from across the country." An example: four sizes of hearth brooms (with natural handles left in the shape they had on the tree, sweeps made from the tassel of broom corn plants and hand tied, and information on their origin) are hand made by the Gates family in Asheville, North Carolina. The craftsmanship is exceptional. Other accessories include bellows, foot scrapers, lanterns, and tinware. Several firebacks are offered, including a sun face design and a field of stars. Sizes run about 18 in × 20 in. Weight is about 40 lb. Fireboards (decorative wood covers for flueless chimneys) are offered with different primitive style paintings on the faces (a Shaker tree of life, a southern plantation, for example). Custom painting from your sketch or photograph can be arranged.

Business operation The firm sells nationally, wholesale to dealers and retail through the mail. Write for current price list and exceptional catalog.

Gold Leaf

M. Swift & Sons, Inc.
10 Love Lane
PO Box 150
Hartford, CT 06141
(203) 522-1181

Gold leaf, that is, real gold leaf, is not a material you need very much of or very often unless you're in the business. Consequently, there are very few sources of old-fashioned, hand-beaten gold leaf. Swift has been making it this way for almost one hundred years. It sells to decorators, sign painters, furniture repairmen and manufacturers, museums, and others, including the firm that leafed the Connecticut state capitol dome. Swift also makes hot die stamping foils.

Business operation Swift has produced an informative booklet, *A Guide to Genuine Gold Leaf Application*, which explains the different purity grades (by the karat, just like jewelry), how leaf is sold (by the "book"; 25 3⅜-in × 3⅜-in sheets), how to gild on glass, wood, and other applications. The company responds to all inquiries from the Hartford office, or one of their branches in Glendale, California; St. Louis, Missouri; and Chicago, Illinois.

Hand-Planed Restoration Millwork
Piscatiaqua Architectural Woodwork
  Company
Bagdad Rd.
Durham, NH 03824
(603) 868-2663

The tools used here, and the method of manufacturing, are as interesting as the products. Original seventeenth- and eighteenth-century hardwood moulding planes are used to turn out a variety of Colonial, Georgian, and early Federal-style millwork, including cornice mouldings, architraves, baseboards, chair rails, and picture frame moulding. Ten styles are in stock, all made of New Hampshire white pine.

Business operation Owner Malcolm MacGregor states, "We can reproduce almost any eighteenth-century profile, with no minimum footage, and no set-up charge. We also make raised panel interior and exterior doors, shutters, and any other architectural

woodwork from cupboards to entire rooms," Restoraiton consulting services are offered.

Pricing Work is sold by the linear foot: from 90¢ for small, ovolo and ogee backbands to $3.50 for a complete architrave. Custom orders are quoted on request. Serious inquiries are answered with an illustrated flyer, price list, and silhouette drawings of stock items and combinations.

Hardware—Lamp Parts
Paxton Hardware Company
Upper Falls, MD 21156
(301) 592-8505

Paxton's hardware catalog covers many varieties of Chippendale and Hepplewhite pulls, Victorian pulls and knobs and keyhole escutcheons, hinges, castors, and catches—a full complement of restoration furniture hardware. Also, Paxton has 10-plus pages of lamp parts and glass shades, a good selection of slightly oddball wiring pipe stems, and arm clusters and such that are difficult to find in hardware stores or electrical supply outlets.

Business operation Paxton ships nationally. The catalog is sent on request. Minimum order is $10.

Hardware—Millwork
Restoration Hardware
438 Second St.
Eureka, CA 95501
(707) 443-3152

Restoration Hardware is a national mail-order firm with a catalog (36 pages for $3 refunded on initial order) that covers a lot of ground: brass hardware, plumbing and lighting fixtures, millwork, switchplates, and the like. The Houseparts catalog is a nice, if concise, collection of restoration products.

Hardware—Sundries

Restoration Works, Inc.
412½ Virginia St.
Buffalo, NY 14201
(716) 882-5000

Restoration Works' mail-order catalog has a limited selection covering several areas: brass rim locks, wrought-iron hardware and hinges, Victorian turn bells, and many specialty items like solid brass door kickplates, marble mantels, a few security devices, energy-saving gadgets, and more.

Business operation   For $2, I would like to see a little more than 30 very uncrowded pages of products, particularly when the scope is so broad. But it does carry several items that are difficult to locate.

Lighting/Structural Antiques

Rejuvenation House Parts Company
901 N. Skidmore
Portland, OR 97217
(503) 249-0774

The Rejuvenation mail-order catalog consists almost entirely of antique lighting fixtures and shades and lamp parts. But they also carry ten patterns of anaglypta, a Victorian wall covering made of heavy, embossed paper that is quite difficult to find. Typically, it was painted and then glossed with shellac to resemble tooled leather. Two floral patterns of supaglypta, a heavier covering made of cotton fibers, are also available. All patterns come in 33-ft rolls 20½ in wide and cover 50 to 55 sq ft.

Business operation Relocated now at larger facilities, Rejuvenation sells many architectural antiques and light fixtures locally as well. The illustrated, comprehensive catalog for mail order is $2.

Materials/Fixtures

Remodelers' & Renovators' Supply
611 E. 44th St.
Boise, ID 83704
(208) 377-5465

This strictly mail-order firm offers a catalog for $2 that covers a lot of territory. A quick tour includes storm lamps, architectural antiques, beveled and stained glass, chimney pots, firebacks, oak and wicker furniture, tin ceilings, weather vanes, and more. The catalog is well-illustrated with about 20 pages of photographs and artwork showing details of door hardware, fretwork, and the like.

Period Building Supplies

Renovation Concepts, Inc.
PO Box 3720
Minneapolis, MN 55403
(612) 377-9526

Renovation Concepts represents themselves, and forty other manufacturers who make period lighting fixtures, moulding, brass rail, metal ceilings, wood columns, plumbing fixtures, beveled glass, and more. Many of these firms are listed in this sourcebook, but not all of them. The idea is to have a single source of supply for all the different materials you might need to restore or faithfully renovate an older house.

Business operation Renovation Concepts will provide its professional, three-ring-type catalog for $10 and a condensed, consumer retail catalog for $5. Many of the pages may be obtained direct from the manufacturers of course, some at no charge. But this firm also offers free consultation service and has an architect and a renovation contractor on staff to answer your questions about products and their applications. It will send a small brochure free. Catalog costs are refundable with your first order.

Porcelain Reglazing

Tennessee Tub
905 Church St.
Nashville, TN 37203
(615) 242-0780

This firm has been collecting cast iron, roll rimmed, porcelain glazed tubs that have been junked because they are scratched, stained, or just seemed out of date to the people who used them. It also has a collection of pedestal lavatory sinks and pull-chain toilets. So now, a lot of people who have discovered the soundness and wonderful detailing of older homes and who want to restore rather than modernize can get these fixtures back from Tennessee Tub, completely reglazed. The firm will refinish your old fixtures in white, will match the colors available from any major plumbing manufacturer, or will even have an artist inscribe the finish to your specifications. You can get your old fixture to Tennessee Tub (shipping costs can be prohibitive here), or order one of its old fixtures reglazed.

Business operation The company carries Chicago Faucets Renaissance Collection (50¢ for this brochure of porcelain handle fittings). If you send them $1 and a description of the fixture you want, the firm will match it against its stock and send you a photograph of what it comes up with.

Pricing The service is expensive: between $45 and $175 for one of its tubs; $450 to reglaze it in white, pastels, or beiges ($50 to $75 more for dark tones); and $150 for crating; plus shipping. Write for a complete price list, including specs for an array of decorative tub legs.

Reproduction Hardware

Newton Millham-Star Forge
672 Drift Rd.
Westport, MA 02790
1 (617) 636-5437

This blacksmith offers a selection of seventeenth- and eighteenth-century hardware, including bolts and latches, hinges, shutter dogs, and ironware cooking utensils. A complete illustrated catalog will be sent for $1 to cover costs.

Reproduction Mouldings and Woodwork

Turnbull's Custom Mouldings
Box 602
Sumner, MI 48889
(517) 833-7089

Turnbull's specialty is duplicating any wood moulding from a small sample or measured drawing you send them—an invaluable service for restorers who reluctantly must do away with damaged or rotting woodwork and want to do a lot better than a pine clamshell replacement. Turnbull maintains a limited stock of coves, chair rails, and such and sells select hardwood and softwood lumber with custom milling and planing.

Business operation Turnbull's sells nationally, mainly by mail. Write for an illustrated brochure of stock silhouettes and prices. Write or call to come to terms on duplicating services.

Reproduction Wood Mouldings
Silverton Victorian Mill Works
Box 877
Silverton, CO 81433
(303) 387-5716

Silverton is a relatively new, expanding millwork firm offering a thorough selection of Victorian mouldings in kiln-dried oak, pine, or redwood. Items include baseboard, ceiling cornice, decorative siding, door and window casing, drip cap, wainscot, headblocks for door trim, chair rail, grooved plate rail, and ornamental brackets. Mouldings are shipped in random lengths from 5 to 12 ft unless specified otherwise.

Business operation For $3 Silverton will send a 35-page catalog illustrated with profiles, section views, and dimensions of all items. Sample packages containing most of its stock blocks, and mouldings are sold for $12, which includes UPS and handling.

Pricing Ranges from under 50¢ per linear foot for plain quarter and half rounds in pine (about 50 percent more in oak), to over $3 for oak window sills. Decorative Victorian rosette head and base blocks for door and window trim are $6 in pine to $10 in 1 1/16-in thick oak.

Restoration Lighting Fixtures
Alcon Lightcraft Company
1424 W. Alabama
Houston, TX 77007
(713) 526-0680

Alcon's brochure shows a small sampling of its Victorian lamp fixtures. All are polished and lacquered brass with (at least in the brochure) tulip-shaped, milk glass shades. Selling mostly to restorers and restauranteurs, Alcon has now assembled a catalog showing homeowners its wares. Although it carries many stock items, most of its work is custom, done to specifications. It also carries antique lamps and lamp parts. All wiring, minus bulbs, is included, and the fixtures are set up to mount to modern electrical boxes.

Business operation Alcon sells wholesale, retail locally in Houston, and via mail order. Write for ordering instructions (no CODs or personal checks) and a complete price list.

Pricing Starting at approximately $60 for wall sconces, its curly arm (it does a 360 running from the brass wall plate to the tulip shade), is currently $57.50. Two-pole, curly arm ceiling fixtures are about $125. Larger, four-pole ceiling fixtures are $225 and up.

Roy Electric Company, Inc.
1054 Coney Island Ave.
Brooklyn, NY 11230
(212) 339-6311

Roy Electric are licensed electrical contractors working in the New York City area, particularly on older brownstones and other homes where the wiring and the fixtures require special skills. Over the years they have accumulated a stock of antique lamps, gas, oil, and early electric fixtures with sconces, brackets, and unusual pieces of fixture art. These fixtures are restored in the shop and sold, mostly to decorators, contractors, and the like, but also to the public.

Business operation Roy sells wholesale, retail locally, and via mail order. They will supply an illustrated catalog showing dozens of fixtures, and will answer questions on the phone.

Restoration Materials

Kingsway
4723 Chromium Dr.
Colorado Springs, CO 80918
(303) 599-4512

Kingsway offers several related services: furniture stripping and repairing, cane weaving, upholstering, how-to classes on refinishing, written moving damage estimates on antiques (all locally), and a national mail-order service covering Victorian restoration materials. The catalog includes a moderately thorough selection of brass hardware, decorative mouldings, turnings, and stair parts, door and window casing (including five different styles of bull's eye corner block and one in a nice daisy-wheel pattern), wainscot cap, astragals and other panel moulding, plaster cornice and capitals, plus two very nice, heavy, anaglypta papers. One is a flowing but sparse floral pattern; the other a highly moulded box pattern resembling tin ceiling motifs. I received two substantial samples of the anaglypta papers with the catalog, priced at about $13 and $20 (depending on pattern) for rolls of about 58 sq ft.

Business operation Kingsway, which is able to come up with special items on inquiry, is worth a visit locally. The catalog is, at this point, sent at no cost on request.

Restoration Mouldings/Hardware Specialties

San Francisco Victoriana
2245 Palou Ave.
San Francisco, CA 94124
(415) 648-0313

San Francisco Victoriana produces a large selection of restoration mouldings in clear redwood, moulding-grade pine, in random lengths from 6 to 14 ft, including picture rail, headblock, crown, astragal, cove, nosing, etc. It also carries a good selection of ornamental plaster, from small, 5½-in acanthus leaf shapes (about $25) to 38-in diameter, high-relief Elizabeth center medallions (an incredible piece with four fully sculpted heads centering the leaf and flower pattern). This firm is one of the few carrying anaglypta (embossed wall covering) in thirteen patterns with eight different borders in rolls from 3 to 14 in wide. In addition to this, the firm handles a nice line of fireplace mantels, Victorian light fixtures and glass shades, and an amazing array of ornate door and window hardware, including hinges, knobs, and keyhole escutcheons, all deeply sculpted and replicating some of the most unusual mass produced hardware made in this country between 1870 and 1915.

Business operation Complete catalogs are $3; free in the company's showroom. Sample packets of wallcoverings can be ordered. Also, this firm handles the Steptoe cast iron spiral stair; a classic.

Restoration Plumbing Fixtures

S. Chris Rheinschild
2220 Carlton Way
Santa Barbara, CA 93109
(805) 962-8598

This firm provides a limited line of restoration plumbing products, including two wood tank toilets (one high, one low), bath sinks, hand-made, 48-oz copper kitchen sinks, a 64-in long copper bathtub, and six different types of faucets, including the classic Chicago J-spout tub faucet.

Business operation Rheinschild will send a well-illustrated catalog to you for $1.35: a nice layout, with one or two large product pictures per page, and a friendly, no-nonsense explanation. Price list is included. Additionally, the firm is ready to respond to your questions on antique plumbing.

Pricing Oak cabinet high and low tank toilets, with accessories, are in the $400 range; the 22-in × 32-in × 6-in copper kitchen sink (unfinished and without faucets or drain) is $275; brass basin faucets start at about $50.

Stenciling

Timeless Patterns
465 Colrain Rd.
Greenfield, MA 01301
(413) 774-5742

What can you do with the bare walls of a 200-year-old house when restoration wallpaper is too expensive and may be too difficult for you to put up in any case? Cynthia Nims, the proprietor of Timeless Patterns, solved her problem with stenciling. She writes, "The results were astounding. (Keeping my kids off the ladder was another matter.) Stenciling became a much loved hobby which eventually grew into a business. I focused my attention on presenting complete room designs which eliminate guesswork and save many hours of your time." Her stencils are presented uncut on polyester film. The tracings can be cut out or simply transferred to the wall. Patterns are taken from stencils that have survived painting, wallpaper, and wallboard for 150 years or so. The patterns can be used on bare plaster, fabric, painted woodwork, and other surfaces.

Business operation Timeless Patterns' catalog is in the form of a long letter from the owner, with several color prints of completed stencils in furnished rooms. It is warm, conversational, and informative—a unique presentation. The catalog (for $3)

includes order forms for red sable painting brushes and comprehensive instructions.

Pricing 18-in × 26-in sheets of carbon transfer paper are 95¢ each. Stencil film (7½ in × 16 in, 14 in × 11 in and other sizes that include a complete pattern before repetition) range from $8 to $16 depending on size and complexity.

Victorian Bath Fixtures

Environmental Restoration & Design
(ERD)
2140 San Pablo Ave.
Berkeley, CA 94702
(415) 548-3967

ERD manufactures period bath fixtures slip cast by hand in porcelain vitreous china. It has the capacity to custom design or match a design in any porcelain product. ERD's catalog includes pedestal basins, pill toilets, and soap dishes. It is a limited stock line.

Business operation ERD's. catalog is sent on request with care and cleaning instructions and prices.

Pricing Small soap dishes are about $20; a self-rimming scalloped sink, $120; a pedestal sink, $400.

Victorian Millwork

Mad River Woodworks
4935 Boyd Rd.
PO Box 163
Arcata, CA 95521
(707) 826-0629

Mad River makes reproductions of Victorian millwork, including screen doors, fret and grillwork, brackets, corbels, stair balusters, ornamnetal shingles and fence pickets, and a variety of trim. It will provide a catalog on request.

Business operation　Mad River ships nationwide. You may see its ads in *Victorian Homes* and *Old-House Journal*, two of the most prominent Victorian-era proponents.

Remodeling

Cabinets

Quaker Maid, Division Tappan
Rte. 61
Leesport, PA 19533
(215) 926-3011

Quaker Maid has been in the custom cabinet business for over thirty years. They make kitchen cabinets, vanities, and a relatively new line of custom furniture. Many styles and sizes are available, but the distinguishing characteristic of Quaker Maid is the ingenious storage systems behind the cabinet doors. They have corner revolving trays, pullout storage bins and work surfaces, storage shelves that have storage shelves behind them that swivel, and a lot more space-saving hardware.

Business operation　Quaker Maid sells direct from the factory through over 700 distributors nationwide. They advertise through the Yellow Pages, or you can write or call Leesport for the dealer nearest you. They will send you several pieces of literature on request, but for planning purposes, get, at least, two of them: Cabinet Specification & Accessory Guide, and Convenience & Decorator Features. Their booklet, "Fact Tag," lists construction specs: 45-degree interlocked miter at corners, ⅝-in thick shelving, hand-rubbed finish, and more goodies.

Colonial Millwork

Michael's Fine Colonial Products
Rte. 44 RD 1
Box 179A
Salt Point, NY 12578
(914) 677-3960

This small firm specializes in sash windows suited for restoration projects and a variety of mouldings. Most of its millwork is custom made. Its 1⅜-in white pine, double hung sash (supplied open or glazed) is sold in 1/1, 2/2, 6/6, 6/9, 8/8, 8/12, and 12/12 (denoting individual panes in top and bottom sash, respectively). The 1/1 sash is available with double glazing. Other work includes fixed-slat shutters, raised panel cabinet doors, octagon windows, and stair parts.

Business operation　For price quote send a sample or drawing with measurements, and specify quantity, size, kind of material (oak, pine, walnut, poplar, etc.). For moulding quote, specify lengths. The company sells nationally.

Pricing　1–0 × 3–2, 1/1 sash sells for about $25. The largest unit, a 3–0 × 5–10, 6/6 sash is about $70. Special orders can be made using 1¾- and 2¼-in stock. Send SASE for complete price list and rudimentary catalog.

Custom Millwork/Woodworking

Carpenter Associates, Inc.
Timber Swamp Rd.
Hampton, NH 03842
1 (603) 926-3801

Carpenter Associates is a custom architectural millwork shop that also is able to provide design, building, and installation services. Working largely on word of mouth recommendations for the past 16 years, the firm is now completing a brochure describing its services. You can write for it. The firm works with architects and directly with clients to authentically reproduce almost any piece of woodwork and to design and install complete kitchen cabinets and interiors. It maintains a library on historical architecture and can construct interiors to period style.

Business operation Generally, the firm works regionally. Write for quotes and travel limits.

Insulation

Owens-Corning Fiberglas Corporation
Fiberglas Tower
Toledo, OH 43659
(419) 248-8000

One of the largest insulation manufacturers, Owens-Corning, quite naturally, has, pushed more insulation as the be-all and end-all, *the* way to save energy dollars. But not everyone needs more insulation. If you live in a northern climate and have in the neighborhood of 6 inches in the attic, but no storm windows, more insulation is probably not the cost-effective answer. Remember, the first inch of insulation saves more energy than the second, that one saves more than the third, and so on; the law of diminishing returns, as every inch costs the same. Within this common sense framework, adding some insulation when you have none or only a little is essential. Owens-Corning has extensive literature that tell you how. Their basic product line is as follows: batts in 48- and 98-in lengths and 16- and 24-in widths, in thickness to give up to an R-38 rating; polyisocyanurate foam sheathing (no formaldehyde here); pouring wool; blowing wool (usually reserved for contractor installations); pipe wrap; grid ceiling systems; flexible ducting, and fiber glass mat roofing shingles (all have a Class A fire rating).

Business operation Owens-Corning materials are sold through most lumber yards and building supply outlets. You can find them almost everywhere, along with extensive, generally high quality consumer information, or you can write for free booklets and brochures from the headquarters if not available locally.

Masonry Fabric

Flexi-Wall Systems
101 Carolina Ave.
PO Box 88
Liberty, SC 29657
(803) 855-0500

This unique product is a patented, flexible, gypsum-impregnated, jute fabric wallcovering that resembles thick, open-weave wallpaper with a masonry base. It can be used in a one-step application over concrete or block foundation walls in a basement, over drywall, over chipped and deteriorating plaster, and even directly over old paneling. The material has passed rigid fire and toxicity tests required by the New York City Buildings Department (just about the most rigid codes going), and has a Class A flame spread rating under ASTM. The material is applied with special Flexi-Wall adhesive, and generally follows procedures similar to the application of conventional wallcovering. Many color tones are available.

Business operation Flexi-Wall is sold through national distributors such as Sherwin-Williams (you should be able to get product information at its dealers) and retail direct. The company will send catalogs and a price list to consumers at no charge.

Pricing Flexi-Wall is sold in 40 sq yd rolls, in three different jute weaves, for about $5.30 per sq yd. Shipping weight is 55 lb per roll.

Stair Components

Mansion Industries, Inc.
14711 E. Clark
Industry, CA 91745
(213) 968-9501

Mansion tries to work around the problem that each stairway installation is a little different from all others by providing a line of stair component parts, including a wide selection of turned posts and spindles, railings, finials, balusters, and a series of shelf and room divider components. The flexibility of this system is based on a clever idea. Top and bottom rails (the balusters in Mansion's many systems do not attach to stair treads) are set parallel to each other within posts. Under normal circumstances balusters would have to be carefully cut with angles at both ends to get a good fit. But Mansion's balusters end in a small horizontal cylinder—like a dowel set at right angles to the upright baluster—which slides in sideways to corresponding holes in the railings. Since the dowels and holes are round, the angle between baluster and rail is not a problem.

Business operation Stair components in clear, kiln-dried hemlock are sold in small component groups at home centers and other building material retailers. The company will provide descriptive product literature on request. Its installation manuals are quite thorough and well illustrated.

Stair Stringer Hardware

United Stairs Corporation
Hwy. 35
Keyport, NJ 07735
(201) 583-1100

United makes wood stairs, railings, and stair parts. One of its systems, called E-Z Rail, made for do-it-yourself remodeling projects, uses a system of U-shaped top and bottom rails into which balusters can be set at any angle. Then small snap-on trim pieces cover up the spaces between balusters, giving the appearance of a solid rail with conventional balusters. In addition to 360- and 180-degree spiral stairs, United carries a stock of starting steps (scrolled, half circled, etc. to conform to different landing designs) and many sizes and shapes of balusters, nosings, and rails. Finally, it carries an ingenious stair tread hardware system imported from England called Turbo. (That seems to be the new hot word in marketing.) An ideal way for do-it-yourselfers to fasten treads to stringers, it consists of a series of brackets made of mild steel in a crimped U-shape, into which wooden treads are slipped. The bracket is rated to approximately three tons of load-bearing capacity. While this device provides all the structural strength you could possibly need and makes installation strictly a matter of proper layout, it doesn't look very good until the moulded polypropylene sleeve is fitted around the bracket. And this sleeve is a little weird up close. It is plastic after all. But against a dark wood, and from a distance, the effect is no more obtrusive than a few strips of quarter round.

Business operation United will respond to inquiries with a brochure at no cost. It sells retail and direct to builders.

Wall Pattern Printers

Rollerwall, Inc.
PO Box 757
Silver Spring, MD 20901
(301) 649-4422

Rollerwall tools provide an interesting alternative to painting and wallpapering. In essence, the system works just like a commercial wallpaper printer, i.e., the pattern is raised on a metal roller that rests next to a feeder roller. As the raised portions of the metal roller (holding the pattern) contact the feeder, they pick up paint or other colorants, and lay the pattern on the wall.

Business operation   Rollerwall has dozens of different patterns and will send you a brochure, free, illustrating the styles, and the two different types of applicators. They sell nationally via mail order.

Pricing   The basic, double-roller applicator is about $15; the same configuration with an integral container for colorant (so you can stay on the wall longer without going back and forth to the supply) is about $30. Raised pattern rollers are $12 each.

TRADE ASSOCIATIONS

Paint and Stain Use

National Paint and Coatings Association
1500 Rhode Island Ave. NW
Washington, DC 20005
(202) 462-6272

This trade association is in business to further the uses and applications of paints and stains. In addition to providing magazine stories, news releases, and other materials to editors, the association will send consumers a series of information booklets (for 50¢ and an SASE). The booklets are informative and contain many specific hints and do-it-yourself tips. However, try to track down a copy of the *Household Paint Selector*, a well-illustrated and very informative book the association prepared and sold through Harper & Row Publishers.

GOVERNMENT AGENCIES

Home Weatherization

Department of Energy
Division of Weatherization Assistance
    Programs
(202) 252-2207

The Weatherization Assistance Program provides low-income households with help in energy conservation. To date, about 1.3 million homes have had some form of weatherization improvement under this program, and the DOE estimates the savings that result are the equivalent of some 4.8 million barrels of fuel oil a year.

Business operation   Write the above address for information on eligibility and application instructions. Applications are granted according to a priority rating system based on need and whether the applicant is handicapped or elderly. Much of the work done is caulking and insulating. Other work includes furnace upgrading, installing vapor barriers, clock thermostats, water heater insulation, and the like. The maximum expenditure per household is generally $1000.

Restoration Contracting/Training

Restoration Workshop, National Trust for
Historic Preservation
635 S. Broadway
Tarrytown, NY 10591
(914) 631-6696

In addition to doing careful, documented restoration work, Restoration Workshop is the only arm of the National Historic Trust (the only private, nonprofit organization chartered by Congress to encourage preservation of sites, buildings, and objects significant in American history), that provides full-time apprentice training in restoration crafts. To help support their organization, the workshop does a variety of restoration contracting—on buildings, churches, old waterwheels, and more—for a price, as private contractors would. They have done work for the National Park Service, and National Trust member organizations from Massachusetts to South Carolina. They work predominantly for these groups, private owners of landmark houses and registered properties, although under the constraints of a limited budget they just may be able to find something historically interesting about your old house. It's worth a try, anyway. Be advised that they are not cheap. The crew, currently, consists of a workshop director, foreman, and seven apprentices. They expect to have more openings soon, and accept people committed to restoration with at least one year in the building trades. They stay one to three years receiving on-the-job training, education, and a salary. Their small shop also turns out a modest amount of millwork. Write for free brochures describing the workshop, and, if interested, details about the apprentice training program. A unique source.

CONSUMER EDUCATION

Information and Services

Renovation and Rehab Process

U.S. Department of Agriculture, Forest
Service
12th St. and Independence Ave. SW
Washington, DC 20250
(202) 447-6661

New Life for Old Dwellings (Handbook No. 481, Catalog No. 1979–300–038) is an excellent, well-illustrated manual with glossary devoted to appraising the condiiton of and rehabilitating older structures. The text covers structural and mechanical details, painting and finishing, recapturing attic space for living, remodeling kitchens and baths, and more. Sometimes a request nets meaty books like these at no cost. Sometimes you are referred to the U.S. Government Printing Office where you will be charged, but not much.

Practical Training

Paperhanging

U.S. School of Professional Paperhanging, Inc.
16 Chaplin Ave.
Rutland, VT 05701
(802) 773-2455

Maybe you don't want to quit the job you have now and go straight into the paperhanging business, but it can be a lucrative craft. I know several people—in fact, several women—who have turned paperhanging into a successful part-time job. They get some training and practice on their own place, use it as an advertisement, start small doing favors for people, offering hints, then take on occasional small projects, and after some perseverance it all turns into a small business. It may not be that easy, and if you need a concentrated shot of training and experience, this school is one place to get it. Its instructor to student ratio is 12 to 1. Ten-week programs cover all aspects of the work and all materials except clothing are supplied by the school.

Business operation   You can write for a free booklet that describes the school and course in detail. Several scholarship programs are available and also a placement service.

READING AND REFERENCE

Colonial Design and Construction
Early Domestic Architecture of
   Connecticut, by J. Frederick Kelly
Dover Publications

One of the excellent Dover series on early American architecture and building, this large-format book is loaded with illustrations (many of them in great detail and well documented, i.e., framing and sash, and door construction out of particular homes built in the 1600s and 1700s) and photographs. Very interesting if you have an old New England home, or if you want to see how timber framing details have stayed about the same for over three hundred years in this country.

House Boats
HouseBoats—Living on the Water
   Around the World, by Mark Gabor
Ballantine Books

If it hasn't occurred to you yet it should have: how-to information and how-to books can be a lot of fun sometimes. Admit it: at some point you have probably thought about the romance, the drama (and probably the endless maintenance) of living on the water. This book covers the field, or the waves, of an incredible variety of homes on the Atlantic, Pacific, the Seine—all over. A treat; 130 pages; about $9.

Insulation
Insulation Manual
National Association of Homebuilders
   Research Foundation
PO Box 1627
Rockville, MD 20850

A prime concern for people renovating and restoring old buildings, built before energy costs soared, is how to get thermal protection into walls, ceilings, and floors without tearing everything apart. Frequently this job is a compromise between the way your home looks and how much it costs you to run it. This manual will help. Intended for contractors, it is a bit technical and contains state by state data for calculating heating and cooling loads. Many different insulating materials are covered, offering choices that may make the compromises a little more successful.

Moving and Hauling
Moving Heavy Things, by Jan Adkins
Houghton Mifflin Company

A wonderful book on a very specific and limited but nonetheless crucial subject. If you have ever gotten involved in major renovation work or restoration, or in helping a friend move, several large and heavy objects will still be embedded in your memory. For me, the absolute winners are an old butcher block (maple and plenty thick) I got off the street and recut, and a giant cookstove (the kitchen kind with six burner plates) bought for peanuts in upstate New York and carried up two very long flights of narrow stairs to a loft in Manhattan. Looking at the illustrations in this book, I could have done it better, or at least worn out fewer muscles. All kinds of ramps and rigging and knots and loops and fulcrums and rollers are shown and explained. The title tells it all.

Old Home Rebuilding
Old Houses, by George Nash
Prentice-Hall

A little different from many restoration and remodeling books, this one spends over 350 pages dealing with the practical and technical concerns of bringing a deteriorated old house back to life. The book is particularly strong in an area missed by many books in the field—dealing with structural flaws, rotting corner posts, overloaded girders, and more. The text is sprinkled with a very friendly voice offering tips on making this sweat

equity excursion a rewarding experience, emotionally as well as financially. About $14.

Old Homes
The Old-House Journal Compendium,
    by Clem Labine and Carolyn Flaherty
Viking Press

If you subscribe to the magazine you won't need this book because it is a compilation of selected articles from the *Old-House Journal.* In almost 400 well-illustrated pages (about $21) there is not much you may have to do to an old house that is not covered. The journal strikes a nice balance between the ooh and aah stories and the very thorough, nittiy-gritty pieces. This books tends to the latter; offers a lot of detailed help.

Old House Case History
This Old House, by Bob Vila
    and Jane Davison
Little, Brown and Company

This is not really a how-to book, although it does provide some of that type of information. And it's not really a book on restoration because the house covered in detail was partly restored but also remodeled complete with skylights and a trash compactor. As a companion piece to the PBS television series, the book makes it clear between the lines that the two projects (filming and building) were at odds on occasion. But the full-color illustrations help along an amiable text. The strength of the book winds up in an odd place: teaching how to subcontract a large project and deal with endless subcontractors—their schedules, specialties, and more. Unfortunately, the actual job process presented here—going to expert after expert for advice and work—is not always the way it works, or the way it is financially possible. And although the book is very readable, even entertaining, my reservations stem from the budget: an estimated $30,000 worth of repairs and restorations wound up costing $80,000, not including the value of donations. At close to three times the original estimate the project starts to leave the real world and become an entertaining television program. The high-quality color photographs make it work.

Preservation Information
    The Association for Preservation
        Technology (APT)
    Box 2487, Station D
    Ottawa, ON
    Canada K1P 5W6

APT is an excellent source for specialized information on architectural restoration and preservation. Membership ($35 per year) nets a quarterly publication and a bimonthly newsletter containing information on projects, publications, courses, and more. The association offers a brief brochure that lists reasons for joining but doesn't say much of anything about the organization. Anyway, the APT was formed in 1968 as an organization of professional preservationists, restoration architects and others, to promote research, encourage the training of professionals and craftsmen, and to serve as a central source of information on preservation, through book lists, and a useful catalog, *Conservation & Architectural Restoration Supply Sources and Brief Bibliographies.* Brief it is, giving names and addresses of many firms, manufacturers, and professionals in a variety of fields: adhesives, chemical suppliers, hardware reproduction, masonry conservation, and more. Unfortunately, you

get only the names—no comments, evaluations, or descriptions. Anyway, a starting place. The catalog currently costs $5.50.

Preservation News
    Historic Preservation
    National Trust for Historic Preservation
    1785 Massachusetts Ave. NW
    Washington, DC 20036

This is the bimonthly magazine (for $15 per year including membership in the organization) of a very active group that is into a lot more than old mansions. For instance, it is involved with the art deco restoration of the Chrysler building in New York and runs small training schools for young artisans learning restoration trades—training schools that largely support themselves by taking on jobs. A very good looking magazine too.

    American Preservation
    Bracy House
    PO Box 2451
    Little Rock, AR 72203

One of the few good magazines on the subject, this bimonthly (for $15 per year subscription) uses excellent photography to help tell the current story of historic building and neighborhood preservation.

Remodeling
    Remodelers Handbook
    Craftsman Book Company

Over 400 pages of completely practical, well-illustrated information for remodeling, including chapters on deteriorated framing, planning, kitchens, baths, adding living spaces, roofing, ventilation and insulation, painting, estimating, and more; very thorough; geared to professionals but readable and nontechnical.

Renovation
Renovation: A Complete Guide,
by Michael W. Litchfield
John Wiley & Sons

Litchfield started *Fine Homebuilding* and has maintained the more practical side of that magazine in this comprehensive, 500-plus-page, illustration loaded book. You will find a lot of information on subjects rarely covered by do-it-yourself books of any kind: cleaning and tuning old thermostats, working with anaglypta wallcovering, for example; cost is about $35 hardcover.

Repairs/Improvements
Home Repairs and Improvements
Time-Life Books

The widely publicized and promoted thirty-six-volume series titled *Home Repair and Improvement* is a good, basic introduction to the tools, materials, and skills of home repair and improvement. For now, the series splits the field into thirty-six sections, many of which overlap a bit too much. You can write for an information packet on the series. Time-Life usually gives you a bonus of some kind for signing up, then you get a book every so often. The cost is quite good, about $10 per hardbound copy. Try one. You can always get your money back. Remember, these books are thorough but very basic and somewhat padded with artwork; pictures and illustrations tend to run with needless background and are often much larger than they need to be to get the message across. Many bookstores carry part or all of the series.

Restoration and Crafts
Talas
130 Fifth Ave.
New York, NY 10011
(212) 675-0718

Talas, a division of Technical Library Services, offers a limited supply of equipment for a variety of specialized arts and crafts. Write for its free book list, which covers subjects such as bookbinding; hand-made paper; the restoration and care of paintings, photographs, ceramics, and furniture antiques; and more.

Restoration Districts and Buildings
Restored Towns and Historic Districts of America, by Alice Cromie
E. P. Dutton

This tour guide can be very useful for owners of old houses. It covers the entire country, detailing specific historic buildings and homes, town by town and county by county. The well-known places are here: Williamsburg, Old Sturbridge, Shelburne, and others, but so are countless other, less familiar sites (in Canada too). The book makes it possible to travel locally for first-hand reference on facades, interiors, structural details, etc. About 400 pages, unfortunately, with only a few illustrations; about $18.

Restoration Techniques/Supplies
The Old-House Journal
69A Seventh Ave.
Brooklyn, NY 11217
(212) 636-4514

This monthly publication is an ideal source for relatively experienced and very commited do-it-yourself restorers. It's a specialized publication, as Patricia Poore, the managing editor, writes "for people who live in or work on houses built before 1930. Most articles focus on how-to techniques, stressing high-quality, do-it-yourself work. Other articles explain architectural styles, maintenance, restoration products currently available, new books of special interest to our audience, and readers' tips." You will not find articles on aluminum siding. These folks make all the distinctions between restoration and remodeling. Of special interest is their annual buyer's guide, *The Old-House Journal Catalogue*, which lists some 1000 companies that provide products specifically for restoration work. As limited as this field is (the 1930 cutoff date will have to be changed at some point or the audience will shrink as some old homes deteriorate), it is still growing. The *Journal* reports that in 1976 its annual guide listed only 208 companies compared with over 1000 now. The monthly now has about 65,000 subscribers.

Business operation   An annual subscription is $16. The annual guide is $12 mail order, only $9 to subscribers. The most recent 5 years of monthly issues are held in print and can be purchased in bound volumes. Finally, the *Journal* staff, whenever possible, offers help by mail or phone on specific restoration questions from its subscribers.

Retrofitting Old Homes
From the Walls In, by Charles Wing
Little, Brown and Company

This book will help you make hard, practical decisions about upgrading the energy efficiency of older homes. Of particular interest are detailed and ingenious plans for re-orienting heat supply and improving the thermal efficiency of existing walls without destroying their appearance. The 225 pages are well illustrated with details notated to cover every retrofit stage. An interesting book for most of the homeowners who have the combination of an older, well-built home without the benefits of energy-efficient appliances and design built in.

Stencils
Early American Stencils,
    by JoAnne C. Day
Dover Publications

This interesting book is a collection of full-size, historically documented stencils from early American homes presented on heavy manila stencil paper—a book truly intended for hands-on use. The companion book by the same author, *The Complete Book of Stencilcraft*, is worthwhile as well.

Urban Restoration
Return to the City, by Richard Ernie Reed
Doubleday & Company

Subtitled *How to Restore Old Buildings and Ourselves in America's Historic Urban Neighborhoods*, this book is excellent reading for anyone eyeing an old brownstone or row house and wondering about the price, the neighborhood, the investment, the sweat equity, and the results. This book will bring you current with a subject that ranges from remodeling to urban homesteading to gentrification. The revitilization of areas in New York to Portland is covered in detail; 190 pages; about $9.

Victoriana
Victorian Homes
Renovator's Supply, Inc.
PO Box 61-A
Millers Falls, MA 01349

This is a colorful, quarterly magazine sold by subscription only ($12 per year) with articles that cover everything Victorian, particularly interiors, fixtures, and furnishings. It is not a how-to book for structural work. You are likely to find coverage of paint matching, wallpaper patterns, and stories on Victorian Lady Ferns, stereoscopes, sponge painting, anaglypta and supaglypta, and more. The liberal use of full color makes the magazine a lot of fun. Single issues are $3.50. Worth a try; some incredible interiors.

SIX

REPAIRS
AND
MAINTENANCE

PRIVATE FIRMS

Exterior

Bird Control
Bird-X, Inc.
325 W. Huron St.
Chicago, IL 60610
(312) 642-6871

The company name says it all, and some of the equipment it sells to keep birds from landing strikes me as overkill, for example, lengths of needle-nose spikes billed as "razor sharp strips of needles" that "prevent" birds from landing, at least from landing and staying alive. However, there are some situations—around high tension wires and water supplies, for example—where nesting and perching, particularly by great waves of birds, can cause trouble. And there are less aggressive and grotesque ways of getting rid of them, with noise and lights for instance. Bird-X does manufacture several such systems, including indoor and outdoor ultrasonic systems, large scarecrows resembling hawks designed to "fly" in the wind, and more.

Business operation Write for free brochures illustrating the systems, but even if you don't mind laying out weapons-of-war-looking hardware on your window sills, I would check with the local building department and maybe your home insurance agent before leaving yourself open to potential liability for accidents.

Nixalite of America
417 25th St.
Moline, IL 61265
(309) 797-8771

Nixalite makes several models of spiked mountings for parapets, fencing, and such that prevent birds from landing (and people from touching). As the ends of these small spikes are cut extremely sharp, be sure you do not open yourself to injury liability and that local codes permit their use.

Business operation The company responds to inquiries with product brochures and offers consultation by phone. A necessary alternative in some cases.

Chimney Cleaning Equipment
Neuman Chimney Cleaners
Rte. 2
Ogema, WI 54459
(715) 767-3586

Neuman makes a unique tool for cleaning chimneys, eliminating the need for hiring professional chimney sweeps, and, as they say, an expensive selection of wire brushes, cables, and extensions. This system is expandable—simply a rigid wire basket with curled ends that can be lowered into the chimney, then expanded against the flue walls with a second rope. If the wire basket gets stuck, and it happens, particularly in older, irregular flues, and flues with heavy creosote buildup, releasing the tension collapses the basket so it can be removed. Obviously, this system will not do the type of finish cleaning that a fine steel brush can do. But creosote can be stubborn, and just may need a heavy-duty scraping before it breaks loose. The basket wires are a lightweight, rustproof alloy. The company estimates that you'll need five to ten pulls up and down to do the job.

Business operation You can write to the factory at the above address for a simple brochure explaining how the system works, with illustrations and directions for chimney cleaning. Write the company for the retail outlet nearest you.

Exterior Cleaning

ProSoCo, Inc.
PO Box 4040
Kansas City, KS 66104
(913) 281-2700

ProSoCo makes Sure Klean masonry cleaners, used almost exclusively by professional cleaning contractors. Its products, which have been used on many landmark buildings, include materials to remove and control graffiti, asphalt, and tar; two types of restoration cleaners for removing atmospheric carbon and dirt, paint oxidation, and embedded clay and mud stains from .brick, granite, marble, and other masonry materials; a limestone cleaner; and more. If you have a painted brick wall that you would like to "unpaint," ask about ProSoCo's paint stripper for brick.

Business operation   The company notes, "While we cannot recommend general use of the materials by consumers, we frequently are asked to refer cleaning contractors to homeowners who have smaller projects." Sure Klean is sold through a network of 700 distributors. Your best bet is to write or call ProSoCo for a local referral.

Façade Cleaning/Restoration

American Building Restoration, Inc.
9720 S. 60 St.
Franklin Industrial Park,
Franklin, WI 53132
(414) 761-2440

ABR is in the cleaning business. But it cleans special surfaces with special chemicals and equipment—things like the Five Flags Civic Center in Dubuque, Iowa; the 1800s façade of Jefferson College in Natchez, Mississippi, and many other buildings. It offers an alternative to sandblasting, which certainly will clean masonry surfaces but often leaves brick and stone severely pitted and looking completely different than intended by the original architects and builders. Also, ABR uses similar expertise to seal exterior masonry to prevent deterioration. You can write for brochures describing its three basic products: a multilayer paint remover, a masonry cleaner, and a masonry sealer. The cleaner is water soluble, biodegradable, and applied by spray, roller, or brush. It will not harm painted surfaces or damage grass or shrubs that catch excess spray.

Business operation   The company sells its products nationally and via mail order. It will send brochures with complete technical specs and instructions for use of the cleaner, paint remover, and sealer on request. Also, John Tadych, the president, writes, "We will provide free consultation services plus free analysis of difficult finishes to be removed."

General Maintenance

Institute of Maintenance Research
2217 Evergreen Ave.
Salt Lake City, UT 84109
(801) 485-3185

While you might expect, given this organization's name, that it would provide do-it-yourself information, brochures on preventive maintenance, tips on energy efficiency, and more, what you get is a confusing array of information sheets that seem to be little more than an elaborate advertisement for one man's lecture career. I looked for more but continued to find statements like, "Operations Engineering is primarily a deliberate, systematic series of exercises designed to give directions, not only in problem solving but in making growth and improvement projections." How's that? One of the information sheets provides an elaborate pay schedule to cover lectures, travel expenses, consultation fees, even product testing. One of the more choice quotes: "Operations Engineering is an art and science devoted to making the most of every asset, situation, or turn of events available within reason." I could surmise only that this is a kind of "power of positive thinking" approach to nuts and bolts subjects, minus the nuts and bolts information.

General Repair Supplies/ Hardware

Defender Industries, Inc.
255 Main St., PO Box 820
New Rochelle, NY 10801
(914) 632-3001

The Defender mail-order catalog is a marine buyer's guide—marine as in Evinrude outboards and boat hooks and bilge pumps. It has a lot of that, but a lot more, particularly a diverse collection of hardware, tools, and repair products like fiber glass tape and epoxy paints, and more. The extensive, 168-page catalog is available for $1.25.

Business operation Defender has a policy of allowing you to place an order with them at any price less than the one listed in its catalog if you include a tear sheet from the less expensive source as proof. Of course, you could simply order from the other source instead.

General Supplies—Marine

E&B Marine Supply, Inc.
150 Jackson Ave.
Edison, NJ 18818
(201) 442-3940; telex 844538

A general marine supply, mail-order house (with six retail stores as well), stocking thousands of items, including the heavy-duty marine equivalent of many home repair and maintenance products: paint, strippers, sealers, cleaners, rust disolvers, fiber glass kits, and an array of hardware that is commonplace to boaters but may serve as a missing link to homeowners.

Business operation E&B will send a free discount catalog three times a year—fun if you like this kind of thing and even if you don't own a boat. Stores do retail business in Fairfield, Connecticut; Lanham and Glen Burnie, Maryland; Perth Amboy, New Jersey; Norfolk, Virginia; and Providence, Rhode Island.

Heat Tape

Cox & Company, Inc.
215 Park Ave. S.
New York, NY 10003
(212) 674-4727

Cox manufactures heat tape, which is like a thin extension cord designed to give off small amounts of heat generated by electrical resistance. Its primary purpose is to prevent pipes from freezing. Cox tapes are available in many lengths, and several are made with small, plastic-packed automatic thermostats and pilot lamps. With these units you can wrap problem pipes before cold weather sets in, plug in the tape, and forget about the problem. The tapes will not draw any current until cold temperatures trigger the thermostat, which is factory-set slightly above freezing. Where pipe insulation may fail, heat tapes are vulnerable only to power failures. Cox also makes heat tapes for roof installations, which are used to clear snow loads and to keep gutters free of ice and snow and free flowing.

Business operation Cox sells through a network of wholesalers and retail distributors but will deal direct with consumers. It offers product specs on request, including electrical usage data, which is marginal, particularly compared with the trouble and expense of repairing a burst water pipe when it lets go in the middle of a cold winter night.

Masonry Waterproofing/Repair
Thoro System Products
7800 N.W. 38th. St.
Miami, FL 33166
(305) 592-2081

Thoro manufactures commercial grade and now a do-it-yourself line of masonry waterproofing, repair, and maintenance products. Generally for home use, they fall into four groups. Thoroseal is a heavy, cement-based concrete coating (also for block and brick walls) that can be applied with a brush or heavy-napped roller to reduce or possibly eliminate below-grade water seepage through foundation walls. Waterplug is a quick-setting hydraulic cement that can be used to stop leaks even while they are flowing. Thorocrete is a patching and resurfacing compound that may serve also as an underlayment or leveling layer for tile floors. Thorogrip is an anchoring cement, quick setting and waterproof. All products clean up with warm water and soap.
Business operation Thoro will send product brochures on request. Circular CP–2 sums it up pretty well.

Metal Siding Cleaner/Sealer
H. B. Fuller Company
Multi-Clean Products Division
2277 Ford Pkwy.
St. Paul, MN 55116
(612) 698-8833

Many metal siding manufacturers (that includes steel and aluminum) offer twenty-year-and-up warranties. And surveys have indicated that after this time the material is still structurally sound. But with many types of metal siding fifteen years or so seems to be the point where problems start with color fading. One solution to the problem of general dinginess is repainting. But that's why you probably chose aluminum in the first place—so you would never have to paint again. There are other options. This company offers a two-stage system of cleaning and sealing. The two products, called Tackle and Guard, are intended to remove paint chalking, mildew, and dirt, and then protect the cleaned surface. Tackle, the cleaner, is phosphate free, containing sodium carbonate and detergents. The sealer, Guard, is water based.
Business operation The company will respond to consumer inquiries and can provide the name of a retail outlet near you, as well as exposure test data on its products. Small samples may be available for a nominal charge. One gallon is said to cover approximately 1500 sq ft. Cost will vary but the job may run about $60.

Water Repellent Coatings
Hydrozo Coatings Company
1001 Y St.
PO Box 80879
Lincoln, NB 68501
(402) 474-6981

Hydrozo manufactures clear, water repellent coatings and concrete sealers. In business since 1902, its commercial garage deck coatings have been applied to over 50 million sq ft of space in the last fifteen years. Its concrete coating is designed to protect the masonry surface against salts, de-icer chemicals, acids, and water penetration. It is a penetrating sealer, not a surface membrane.
Business operation You can write the company for technical specification sheets,

including wood, brick, and vertical masonry sealers. It will send you the name, address, and phone number of the distributor nearest you.

Weatherstripping
Mortell Company
Kankakee, IL 60901
(815) 933-5514

Mortell manufactures all kinds of weather-stripping for doors, windows, air-conditioners, and so forth. It makes flexible varieties for wrapping pipes, temporary seals for openings, rigid mounts for sealing the seam between door and sill, and small wood moulding strips with a foam edge for additional protection around windows and doors. Generally, these products are modestly priced and return significant energy savings. Unfortunately, many people overlook these easy do-it-yourself jobs in favor of the big projects like adding more insulation in the attic.
Business operation Mortell weather-stripping products are widely distributed in home centers and lumber outlets across the country. A brief illustrated catalog with drawings showing proper applications is sent on request if you cannot find it at a retail outlet.

Thermwell Products Company, Inc.
150 E. 7th St.
Paterson, NJ 07524
(201) 684-5000

Therwell sells Frost King weatherstripping and related products such as water heater insulation blankets and heat cables for piping and roofs. Its large selection of window and door weatherstripping, both temporary and permanent, is widely available in home centers and lumber outlets.

Business operation The company sends a small, illustrated brochure, *Guide to Saving Energy*, on request if you can't get it locally. Its catalog (No. 682A) shows the full range of available products, including pipe cables up to 6 ft long, waterproof stock tank heaters, and many other specialty items.

Interior

Adhesives
Franklin Chemical Industries, Inc.
2020 Bruck St.
PO Box 07802
Columbus, OH 43207
(614) 443-0241

Franklin is a major supplier of adhesives to the woodworking and furniture industry. Also, they make a wide selection of adhesives for consumers, concentrating in four areas: wood glues, caulking and sealants, flooring adhesives, and construction adhesives. The latter are often overlooked by consumers who do not realize the great holding power panel adhesive, for instance, can have when used in addition to conventional nailing. Including adhesive for securing panels to metal frames, contact cement for laminates, tile adhesive, and more, Franklin offers a subfloor and plywood adhesive approved by the APA (American Plywood Association), a nonflammable, water-based mastic used with polystyrene foam insulating panels, and a general purpose construction adhesive that exceeds APA Specification AFG-01, and FHA/HUD Use of Materials Bulletin #60.
Business operation Franklin can supply a great many product booklets. For economical new construction you might be in-

terested particularly in booklet CA25-82 on construction adhesives that discusses the APA Glued Floor System. The company sells nationally through wholesalers into building material chains, hardware stores, lumberyards. Write for a product listing and technical data.

Exterminating

Acme Exterminating Corporation
460 Ninth Ave.
New York, NY 10018
(212) 594-9230

A pest control company working in the New York, New Jersey, and Connecticut area, Acme is responsive to inquiries covering all exterminating subjects and sells retail products for the control of vermin and rodents. All chemical treatments must have an EPA (Environmental Protection Agency) registration number.

Pest/Toxin Control

Urban IPM Resource Center
1010 Grayson St.
Berkeley, CA 98710

IPM stands for Integrated Pest Management, and that includes insects and rodents. The center, which is affiliated with the John Muir Institute for Environmental Studies, dispenses information to homeowners, renters, gardeners, and professionals who need to know how to deal with pests in a relatively nontoxic way. To this end the center provides technical reports on research, how-to guides for lay persons, and educational materials. Although it is somewhat swamped with requests for information, IPM offers to respond individually. You might start by writing for its list of publications.

Wood and Masonry Treatments

United Gilsonite Laboratories
Box 70
Scranton, PA 18501
(717) 344-1202

UGL makes an extensive variety of wood and masonry related products, including wood stains and clear finishes for interior and exterior use, masonry waterproofers, caulks and sealants, asphalt roofing compounds, and paint specialties. These products are sold nationwide in retail hardware stores, paint stores, lumberyards, and home centers and are supported with extensive consumer literature.

Business operation   UGL product sheets are available at no cost. The company offers several information booklets (for 25¢ to cover mailing), including one of particular value, *How to Waterproof Masonry Walls.* UGL provides toll-free lines for consumer questions: 1 (800) UGL-LABS; and in Pennsylvania only, 1 (800) 262-LABS.

Furnishings and Fixtures

Adhesive/Tools

Roberts Consolidated Industries
    (Weldwood)
600 N. Baldwin Park Blvd.
PO Box 1250
City of Industry, CA 91749
(213) 338-7311

Weldwood makes an extensive line of adhesives and tools used in laying floors, carpets, tile, and more, as well as Penta brand preservatives and Woodlife brand water repellent preservatives. Adhesives include contact cements, epoxy glues, and woodworkers glue for home and hobby use, contact cements and solvents for laminates, flooring adhesives, construction adhesives for ceramic, plastic, and metal tile, drywall, wood subfloor and general structural applications.

Business operation Weldwood products are widely available. For a complete look at tools and materials write for Catalog RFC/WC, "Roberts Weldwood Flooring Specialties." Several specialized tools may be difficult to find elsewhere, such as electric carpet cutters or complete carpet tool kits.

Carpet/Floor Care
The Hoover Company
North Canton, OH 44720
(216) 499-9200

Hoover is a well-known manufacturer of upright and canister vacuum cleaners, hand cleaners, rug and carpet shampoo, and polishing machines—a step in between simple cleaning and complete sanding and refinishing that is often overlooked.

Business operation Hoover has seventy factory service centers and over 800 authorized service dealers across the country. You may be able to get Hoover's informative brochure, *Consumer Guide to Carpet Cleaning*, from one of them. If not, write the company for a copy, and for any product literature.

Caulk/Grout Tools/Hardware
Modern Industries, Inc.
515 Olive Ave.
Vista, CA 92083
(714) 724-2161
(800) 854-1045 (Toll-free)

Modern manufactures a modest, relatively unconnected selection of products: two small

tools, one that has a convenient crooked handle and V-shaped blade for removing old grout, and a small caulking tool with a nylon former available in different widths. It also manufactures a series of adjustable automatic hinges that work for lip and overlay doors and, as the company states, "have easily passed our extra-long 300,000 slam test." (That must have been a fun job for someone; probably got rid of all his aggression.)

Business operation The company will send illustrated product literature on request. Florence Otis, the president, writes that most of its products are available throughout the country, but if you can't find them you can use the toll-free line for information.

Electronics/Motors Surplus Supplies
C and H Sales Company
2176 E. Colorado Blvd.
Pasadena, CA 91107
(213) 681-4925

C and H has thousands of items (and the catalog does not list them all, even though it is 112 pages long). All are surplus in one way or another.

The company says all equipment is fully tested, and offers a ten-day full-credit policy if you are not satisfied. Just to give you a sense of what they have: sixty-one different kinds of small blowers, including a 15 cfm Gould fan (11 watts, single phase, 2900 rpm, about 3 in $\times$ 3 in $\times$ 2 in, for $2.95); eighty-one different kinds of DC motors, including several from GE, Globe, Oster, Electrolux—and you thought when the motor went, you had to throw the appliance away. C and H also carries batteries, heating elements, hydraulic cylinders, heat shrink tubing, a wide range of optics including a few really esoteric items such as aerial cameras and beam splitters, a reasonable selection of small precision hand tools (tweezers, snips, etc.), pressure gauges, pumps, all kinds of solenoids and switches and transistors, plus, just when you think you've found the limitation of the selection, a page of universal joints.

Business operation   As far as I can tell the catalog is still free—quite a good deal. Mail order sales are made nationwide. There is a minimum order of $20.

Furniture Wax
Marshall Imports
713 S. Main St.
Mansfield, OH 44907
(419) 756-3814

Marshall is the sole U.S. importer of Antiquax waxes, cleaners, and polishers. They are made to exacting standards by James Briggs & Sons, Ltd., Manchester, England. Much of Marshall's sales are to commercial firms, but they do maintain a retail mail-order department. Antiquax paste wax is a formulation of pure beeswax, Number 1 Primeira Yellow Carnuba wax, and several other vegetable waxes. A tiny tin (a thick half-dollar size) retails for $4.50.

Glass/Mirrors/Resilvering
Atlantic Glass & Mirror Works
439 N. 63 St.
Philadelphia, PA 19151
(215) 747-6866

Atlantic sells plate glass and Lexan, does storefront and custom mirror installations, and more. But that's not why it's listed here. It's here because it has a solution to a common problem: what can you do with a mirror that you like, that's beveled, that's wonderful in every respect except that the silvering is going and the mirror looks blotched. The answer is quality resilvering, as Joyce and Mark Taylor, the proprietors of Atlantic write, "a bona fide historical craft. We are established for 47 years, specialists in custom resilvering of antique beveled and/or engraved mirrors. Real silver is used in this process. Up to 6 weeks' time may be needed to complete one mirror. Cost is based on the silver market." And that's the problem. Silver is a volatile commodity, particularly when a couple of brothers from Texas try to corner the market.

Business operation   Atlantic's minimum fee is $30 for setup and labor, plus a fee per square footage depending on the mirror style and condition. (Again, depending on the market, the fee could be $20 a square foot.) Atlantic has no literature to send you. It deals regularly with decorators, architects, and antique dealers but welcomes your inquiry. You may spot one of its ads in the *Old House Journal.*

Gold Leaf
M. Swift & Sons, Inc.
10 Love Lane, PO Box 150
Hartford, CT 06141
(203) 522-1181

There are very few sources of old-fashioned, hand-beaten gold leaf. Swift has been making it this way for almost 100 years. They sell to decorators, sign painters, furniture repairmen and manufacturers, museums, and others, including the firm that leafed the Connecticut state capitol dome. Swift also makes hot die stamping foils.

Business operation   Swift has produced an informative booklet, "A Guide to Genuine Gold Leaf Application," which explains the different purity grades (by the karat, just like jewelry), how leaf is sold (by the "book"; 25 3⅜-in × 3⅜-in sheets), how to gild on glass, wood, and other applications. The company responds to all inquiries from the Hartford office, or one of their branches in Glendale, California; St. Louis, Missouri; and Chicago, Illinois.

Lamp Electrification/Restoration
Aladdin Lamp Mounting Company
118 Monticello Ave.
Jersey City, NJ 07304
(201) 434-2869

Lamp mounting is the process of electrifying nonelectric lamp fixtures. In addition to this specialized service Aladdin can fabricate fixtures to your specifications, even from an old photograph, and will clean and polish all types of metal fixtures.

Business operation Aladdin is open to the public, although 90 percent of its customers are interior decorators and antique dealers. No illustrative literature is available, so you must write with your specific request for information and prices.

Lubricants/Cleaners
WD–40 Company
1061 Cudahy Place
San Diego, CA 92110
(714) 275-1400

WD–40 is basically a lubricant, although it is also advertised as a penetrant, rust preventer, and cleaner. This firm makes only the one product, although it is available in all sorts of containers.

Business operation WD–40 will send you a free copy of its booklet, *Easy Fix-It Guide*, which details about forty (what a coincidence) applications of the product around the home.

Marble
New York Marble Works, Inc.
1399 Park Ave.
New York, NY 10029
(212) 534-2242

New York Marble, in business since 1900, sells marble in many different shapes and sizes, stock pieces and custom work, in approximately 120 different color tones. They also repair and restore marble furnishings and have done work for Sotheby Parke Bernet and the Metropolitan Museum of Art. Commonly asked for items include ¾-inch-thick countertops (about $20 per square foot and up), and natural tiles (about $4.25 and up for 12-in squares). As to their repair and restoration services, you can bring in your piece (call first), or send a photograph or two illustrating exactly what the problem is, and New York Marble will quote you a rough price on the spot. Their retail store (you should be able to find one in Los Angeles soon) shows much of what they carry.

Business operation Repair and restoration work should be arranged by appointment. New York Marble will arrange shipping. The work generally takes about two weeks. They welcome inquiries from architects, contractors, and consumers. Write for brief product descriptions and an interesting, short, but thorough piece on marble cleaning and care. They carry marble cleaners and adhesives.

Metal Cleaners
Bradford Derustit Corporation
PO Box 151
Clifton Park, NY 12065
(518) 371-5420

Bradford specializes in chemical metal cleaners, including one of particular interest, B-P Rust/Oxide Remover, which is safe for hands, paint, metals, rubber, and wood. Lois R. Squire of Bradford writes, "It is used and recommended by many of the most famous companies and museums in the United States. It is recommended by the Society for Historic Preservation, and used in ordinary homes as well as historic ones." B-P Remover works for ferrous and non-ferrous metals and has a nonacid base, so that machine parts, tools, and other equipment can be emersed without disassembling rubber, wood, or other component parts. This mix is packaged in a concentrate to use in a ratio of 1 to 20 with water. Bradford also makes a metal brightener for use on steel, chrome, nickel, copper, and brass that removes heat stains, discoloration, and tarnish.

Business operation   Write for product brochures with full technical specs. Bradford sells through local distributors and directly from the factory. Write for quotes. It writes, "We are pleased to offer specialized advice from our office at the address and phone above."

Paint Specialties
Illinois Bronze Paint Company
Lake Zurich, IL 60047
(312) 438-8201

Illinois manufactures a limited line of paint specialties, in particular a rustproof garden and farm enamel, a gutter repair paint, and an appliance touch-up paint. The latter is available in colors matched to the best-selling appliance colors among major manufacturers and available in 1-ounce containers. Its gutter patch kit consists of either black or aluminum compound and fiber glass mending tape.

Business operation   Write for free product information and color cards for matching. Illinois sells nationally.

Zynolyte Products Company
18915 Laurel Park Rd.
Compton, CA 90220
(213) 604-1333

Zynolyte manufactures many paint specialties—rust preventers, epoxies, chalkboard finish, spray paint in fluorescent finishes, 1000 degrees F heat paint, epoxy chrome finish, wrinkle finish, and more, all in addition to colors and stains and such in regular old paint cans. A surprising variety come in aerosol form.

Business operation   Write to the headquarters listed above for information on local distribution. Zynolyte also carries commercial-grade wooden step ladders, something that can be quite hard to find.

Solder
Kester Solder, Division Litton Systems, Inc.
4201 W. Wrightwood Ave.
Chicago, IL 60639
(312) 235-1600

Kester makes all types of solder and sells through hardware stores and chains, including True Value, Sentry, K-Mart, and others. To eliminate confusion, Kester color-codes all solder packages with symbols and applications so that you can tell which product to use for which job.

Business operation   Kester offers a 12-page booklet called *Soldering Simplified* for 50¢, although much of the information inside is what you'll find in a decent how-to book. Brief application guides are free at purchase.

Stripping/Refinishing
Kingsway Stripping & Refinishing
4723 Chromium Dr.
Colorado Springs, CO 80918
(303) 599-4512

Kingsway is a small firm that handles all kinds of furniture refinishing work, particularly for Victorian pieces, for which it carries a line of reproduction mouldings, brass, cane, and even upholstery. Nationally, the company produces a catalog ($3 refundable against first order) of mouldings, gingerbread work, and embossed wallpaper.

Business operation Kingsway will send wallpaper samples free with the catalog and will work to help you track down hard-to-find items it does not carry.

Surface Preparations
The Savogran Company
PO Box 130
Norwood, MA 02062
(617) 762-5400

Savogran makes a complete line of surface preparation products—everything from "Strypeeze," probably its best-known product, to commercial floor levelers, cleaners, grout, and more.

Business operation Savogran products are distributed and sold nationally. In general, products like these are hard to get excited about because they are care and maintenance products. Thus they don't get much coverage in how-to-magazines. But Savogran has put together a reasonable, 30-page brochure on the jobs you can do with their products. It's worth obtaining, for it covers the basics of stripping masonry and furniture; rescuing decayed wood surfaces; cleaning and maintaining asphalt, tile, metals, and grout; and more. For a rundown on products, ask for Catalog 40. Savogran responds to consumer inquiries, first with their how-to- booklet, then with one-to-one help, if you write in again, or call.

TRADE ASSOCIATIONS

Paint and Stain Use
National Paint and Coatings Association
1500 Rhode Island Ave. NW
Washington, DC 20005
(202) 462-6272

This trade association is in business to further the uses and applications of paints and stains. In addition to providing magazine stories, news releases, and other materials to editors, the association will send consumers a series of information booklets (for 50¢ and a SASE). They are informative and contain many specific hints and do-it-yourself tips. However, try to track down a copy of *Household Paint Selector*, a well-illustrated and very informative book the association prepared and sold through Harper & Row.

Pest Control

National Pest Control Association
(NPCA)
8150 Leesburg Pike
Vienna, VA 22180
703-790-8300

Encompassing about 3000 members and close to 50 state groups, NPCA provides advisory services on pest control, new products, and safety and sponsors research at several universities that result in pest control standards for commercial and residential applications. The association provides an informative, illustrated brochure showing the telltale signs of various kinds of pest damage, passes along referrals of local PCOs (pest control operators, as they prefer to be called), and keeps up-to-date information on state licensing requirements as well as the status of pesticide products. Also, it maintains a grievance committee to sort out consumer problems with its members. Generally, the association is very helpful over the phone and responsive to diagnostic questions from home consumers.

GOVERNMENT AGENCIES

Damage Costs

Department of Consumer Affairs
PO Box 1157
Jefferson City, MO 65102

Preventive maintenance, one of the most important aspects of home repair, is usually the aspect that gets the least attention. We hope that when things break, whether it's a pane of glass that collided with a baseball or half a roof that cushioned a falling tree, the costs of repairs may be covered by our homeowner's insurance. But there are many types of insurance, and they come with a varying number of exclusions. To find out what kinds of home insurance cover what kinds of damages and repair work, contact home insurance agents, your state insurance department and write for the booklet, *The Consumer Shopping Guide for Homeowners and Renters Insurance.* Among other things, it details a survey of insurance rate comparisons.

Home Repair Help

Volunteers in Service to America
(VISTA)
Action
Washington, DC 20525
(800) 244-8580

Folks at the toll-free Washington number generally answer "Peace Corps," although Action is the umbrella name for the country's volunteer service agency that includes the Peace Corps, VISTA, and other programs. VISTA in particular is worth contacting if you are at or near the government's criteria for poverty and need help. Programs vary dramatically from region to region. In New York State, for instance, VISTA volunteers help with tenant negotiations with landlords. In many cases this is the only way someone in a substandard apartment with limited funds is going to get anything fixed. Unfortunately, this program has a low funding priority and only some

200 or so volunteers working in the Northeast. If you're interested in volunteering, VISTA personnel get a subsistence stipend for a 40-hour minimum work week.

Pesticides
Environmental Protection Agency (EPA)
Office of Pesticide Programs
Washington, DC 20460
(202) 557-7460

In addition to setting federal standards and regulating a wide range of environmental industries, this particular office of EPA maintains a constantly updated list of pesticides that may and may not be used and the special restrictions on their use. Every pesticide you or a pest control contractor may use must have an EPA registration number right on the box or bottle. Write this office for the current list. For more information on pest control, write to EPA Office of Public Awareness, Washington, DC 20460.

Rehab Loan Insurance
U.S. Department of Housing and Urban
   Development
Single Family Development Division,
   Office of Single Family Housing
Room 9270
Washington, DC 20410
(202) 755-6720

The purpose of this HUD program is to help individual homeowners repair and improve homes that need work and are more than one year old. (That one-year requirement doesn't say much about the condition of new housing.) HUD doesn't do the work for you or pay for it, but this program will insure the loan you get to do the work, and that can make all the difference to a bank. And why not? There's no way it can lose its money—not a bad way to make a profit. Loans are guaranteed up to $92,000 and can be used for repair and improvement, purchase and improvement, or refinancing and improvement. Write for details of qualifications.

Structural Repairs
Department of Housing and Urban
   Development
Office of Consumer Affairs, Suite 4100
Washington, DC 20410
(202) 755-6473 (Or contact regional
   office)

One of HUD's many programs, this one provides federal funds in the form of reimbursements for the repair of structural defects (serious problems that affect your safety) in some HUD-insured homes, particularly in older, declining neighborhoods. Write for details of the program. Since you are dealing with the federal government here, you'll meet all kinds of restrictions and limitations—red tape.

CONSUMER EDUCATION

Vocational Training

Alaska Vocational Technical Center
PO Box 615
Seward, AK 99664
(907) 224-3322

For Alaska residents only, this active center offers training in building maintenance, forestry, heavy equipment mechanics, welding, and more. Organizations like this one exist in most states and generally help young adults (twenty to thirty years old) improve or learn skills that can be turned into careers or used for successful self-sufficient living.

Business operation   A brochure with complete course descriptions, fees (from $160 for a 16-week welding course to $440 for a 14-month forestry technician course), and schedules, is sent on request.

Ogden-Weber Area Vocational Center
1100 Washington Blvd.
Ogden, UT 84404
(801) 621-2373

This area center provides short-term training and entry level job placement for residents of northern Utah. It works closely with employers to assure that students receive the training needed in industry. A few of the subject areas covered are furniture upholstery, small engine mechanics, drafting, and electrical appliance repair. The center takes about 500 students every month, a group that includes displaced homemakers,

veterans, high school students, and others. The center, which also goes by the name Skills Center North, recently received the U.S. Secretary of Education's Award for Outstanding Vocational Education Programs.

Business operation   A descriptive brochure is sent on request, and any questions will be answered by phone or in person if you go to the center.

Reid State Technical College
I–65 and Hwy. 83
Box 588
Evergreen, AL 35401
(205) 578-1313

Reid State is located at a point central to six counties in Alabama and offers training in electronics, forestry, air conditioning, cabinet making, masonry, maintenance technology, welding, and more. You must be 16 or older and a high school graduate (or the equivalent) for full-time study. Up to 25 percent of many shop-related courses may be completed on the job. The school notes that in addition to young adults, it is training an increasing number of what it calls *displaced workers* (an interesting phrase when you think about the World War II phrase it conjures up; *displaced persons*) and also retired persons who want to re-enter the work force, if only part time, to work from the home or out of the garage.

Business operation   A comprehensive catalog is sent on request.

READING AND REFERENCE

Asphalt Drives
Asphalt in Pavement Maintenance
The Asphalt Institute
College Park, MD 20740

An excellent example of books prepared by industry on specific subjects. This thorough manual (write the institute for current cost) covers commercial roadwork and all categories of repairs, small and large patches, recoating, and more. It's a bit technical but leaves no stone (sorry) unturned. Worth writing for. Ask for a complete information and book list from the institute at the same time.

Carpentry Repairs
Carpentry (Some Tricks of the Trade from an Old-Style Carpenter), by Bob Syvanen
179 Underpass Rd.
Brewster, MA 02631

Most books on carpentry start with the basics: "This is a saw." Everything is explained theoretically, the way you're supposed to do it, the way the results should look. But anyone who has tried to work on existing, out of kilter buildings knows that along with a miter box, you may well need a scriber to match existing conditions. That's what this book is about. In fact you won't find any basics, only the little goodies, all illustrated and almost all commonsense solutions to small but nerve-racking problems. One hundred pages of ingenious and interesting details; one carpenter's tips, some of which will work for you, some of which I recognized, some of which I found more

troublesome than helpful. But it is fun; about $7.

Contractor Repairs
Getting Your Money's Worth from Home Contractors, by Mike McClintock
Harmony Books

Doing it yourself can get out of hand. And many people don't want to, can't afford the time, and can afford to have a professional do the work instead. Still, it pays to hire wisely. This book covers all types of home contractors, including carpenters, electricians, asphalt pavers, exterminators, roofers, locksmiths, and more, telling in each case the services they provide, qualifications you should look for, standard professional practices, how to evaluate the services you do get, and a section on grievances just in case things don't work out. Products are reviewed and analyzed by many magazines and books. Services, forgotten in most publications, are an equally important part of the puzzle. An appendix of consumer sources, state by state, is included. About 180 pages; $6.

Energy-Efficient Repairs
Home Remedies, by Tom Wilson
Mid-Atlantic Solar Energy Association
2233 Gray's Ferry Ave.
Philadelphia, PA 19146

This book presents commonsense solutions, alternatives first covered at the National Retrofit Conference in 1980. In 250 pages, Mr. Wilson covers windows and doors, weatherstripping, insulation, vapor barriers, heating appliances, and more, in an interesting book that includes different points of view from different sources. Interesting, eye-opening reading; more than nuts and bolts how-to-; about $10.

Fixture and Furnishing Repair
Fix-It Yourself Manual, by
Reader's Digest

Picking up where the *Do-It-Yourself Manual* stopped, this somewhat shorter book (about 480 pages instead of 600; still for $20) covers the nitty-gritty repairs inside the house—things like getting the loose rungs of a chair back together, replacing washers in faucets, changing electric plugs and lamp parts, fixing small appliances, and much more. Like the other Reader's Digest manual, this book is lavishly illustrated, clear, and concise. The only limitation is that repair sequences on a camp stove, for instance, must be generic. If you have an import, something you found at a mail-order house, the careful, step by step sequences may show terrain you can't locate on your model. Still, a valuable tool for homeowners and apartment dwellers. What it lacks in depth it makes up for in scope. And an excellent buy.

Home Inspection
The Complete Book of Home Inspection,
by Norman Becker
McGraw-Hill

It is becoming more commonplace for home buyers to hire a professional inspector to take a thorough look before they sign a contract of sale. General contractors, architects, engineers, and professional home in-

spectors (many of them are engineers) can do the job. That's what this book is about: a trip through the house, both inside and out, looking for problems. Pictures help, although there are not nearly enough of them, and the book concentrates on existing problems that are fairly obvious if you know what to look for. It's a help for home buyers and a reasonable guide for homeowners concerned with maintenance and repair.

Household Hints
Help From Heloise
Avon Publishers

Yes, this is a valuable book for owners and renters, even though you have to wade through a huge number of awfully cute remedies for some incredibly insignificant problems. That's the drawback. But for $3.50 in paperback and 400 pages of questions and answers gleaned from the syndicated column, there is a fair amount of time and money-saving repair information. Heloise is particularly good on home remedies for cleaning problem stains off just about everything you have, from clothes to furniture. To her credit, many of the ideas come from readers who have tried them out. Heloise does likewise enough of the time to make the tips reliable.

House Repairs
Complete Do-It-Yourself Manual
Reader's Digest
1973

When it arrived back in 1973, this massive book (about 600 liberally illustrated pages) was derided by many home how-to purists, who claimed it was too shallow and tried to cover too much. But it is probably the best repair book available for people who do not have the time or inclination to become involved with the endless details of home maintenance. There is a lot to know, after all. This book is so organized that inexperienced homeowners can find a case close to the problem in front of them, look at some pictures, get a little help with tools and materials, and take an informed crack at a solution. The book does cover a lot, mainly the house itself, not what's inside. You may find that as you learn the basics you outstrip this book, that, as thorough as it appears, the strange case of siding rot or roof leakage you have won't behave the way the book says it will. Still, a massive amount of illustration and photography, both exceedingly clear, help a lot. And an excellent buy at $20.

Repair Diagnosis
The Homeowner's Handbook, by Mike McClintock
Charles Scribner's Sons

In addition to a checklist for home buyers, information on the costs of home improvements, making contracts with home professionals, and other background information for how-to owners and renters, this book provides a visual diagnosis section with photographs and captions detailing most building materials from foundations to roofs as they ought to look and in varying stages of normal deterioration. The visual guide is helpful even for inexperienced owners, letting them identify what's happening without going into all the details of why it's happening. Sometimes this is the most crucial part of a home repair project. A preventive maintenance schedule is included, which may forestall many of the conditions shown in the diagnosis section; about 230 pages; $15.

Repairs/Improvements
Home Repairs and Improvements
Time-Life Books

The widely publicized and promoted 36-volume series entitled *Home Repair and Improvement* is a good basic introduction to the tools, materials, and skills of the field. The series splits it into 36 (for now) sections, many of which overlap a bit too much. You can write for an information packet on the series to the above address. The deal is that Time-Life usually gives you a bonus of some kind for signing up, then you get a book every so often. The cost is quite good, about $10 per hardbound copy. Try one. You can always get your money back. Remember, they are thorough but very basic and somewhat padded with artwork, i.e., pictures and illustrations tend to run with needless background, often much larger than they need to be to get the message across. Many bookstores also carry part or all of the series.

Restoration Techniques/Supplies
The Old-House Journal
69A Seventh Ave.
Brooklyn, NY 11217
(212) 636-4514

This monthly publication is an ideal source for relatively experienced and very committed do-it-yourselfers. It's a specialized publication, as Patricia Poore, the managing editor writes, "for people who live in or work on houses built before 1930. Most articles focus on how-to techniques, stressing high quality do-it-yourself work. Other articles explain architectural styles, maintenance, restoration products currently available, new books of special interest to our audience, and readers' tips." Of special interest is their annual buyer's guide, *The Old-*

House Journal Catalog, which lists some 1000 companies that provide products specifically for restoration work. The *Journal* reports that in 1976 their annual guide listed only 208 companies compared to over 1000 now; also that the monthly has about 65,000 subscribers.

Business operation   An annual subscription is $16. The annual guide is $12 mail order, only $9 to subscribers. The most recent 5 years of monthly issues are held in print and can be purchased in bound volumes. Finally, the *Journal*'s staff, offers help whenever possible by mail or phone on specific restoration questions from their subscribers.

Retrofitting

Retrofitting an Existing Wood Frame
Residence for Energy Conservation—
An Experimental Study
Burch and Hunt, Center for Building
Technology, Institute of Applied
Technology, National Bureau of
Standards
Washington, DC 20234

With such a catchy title you know this report has to come from the government. By now some of the information is dated. The report was issued in 1977, just prior to the onslaught of superinsulation, and includes a discussion of urea formaldehyde foam, now banned by CPSC. However, even with these limitations it is an extremely thorough and useful guide to energy retrofitting, covering insulation, air infiltration, moisture barriers, taking energy measurements, and more. Some of the information is technical and takes work before you can put it to practical use in the place where you live. It will help you decipher what contractors are talking about and help you evaluate retrofit proposals.

Weatherization Improvements

All Through the House, by Thomas
Blandy and Denis Lamoureux
McGraw-Hill

This is a reasonable energy workbook with lots of charts and formulas, and a do-it-yourself home energy audit. The illustrations are incredibly sloppy, which gives the book a bad look even though the information is all there; a reasonable alternative to the superior *New Hampshire Energy Saving Manual* (also in a workbook format), which may be difficult to obtain; 183 pages; about $8.

FURNISHINGS
AND
FIXTURES

PRIVATE FIRMS

Factory Built

Cabinets

Kitchen Kompact, Inc.
KK Plaza, PO Box 868
Jeffersonville, IN 47130
(812) 282-6681

Kitchen Kompact turns out an incredible number of kitchen cabinets and vanities for baths, all in fairly ordinary styles with some woods a little lighter or darker than others, some door panels raised and some not.

Business operation The company sells through about 250 building supply wholesalers to several national home center chains. Their factory-built cabinets are literally built on an assembly line (about 30 miles of conveyor under 600,000 sq ft of shop space) and pop off the line at the rate of 1000 per hour. The firm offers a *Cabinet Design Guide*, which is very general and not much practical help, but includes a *Cabinet Planner*, which is helpful. It is a giant fold-out with graph layouts and typical kitchen appliances and furnishing laid out to scale along with all the company's cabinet components. The planner is included with the *Design Guide*, which costs $3. Try for individual product sheets (locally or from the company) and a copy of the planning page.

Long-Bell Cabinets, Inc.
Box 126
Longview, WA 98632
(206) 425-2110

Long-Bell makes stock wood cabinets sold through distributors, dealers, and national retail chains. In addition to full product sheet, the company offers two design booklets, *Long Bell Cabinet Ideas* and *Create-a-Cabinet Ideas*, provided free to consumers who write in their request. Valerie LaBerge, manager of sales and service. is one of the few executives in this industry to comment on a very interesting trend. She says that Long-Bell is moving toward selling kitchen cabinets in knock-down form to save on freight and inventory space but also to enable customers to design and assemble their own kitchen storage systems.

Dumbwaiters

Sedgwick
PO Box 630
Poughkeepsie, NY 12602
(800) 431-8262

Sedgwick manufactures dumbwaiters and several small residence elevators that are sold through elevator companies. These are hardly do-it-yourself items, and the company stresses that it does not sell direct because proper installation and service is so crucial. Sedgwick's catalog carries the slogan, "Giving a lift to the world since 1893," which is when the company started to make hand-operated dumbwaiters and hand-operated sidewalk elevators. Its product line has grown some to include 70,000-lb freight elevators but still includes a 5-lb, hand-pulled dumbwaiter. Although a 150-lb capacity "parcel lift" dumbwaiter may seem like a luxury, to many who are handicapped or live in homes on mountainous sites where you need Sherpas to get the groceries into the kitchen, a simple, motorized machine like this may be essential. Generally, no extensive rebuilding or structural work is required for installation as many of the loads (that's engineering loads) are canceled within the dumbwaiter structure. Standard speed is 50 ft per minute. (Your package will probably get upstairs before you.)

Business operation   Sedgwick has recently completed new product literature. It responds to inquiries with a complete product catalog and typical layout drawings. Ask for contractor recommendations.

Traditional Furniture

Bassett Furniture Industries, Inc.
PO Box 626
Bassett, VA 24055
(703) 629-7511

Bassett is one of the largest manufacturers of furniture of any kind. Its extensive line is largely traditional and Colonial, featuring standards such as dovetail drawers, and Micarta tops. It has thirty-four manufacturing plants in thirteen states. You can write the headquarters for the name and address of the dealer nearest you (dealers are widely available) and for a series of free, illustrated product brochures.

Wood Furniture

Thomasville Furniture Industries, Inc.
PO Box 339
Thomasville, NC 27360
(919) 475-1361

Thomasville is a major manufacturer of quality furniture, most of it traditional but some displaying "oriental" designs and a few other departures. A complete view of products is presented in its book (for about $11) of full-color photographs, which includes planning pages. sections on construc-

tion details, hand-carving and finishing, and more. More limited product catalogs are sent on request.

Business operation   Sales are national direct from the manufacturer to retail dealers.

Kits and Plans

Chairs/Stools/Seat Weaving

Cane & Basket Supply Company
1283 S. Cochran Ave.
Los Angeles, CA 90019
(213) 939-9644

Selling primarily cane, rush, basket weaving supplies, and tools for the work via mail order nationwide, this company offers a limited line of do-it-yourself furniture kits, including factory sanded all wood turnings, glue, instructions, and, depending on the style, either cane or rush for seat weaving.

Business operation   Write for free brochure describing products and prices.

Pricing   An 11-in sq, 9-in high, hardwood foot stool kit (four plain legs and eight plain rungs) is about $5—right, that's not a typo—for frame only; about $7 with either #5 GB fiber rush, ½-in flat reed, or 6 mm binding cane. A 36-in high, simple ladder-back chair frame kit is about $25.

Clock Kits/Tools/Case Hardware

Craft Products Company
2200 Dean St.
St. Charles, IL 60174
(312) 584-9600

Craft Products makes hardwood clocks, music boxes, and weather instruments in kit form. Products range from an 82-in-tall grandfather clock with solid oak case, ¼-in-beveled glass door front, solid brass movement, and Urgos Tubular West German chime movement (for about $1000), to small wall and desk clocks in the $50 to $100 range. All pieces are precut and sanded. Complete instructions are furnished with each kit.

Business operation The company sells via mail order from the factory and will supply an illustrated brochure describing their products. Write for information on assembly requirements first, although the kits are shipped with many of the small pieces preassembled. No trimming or mitering is required.

Emporer Clock Company
Emporer Industrial Park
Fairhope, AL 36532
(205) 928-2316

Emporer is one of the nationally advertised manufacturers of clock kits, Craft being its main competitor. Its catalog is available for $1 and includes mantel chiming clocks, regulator wall clocks, grandfather clocks, and several pieces of hardwood furniture. Its kits come with instructions, brass movements, and dials, all offered with a no-questions refund policy within 30 days of purchase. All pieces are precut and sanded.

Business operation Emporer's business is strictly mail order, although Robert Taupeka, the president, writes, "We service our customers by maintaining an inventory of spare parts and a customer service organization to assist a customer in assembling his product or maintaining his clock mechanism."

Pricing Also available as assembled and finished pieces, representative kit prices are black walnut mantel clock, $190; oak regulator wall clock, $170; grandfather clocks, $150 to about $300 for the case kit and about $150 for the movement, although several more exotic designs with moving moon dials and such can run over $300. Blueprints, so you can cut your own pieces, are available for $3.

Mason & Sullivan Company
586 Higgins Crowell Rd.
West Yarmouth, MA 02673
(617) 778-1056

Mason & Sullivan makes a really fine line of clock kits, from extremely elaborate and detailed grandfather clocks complete with solid brass reproduction hardware to small, simple mantel clocks. Many of the kits are available in several "skill levels." It's an interesting idea. At Level 1 all parts are precut and all holes are drilled. You need a screwdriver, some glue, a clamp, and that's it. But at Level 4 many parts must be cut to blueprint specifications, and you'll need a router and maybe a jointer to cut grooves, mouldings, and so forth. And this alters the prices considerably. Grandfather clocks with cherry cases cost about $500 at Level 2 but about $320 at Level 4. In addition to an extensive selection of kits and movements (grandfather movements are guaranteed for 3 years, which is unusually long), the company carries skeleton kits (you assemble the movements); a good selection of brass case hardware, including hinges, lock hardware, pulls, and handles; and a modest collection of beautiful professional clockmaker's tools imported from Switzerland.

Business operation Mason & Sullivan's excellent, 30-page, full-color catalog is sent on request.

Selva Borel Company
PO Box 796
Oakland, CA 94604
(415) 832-0356

This firm produces a limited number of kits that are reproductions of old German clocks.

Also, it stocks parts for repairing and making clocks from scratch (without a precut kit).

Business operation Borel's illustrated catalog (some 60 pages of color) is available for $2.

Viking Clock Company
Box 490
Foley, AL 36536
(205) 943-5081

Viking makes several types of clocks in kit form. Some are available factory assembled, including a 75-in-tall grandfather model, and a 15-in-high desk clock. All styles are somewhere between Colonial and Victorian. On the positive side, all the stock is solid wood; the 100-plus pieces of the grandfather clock, for example, are steam- and air-dried for 60 days, then kiln-dried for 30 days; the all-brass clock movements are shipped only after 260 accurate hours of time testing. I would request details, assembly instructions, and more before buying because of two negatives. First, Viking's literature makes a bit too much of the easy assembly while claiming a 75 percent saving over comparable, finished clocks by using the kit. But if assembly is such a snap, labor costs should not be such a large share of the total price. In fact, a 75 percent saving on its factory-built, $950 grandfather clock ($712) should price the kit at $238. It lists for $535. Also, it offers a limited warranty that is outstripped by a one-time purchase of a lifetime service contract. That rubs me the wrong way. I don't go for so-so warranties for free and really good ones for extra money.

Business operation Viking sells nationally via mail order. Write for details, current prices, and color brochures showing the ornate and elegant clock faces.

Pricing The large grandfather kit cabinet is about $200 in oak, $300 in walnut. Movement, pendulum, etc., are extras.

Colonial/Shaker Kits

Cohasset Colonials
733 Ship St.
Cohasset, MA 02025
(617) 383-0110

The best furniture kits I've put together for the price, Cohasset uses high-quality woods, and ships all pieces, including hardware, stain, and sandpaper for touch-ups—everything you need plus directions. The wood comes through like velvet and ready to stain. Many of its pieces (generally Colonial, also a lot of Shaker chairs and tables) are reproductions of museum pieces. You can't just walk into a museum and copy its pieces. You have to get permission and that means the museum looks you over pretty carefully first. Cohasset makes kit reproductions from pieces in the Metropolitan Museum in New York, the Museum of Fine Arts in Boston (some of Cohasset's kits are even sold through the museum catalog), the Shelburne Museum, Fruitlands, and others, so you don't have to take my word for the exceptional quality. The catalog (for $1) covers Windsor chairs, Shaker chairs, fourposters, a classic Shaker rocker ($119) with ladle arms and woven web seat reproduced from a chair at Fruitlands, writing desks, cabinets, lamps, brass, and a limited selection of fabric—even handmade quilts to order.

Business operation I've been through Cohasset's workshops and have seen the attention given to tolerances and fittings. The company ships anywhere. It is happy to answer questions by mail or phone. Its showroom overlooking Cohasset Harbor is a treat.

Corner Cabinets
Outer Banks Pine Products
Box 9003
Lester, PA 19113
(215) 534-1234

Outer Banks makes eight different styles of Colonial corner cabinets—cabinets with a triangular back. Most have glass front doors for china display, and some combination of shelves and storage below. The pieces are available finished or in modified kit form, so some assembly is required (hinges for the doors, etc.), and the wood is unfinished. The price reduction for pieces in this semi-assembled form is not significant, but it does give you an opportunity to finish the piece exactly as you want, say, to match other wood tones in the room. All pieces are complete with glazing, hardware, plywood backs, shelves for the upper and lower sections, and instructions. Almost all stock is clear pine. Detailing includes features like true, raised-panel doors, scalloped-edge shelves, fluted pilasters, and more. The pieces do not look like budget, unfinished furniture. Door stock, for example, is a full 1⅛-in thick.

Business operation Outer Banks will send you several well-illustrated brochures giving the different styles available, a nice little piece on finishing raw wood, the differences between fully assembled and kit form, shipping, and prices.

Pricing The corner cabinets, all about 7 ft high, are priced from about $215 to $350 in kit form. (Three styles are available in the lower price range.) Fully assembled, ready-to-finish pieces run about 10 percent more.

Eighteenth-Century Reproductions
The Bartley Collection, Ltd.
747 Oakwood Ave.
Lake Forest, IL 60045
(312) 634-9510

The Bartley Collection carries approximately twenty-five authentic furniture reproductions in kit form. Quality is first rate. Instructions are complete. All hardwood pieces are Honduras mahogany and Pennsylvania cherry and all precut, sanded, and ready to assemble. Among several credits for the company, the Reproduction Committee of the Henry Ford Museum and Greenfield Village selected Bartley as the exclusive manufacturer of several pieces from the Ford Museum collection. All items are available assembled and hand finished for about twice the price of the kits. The collection includes bow-back Windsor chairs ($190), tip-top tables with solid hardwood top ($345), a Chippendale block-front chest of drawers with mortise and tenon construction, and 2-in-thick dovetailed drawer fronts ($935), Queen Anne drop-leaf tables ($495), and several other wonderfully detailed pieces. A complete finishing kit is included.

Business operation Bartley maintains a showroom in Lake Forest but sells predominantly by mail order. Write for a catalog ($1), which shows each piece, finished and in color, with ordering information.

Furniture Plans/Tools/Materials
Armor Products
PO Box 290
Deer Park, NY 11729
(516) 667-3328

This is a company with a lot to offer: an extensive list of clear, clean, full-scale plans for furniture pieces; a good selection of furniture hardware, clock movements, and tools. The pages and pages of plans cover hobby horses, small wall plaques, basic end tables, and more elaborate pieces such as Colonial corner cabinets. But the proprietor is experienced at putting projects like these together. John Capotosto provided detailed woodwork projects for *Popular Mechanics* when I was an editor there and has done so for many other publications. That's probably why the plans include key photographs on the sheet and detail drawings so you don't get dumped in the ditch between Steps 21 and 22. Definitely a catalog worth writing for. Also, Armor sells a really interesting booklet for shop workers, *Making and Using Simple Jigs*, a well-illustrated, imaginative book that can solve a lot of cutting and drilling problems.

Glass Tools and Materials
Whittemore–Durgin Glass Company
PO Box 2065
Hanover, MA 02339
(617) 871-1743

Whittemore–Durgin is an excellent source for all kinds of glass, kits, supplies, spare parts, tools, pre-cut stained glass kits, complete tool kits for stained glass craftspeople, project sheets with pieces laid out to scale, endless styrene lampshade forms on which leaded framing is laid out, an extensive selection of tools, including cutters, etching equipment and patterns, lamp stems and hardware, beveled glass supplies—really a complete selection at moderate prices.

Business operation Whittemore–Durgin has two retail stores: one in Rockland, Massachusetts (825 Market St.; (617) 871-

1743), and one in Middlesex, New Jersey (436 Lincoln Blvd.; (201) 469-5350). A full catalog with a price list is sent on request. It describes the contents as "the choicest and most elegant materials for the perpetrating of STAINED GLASS ARTISTRY . . . CERTAIN PATENTED DEVICES . . . for every variety of GOODS and PATTERNS for the production of QUALITY LEADED GLASS WORK."

Kitchen Cabinets
Belwood, Division U.S. Industries
PO Drawer A
Ackerman, MI 39735
(601) 285-6281

Belwood manufactures what it calls *unifront cabinets*. The idea is to extend the use of traditionally kitchen cabinet styles and designs to other rooms in the house. Of particular interest is the component packaging of cabinet fronts with prehung doors, precut filler assemblies, and more, all to provide a lot of flexibility in cabinet design. This works well in kitchens, although when these units are used in dens and living rooms they still look like kitchen cabinets to me, even though you can get them in many different finishes and styles.

Business operation Belwood sells through home centers and building supply outlets and says that this enables it to price items about 30 percent below comparable units sold in conventional furniture stores. Eugene Kirk, director of sales, writes, "We provide total guidance to the do-it-yourselfer through assembly manuals, installation manuals, and specification sheets which guide them in the actual layout and design of the kitchen." Product literature is sent on request.

Kits—General Supplies
Wikkmann House
Box 501
Chatsworth, CA 91311
(213) 349-5148

Wikkmann's $2 catalog offers quite a wide range of furniture kits; a limited selection of tools and hardware; and an extensive selection of full-size plans and blueprints for grandfather clocks, models of all sizes and descriptions, toys, chests, and more. It carries the "Careful Wrecker's Friend" salvage pry bar (one of my favorites because it is so simple and does its job so efficiently), Duplimaster lathe attachments, and full plans for home workbenches. Generally, the styles are decorative, maybe even a tad gadgety as opposed sleek and efficient, although you should probably look for yourself as capsule descriptions of style can only hint at what you'll find.

Business operation Wikkmann sells nationally via mail order and will sometimes locate a source if it cannot fill your needs. Its large-scale plans are exceptionally clear and uncomplicated, probably just right for a near novice.

Pricing Plans range from under $2 for small projects to $7 and $8 for larger ones.

Nineteenth-Century Kits
Heritage Design
PO Box 103
Monticello, IA 52310
(319) 465-5374

Heritage sells furniture kits for nineteenth-century platform rockers, plant stands, two Roycroft service tables, plant stands, music boxes, and more. Selection is limited. Kits include all precut hardwood parts, presanded and ready for finishing, along with required hardware and assembly instruc-

tions. It is good policy to request a sample set of directions and details about a piece before ordering.

Pricing The rocker with caned seat and back is close to $300. Write for complete price list.

Seat Weaving Kits and Supplies
Newell Workshop
19 Blaine Ave.
Hinsdale, IL 60521
(312) 323-7367

Newell offers complete seat weaving kits such as a package of caning materials, tools, and instructions. Refills are sold so you can start small and take on more projects without paying twice for the basics. Newell stocks seven thicknesses of cane, binder, plastic cane, reed spline, fiber rush in three sizes, Oriental sea grass, flat fiber reed, and two sizes of flat natural reed. It offers precut cane webbing to your specifications as well.

Business operation Write for Newell's illustrated brochure, which describes products, kits, and tools very briefly and gives estimating and ordering information. Materials are sold nationwide via mail order.

Pricing ½-in flat fiber reed is about $2 per pound (a pound should be 130 linear ft); caning kits are about $7 per seat. State the center to center distance between seat holes with kit orders, which include cane, holding pegs, awl, sponge, and instructions.

Shaker Kit Reproductions
Shaker Workshops
PO Box 1028
Concord, MA 01742
(617) 646-8985

This is one of the few sources of quality Shaker reproductions in kit form. It offers a complete selection of pieces, including Shaker rockers, candle stands, trestle tables, and many furnishings like veneer boxes, wall pegs, and such. I've put together a few of its pieces and generally the wood is very clear, very good quality (most seems to be northern pine), and sanded very smooth. The kits include instructions, of course, and any other materials you need for assembly, for instance, glue, woodscrews, and hardware. You may have to do just a little fiddling to get the dovetailed leg on a Shaker candle stand table into the dovetailed mortise on the table stem, for instance, but only a little. On many of its chair kits, you can order different colors of chair tapes, a very comfortable seat weaving material that is completely authentic and pretty straightforward. You also get a choice of wiping stains or oil.

Business operation Shaker Workshop's catalog is very attractive. Shipping is prompt and reliable. A nice firm with a nice, modest showroom if you ever get in the neighborhood. It wants 50¢ for the 32-page color catalog. It's worth it to get a look at the wonderfully simple, efficient, and beautiful Shaker designs, which are very reasonably priced.

Window Insulation
Homesworth Corporation
18 Main St.
Yarmouth, ME 04096
(207) 846-9726

Homesworth manufactures Sunsaver thermal shutter kits. They are available in three sizes but must be final trimmed by the installer. The shutters are hinged to the window casing and weatherstripped to form a tight seal. The design does not interfere with normal window operation. All materials are provided in the kit (including installation instructions), except the final decorative cov-

ering, which can be fabric or wallpaper to suit. The company notes that in 1978 there were only six commercial products available for controlling heat and cooling through windows. Now the movable window insulation industry includes some sixty firms producing an array of products.

Business operation Homesworth sells through a dealer network in New England but does fill orders direct from the factory. It will send you illustrated product brochures and an order form on request.

Pricing The insulated shutters retail for $3.25 per square foot, so a standard 5-ft × 3-ft double hung window would cost about $50 to cover. (In some states a tax credit is given for this type of energy-saving expense.)

Wood Turnings/Specialties
Emco Specialties, Inc.
PO Box 853
Des Moines, IA 50304
(515) 265-6101

Emco makes several product lines, some of which have nothing to do with each other, which, I guess, is why *specialties* is the right word. Of particular interest is its kit-packaged sets of legs and wood turnings, brackets, and other table hardware that can turn a sheet of veneered plywood with some edge detailing into a serviceable, nice-looking table. It also sells wood letters and an interesting, modular shelving system with turned spindle sections that can be screwed together (an interior, double-threaded bolt is provided) to customize your own wall system.

Business operation Sold nationally, mainly in larger home centers that have the room for the large spindle and leg displays; also in some mail-order catalogs. Illustrated literature on all Emco's products is available. Write to its customer service department at the address above. It can tell you about pricing and where its products are available near you.

Reproductions and Custom Work

Blacksmithing
Ian Eddy Blacksmith
RFD 1, Box 213
Putney, VT 05346
(802) 387-5991

Ian Eddy handcrafts many kitchen, bath, and fireplace fixtures like trivets, plant hangers, pot hooks, and utensil racks and custom orders to your specifications. As Mr. Eddy puts it, "I try to create things using traditional methods to solve contemporary problems."

Business operation   Ian Eddy sells wholesale, retail, and via mail order. Write for detailed brochure with accurate ink drawings and prices.

Pricing   Costs are modest, ranging from $3 for small, simple hooks and holders to about $25 for larger, more elaborate utensil racks.

Country Store General Supplies/ Newsletter
Cumberland General Store
Rte. 3
Crossville, TN 38555
(615) 484-8481

Cumberland puts just about everything into their mail order catalog. It is an amazing collection of old, and a few new, items cover-

ing over 250 illustrated pages. What a treat! Here's a brief sampling of the variety: 25-qt pressure canners, a cherry pitter, antique coffee mills with hand cracks (about $30), small and large cider and wine presses, Queen Atlantic woodburning kitchen ranges, oil lamps, force pumps, windmills, cow anti-kickers (keeps them from kicking in case you grab something you shouldn't), calf feeder pails, white oak pitchforks, portable forges ($333), portable bench grindstones ($50), horseshoe nails, wagon harnesses, surreys (yes, one does have a fringe on top; $3750), Lee jeans, dulcimers, porch swings. Almost every page has something fun, something interesting, or something you never saw before.

Business operation   Prices are generally modest. Do not miss this one, or the *Cumberland Country Reader,* a newsletter that keeps you up to date on new additions to the catalog and reviews of new books. A typical issue might have one large page devoted to Tennessee ghost stories or a page of "Country Wisdom Bulletins" (about $2 each) on an endless selection of how-tos on self-sufficiency subjects.

Craft Artisans
The Goodfellow Catalog Press
PO Box 4520
Berkeley, CA 94704
(415) 845-7645

The Goodfellow Catalog of Wonderful Things contains over 700 pages with about 1500 illustrations and is the largest direct mail-order source of handcrafted items. Readers can order directly from the workers represented in the catalog. There are about 700 of them, and some 3000 different items. These are finished products, including a lot of clothes, not a lot of woodwork, but some of almost everything.

Business operation   The current price for the book in soft cover is $19.95 plus $2.50 shipping from Goodfellow Press.

Furniture Repair and Construction

Sawdust Room
PO Box 327
Stevensville, MI 49127
(616) 429-5338

D. L. Fife, the owner, specializes in custom making nearly any wood object to your specifications. He writes, "I produce custom items of wood per request, repair and make the missing parts for new and antique furniture." The work includes canopy beds, lathe duplications, spinning wheels, rockers, and more.

Business operations   Products are sold nationally via mail order and retail locally.

Pricing   Quotes are furnished on request when clients send along a sample or measured drawing and an SASE.

Ironwork

The BlackSmith Shop, Inc.
Mount Holly, VT 05758
(802) 259-2452

Pete Taggett of the BlackSmith Shop, writes, "Our village blacksmiths with their dedication to fine workmanship, honed by a keen appreciation of the quality of yesterday, preserve the art of smithing." The small business was started in 1971 and produces hand-wrought lamp stands, hooks, log holders, fireplace tools, and such, as well as a handy ash bin called the Ash-Away, designed at the shop. The Ash-Away is a 5-gal-capacity ash box on short legs, with folding top doors and a series of handles so that ashes, even with hot embers, can be removed from woodstoves cleanly and safely.

Business operation   The BlackSmith Shop's illustrated catalog with price list is sent on request.

Pricing   Costs are modest. Several fireplace tool sets that include shovel, poker, broom, hoe, and hanger are $40 to $50.

Robinson Iron Corporation
Robinson Rd.
Alexander City, AL 35010
(205) 329-8484

Robinson fabricates a collection of ornate cast iron specialties, including fountains, urns, furniture, and statuary. It also has the capacity for custom restoration castings. The company's insert file in *Sweet's Catalog* is well illustrated and covers a good selection of its gates, fencework, lamp posts, and more.

Business operation   Robinson's complete catalog is sent for $3. The company ships nationally.

Pricing   Cast pieces range from simple urns and vases in the $200 to $400 range up to crane fountains for $2000 and $3000.

Schwartz's Forge and Metalworks
PO Box 205
Forge Hollow Rd.
Deansboro, NY 13328
(323) 841-4477

Joel Schwartz's catalog of iron gates, fire screens, and grillwork is a limited portfolio of unusual, original, and generally light-hearted pieces. He does custom work. The portfolio shows samples (the full-page photographs of some fifteen pieces sells for $3.50) of style. To give you a general impression, the work has a lot of vine tracery that is minimal rather than florid and Victorian, and a lot of hoopwork, with fine detailing. Several of the free-form tracery designs for gates, and one for a complete stair railing, are full of motion, pleasingly asymmetrical. I hope this tells you enough so you can make a reasonable decision about investing the $3.50. It would be easier if small firms doing custom work offered a small flyer, even with one or two pictures. But I understand that one way to stay at the forge and not at the desk is to weed out idle requests up front. If the short description here appeals to you, the portfolio will not be a disappointment.

Wallin Forge
Rte. 1, Box 65
Sparta, KY 41086
(606) 567-7201

Wallin's brochure is four years old and has not been updated because, as S. R. Wallin writes, "our business is now 99 percent custom, since we have found that our clients, whether they need shutter hardware or a chandelier or fireplace accessories, have very specific needs." Even so, the brochure illustrates a limited collection of ironwork done with an unusual and surprisingly light touch—not a style you often see. Railing sections, for instance, incorporate oval hoops finished with a filigree curlicue on each side and a center medallion holding two fish. Nice stuff. The free catalog may bring you into Wallin's fold of custom work clients.

Lighting and Seating

Silver Dollar Trading Company
1446 South Broadway
Denver, CO 80210
(303) 733-0500

Silver Dollar makes reproduction metal chairs, benches, street lights, fountains—even a shoeshine stand—generally in a very ornate Victorian style. All items are available in black, white, green, or brown. All wooden parts are oak. Trim metal is solid brass. Some of the pieces are incredibly detailed, and seem to be growing new curls, swirls, and fretwork before your eyes.

Business operation Silver Dollar Trading ships predominantly to dealers, restaurant chains, designers, and builders, but welcomes consumer inquiries. Shipping charges can be substantial on some items, like the 320-lb raised shoeshine stand. Most items are shipped from Silver Dollar's warehouse in Texas.

Pricing FOB prices from Denver are in the $150 to $250 range for a variety of benches; $600 for a solid brass, 5-ft-long Federal-style bench on special order; $1800 for the shoeshine stand, complete with iron foot rests, brass and green canvas canopy, oak base with storage drawers, brass scrolling, and trim.

Seventeenth- and Eighteenth-Century Beds/Lumber Supply

The Country Bed Shop
Box 222
Groton, MA 01450
(617) 448-6336

This shop produces seventeenth- and eighteenth-century reproductions of beds, chairs, tables, and case furniture. Initial roughing operations are done by machine, but all dovetail work, mortising, turnings, carvings, raised panel construction work, and so on is done by hand. The proprietor, Charles E. Thibeau, one of the few Americans elected to The Guild of Master Craftsmen in London, produces work on commission but does offer a sampling of work in the Bed Shop catalog. It includes pencil-post beds, Sherton field beds, and a wonderful collection of bow-back Windsor chairs, tilting-top chair tables, Pennsylvania German cupboards, and more. Other operations of this firm include the production of old-fashioned hand-made milk paint for restoration work and the milling of wide board flooring and paneling, in oak from 4- to 16-in wide and in pine from 12- to 24-in wide.

Business operation The Country Bed Shop's catalog is available for $3 and includes photographs of all pieces, plus interesting notes on the history of bed construction, roping bed frames, and other subjects. Small brochures on milk paint products and wide board lumber is sent for 60¢ in stamps to cover postage.

Pricing A Hepplewhite field bed with headboard and gracefully raised ogee canopy frame is about $1600 with cherry, maple, or mahogany posts. Less elaborate chairs and tables range from $375 (for the bow-back Windsor) to about $600.

Shaker Stoves/Clocks
Adirondack Hudson Arms
60 Kallen Ave.
Schenectady, NY 12304
(518) 374-7200

This firm has museum-quality Shaker stoves, clocks, and an assortment of wares such as pewter spoons, moulds to make them, and more. Its stoves are replicas in design and workmanship of the original Shaker versions. All hardware is hand wrought and filed. All castings are gray cast iron. Roughly 38 in long (12 in of that is the hearth extension in front of the door) and 9 in wide, the stoves are available with or without an afterburner—an L-shaped extension to the firebox, drawing the flame path up into the leg of the L at the back of the firebox and

forward to the flue pipe. Museum-quality "dwarf tall case alarm clocks" are reproductions of Shaker clocks built at the Watervliet, New York, settlement around 1800. They are about 36 in high. Reproductions can be made for almost all Shaker clocks in existence and available to the firm's pattern maker.

Business operation The company sells nationally to serious collectors.

Pricing The small clocks (with battery powered pendulum, not quite a Shaker invention) is $125. The Shaker stoves are $350 without L-shaped afterburner, $400 and $550 with small and large afterburners respectively.

Turnings/Cabinetry
Haas Wood & Ivory
64 Clementina
San Francisco, CA 94105
(415) 321-8273

Haas has been in business since 1887. It provides custom wood turnings and just about any type of Victorian ornamentation, including complete cabinet systems. Since it works from your plans and specifications, it does not offer a catalog of stock items but invites inquiries on new work or restoration projects.

Victorian Lighting
Nowell's Victorian Lighting
490 Gate 5 Rd.
PO Box 164
Sausalito, CA 94965
(415) 332-4933

Nowell's manufactures authentic reproduction period light fixtures for wall and ceiling mounts, all solid brass and with a very wide variety of glass. In addition to catalog sales, Nowell's handles repair and restoration work and maintains a stock of antique parts and glass shades.

Business operation Nowell's excellent catalog is sent on request. Special questions will be handled, even helping you to track down hard-to-find items. Nowell's is one of only a few sources of parts for antique oil lamps.

Wall Phones—Antique and Reproduction

Billard's Old Telephones
21710 Regnart Rd.
Cupertino, CA 95014
(408) 252-2104

Talk about specialization. This is the only place I know of that does this kind of thing. I picture all of its phones going off at once when I call. It has many, and a stockpile of parts and supplies to rebuild, repair, or modernize all types of vintage phones. It also sells reproduction oak wall phones (modernized with a concealed dialer and modular plug jack), complete with ringing brass bells, finger joint corners, and brass crank ringer. Billard's has original old cases, reproductions, books on telephone history, and even a reprinting of the 1881 Boston telephone directory that lists A. Graham Bell as a subscriber to the fledgling system. These folks are *involved* in phones.

Business operation Billard's sells nationally by mail order and retail locally. It will send you a catalog for $1 (refundable with your first order), which is primitive, typed, sketched, and includes four wonderfully crazy pages of phone-type illustrations so you can identify the one you have and get the right parts for it. The catalog also has someone that looks like a real cute 8-year-old daughter of the proprietor demonstrating

the assembly steps (band sawing, "close scrutiny," and more) of the two-bell, oak wall phone. Special interest at its weird but wonderful best.

Pricing Original old oak wall phones cost between $150 and $200, depending on size and extras.

Wood Signs/Carving

Shelley Signs and Carvings
Box 94
West Danby, NY 14896
(607) 564-3527

Mary Shelley hand-carves and paints signs for stores, restaurants, and your house and also does custom artwork, like a picture of your house that she can do from a good photograph, in the form of low-relief, painted wood carvings. A unique service.

Business operation Mary Shelley will send you several prints showing her work. One of her signs has been shown at the Smithsonian. Signs can be made from photographs or your sketches and suggestions, to hang over your fireplace, mount into a door panel, or wherever you want. Write for more information and prices.

Finishing and Repair

Antique and Instrument Restoration

The Musical Museum
Deansboro, NY 13328
(315) 841-8774

"An amazing collection of things that go toot, whistle, plunk, and boom." Positively unique, this line from the museum's literature accurately sets the stage for what you'll find. The museum acquires, displays, repairs, and restores music boxes, zithers, pipe organs, nickleodeons, even a mechanical bird that flies from branch to branch and chirps. The Museum also stocks old lamps and lamp parts, including bent glass, painted china shades, and Woodstock cloth shades. Art, the proprietor, writes, "We have had to repair too many botched jobs to be in favor of the do-it-yourself approach. We will work with those who are talented enough to do things the right way, and we can furnish hints, parts, ideas, historical research, etc."

Business operation   Write for a brochure describing the museum and lamp shop. Restoration services should be arranged face to face. The Museum staff offers an antique workshop (informally) year round during business hours (10:00 to 5:00). Tours are given at special rates for scheduled groups and senior citizens. Deansboro is north of Cooperstown (Baseball Hall of Fame). If that doesn't help you, it is south of Utica on Rte. 12. If that doesn't help you, call Art for directions.

cluding a limited range of chair and stool kits ready to assemble, finish, and weave.

Business operation   The company sells nationally via mail order.

Pricing   A 250-ft coil of fine (1½ mm) carriage cane is about $5; same length of 3½ mm common cane is the same price, increasing by about a third for 1000-ft hanks. Cane is select quality, freshly cut from rattan with strands 8 ft or longer. Terms are cash with order or COD or approved credit with charge cards; shipping within 24 hours of order.

Frank's Cane & Rush Supply
7244 Heil Ave.
Huntington Beach, CA 92647
(714) 847-0707

This mail-order house has a moderately priced selection of supplies that includes many grades of cane, rush, sea grass, plus spline material, machine-woven cane, complete do-it-yourself kits, and a huge poster that details seat weaving steps start to finish. It also carries related tools. The catalog is free.

Cane, Rush, and Splint Supplies

Cane & Basket Supply Company
1283 S. Cochran Ave.
Los Angeles, CA 90019
(213) 939-9644

In business as importers and distributors since 1934, this company supplies a complete selection of cane, fiber rush, Hong Kong sea grass, Danish seat cord, flat and oval reed splint, basket reed, machine-woven cane webbing in some eighteen patterns, and specialty tools for the work. A free, illustrated catalog with useful do-it-yourself information is sent on request, in-

Cleaners/Polishes

Pacific Engineering, Inc.
PO Box 145
Farmington, CT 06032
(201) 674-8913

Pacific makes a limited variety of furniture waxes and polishes, specifically a carnuba paste wax, a pigmented wax for dark wood finishes, a sealer and polisher for new wood surfaces, and another, somewhat hard-to-find item, silvering powder. This is a powder made from true silver and used to permanently plate copper, brass, or bronze and to resilver antique clock dials and other items.

Business operation Pacific sells nationally through dealers and by mail order. It will answer inquiries with product brochures and a price list for mail-order customers. Also, they write, "We have a full line of information and can offer personal advice in the use of our products."

Pricing Retail costs are approximately $4.50 per ½-lb can plus shipping.

Clock Repair/Restoration
Clocks, Etc.
1506 N. Main St.
Walnut Creek, CA 94596
(415) 932-7787

This firm handles complete restoration of all time pieces but specializes in restoring antique clocks and pocket watches, including case, dial, and works. It also does appraisals on these items.

Business operation Serving the Bay area, Clocks, Etc. will respond to inquiries about specific antique pieces with a Polaroid of the item (for $1) if they have it or can locate it.

Furniture Refinishing
The Hope Company
2052 Congressional Dr.
St. Louis, MO 63141
(314) 432-5697

Hope sells a refinishing agent it claims will not disrupt wood patina, wood fillers, or glue joints but will remove only the surface finish of lacquer, varnish, or shellac. It is not recommended for removing paint or urethane finishes. The mixture contains methanol and toluene and is poisonous. Hope also

sells 100 percent pure tung oil (also available in aerosol spray), tung oil varnish (a mixture of the oil and varnish that produces a higher sheen), a furniture cleaner, and pure lemon oil. A new product for Hope is stove black, rated heat resistant to 1200 degrees F.

Business operation Hope sells nationally through wholesalers, retailers, home centers, and discount stores. Write the company for several small brochures on its products with general application instructions.

Pricing Varies at local level.

Glass/Mirrors/Resilvering
Atlantic Glass & Mirror Works
439 N. 63 St.
Philadelphia, PA 19151
(215) 747-6866

Atlantic sells plate glass, Lexan, and does storefront and custom mirror installations, and more, including quality resilvering. It is, as Joyce and Mark Taylor, the proprietors of Atlantic write, "a bona fide historical craft. We are established for forty-seven years, specialists in custom resilvering of antique beveled and/or engraved mirrors. Real silver is used in this process. Up to six weeks' time may be needed to complete one mirror. Cost is based on the silver market." And that's the problem. Silver is a volatile commodity.

Business operation Atlantic's minimum fee is $30, for setup and labor, plus a fee per square footage depending on the mirror style and condition. (Again, depending on the market, the fee could be $20 a sq ft.) Atlantic has no literature to send you. They deal regularly with decorators, architects, and antique dealers, but welcome your inquiry. You may spot one of their ads in the *Old House Journal*.

Insulated Window Shades

Appropriate Technology Corporation
PO Box 975
Brattleboro, VT 05301
(802) 257-4501

Window Quilt is an energy-saving material made of a sheet of aluminized polyester plastic acting as a heat reflector and vapor barrier and sandwiched between two layers of fiberfill insulation, and covered with polyester fabric. Available in some fifty colors, the thin, rollable package is ultrasonically welded to simulate a quilting stitch. Tests conducted for the company show that while single glazing has an R value of .9, adding a Window Quilt with magnetic or velcro seal to the window frame rates R-4.3.

Business operation   Standard units and a commercial quality material meeting strict flame tests are available through a national network of 1800 dealers. Each is required to have measuring and installation capabilities. There are twenty-two professional field representatives across the United States and Canada to deal with technical and installation questions. Inquiries net a color brochure, several mini-samples, and dealer list.

Pricing   Varies at local level.

Lamp and Chair Repair

E. W. Pyfer
218 N. Foley Ave.
Freeport, IL 61032
(815) 232-8968

Pyfer offers a wide variety of repair services and parts but only in two specific areas: lamps and chairs. The lamp service includes rewiring, brass plating, replacing missing parts, restoration, conversion to electricity, and shade repair. He maintains a stock of Aladdin parts and other chimneys, globes,

and shades. Chair caning and seat weaving with natural rush, reed, and hickory split can be done as well.

Business operation   This is a retail business that responds to mail orders. Mr. Pyfer reports, "We will answer all questions at no charge. Customers may write for specific items and/or information."

Ornamental Metal and Stone

Kenneth Lynch & Sons
78 Danbury Rd.
Wilton, CT 06897
(203) 762-8363

Practically every possible piece of architectural and ornamental sculpture, fountain, bench, gate, sundial, and weather vane can be found in one of Lynch's catalogs or books. Traditional craft skills are used to produce items like a 48-in weather vane in gold leaf or verde antique copper representing an American eagle with wings spread (about $1700) and a bronze horizontal sundial ($65). Kenneth Lynch, Sr., reports, "We sell mainly to architects and decorators all over the United States, and we make over 10,000 items, our principal interest is garden ornaments, sundials, and weather vanes." Lynch offers a 750-page encyclopedia of garden ornaments with over 3000 illustrations and fully illustrated catalogs on the following: hand-wrought lighting fixtures, gallery and museum supplies, benches, gesso, architectural sheet metal, ironwork, weather vanes and cupolas, and sundials—fun for enthusiasts, collectors, and craftspeople.

Business operation   Lynch sells nationally.

Pricing   Write for current catalog prices or quotes on custom work from your plans and specifications. Bound catalogs for the specific categories listed above, which include detailed specs, may be ordered at $2.50 each for softcover, $5.50 for hardcover, plus $1.50 postage' and handling— all refundable on your first order.

Paint and Supplies
S. Wolf's Sons
771 Ninth Ave.
New York, NY 10019
(212) 245-7777

Wolf's has been in business in New York for about 115 years. It sells paint, wallpaper, tools, and allied supplies in small and large quantities. (It supplied several several thousand gallons to the Empire State Building recently.) Wolf's stock a really complete selection of paint and stain, including many specialty items such as heat resistant and fire retardant paints, antibleeding aluminum sealer, blackboard coating, luminous paint, and more.

Business operation People behind the counter at the Ninth Avenue store will supply color cards and a lot of practical advice. Do-it-yourselfers don't realize how many special products for special cases there are until they get a look at a catalog like Wolf's that's really complete.

Photo and Frame Supplies
Light Impressions
439 Monroe Ave.
PO Box 940
Rochester, NY 14603
(716) 271-8960

Light Impression's catalog covers a wide range of photographic supplies and also displays many tools and materials for framing, mounting, and mat cutting, plus brad drivers, miter clamps, and even the Lion Miter-Trimmer (above $200 now, but still the ultimate moulding tool). Photography hounds will appreciate the book list, available prints, specialty slide storage, and even slide making equipment.

Refinishing Products/Stains
Formby's, Inc.
825 Crossover Lane
Memphis, TN 38117
(901) 685-7555

I'm not sure why I am skeptical when a company that makes a decent line of products suddenly bursts on the scene with aggressive, national advertising. I guess I worry that it's the same old product all hyped up or that the product may suffer in order to pay for all that advertising. But Formby's, which makes furniture refinishing products, wiping stains, cleaners, and even complete' refinishing kits with gloves, steel wool, and the works, shows two positive indicators. First, while its literature does a lot of self-selling its *Furniture Fact Book* answers real questions with real information, not advertising hype as so many do. Also, J. Michael Ward, product manager at Formby's, writes, "Consumers can receive a personal reply regarding any furniture refinishing, staining, or finishing questions by writing to Homer Formby, PO Box 667, Olive Branch, MS 38657." Maybe homespun Homer really does sit down and write out all the answers. Maybe not. It's still an unusual offer, worth trying before or after you try their products. I doubt that you are impressed much by advertising platitudes, but that, like me, you're willing to take a good look at a company's products when that company is willing to give you usable help and advice.

Business operation Formby's sells retail

in paint, hardware, and department stores, plus many lumberyards and home centers. Write the headquarters for free literature.

Stripping/Restoration

Chem Clean Furniture Restoration Center
Rte. 7
Arlington, VT 05250
(802) 375-2743

Chem Clean is a nationally franchised system of paint and varnish removal. No central source of advertising and information is available, although you might try looking up Chem Clean in your local yellow pages. In any case, this particular shop combines the stripping service with related services like hardware and paint sales.

Business operation The firm will be happy to talk to customers about any phase of furniture restoration. It supplies do-it-yourself materials; stripping, repair, and refinishing materials; and seat weaving, stenciling, and other services.

Wax/Cleaners

The Butcher Polish Company
PO Box G
Marlborough, MA 01752
(617) 481-1700

In business since 1880, this company is best known for Butcher's Wax, both Bowling Alley Paste, which is clear, and Boston Polish, which has an amber tint and is recommended to hide nicks and scratches. However, this company also makes a full line of wax for kitchen floors, tile, and both cleaners and liquid black for woodstoves. Tried and true products.

Business operation The company will send you two product sheets giving very brief, general descriptions of its products free and, for 50¢, a small booklet containing very basic but reasonably thorough cleaning and care instructions. But why bother? It's an established company with a good reputation. So try a small can and then make up your mind if you want more. You can buy the products at almost any hardware and home lumber outlet.

S. C. Johnson & Son, Inc.
Racine, WI 53403
(414) 631-2000

Johnson Wax makes a full line of waxes, sealers, polishes, and other furniture and floor care products, generally available. Of interest to consumers are two booklets the company offers at no charge, one called *Floor Care* and the other, *Furniture Care*. Both are well detailed, illustrated booklets (about 30 pages each) that do not waste your time with a lot of advertising hype but get to the point, including practical instructions, tips on refinishing, dealing with everyday scrapes, burns, and so forth. Worth writing for.

Window Coverings

Perkowitz Window Fashions, Inc.
135 Green Bay Rd.
Wilmette, IL 60091
(312) 251-7700

Perkowitz is a major supplier of all types of window coverings, including stock and custom shutters in unfinished pine that are painted or stained and louvered shutters, blinds, and shades.

Business operation Perkowitz sells nationally wholesale, retail, and via mail order.

Write for comprehensive product information, including do-it-yourself advice and graphic installation instructions.

Window Shutters
Pease Industries, Inc.
2001 Troy Ave.
PO Box 510
New Castle, IN 47362
(317) 529-1700
1 (800) 543-1180 (Toll-free)

Pease manufactures rolling window shutters that mount outside and are controlled from inside. The shutter is made of horizontal PVC slats that are linked together and travel in guide rails mounted along the outside of windows or doors. The roller housing can be mounted on existing walls or recessed into soffits. The hollow slats not only offer a degree of protection but also trap a layer of air between the slats and the glass. It is an interesting system, even though it may make your home look a bit like a store closed up for the holidays.
Business operation Illustrated product literature is sent on request, along with an architectural spec sheet.

Wood Care/Finishing
Wood Tender Finishing Products
4611 Macklind Ave.
St. Louis, MO 63109
(314) 481-0700

The Wood Tender's catalog offers a diverse selection of tools and materials used by manufacturers and many specialty items that most home centers don't stock and can't order for you either—things like small diameter, brad point drill bits, breast drills, complete furniture repair kits with small amounts

of wax, solvents, lacquers, and more, to deal with any repair problem.
Business operation The catalog is sent on request.

Wood Finishing
Daly's, Inc.
1121 North 36th
Seattle, WA 98103
(206) 633-4204

Daly's offers a complete line of wood finishing products, including bleaches, removers, stains, and surface sealers. It carries teak oil, marine sealer, teak cleaner, oxalic acid crystals, aniline stain remover, paste wood filler, and even a modest line of equipment like scrapers and gloves.
Business operation After selling regionally for over 30 years, Daly's has, for the past 5 years, sold via mail order. A booklet, available free, gives brief descriptions of its products. A terrific manual, titled *Wood Finishing Class Notes* (for $2) is a thorough treatment of many wood finishing subjects and even includes a kind of troubleshooting flow chart where you ask questions and work your way through a tree of solutions to get the job done. Naturally, at the end of some of those trees are Daly's products. But the information here is quite specific and definitely helpful.

Deft Wood Finishing Products, Inc.
PO Box C-19507
Irvine, CA 92713
(714) 549-8911

Deft manufactures clear wood finishes, polyurethanes, Danish oil finishes, an acrylic coating called Wood Armor, and a full line of stains and wood tints. Most are available in liquid and aerosol.

Business operation Write to the head-quarters listed above for the Deft catalog.

Finish Feeder Company
PO Box 60
Boyds, MD 20841
(301) 972-1474

Finish Feeder is an exotic combination of penetrating natural plant oils and beeswax used to "feed," restore, and protect natural wood resins that seal the surface of all woods. The idea is to duplicate a natural sealing process where resins bleeding from cut wood crystallize and harden on or near the surface. A modest but informative flyer explains Finish Feeder, its use on wood after old finishes are removed, and its application on raw wood. One pint is specified to cover 400 sq ft. Penetrating stains or clear liquid sealers may be used under a first coat.

Business operation Manufactures and distributes nationally by mail order, primarily to antique dealers and professional furniture refinishers. That should tell you something.

Pierce & Stevens Chemical Corporation
PO Box 1092
Buffalo, NY 14240
(716) 856-4910

This company produces wood finishes, one of which you may know by its trade name, Fabulon. The current version of this product is called Aqua Fabulon, denoting that this is a water-based acrylic wood finish. According to product specifications, Aqua Fabulon covers 300 to 500 sq ft per gal and produces a dust-free surface within ½ to 1 hour of application. The object can be re-coated in 1 to 2 hours and used in 12 to 15 hours. It is nonflammable, cleans up with water, and comes with a pad applicator.

Business operation The company sells nationally through retail stores. It will supply product information free on request, including a short brochure on preparing and refinishing old or new wood floors.

Sutherland Welles, Ltd.
206 W. Main St.
Carrboro, NC 27510

Sutherland carries several different tung oil wood finishing products, including sealers, low- and high-luster finishes, polymerized tung oil, and antiquing oil, plus custom stains. The polymerized oil produces a hard surface finish that is suitable for flooring.

Business operation Sutherland sells through Garrett Wade, Fine Tool, Wood-craft, and other mail-order houses and also direct via mail order. It will send a catalog with prices on request and soon will introduce a complete line of marine products, including an ultraviolet shield and an anti-fouling ingredient.

Hardware

Antique Hardware Reproductions
Antique Hardware Company
PO Box 1592
Torrance, CA 90505
(213) 378-5990

Antique Hardware makes a line of small hardware such as knobs, keyhole escutch-eons, teardrop pulls, bails and trim plates, halltree hooks, and many drawer pulls. All are replicas of antiques and generally ornate. The castings are hand sanded to remove burrs, then tumbled with nuggets to remove sanding marks and impart an antique appearance.

Business operation The catalog is sent on request and shows all hardware in actual size photographs. The minimum order is $10.

Brass Fixtures/Fittings/Hardware
Sign of the Crab
8101 Elder Creek Rd.
Sacramento, CA 95824
(916) 383-2722

It costs $2, but it is an "ooh-aah" catalog, with a stunning cover—a large, solid brass crab, incredibly detailed, in a splash of water on a black background. The full-color catalog offers some gadgets and gizmos like a 19-in-high replica of a Mark V diver's helmet, a good selection of brass bells, barometers, clocks, door knockers and handles and letterboxes, plus a lot of bathroom brass: exposed brass piping, faucets, etc. Really nice stuff.

Business operation Sign of the Crab's main office has a showroom and other retail outlets across the country (nine of them) can be located by writing the headquarters at the address above. The brass "watering can" shower heads, hammered brass bar sinks, wall-mounted glass holders are something to see.

Brass Locks/Hardware
Baldwin Hardware Manufacturing
  Corporation
841 Wyomissing Blvd.
PO Box 82
Reading, PA 19603
(215) 777-7811

Baldwin makes no bones about it—"Baldwin is a manufacturer of the finest hardware products available in America." Its sales manager's enthusiasm is unbounded.

And in the category of early American rim locks, keyhole latches, knob and lock trim, I don't know another firm that matches its reputation. Baldwin manufactures all kinds of brass hardware such as recessed pulls, door knockers, hinges, and such, beautiful lever handle hardware (some with Limoges porcelain handles that are delicately hand painted and absolutely astonishing), and a fine line of mortise locks and hardware. But the cream of the crop is covered in Baldwin's catalog, *18th Century Colonial Lock Makers*. The simple but elegant brass rim locks, beveled edge rim locks, Dutch elbows, and the like are specified for many historic restoration jobs. Baldwin's brass is manufactured using a forging process that the company estimates improves tensile strength by 250 percent over conventional castings and produces a surface without imperfections.

Business operation Baldwin sells exclusively through distributors (no mail order), and has started a series of privately owned stores called Baldwin Brass Centers. The company will provide distributor referrals on request. Its catalogs are exceptional.

Ceiling Fans
Casablanca Fan Company
182 S. Raymond Ave.
PO Box 37
Pasadena, CA 91109
(213) 960-6441

Casablanca, aside from grabbing one of the best possible names for a fan company, has one of the best owner's manuals for fans or any other electrical product. First, though, Casablanca makes many different ceiling fans. Its Centennial model has many solid bronze decorative fittings, etched rosewood blades, and hand-cut crystal light shades, all done in a limited signed and numbered production run of 5000. Most of the fan designs have real, albeit intricate and ornate, character. Also, Casablanca makes sixteen different kinds of blades in teak, walnut, cane, and other woods and twenty-five different kinds of lamp shades for fans with fixtures attached below the motor housing. Its catalog covers it all. The owner's manual I looked through has 18 pages filled with photographs and illustrations and covers electrical safety, mounting locations for maximum energy efficiency, and installation and wiring, including optional wiring applications, plus troubleshooting and specs. It leaves nothing out. Too bad most companies don't take this kind of care with the customers who buy their products.

Business operation Casablanca has about 1000 retail outlets across the country where you can get product information. The company will handle inquiries direct and offers a toll-free line: (800) 423-1821; in California only, (800) 352-8515.

The Ceiling Fan Company
4212 S.W. 75th Ave.
Miami, FL 33155
(305) 261-3356

This fan company has a modest collection of fans that have specific motifs, like shell designs, leaves, or birds. They are offered in a variety of finishes, including dark and light paints, polished brass, bright copper, nickel-chrome, and antiqued copper, with paddles in oak, mahogany, rosewood, teak, ash, pecan, and maple. It carries Hunter's line of light kits and motors.

Business operation This firm has recently finished a book called *A Consumer's Buying Guide* on ceiling fans, which covers a little ceiling fan history, motor workings, installations, and more. You can write for product literature (Catalog No. 5), and information on the consumer guide.

Pricing Prices range from about $200 to $350 depending on metal and wood finish.

Robbins & Myers, Inc. (Hunter Fans)
Comfort Conditioning Division
2500 Frisco Ave.
Memphis, TN 38114
1 (800) 238-6872 (Toll-free)

Robbins & Myers makes more than 50 models of Hunter fans that are available with some 100 accessories such as decorative ceiling plates and light kits to mount just below the blade spindle. The basic design of Hunter fans has remained the same since 1903. (The company was founded in 1886.) Paddles are available in colors and wood finishes, with cane inserts, from 38- to 52-in diameters.

Business operation Through the toll-free line consumers can reach Hunter's "fan doctor" any weekday. The company's catalog includes sizing information and installation requirements. Independent service centers are located in most major cities. If they do not have product catalogs, write the company at the address above or use the toll-free line. Form CF–75 provides a full listing of products and features. Hunter estimates that a fan can make a 78 degree room feel like 72 degrees when used with air-conditioning. Savings are equally significant when warm air at ceilings is brought down where the people are during the winter.

Colonial Hardware

Acorn Manufacturing Company, Inc.
PO Box 31
Mansfield, MA 02048
(617) 339-4500

Acorn forge has been producing Colonial builders hardware, decorative hardware, fireplace equipment, and similar items for about 35 years. Its wide selection, which includes cabinet latches, door and drawer pulls, strap hinges, H and H-L hinges, and thumb latches, is generally available in four different finishes: hand-wrought black iron, pewter finish, antique copper, or antique brass. Most of its pieces can be purchased with plain or forged edges.

Business operation   Robert M. DeLong, Acorn's president, writes, "If consumers are unable to purchase through a local retailer, they may order direct from the factory at the suggested retail." A complete catalog is available with price list.

Decorative Hardware

The Decorative Hardware Studio
160 King St.
Chappaqua, NY 10514
(914) 238-5251

The Decorative Hardware Studio's catalog is a massive compilation of fine hardware, including basin and tub sets, seashell basins, forged brass door knockers, heavy-duty mortise locks, forged brass door knobs and lever handles, carpet rods, and the like.

Business operation   For information on prices and availability write the company.

Decorative Hardware/Fixtures

W. J. Weaver and Sons, Inc.
1208 Wisconsin Ave. NW
Washington, DC 20007
(202) 333-4200

Weaver is a decorator supply house with an extensive catalog of locks, door knockers, light fixtures, all kinds of hardware, mouldings, signs, weather vanes, and a lot more.

Business operation   They feature a selection of molded styrene ceiling ornaments—

like very detailed shell and sunburst patterns in which, for example, you might center a chandelier. They are applied with contact cement.

Pricing   Ceiling medallion prices range from about $7 for small (2 in × 4 in) designs, up to approximately $15 for intricate 34-in-diameter designs. The catalog, 60 pages of pictures and descriptions to ooh and aah at, is available with a complete price list for $2.50. This firm has been in business since 1889 and ships nationwide.

Fireplace Equipment

Lemee's Fireplace Equipment
815 Bedford St.
Bridgewater, MA 02324
(617) 697-2672

Lemee's catalog includes all kinds of decorative and functional fireplace equipment such as screens, andirons, wood baskets, hearth brooms, and more. Also, Lemee's will send details with photographs of its firebacks and line of fireplace cranes.

Business operation   Lemee's nearly 40-page catalog is available for $1. Lemee's ships nationwide.

General Repair Supplies/Hardware

Defender Industries, Inc.
PO Box 820
255 Main St.
New Rochelle, NY 10801
(914) 632-3001

The Defender mail-order catalog is a marine buyer's guide, as in Evinrude outboards and boat hooks and bilge pumps. They have a lot of that but a lot more, particularly a diverse collection of hardware, tools, and repair products like fiber-glass tape and epoxy paints, and more. The extensive, 168-page catalog is available for $1.25.

Business operation Defender has a policy of allowing you to place an order with them at any price less than the one listed in their catalog, if you include a tearsheet from the less expensive source as proof. Of course, you could simply order from the other source instead. A catchall source of specialty items.

Industrial Security Products

Sargent & Greenleaf, Inc.
One Security Dr.
Nicholasville, KY 40356
(606) 885-9411

This firm makes high-quality, sophisticated security products and locking mechanisms, particularly for the safe and banking industry. But it does make some equipment rated commercial. In most cases that means heavy-duty and appeals to many consumers. Although most of its sales are to the OEM (original equipment manufacturers) market, Judee Brummette writes, "We do have a customer service department that would be happy to supply specific information on locking mechanisms for safes and vaults along with digital access control padlocks and deadbolts."

Ironing Board Built-In

Dorz Manufacturing Company
Box 456
Bellevue, WA 98009
(206) 454-5472

Since I grew up watching "Ozzie & Harriet" and similar programs that displayed family and rec rooms the size of football fields, all with built-in this and gadget that, it figures

that one of the little extras that really appeals to me is a product like this one—a recessed ironing board, fitted into a wood cabinet with your choice of birch or pine doors with hardwood frame, all of which tucks into the 3¾-in recess between wall studs. What fun. Is it a fuse box, a closet? No. It's the Murphy Bed of household appliances, and eliminates finding a storage space for one of the truly gangly and ugly but essential pieces of household equipment.

Business operation Although Darrel Razor writes that his product is distributed nationwide, he will fill orders at the factory, shipping direct. For a look, you can get an illustrated brochure on request that shows the door options, gives rough openings, etc.

Iron-A-Way, Inc.
220 W. Jackson
Morton, IL 61550
(309) 266-7232

Iron-A-Way calls its unit a "compact pressing valet." Oh well. It is a nifty piece of hardware complete with fold down ironing board; pressing arm board and light (as options); electrical panel with automatic timer, outlet, and pilot indicator light; and built-in insulated storage for an iron, all tucked neatly into a narrow cabinet that can be recessed between 16-in centered wall studs. Several different sizes are available with other options like a raised wood panel for the door or a cane door. It's a great way to save space.

Business operation Iron-A-Way responds to inquiries by referring you to a local dealer and including a full brochure and ordering information with its response. You can order direct from the company as well. In fact, Jana L. Diegel, the sales secretary, writes, "If they [consumers] are within the continental United States and send in the order blank within 60 days of the date marked on it, we will pay the freight."

Joint Fasteners/Clinches

Superior Fastener Corporation
9536 W. Foster Ave.
Chicago, IL 60656
(312) 992-3777

Superior makes Skotch wood fasteners. Shaped like a large, toothy staple, the fastener has two prongs at each corner that are splayed slightly to draw together the joint between them as the staple is set. A variety of flat fasteners are available, from a small ⅜-in × 1-in unit to a ¾-in × 2-in model. They are made of rust resistant cadmium steel. Superior also makes a round version of the fastener for repairing and securing chair rungs, the idea being that the small teeth protruding from the fastener sleeve grab onto the sides of the socket, preventing the rung from coming loose.

Business operation Superior sells nationally retail and wholesale. You can write for free product pages or directly to Paul R. Armstrong, who writes, "I would be happy to answer any letter sent to my attention." This kind of fastening system may appeal particularly to do-it-yourselfers who regularly make a mess of themselves and the wood they are working on when they use glue. The rung fastener, for instance, eliminates the need to glue or clamp.

Kitchen Storage Equipment

Rubbermaid, Inc.
Home Products Division
1147 Akron Rd.
Wooster, OH 44691
(216) 264-6464

Whatever you have that is remotely connected to kitchens and food, Rubbermaid makes something that will hold it, seal it, or store it—well, almost anything you have. The company makes all kinds of garbage cans (they call them *household containers*), space organizers, bowls, canisters, shelf liners, and even flower pots and watering cans. Some of its items have obvious utility —a moulded silverware tray to make some sense out of a drawer, plastic inserts that hang from steel refrigerator shelves to store bottles and cans in space that is usually wasted, and more. But some of its products really have nothing special going for them— a soap dish that is just a soap dish. It's no big deal, but in some instances the company seems to have been carried away by the idea of organization so that the four items on your dresser now sit neatly in a fifth item.

Business operation Rubbermaid products are available nationwide in many home centers and other retail outlets. The company has voluminous product literature, summed up in their Catalog HC–250, *Housewares Catalog.*

Kitchen Storage/Hardware

Amerock Corporation
4000 Auburn St.
Rockford, IL 61101
(815) 963-9631

Amerock manufactures cabinet and decorative hardware, drawer suspension systems, and kitchen storage equipment. For those interested in what Amerock calls a *unified decorative motif*, switchplates, bath, and general lock hardware is available in the same styles so that once you decide to go Georgian, you can go all the way. In any case, I think the outstanding feature here is a line of kitchen storage hardware sold under the name Cabinet Aides. For instance, it includes a shelf system with solid brackets made of the shelving materials and fitted to a concealed metal bracket. The system has clean lines and dispenses with the need for shelf standards. Also, Amerock makes several inventive storage systems: cookbook racks that pop down from beneath upper kitchen cabinets, knife racks that do the same thing, a medical cabinets with child resistant latch for mounting on the door of a high cabinet, small storage trays to fit on the back of false front drawers that are normally fixed in front of sinks and such, plus the more conventional array of lazy susan cabinet organizers, etc. Many of these simple products show a practical sense of design and will help you use kitchen space more effectively.

Business operation Products are sold nationwide through an extensive network of retail stores. The company will send along two small brochures at no cost: one covers decorative hardware, the other illustrates the kitchen storage systems.

Legs and Hardware

M. Wolchonok & Son, Inc.
155 E. 52 St.
New York, NY 10022
(212) 755-2168

Wolchonok is a major distributor of furniture hardware, including an extensive selection of legs in wood (turned, carved, etc.), and cast legs with brass plating, which are highly detailed. It also carries a full line of Sheperd casters, sockets, glides, door stops, and such. The company handles a modular polished chrome furniture framing system—the clip-together type that can be attached to make coffee table frames and so forth. Wolchonok carries decorative hardware a step further to include a full line of Artistic Brass plumbing valves and faucets, including Victorian porcelain and grass fittings as well as ultramodern sculptured chrome and lucite fittings.

Business operation The company sells

wholesale and retail locally and will ship goods. I asked them what help, information, and literature consumers could receive by contacting them. The reply was straightforward: "They state their problems—and we'll solve them." Write for catalogs, or if you are in New York, wander in.

Locks

Master Lock Company
2600 N. 32 St.
PO Box 10367
Milwaukee, WI 53210
(414) 444-2800

Master makes all types of padlocks, residential alarm systems, and several specialty locks, all covered in their Catalog No. 77. Some of the special application products include hasplocks, gun locks that encircle the trigger area, trailer locks that secure standard ball and cam connections, even locking bars that protect the pressure screws on outboard motors.

Business operation If literature is not available locally write the company.

Simplex Security Systems, Inc.
Front and Main Sts.
Collinsville, CT 06022
(203) 693-8391

Simplex manufactures locks that do not resemble ordinary locks. They are push-button operated combination locks. Generally the entry door locks have a numbered panel above the cylinder (one to five, for instance) that can be set to open only when a certain sequence is pushed, and on some models this can include pushing two buttons at the same time, which yields a staggering number of possible combinations. This certainly eliminates the problem of losing your keys.

Business operation Simplex has extensive literature covering products, installation, combination changes, and full technical data, all available to interested consumers.

Pricing Deadbolt push-button locks cost about $80 with all hardware and range upward of $200 for sophisticated systems with time delay, inside key and latchbolt controls, and other features.

Restoration Mouldings/Hardware Specialties
San Francisco Victoriana
2245 Palou Ave.
San Francisco, CA 94124
(415) 648-0313

San Francisco Victoriana produces a large selection of restoration mouldings. They also carry a good selection of ornamental plaster, from small, 5½-in acanthus leaf shapes (about $25), to 38-in diameter, high-relief "Elizabeth" center medallions (an incredible piece with four fully sculpted heads centering the leaf and flower pattern). This firm is one of the few carrying anaglypta (embossed wall covering) in thirteen patterns with eight different borders in rolls from 3- to 14-in wide. In addition to this, the firm handles a nice line of fireplace mantels, Victorian light fixtures and glass shades, and an amazing array of ornate door and window hardware, including hinges, knobs, keyhole escutcheons, all deeply sculpted, replicating some of the most unusual mass-produced hardware made in this country between 1870 and 1915.

Business operation Complete catalogs are $3; free in the company's showroom. Sample packets of wallcoverings can be ordered. Also, this firm handles the Steptoe cast iron spiral stair; a classic.

Storage Organizers
Akro-Mils
1293 S. Main St.
Akron, OH 44301
(216) 253-5593

Akro-Mils manufactures plastic and metal storage organizers, including metal cabinet, plastic drawer units for all kinds of small shop hardware (like sixty-drawer cabinets), and all kinds of large, bulk storage systems, multiple plastic bins on wheels, and more. Many of the applications are commercial and industrial, but many of the moulded plastic items (like extremely compact swing bins) are ideal for recapturing some dead kitchen cabinet space.

Business operation The company offers to respond to inquiries by phone or mail and will send illustrated product literature with prices on request. David Moreland of Akro-Mils writes, "With smaller homes and more people living in apartments than ever before, their space is more valuable and they need to be able to store things economically and efficiently, which Akro-Mils offers the consumer." Pricing is quite reasonable, and it is almost certain that you will find a good use for one of the storage systems in the catalog.

Timing Controls
Intermatic, Inc.
Intermatic Plaza
Spring Grove, IL 60081
(815) 675-2321

Intermatic is the world's largest manufacturer of all kinds of timing controls, both electronic and electromechanical, for home and industry. When you see 24-hour timers with labels that say Sears, Ward's, Penney's, Radio Shack, Ace Hardware, True Value Hardware, and other such well-known names, they are made by Intermatic. If this is news to you—that giant retailers don't actually manufacture all the products they sell—you qualify as a truly naïve consumer. Intermatic also sells retail through many catalog outlets. Probably its most useful device for owners and renters alike is the simple, very inexpensive 24-hour timer. You can use it to control appliances—something as simple as turning off the TV so that it doesn't run all night after you fall asleep halfway through the late movie. Also, a few timers can be set up to turn on and off lights, radios, TVs and more to simulate occupancy even when you're not home. This very basic burglary protection turns out to be quite effective. Basic Intermatic timers I have used have proven to be reliable and a good buy—particularly if you use your imagination to use them to save on energy costs.

Business operation   Although Intermatic has no special consumer department, they are responsive to consumer inquiries. Paul Saxton, vice-president of marketing, writes, "They can talk to anyone in the company from the president on down."

Tools and Hardware—General

The Stanley Works
PO Box 1843
New Britain, CT 06050
(203) 225-5111

Stanley is one of the largest, best-known manufacturers of hand tools. Also, they make an extensive line of hardware. Stanley is very responsive to consumer questions, offers good instruction and application literature—even a selection of thorough do-it-yourself construction plans for various home projects. Try to get hold of their massive Catalog No. 130, which includes an extensive, single-source selection of everything from fence hardware to brass drawer pull.

Business operation   Stanley sells only

through wholesalers and retailers and has no mail order. Inquiries about products, plans, etc. should go to Stanley at Department PID, PO Box 1800, New Britain, Connecticut 06050.

U.S. General
100 Commercial St.
Plainview, NY 11803
(516) 349-7275

This large catalog (over 6000 items) is free for the asking and carries a tremendous selection of many name brand tools at reasonable prices. For instance, the last catalog I saw had Milwaukee's Sawzall (the two-speed model plus case and blades) for $137, a pretty good price for a construction classic. Their drill section also covers B & D, Skil, Makita, and Rockwell. They have hoists, machine tools, four kinds of bolt cutters, shop vacs, fire extinguishers, furniture casters—tons of stuff. Write for the catalog, order small to start to make sure you're happy with quality, shipping, etc. Mailing is pretty reliable, prompt.

Wire Rack Storage

Schulte Corporation
11450 Grooms Rd.
Cincinnati, OH 45242
(513) 489-9300

Schulte manufactures welded wire products —epoxy-coated wire grids shaped into all kinds of storage and shelving units. It makes full closet systems with bracket mounts, door back racks for closets and kitchen pantry cabinets, and a full line of pull-out wire rack drawers. These units are not inexpensive, but when you think that they are very easy to install, require no fabrication on the job, and leave more room for storage than conventional wood shelving, the cost becomes more reasonable.

Business operation   Schulte sells to major catalog houses like Montgomery Ward and J. C. Penney as well as direct to home centers and hardware chain stores. Schulte's product booklet, "Space Efficient Storage Systems," covers product types and sizes in detail. Referrals to local retail outlets can be made if required. All in all, these systems let even inexperienced do-it-yourselfers get 50 percent more into a closet without having to nail the door closed to keep everything inside.

Woodwork/Hardware Supplies

The Woodworker's Store
21801 Industrial Blvd.
Rogers, MN 55374
(612) 428-4101

This is one of the best presentations of tools, materials, and supplies in this field; 112 pages of large, crystal-clear, color photographs, color artwork with cutaway views showing hardware details and operation—a beauty, and a bargain for $1. General coverage includes veneers, inlays, hardwood lumber, carved mouldings, cabinet and specialty hardware, all kinds of hand tools, finishing materials, kits, and books. Here are a few goodies: concealed, self-closing hinges; thirteen different kinds of lid and drop-leaf supports; magnetic touch catches (you really ought to try one of these); Tite Joint furniture fasteners; platform rocker springs; Ulmia hardwood planes. The latter are carried in several mail order catalogs but indicate the general quality of the selection here.

Business operation   Retail stores are in Minneapolis, Denver, Seattle, and Boston; in business for thirty years; mail order nationwide; mailing list of 125,000. A dollar well-spent for the catalog.

TRADE ASSOCIATIONS

Carpeting

Carpet and Rug Institute (CRI)
Director of Consumer Affairs
1629 K St. NW, Suite 700
Washington, DC 20006
(202) 223-2578

The Institute represents manufacturers and has on hand a variety of brochures and technical publications on carpet construction and maintenance. CRI may be helpful with unreconcilable complaints against manufacturers, although their full-time consumer panel has been disbanded.

Furniture Complaints

Furniture Industry Consumer Advisory
  Panel (FICAP)
Box 951
High Point, NC 27261
(919) 885-5065

FICAP was established in 1973 to help consumers with problems concerning new furniture. The panel is sponsored by the Southern Furniture Manufacturers Association and the Southwestern Furniture Manufacturers Association. It works with consumers nationally but only after you have exhausted conventional grievance channels; that is, going back to the point of sale or back to the manufacturer if the piece was defective in some way. FICAP, at that point, will step in to obtain a review of your complaint by management personnel in a position to do something about it, recommend affirmative action on your complaint to the retailer and manufacturer if called for, suggest alterna-tive solutions to an impasse, and so forth. It's worth trying, although it is an advisory body only and can't make a retailer or man-ufacturer do anything.

Business operation   Write FICAP for an informative brochure that runs through the distinctions in furniture labeling and com-plaint handling procedures.

PROFESSIONAL SOCIETIES

Locksmithing
Associated Locksmiths of America
   (ALOA)
3003 Live Oak St.
Dallas, TX 75204
(214) 827-1701

ALOA, which represents bonded locksmiths who have at least two years of full-time service and installation experience, can pro-vide brochures to consumers covering dif-ferent types of locks, keys, safes, and burglar alarms. It will provide referral services for professionals in your area and maintains a grievance committee to handle consumer problems with its members.

GOVERNMENT AGENCIES

Wood Finishing
USDA Forest Service, Forest Products
   Laboratory
PO Box 5130
Madison, WI 53705
(608) 264-5600

One of the best sources of information on all aspects of wood use, design, and perform-ance, the Forest Service offers a huge array of helpful, although largely technical, infor-mation. Report No. 81–024, *Wood Finish-ing List of Publications*, contains listings of specific reports on such subjects as perform-ance of mildecides in semitransparent stain, bleaching wood, finishing exterior plywood, protecting log cabins from decay, and much more. The publications list is free. And sin-gle copies of the individual reports it lists are free as well, as long as you request only single copies of a limited number (hope-fully in the same general field of interest). Blanket requests don't work.

CONSUMER EDUCATION

Information and Services

Carpet and Rug Care

The Carpet and Rug Institute (CRI)
Box 2048
Dalton, GA 30720
(404) 278-3176

CRI represents manufacturers of rugs and carpets. Although it does not offer mediation and complaint handling services, it does have two small consumer information booklets that may interest you. One, called *Chemical Spots and Stains on Carpet and Rugs*, gives causes and solutions to stains from bleach, food, and an array of chemicals. The other, *Carpet & Rug Care Guide*, is a more thorough treatment that covers do-it-yourself cleaning, wear, professional cleaning, and more. CRI will send both for $1 and an SASE with 40¢ return postage. If you're simply stuck with a carpet problem, I would try a letter first, asking the specific question, before springing for these pretty basic information booklets.

Practical Training

Crafts Instruction

Haystack Mountain School of Crafts
Deer Isle, ME 04627
(207) 348-6946

Haystack Mountain is a summer school in a stunning location on the edge of Penobscot Bay at Deer Isle. Five sessions (of 2 or 3 weeks each) cover subjects such as black-smithing, woodwork, metalwork, glass, and more.

Business operation   Haystack will send a brochure on request. Tuition is approximately $110 per week per person. Room and board is about $150.

Furniture and Wood Finishing

Dakota County Area Vocational-
   Technical Institute
County Rd. 42 at Akron Ave
PO Drawer K
Rosemount, MN 55068
(612) 423-8301

Whether learning a skill for a job or for themselves, Minnesota residents can do it at the Dakota County Area Vocational-Technical Institute for about $3.20 a day. That's the tuition for residents. More than forty different programs are offered, all approved for veteran training, with courses running from 6 months to 2 years. The campus is about 20 miles south of the twin cities area. An example: The 11-month course on wood finishing and wood service includes finishing, upholstery, refinishing, and structural repairs and covers spraying, glazing, regraining, color theory, and other specialties in separate courses. Full information is available free on request.

Locksmithing

Locksmithing Institute
Division, Technical Home Study Schools
Little Falls, NJ 07424

This school, established in 1948, offers a locksmithing course that teaches how to make keys by code number, identify key blanks, depulicate keys, and fit keys to locks. The course is approved by the New Jersey Commission of Education. An interesting way to learn a bit more than you need to know for most residential applications—

enough so that you may be able to use the craft to earn some money. The school will send a brochure describing the course at no charge. Also, it offers to respond promptly to any additional requests for information. Ask a lot and in detail before enrolling.

READING AND REFERENCE

American Furniture
American Furniture, by Helen Comstock
Viking Press

One of the most scholarly and readable tomes on the subject, starting with Jacobean and William and Mary and closing with Early Victorian in 1870. Over 300 pages with endless photographs, many in color, and an exhaustive text. One of the courses I took in college on early American furniture was taught at the Metropolitan Museum. The American wing was the classroom. This book, with details of every important furniture maker, was assigned as the text.

Antique Furniture
Repairing and Restoring Antique Furniture, by John Rodd
Van Nostrand Reinhold Company

There is some difference between repair and restoration. This book concentrates on restoration, which is simply repairing with the extra care required to preserve the style and detailing of an antique. This book covers dismantling, restoring components from even badly damaged parts, gluing and finishing and is very specific. It includes case histories, work on drawers, veneers, marquetry,

and more. A worthwhile investment with solid text and lots of tips from someone in the business.

Antique Reproduction
Make Your Own Antiques,
    by Francis Hagerty
Little, Brown and Company

With the title an obvious contradiction, seeming to head completely in the wrong direction, this book is not one I would have looked at had I not run into the author. Working on a magazine article about Shaker furniture, I discovered that the Boston Museum of Fine Arts recommended and sold a few "authentic" Shaker kits—a rocking chair that was particularly handsome. I tracked it back to Cohasset Colonials, Mr. Hagerty's company, and wound up spending a long morning there. It is unusual to find any company taking such care with everything from wood selection to customer service. The shop was filled with clear pine, shop jigs, multiple hole drilling machines (for doing Windsor chair seats in one shot) that were antiques in their own right but working beautifully. The book is thoughtful, accurate, and includes fine measured drawings for several furniture projects from a simple Shaker shelf to a six-board chest complete with stencil pattern. The book is missing only Hagerty's warm conversation.

Cabinet Making
The Home Cabinetmaker,
by Monte Burch
Harper & Row

This is one of the most comprehensive books you'll find on cabinet making; over 500 pages, with the text consistently supported by good photographs and artwork in the *Popular Science* tradition. The book starts with a solid chapter on wood characteristics, milling, curing, grading, and performance; goes on to fasteners, adhesives, and clamps; covers (in what is probably the strength of the book) all basic cabinet making techniques, joint by joint by mortise by dovetail in first-rate, understandable and usable detail. Other portions of this comprehensive book cover finishing, many specific furniture projects, millwork, the shop with tools and equipment, even a short chapter on carpentry and cabinet making as a career. This book is power tool oriented, making use of jigs and generally any tools and techniques that can be adapted to a home shop. Just about everything I can think of on the subject is there, down to really helpful little tidbits like a small chart listing the proper size pilot holes to drill for different screw sizes. No color photos of all that beautiful wood; that's the only drawback; about $27.

Carpet Selection/Installation
Olin Corporation
120 Long Ridge Rd.
Stamford, CT 06904
(203) 356-2000

One special service offered by Olin, in addition to selling a wide variety of floor covering products, is providing an informative guide called *The Carpet Report*, which contains information on selection and installation. Write Olin for a copy.

Chair Making
Make a Chair from a Tree,
by John D. Alexander, Jr.
Taunton Press

Slatback chairs are Mr. Alexander's specialty, and in this book he shows you how to get one out of a tree, step by step, with great attention to detail. Starting with designs and instructions for a workbench and shaving horse (the pieces of furniture you need to help you make a chair), the book is personalized, expressing a point of view. Using hand tools only, Mr. Alexander thinks each chair should be just a little bit different, depending on who is going to be sitting in it. A thorough treatment of a traditional subject; 125 pages; about $9.

Country Furniture and Tools
Country Woodcraft, by Drew Langsner
Rodale Books

This is a book to enjoy, whether you try to build the pitchforks, wheelbarrows, milking stools, benches, farmhouse tables, and many other projects covered or not. Many good illustrations and photographs and a straightforward text make the projects believable. The designs derive their beauty from simplicity, and that helps convince the reader that with a little practice the results shown can be achieved. If you enjoy working with wood, particularly if you appreciate hand as opposed to power production, you will have fun with this book. Very thorough; very clear; an excellent format that keeps the projects moving and understandable; and a good buy (about $11).

Decorating History
20th Century Decorating Architecture & Gardens, by House & Garden
Holt, Rinehart, and Winston

This book covers eighty years of the most unique pages from *House & Garden*. Someone made the right decision, and instead of doing a current look back, the original text was left in place, including picture captions. It winds up being a wonderful tour through each new wave and rediscovery in American design, architecture, and particularly furnishings from 1900 to 1980. Frankly, from the sixties on it is not exactly fascinating, probably because it is all too familiar. But the 2-page spread on an Adirondack lodge, a 1907 story titled, "A House For One Thousand Dollars" (and it was over 1200 sq ft), and more are real treats. Try the library first; this hardbound book was about $35 last time I checked.

Do-It-Yourself Projects
500 More Things to Make for Farm and Home
600 More Things to Make for Farm and Home
by Glen Charles Cook
Interstate Printers and Publishers

Between these two books there is enough to keep you busy indefinitely. These titles are not new (1944 and 1952 respectively), but

because they serve mainly as design guides and include classic construction and hardware like strap hinges, time is of little importance here. The pages are filled with illustrations that cover all kinds of benches, braces, doors, shelters, bins, troughs, and stock feeders. The straightforward plans are oriented to farm use, i.e., plank and beam construction, facenailing, and hardly a piece of moulding. Interesting design guides with endless specialty structures and contrivances in cutaway views with notes and measurements.

Finishing
Wood Finishing and Refinishing, by S. W. Gibbia
Van Nostrand Reinhold

This book offers a thorough treatment of subjects that are frequently tacked on to the end of books on designing and building furniture. In 270 well-illustrated pages, step by step stages of sanding, staining, varnishing, and sealing—you name it. And the book covers the fine points; killing or enhancing the effects of wood grain; different materials used to achieve different results; and brushing and hand rubbing techniques; about $10.

Furniture Building
The Build-It-Yourself Furniture Catalog, by Franklynn Peterson
Prentice-Hall

The styles are mostly mid-sixties—prosaic—but the book is well illustrated, heavy on details, and presents complete plans for twenty-four chairs, many tables, cabinets, shelf systems, headboards, chests, and more. If you don't decide to follow one of the plans, a look still gives valuable information on cutting patterns for minimal waste in plywood sheeting, gluing, and more.

Furniture—Measured Drawings
Masterpieces of Furniture,
   by Verna Cook Salomonsky
Dover Publications

For students of classic furniture and accomplished furniture makers, this book offers 101 plates with a photograph of a finished museum piece, a few paragraphs on its history, and an accompanying page of measured drawings. However, these drawings are not the how-to illustrations you may be used to —the exploded views and such—but simply elevations and sections with measurements. Chippendale, Sheraton, Queen Anne, Duncan Phyfe, and other styles and makers are represented by pieces from five museums.

Modern Furnishings
High-Tech, by Kron and Slesin
Clarkson Potter, Crown Publishers

At the other end of the spectrum from hand-crafted country tables, this book is more of a catalog, covering close to 2000 suppliers of furniture and fixtures that are sleek, clean, and generally utilitarian. The emphasis is on the industrial side of modern design—a lot of floor grates that might be used on a stairway in a factory. Some of the design applications may stretch the point (as in Tom Wolf's *From Bauhaus to Our House,* where

he talks about those nifty little $400,000 summer cottages that do in fact look a lot like chemical plants), but there is a lot of clean utilitarian equipment here. Try the library unless you love this stuff, as the lavishly illustrated book runs about $32.

Product Evaluations
Gadget Newsletter
116 W. 14th St.
New York, NY 10011
(212) 989-8001

For $15 a year (the U.S. subscription rate; $19 in Canada) you get a 12-page newsletter every month, nicely laid out with photographs and reviews of all kinds of gadgets that are generally a little off the beaten track and at the leading edge of technology or inventiveness or silliness. The newsletter covers audio and video equipment, kitchen appliances, tools, and even solar powered briefcases—weird but fun.
Business operation   The newsletter is fact filled and to the point, accurately subtitled as *The Newsletter for Grown-Up Kids* and is sold nationally by subscription only. See if you can get a sample issue, which may contain a new subscriber offer at a somewhat reduced rate.

Shaker
The American Shakers and Their Furniture, by John G. Shea
Van Nostrand Reinhold

Here is the definitive book on Shaker furniture design and construction, complete with over 100 pages of museum measured drawings. This is a book for woodworkers who can read plans and for anyone interested in the history of Shaker design.

By Shaker Hands, by June Sprigg
Knopf, 1975

A warm and loving look at the Shakers, their work, and all that they produced. Pencil drawings are used in place of photographs, which is the one drawback, but the text is personal. It includes a nice section on Sister Tabitha Babbit, of the Harvard, Massachusetts, community who, in 1810, invented the circular saw.

Upholstery
Upholstering Methods,
    by Fred W. Zimmerman
Goodheart-Wolcox Company
123 W. Taft Dr.
South Holland, IL 60473

This book covers a subject that is generally disregarded in furniture making books. They discuss the frame but not the cushions. The not very catchy title reflects the treatment inside—carefull step by step sequences with good illustrations covering padded and cush-

ion upholstery, seat weaving, how to tie off springs, and more; about 200 pages; $12.

Wicker
*Collecting and Restoring Wicker
    Furniture,* by Richard Saunders
Crown Publishers

It's not all that comfortable to sit on without a pad, and the tables with woven reed surfaces can trap every bit of food that doesn't stay on the plate. But there is nothing quite like a porch full of light, airy, wicker furniture. Be warned that some wicker craftspeople get carried away with the designs, folding rosette upon filigree. This book presents simple and ornate designs, tables, chairs, antiques, and modern pieces. Wicker is expensive now because handwork is expensive. And there are many wicker pieces floating around at garage sales and on scrap heaps, often with only one or two holes in the weave. This book also explains how to patch and rebuild and gives small, practical tips on weaving. Having caned many chair seats, I can tell you that although the results are satisfying, the work itself is repetitive and very tough on the hands. If anything, wicker is even tougher. 120 pages; about $10; well-illustrated.

APPLIANCES

PRIVATE FIRMS

Air and Water Purifiers
North American Philips Corporation
(Norelco)
High Ridge Park
PO Box 10166
Stamford, CT 06904
(203) 329-5700

In addition to making shavers and many kitchen appliances, Norelco manufactures a portable, activated-charcoal tap filter that helps remove chlorine, organic chemicals, sulfur, odors, and many other pollutants from drinking water. This kind of device may be particularly helpful in private homes that use water from shallow wells. Also, Norelco carries a line of air cleaners (even one that is built into a cat litter box) that work on the same principle as large, whole house systems. A screen of positive and negative particles form an electrostatic trap for dust and other airborne matter, while a crystalline wafer filters odors.

Barbecues
Structo
Rte. 75
Freeport, IL 61032
(815) 232-2111
(800) 435-5194 (Service and parts information toll-free)
(800) 892-1176 (Service toll-free, Illinois only)

Structo manufactures gas, electric, and charcoal fired barbecues, both large, free-standing models and small, table-top units. Many of its gas grills have electronic ignitions just like a furnace, stainless steel burners, heat controls for each burner, and capacities from 11,000 to 23,000 BTUs.

·*Business operation* Structo sells through retail dealers nationally and provides a thorough owner's installation manual that makes an attempt to sort out what hardware goes with what parts by keying everything alphabetically; also with toll-free lines for any parts or service questions.

Built-In Intercoms/Security/Vents/Etc.
NuTone, Division Scovill, Inc.
Madison & Red Bank Rds.
Cincinnati, OH 45227
(513) 527-5100
(800) 543-8687 (Continental United States except Ohio)
(800) 582-2030 (Ohio only)

NuTone makes a wide variety of built-in convenience products (that's the way the company sums them up) including intercoms, security systems, fans, ventilators, range hoods, central cleaning systems, kitchen food centers (that neat gadget that mounts flush in the counter and into which you can plug all sorts of appliances), and more.

Business operation NuTone products are sold nationwide through a network of electrical wholesalers, many of whom have retail showrooms. You can use the toll-free numbers above to locate the dealer nearest you. Individual product line catalogs are available for about $1. NuTone's master catalog (fully illustrated and well supported with technical specs) costs about $3.

Cooking Appliance Hot Line

North American Philips Corporation
High Ridge Park
Stamford, CT 06904
(203) 329-5700

North American Philips (Norelco) makes a variety of electric appliances, including (in addition to its well-known razors) a variety of cooking appliances. It will respond to inquiries with product brochures and offers a toll-free number for both consumer information and complaints: (800) 243-7884.

Dishwashers/Kitchen Appliances

Kitchen Aid, Division Hobart Corporation
Troy, OH 45374
(513) 335-7171

Kitchen Aid manufactures dishwashers, trash compactors, waste disposers, hot water dispensers, food processors, mixers, and other kitchen appliances. It sells through a network of authorized dealers across the country. Kitchen Aid dishwashers have an excellent reputation for reliability, and the company offers a lot of literature to help you get the most for your money. (These are certainly not the least expensive models on the market.) In addition to providing product brochures, Kitchen Aid has a series of pamphlets called Consumer Memos. Volume 2, Number 1 deals with energy saving and contains a good explanation of Energy-Guide labeling. Information is available from dealers and free of charge from the headquarters at the above address.

Hot Line—Maytag Appliances

Maytag Corporation
403 W. Fourth St.
North Newton, IA 50208
(800) 228-9445 (For Iowa, Mississippi, Oklahoma, South Dakota, and Wyoming)
(515) 792-7000

Maytag offers a toll-free hot line (only in some states) for action on complaints and to obtain the name and address of the nearest factory-authorized dealer. Remember that "factory parts" is often a bogus listing in classified phone directories. All appliance service centers have to use parts from the factory.

Hot Line—Whirlpool

Whirlpool Corporation
Benton Harbor, MI 49022
(800) 253-1303
(800) 632-2243 (In Michigan)

A 24-hour hot line where you can get the name of the nearest factory-authorized dealer, general information on the company's products and services, and register complaints that cannot be solved at the local level.

Hot Line—White-Westinghouse

White-Westinghouse Appliance
   Company
930 Fort Duquesne Blvd.
Pittsburgh, PA 15222
(800) 245-0600
(800) 242-0580 (In Pennsylvania)

A 24-hour, toll-free hot line for consumer complaints, and information about local, factory-authorized dealers.

Incandescent Oil Lamps

Campbell Lamps
1108 Pottstown Pike
West Chester, PA 19380
(215) 696-8070

Campbell carries some twenty models of Aladdin oil lamps, a good hurricane or emergency lamp for any home, and one used every day (or at least every night) in homes so rural that electrification has not reached them. Teardrop glass chimneys rest on brass burner assembles with conventional mantels —just like the bright white camp lanterns. Maximum intensity matches that of a 60-watt bulb. Campbell also carries fourteen different hand-blown glass shades and supplies of high-grade pink paraffin lamp oil that leaves no deposits on the burner or wick.

Business operation Write for an attractive lamp brochure, prices, and complete parts list. Enclose $1 or try an SASE. The company ships nationwide.

Pricing Simple glass canister, Colonial lamps are about $30. More elaborate brass cannister table lamps are about $60 to $80.

Major Appliances

Gibson Appliance Company
Gibson Appliance Center
Greenville, MI 48838
(616) 754-5621

Gibson makes a wide range of refrigerators, freezers, dishwashers, gas and electric ranges, microwave ovens, room air-conditioners, humidifiers, dehumidifiers, and laundry major appliances. It sells nationally through an extensive dealer network and will supply consumer information on any of its products on request.

Kelvinator Appliance Company
1545 Clyde Parkway SW,
Grand Rapids, MI 49508
(616) 241-6501

Kelvinator manufactures a full line of major appliances, including clothes washers and dryers, dishwashers, ranges, freezers, and refrigerators. All product literature is available from the advertising department on request. Aside from the standard line of feature-loaded appliances, Kelvinator makes a very nice washer/dryer combination that can be purchased with one of several kits to make the units portable, to roll out from under counter, or to stack in a 24-in-wide opening—a real plus for apartment dwellers.

Roper Sales Corporation
1905 W. Court St.
PO Box 867
Kankakee, IL 60901
(815) 937-6120

Roper manufactures a complete line of refrigerators, gas and electric ranges, microwave ovens, disposals, range hoods, trash compactors, and dishwashers. It sells direct to consumers at only two locations; its factory outlet branches in Kankakee and Chattanooga.

Business operation The company will send complete product specs on request, along with the name of a dealer who handles its products in your area.

Sears, Roebuck and Company
Sears Tower
Chicago, IL 60684

If there is one firm in this book that could be listed in almost every section it is Sears. Mike Mangan of the marketing department writes quite accurately that "Sears carries everything for the entire house, be it replacement windows, to heating and cooling appliances, portable and bench power tools, all the elements one needs to tackle most DIY projects." Most of the thousands of products offered for sale (not manufactured) by Sears are covered in the Shop at Home catalog, but your best bet is to write Sears, tell them the specific area you are interested in, i.e., tools, farm equipment, or the "good, better, best" appliances. Each area is now covered completely by what Sears calls "specialogs." Three catalogs that include most of the areas covered in this book are F7410, Home Improvement; F7495, Craftsman Power and Hand Tools; and F7417, Farm and Ranch.

Business operation Sears has more than 2100 selling outlets in the United States, some 865 retail stores, and what they describe as a "brigade" of catalog-selling units. If you cannot get the information or products you want at a local store contact Sears at the above address, attention Department 703.

Whirlpool Corporation
2000 U.S. 33
Benton Harbor, MI 49022
(616) 926-5000
(800) 253-1301 (Toll-free except
   Alaska, Hawaii, Michigan)
(800) 253-1121 (Toll-free, Alaska and
   Hawaii)
(800) 632-2243 (Toll-free, Michigan)

Whirlpool makes a full line of major appliances: refrigerators, freezers, ranges, ovens, cooktops, exhaust hoods, dishwashers, compactors, air-conditioners, washers, dryers—the complete picture. Its selection is tremendous and can be seen in countless dealerships and department stores or through builders across the country. You can write or call for clear, informative, well-illustrated product information. More to the point is Whirlpool's record on consumer affairs. Now it is a popular cause, espoused in one way or another by every manufacturer of every product. But Whirlpool was active before it was expected. Its consumer affairs division was started in 1959, back when gasoline was less than a quarter a gallon and no one worried about saving energy. Since 1967 it has operated what it calls Cool-Line service: toll-free lines manned by people who are technically qualified to give you a usable answer. What's more, unlike many companies that hide services that cost them money and time, Whirlpool does not hide this free service. Cool-Line handles some 200,000 calls a year, 32 percent for dealer referrals, 63 percent for product, parts, and installation information, and 5 percent with issues that require local field service. Another good indicator: Whirlpool can provide an air-conditioner comparison sheet for all its models listing twenty-two different specs, including EER's (ranging from a mediocre 5.4 to a very solid 8.8). Also, it offers a small booklet (Form No. 6H01 Rev. A) on choosing an air-conditioner that has a comprehensive guide to properly sizing BTU rating to cooling load—an excellent benefit that can protect you from high-pressure dealers or salesmen who "discover" more and more reasons why you need a bigger and bigger unit.

White-Westinghouse Appliance Company
930 Fort Duquesne Blvd.
PO Box 716
Pittsburgh, PA 15230
(412) 263-3700

White-Westinghouse is a large manufacturer of major appliances, including refrigerators, freezers, ranges, microwaves, washers, dryers, humidifiers, dehumidifiers, and more. These products are widely available and easy to get a look at.

Business operation In addition to providing any product information you can't get from a local dealer, White-Westinghouse maintains a Home Economics Institute that produces excellent consumer literature. Particularly useful is a 30-page brochure, *Appliances! Appliances!* (Sounds almost like a new musical.) It covers largely generic rules of selecting appliances, includes information on how to select the right-sized humidifier or dehumidifier. It also offers a good explanation of EnergyGuide labeling. The booklet, along with other product information, is free on request. Information on appliance service is available toll-free: 1 (800) 245-0600.

Major Kitchen Appliances

Tappan Appliances
Tappan Park
Mansfield, OH 44901
(419) 755-2011

A major supplier of kitchen appliances with over 8000 retail dealer outlets, this company seemed to take a bleak view of reaching consumers through this book, stating only that if you send $1 to their advertising department at the above address, they will send you literature on what features to look for. My guess is that somewhere at the high comporate level a decision has been made to get you in touch with their dealers at all costs—even at the risk of turning you off by being unresponsive to preliminary inquiries.

Microwave Ovens

Litton Industries
303 E. Wacker Dr.
Chicago, IL 60601
(312) 664-4558

Litton is one of the major manufacturers of microwave ovens, offering all combinations of single and double ovens and wall and cabinet mounts, with many options on each. Of particular interest is its ceramic cooktop. It is flat, really flush with the counter except for the control knobs, and installs like a self-rimming sink. It is ideal for families with young children who may be able to reach and play with front-mount controls and also for remodeling situations. It is electric, though, and that is just about the most expensive source of fuel these days. Litton also makes some hand tools, solder, and a lot more. This huge company will respond to inquiries with full product information.

Ranges/Ovens

Jenn-Air Corporation
Consumer Services Department
3035 Shadeland
Indianapolis, IN 46226
(317) 545-2271

Jenn-Air kitchen equipment is distinctive because of its built-in venting system, which allows cooktop grilling without a vent hood. The systems now offered are really quite sophisticated: all electric, with the option of plugging in different cooktop cartridges (with a grill top or conventional coil or ceramic element), convection ovens, microwave ovens, all combined with the integral vent system. Other cooktop options include rotisseries, deep fryers, and griddles. The drop-in counter top units require access for a venting line to an outside wall or up through a wall cavity to the roof.

Business operation Jenn-Air sells nationally through independent dealers. It is listed in your local Yellow Pages under "Ranges." To find out how these systems work in detail you can write the company for product brochures. Make sure you get Catalog No. 10–360–N, which covers the product selection, accessories, and features, and

Catalog No. 10–206X, *Product Specifications*, which shows typical measured openings and vent requirements.

Small Appliances
Sunbeam Appliance Company
2001 S. York Rd.
Oak Brook, IL 60521
(312) 654-1900

Sunbeam makes an extensive line of small appliances covering kitchen, bath, and even small portable power tools. Free product literature, information on performance, and requests for service should be directed to its Consumer Satisfaction Department at the above address.

Tap Filter
Teledyne Water Pik
1730 E. Prospect St.
Fort Collins, CO 80525
(303) 484-1352

Teledyne's "Instapure" water filter is designed to attach to drinking water taps. On average, this is what it does: reduces chlorine 34 percent, general pesticides by 75 percent, PCBs by 31 percent, sediment by 84 percent. It acts on organics and particulates but does not remove alkalinity or fluoride.

Business operation These units are widely available and easy to install. Suggested retail is about $40. Full performance specs are available, but you may have to get them locally as the company told me it rarely makes literature directly available to consumers—kind of a strange attitude.

TRADE ASSOCIATIONS

Home Appliance Information
Association of Home Appliance
    Manufacturers (AHAM)
20 N. Wacker Dr.
Chicago, IL 60606
(312) 236-2921

AHAM is a respected industry group providing a wealth of consumer information, particularly detailed heating and cooling load estimate forms (outlines that help you decide how much heating and cooling you need) that may equal or surpass the thoroughness exercised by many heating and cooling contractors. The forms make provision for your type of building construction, insulation, glass area, and other details, from which it is possible, after some mathematics, to come up with accurate BTU ratings for mechanical equipment. Write for the forms and publication list.

CONSUMER EDUCATION

Information and Services

Major Appliance Grievances

Major Appliance Consumer Action Panel (MACAP)
20 North Wacker Dr.
Chicago, IL 60606
(312) 984-5858
(800) 621-0477 (Outside Illinois)

MACAP is composed of independent consumer experts. Its mission is to receive comments and complaints from appliance owners, to study industry practices and recommend changes to improve service, and to issue reports to consumers telling them how they can use their appliances most efficiently. Most importantly, MACAP offers mediation services on the following appliance once consumers have worked through local dealers and the customer relations office of the manufacturer's main headquarters: compactors, dehumidifiers, dishwashers, disposers, gas incinerators, water heaters, home laundry equipment, microwave ovens, ranges, refrigerators, freezers, and room air-conditioners. MACAP does not handle complaints on appliances used in rental units, for commercial purposes, or where the complaint is in litigation.

Procedures Documented complaints sent to MACAP are processed and forwarded to the manufacturer with a request for a report on a plan of action to settle the dispute within 3 weeks. If no solution is forthcoming, your case goes before a review panel that may make specific though nonbinding recommendations to the manufacturer. This panel handles over 1000 complaints per year —about 40 percent of MACAP's total complaints. Most of those are satisfied without full review and arbitration. Your complaint must include the name, model number, serial number, and date of purchase of the appliance; the name and address of the dealership where you bought it; and copies of all correspondence with the dealer and manufacturer.

Business operation MACAP's office hours are 8:30 to 4:30 Monday through Friday. Use the toll-free line for instructions. Request its *Answers to Questions* brochure and *The MACAP Handbook for the Informed Consumer*. The privately funded, nonprofit group does not charge a fee for its services.

Practical Training

Skills Training

Akron Public School: Adult Skills Training Center
147 Park St.
Akron, OH 44308
(216) 253-5142 (Akron area only)

Typical of many vocational training sources across the country, this one, which serves only the Akron area (thus, no area code is given with the phone number) offers many programs, including a hands-on course in household appliance repair. It covers reading schematic wiring drawings, troubleshooting, and more—not a quick and dirty "self-help" course but real nuts and bolts. Other courses offered are welding, machine maintenance, and building maintenance.

Business operation Write for the free brochure briefly describing the courses or call for details. The Park Street Center is open 8:00 to 5:00 Monday through Friday.

All programs are approved by the State Department of Education. This center also works on apprenticeship-related instruction (a little more serious than home how-to) in coordination with the tool-and-die makers, insulation workers, carpenters, plumbers, and other unions.

READING AND REFERENCE

Air-Conditioners
Directory of Certified Room
   Air-conditioners
Association of Home Appliance
   Manufacturers
20 N. Wacker Dr.
Chicago, IL 60606

AHAM's directory of air-conditioners lists all brands and all models of certified room and built-in appliances. Published semiannually, the directory lists certified BTU/hour cooling capacity, amps rating, EER (Energy Efficiency Rating based on Department of Energy test procedures), and operating voltage. The 14-page report is sold for 50¢.

Apartment Kitchens
The Complete Apartment Guide,
   by Ardman and Ardman
Collier Books

Much of this book is devoted to design and decorating information, with a few meaty chapters thrown in—one on legal matters and one on apartment kitchens, including advice on appliances and on storage systems that get the most out of limited space. No artwork, and thin on how-to, there is some reasonable advice if you keep reading.

Appliance Efficiency
Guidelines for Communicating with
   Dealers, Distributors and Consumers
   About the EnergyGuide Appliance
   Labeling Program
Association of Home Appliance
   Manufacturers
20 N. Wacker Dr.
Chicago, IL 60606

The catchy title boils down to a thorough, 8-page examination of EnergyGuide labels, explaining the labels blow by blow: annual electrical consumption and costs, efficiency ratings, comparative efficiency ratings, capacity, and more. The program gives you some ammunition against the salespeople who all too often try to "move you up" to larger-capacity and more costly machines. A single copy is 60¢.

Appliance Energy Use
Facts on Major Home Appliance Energy
   Consumption
Association of Home Appliance
   Manufacturers
20 N. Wacker Dr.
Chicago, IL 60606

This modest 15-page report covers average electrical consumption of laundry appliances, dishwashers, refrigerators, air-conditioners, and other home appliances, showing trends in efficiency at the manufacturing level, appliances commonly available in new housing, the EnergyGuide labeling program, and more. Single copies are 25¢ each to cover mailing. AHAM supplies many such booklets, all at moderate cost, except booklets on safety (childproofing an old refrigerator, for instance), which are sent free.

Appliance Repair
Small Appliance Repair Guide,
   by Leo G. Sands
   Tab Books

Major appliances like washing machines and furnaces are backed by warranties that are generally practical. If you buy from a local dealer you can get local servicing. This is rarely true of small appliances. If they didn't save the original carton or send in the owner's registration and they aren't sure what's wrong in any case, many people simply dispense with the appliance and buy another. This book does rely on some knowledge of appliance wiring, of wiring diagrams, multimeters, and some other basic test equipment, but it covers small kitchen appliances, humidifiers and dehumidifiers, electric heaters, fans, and more.

Consumer Information/ Evaluations
   Consumers Union (*Consumer Reports*)
   256 Washington St.
   Mount Vernon, NY 10550
   (914) 664-6400

The first issue of *Consumer Reports* was sent to about 3000 charter subscribers in May 1936. It had articles on the relative costs and nutritional values of breakfast cereals, what the magazine called "fanciful" advertising claims made by Alka Seltzer, the hazards of lead toys, the true costs of credit, and the wastefully high octane numbers of premium gasolines. Many of these issues are still discussed in the magazine today, and Consumers Union notes that back in 1936 just under $15 per person was spent on advertising persuasion. (The amount climbed to over $100 per person back in 1970.) Millions of regular readers trust this source of product information and evaluation, largely because it does not accept advertising or free products for its tests. Consumers Union sums up much of the information it gathers in an annual issue called *Buying Guide* and also in special publications. The Union is uniformly thorough in its approach to product testing. My only reservations are, first, that it rarely tackles service evaluations (much harder to deal with than products), and that on occasion the in-depth laboratory testing loses touch with real issues of why people need certain products and how they actually use them in daily life. My advice is not to follow its recommentations blindly (as many do) but to use its reports as an informed second opinion whenever you can.

Business operation   The magazine is sold by subscription (prices will vary depending on current offers and incentives) and at newsstands. If you can't find information about the union's books in the magazine, write to the address above for a book list.

Country Store General Supplies/ Newsletter
   Cumberland General Store
   Rte. 3
   Crossville, TN 38555
   (615) 484-8481

In small towns with one school, one church, and one post office, the one general store had to stock just about everything. There are still a few towns like this, but you can get a look at the modern version of a general store, because Cumberland puts just about everything into its mail-order catalog. It is an amazing collection of old and a few new items covering over 250 illustrated pages. What a treat. Here's a brief sampling of the variety: 25-qt pressure canners, a cherry pitter, antique coffee mills with hand cranks (about $30), small and large cider and wine presses, Queen Atlantic woodburning kitchen ranges, oil lamps, force pumps, windmills, cow antikickers (keeps them from kicking in case you grab something you shouldn't), calf feeder pails, white oak pitchforks, portable forges ($333), portable bench grindstones ($50), horseshoe nails, wagon harnesses, surreys (yes, one does have a fringe on top; $3750), Lee jeans, dulcimers, and porch swings. Almost every page has something fun, or something interesting, or something you never saw before.

Business operation Prices are generally modest. Do not miss this one, or the *Cumberland Country Reader*, a newsletter that keeps you up to date on new additions to the catalog, reviews new books, and in a typical issue might have one large page devoted to Tennessee ghost stories, a page of "Country Wisdom Bulletins" (about $2 each) on an endless selection of how-to and self-sufficiency subjects.

Food Equipment
Home Food Systems,
   by Roger B. Yepsen, Jr.
   Rodale Books

Subtitled *Rodale's Catalog of Methods and Tools for Producing, Processing, and Preserving Naturally Good Foods*, this 475-page book covers all kinds of kitchen tools and equipment, listing price, model number, and a brief review. Hand and power equipment

is included—food processors, grinders, racks, storage systems, and more; a good buy for $14.

Home Security
Total Home Protection, by Curt Miller
   Structures Publishing Company

A large-format book, loaded with photographs covering burglary prevention, fire protection, and more. The emphasis is on a hardware solution, particularly in the burglary section, and not so much on more commonsense practices as using light timers when you are away. But in addition to reasonable advice, this book covers a lot of products and shows installations. An add-on section at the end of the book tries to make good on the word *total* in the title, with brief coverage of lightning protection, termites, insurance, and more. A good look at home security; a good buy in paperback (about $5); not hysterical or paranoid.

Kitchen Equipment/Supplies
Garden Way Living Catalog,
   by Garden Way Publishing

One of the nice, complete (128 pages) compilations of kitchen gear that includes new appliances, food processors and the like, as well as many nonelectric work savers like coffee mills and meat grinders.

Whole Earth Access Catalog
Basic Living Products
2990 Seventh St.
Berkeley, CA 94710

Fun for kitchen freaks, this low-cost catalog ($3) covers knives, juicers, stoves, you name it. The emphasis is on low-cost products reviewed in a short paragraph covering features; illustrations galore.

Laundry Appliance Repair
How To Repair Home Laundry Appliances, by Ben Gaddis
Tab Books

Although this publisher's books generally have low-budget photography and only moderately good artwork, and although some are very sketchy on expertise and practical information, some, like this one, are very worthwhile. This book covers washer and dryer motors, installation of appliances, electrical systems, general troubleshooting, electric and gas dryers, and water heaters. Because it borders on an extended service manual, some electrical experience will help with the wiring diagrams.

Major Appliance Troubleshooting
The Handbook of Major Appliance Troubleshooting and Repair,
by David L. Heiserman
Prestice-Hall, 1977

Only a bit dated, this is a fairly technical but understandable troubleshooting guide. While for practically any appliance 99 percent of the troubleshooting information at the back of your owner's manual covers deep dark secrets like, "Be sure the appliance is plugged in," this manual will run you through a series of diagnostic steps. Some specialized equipment is called for on some of the procedures.

Product/Service Reporting
Consumers Research Magazine
Washington, NJ 07882

The lesser known of the two general consumer interest magazines, *Consumers Research* reports much as does *Consumer Reports*, covering all types of home consumer products and services, including tests of brand name products and in-depth articles on special issues like health, safety, and nutrition. *Consumers Research* operates a 9-acre testing facility. Subscription rates may vary depending on what offer to new subscribers is under way. Generally one year costs about $9.

Refrigerators and Freezers
Directory of Certified Refrigerators and and Freezers
Association of Home Appliance Manufacturers
20 N. Wacker Dr.
Chicago, IL 60606

This directory lists all brands and all models of certified refrigerators and freezers and includes the AHAM-certified ratings in cubic foot volume (the total and split between food and freezer compartments); the total square footage of shelf area; door configuration; defrosting system; and annual estimated operating costs based on the Department of Energy's tests procedures. The directory is published semiannually; the 20-page report is available for 50¢.

NINE

HEATING
AND
COOLING

PRIVATE FIRMS

Gas, Oil, and Electric

Boilers

Northland Boiler Company
East Haddam, CT 06423
(203) 873-9119

Northland is the sole outlet in the United States for Stelrad wood-, coal-, oil-, and gas-fired cast iron boilers. Complementing this line is the series of Stelrad Accord 16-gauge steel panel radiators (very thin exposed radiators) that are common in Europe but not in the United States, at least not yet. Northland also makes a steel combination and a solid fuel boiler for both hot water and steam heating systems. Its CR–1 boiler is rated 88.5 percent efficient when oil fired, which is outstanding. Bruce Guptill of Northland writes, "The slightly higher price-tag on a multifuel boiler compared with a standard oil- or gas-fired unit is more than offset in a matter of 1 to 3 years by savings on fuel: for example, Number 2 fuel oil at \$1.40/gallon is equal to approximately \$200/cord of wood or \$250/ton of hard coal. With national average prices at about \$100/cord for wood and about \$135/ton of anthracite, the savings can be tremendous by burning solid fuel." These figures may be a bit optimistic, but the point is valid: when you have the capacity to change fuels you have the opportunity to burn the least expensive one, even as costs fluctuate.

Business operation Northland will send along comprehensive product literature on request. Also, it offers to help with heat load calculations and sizing and can direct you to a dealer nearby. It concentrates on the Northeast but is in the process of expanding sales nationwide. I did get hold of one of its owner's manuals (for the NC2 wood and coal boilers), and it is one of the best I've seen: exceptionally thorough, with clear and clean artwork, directions, and operating cautions.

Weil-McLain
Blaine St.
Michigan City, IN 46360
(219) 879-6561

Weil-McLain is the largest manufacturer of cast iron boilers for hot water and steam heating in the country. It sells through wholesalers to heating contractors, not directly to consumers. Among its many products, which vary greatly in size and capacity, the most interesting is its relatively new VHE model line, which is rated 87 percent efficient and extracts so much heat from the combustion process that no chimney flue is required. The exhaust is cool enough to be vented through stainless steel duct pipes, allowing its placement almost anywhere in the house. This is only one of the advantages in this high-efficiency system. Different models in the VHE series have BTU output capacities ranging from 59,000 to 147,000. The largest unit is actually rated 87.4 percent efficient.

Business operation Product literature should be available from local contractors. If not, write the company for any product sheets and a concise, informative booklet, *What Are Your Choices*, which covers efficiency ratings, fuel savings, and even has a brief appendix of information sources on the subject.

Controls

Robertshaw Controls Company
Consumer Products Marketing Group
10 W. Victoria St.
Long Beach, CA 90805
(800) 421-1130
(800) 262-1173 (In California)

Robertshaw is a major manufacturer of heating and cooling system sensors, switches, and controls, including a full line of thermocouples and thermostats suitable for do-it-yourself installations. Of particular interest are two new set-back thermostats, one for heating, one for heating and cooling. A 24-hour timer can be interrupted during the cycle to call for a set-back temperature from 1 to 10 degrees lower than the main setting, which has a setting range of 50 to 90 degrees F. A. replaceable nickel cadmium battery supplies the power. Both models (T30–1041 for heat only, T30–1043 for heating/cooling) are universal replacements for almost all 24-volt thermostats. (Millivolt models are available.)

Business operation Robertshaw offers well-illustrated product brochures, including preliminary installation instructions (so you can see what's required before you buy), and Philip S. Johnson, manager of the consumer products marketing group, writes that consumers can get "aid in installation, advice on the proper model to purchase, where to purchase and where to send it if it needs repair." The company, which sells many other control devices, including pressure relief valves, sells nationwide, mostly at retail, although some catalog houses carry its products.

Pricing Varies at retail level. Write for suggested retail.

Heating Appliance Parts/ Repairs/Sales

Fourth Avenue Stove & Appliance
Corporation
59 Fourth Ave.
Brooklyn, NY 11217
(212) 622-0050

I didn't include this firm only because the proprietor, Peter Mancuso, listens to my home consumer radio program. I included it because it sells parts for gas, electric, wood, and coal heaters and stoves. It is likely to have the unusual piece you can't find elsewhere, even if the manufacturer is out of business. Moreover, it has been in this business in the same place for over 50 years, and that says good things to me, specifically, good word-of-mouth recommendations. Also it provides servicing and sells some new heating appliances, particularly gas heaters, as well as woodburning and coalburning stoves.

Business operation Fourth Avenue is ready to help you with installation details and practical advice on installations. As Peter Mancuso writes, "We are renowned for our supply of old stove parts—gas or coal. We help whenever possible—samples are a must. For units under 15 years [old] the name, model, and serial number may be sufficient."

Heating/Cooling Systems

Intertherm, Inc.
10820 Sunset Office Dr.
St. Louis, MO 63127
(314) 822-9600

Intertherm makes complete heating and cooling systems, including electric-powered baseboard systems. Most of its sales are to home manufacturers and builders (yes, these days there is that distinction). However, its advertising manager writes that Intertherm will "provide product literature and make available service manuals and would also refer anyone calling to the nearest retail outlet for inspecting of equipment."

Heating Plants

Ford Products Corporation
Ford Products Rd.
Valley Cottage, NY 10989
(914) 358-8282

Ford manufactures a wide range of gas- and oil-fired furnaces, boilers, and water heaters. Most of its heating equipment uses Carlin burners (The Carlin Company, Windsor, CT 06095). Ford also manufactures coal- and wood-fired furnaces. Complete product specs are available on request.

Kerosene Heaters

Campbell Lamps
1108 Pottstown Pike
West Chester, PA 19380
(215) 696-8070

A major distributor and authorized parts and service center for Aladdin, Sanyo, and Comfort Glow kerosene heaters. Write for parts and price list, including replacement wicks and exploded, numbered drawings of specific heaters with parts and prices on each.

Business operation Campbell sells nationwide via mail order. A complete, illustrated catalog, including full line of kerosese lamps, is available via first class mail for $1. The company takes phone orders 9:00 to 5:00 Monday through Saturday. A reminder: check with your local fire department or building department before buying. Many localities, particularly around metropolitan areas, have banned the use of portable kerosene heaters. Also, you many want to investigate the consequences to your health, as these heaters are not vented to the outside.

Kero-Sun, Inc.
PO Box 549
Kent, CT 06757
(203) 927-4611

In 1978 Kero-Sun made about a half million dollars. In 1982 it made over 100 million dollars—not bad for anyone who had a piece of the kerosene heater business. The conditions were perfect, for Kero-Sun anyway, as fuel costs went up and supplies went down, and the winters were long and cold. The company now also sells fuel, large-capacity vented heaters, parts, and accessories, and it operates a group of retail stores called Energy America.

Business operation The products are sold across the country. (Kero-Sun has three times the market share of its nearest competitor.) For a good look at its products write for the booklet *Portable Heaters* (No. 200510). And a word of warning: in some areas portable kerosene heaters are not code approved. Check with your building or fire department. And some people have problems with kerosene heaters that are not vented, i.e., the combustion exhaust stays in the room along with the heat. A *Consumer Reports* article last year warned readers off, but the evidence seems inconclusive at this point. I advise potential buyers to ask for a test run to get a whiff of what to expect, literally. Investigate this issue before you buy.

Major Appliances

Carrier Corporation
PO Box 4808
Syracuse, NY 13221
(315) 424-4711

Another one of the very large manufacturers, Carrier produces a very wide selection of heating, cooling, and air-treating appliances for residential, commercial, and industrial applications. It sells through some 5000 dealers across the country.

Business operation Carrier will provide free, detailed literature on any of its residential products you care to inquire about.

Fedders Corporation
Edison, NJ 08817
(201) 549-7200

Why is it that the great big companies don't seem to have a street address? Anyway, Fedders is one of the big companies in this field, making a very wide selection of air-conditioning and heating appliances for residential, commercial, and industrial applications under the trade names Fedders, Airtemp, and Climatrol. It sells through a large network of distributors who sell in turn to dealers and contractors. To its credit, Fedders has moved with the energy-conscious times, making vapor-compression furnaces, heat pump water heaters, and other such systems that use at least a portion of naturally available energy.

Business operation Fedders will respond to consumer requests with detailed product information. Write or call its consumer affairs department.

Pulse Combustion Boiler
Hydrotherm, Inc.
Rockland Ave.
Northvale, NJ 07647
(201) 768-5500

Hydrotherm's pulse boilers do not need a chimney connection because exhaust is cooled, condensed, and drained. The boiler will fit almost anywhere because it doesn't need to be near a flue and is only about 4 ft high and a little over 1 ft wide. EnergyGuide labels rate two natural gas and two propane

gas models at 90.44 to 91.16 efficiency, which means that you get 90¢ worth of usable heat for a dollar's worth of fuel. The system operates so efficiently by drawing outside air through small-diameter plastic pipes (this cuts way down on air infiltration) into the combustion chamber, where it is mixed with gas and ignited by a spark only on the initial cycle. There is no constant pilot light. The hot gases are forced down through heat exchanger tubes inside the boiler where the heat is exchanged, and the water feeds heat in turn to your distribution system. Condensed exhaust is fed back outside at a very low temperature through another small-diameter pipe. The system is very unobtrusive. Storage tanks for hot water can be attached to the boiler with a heat exchange coil, and the system is supposed to work well with a heat exchanger inserted into the blower plenum of a forced air furnace.

Business operation Write for full product specs with voluminous technical data, test reports, and such. The company also has offices at the following locations: 10 Maryland Ave., Dundalk, MD 21222; (301) 285-2300; and 6860 Rexwood Rd., Mississauga, ON L4V 1L8 Canada; (416) 678-9215.

Sprinkler Systems
Grinnell Fire Protection Systems
Company, Inc.
10 Dorrance St.
Providence, RI 02903
(401) 456-5660

Grinnell is the first manufacturer to offer a residential sprinkler system. While smoke and fire detectors are designed to warn you so you can get out, these systems are designed to put out the fire, or at least minimize damage until professional fire fighters arrive. The system uses existing domestic water supply piping. Components of the system are available in kit form, including control valves, water flow alarms, and sprinkler heads.

Business operation This is a new product. Additional information is available on request from the manufacturer. Grinnell's system is UL listed, and meets NFPA Standard 13D.

Wood and Coal

Air Exchanger Stove
Turning Point
South Strafford, VT 05070
(802) 765-4066

This company makes a unique woodburning stove. There are a lot of companies making a lot of different stoves today, so that's a real accomplishment. The stove, presented in a wonderfully illustrated, warm, and personal catalog—also unique and well worth a look—can best be described as a combination of two ideas: a baffled airtight stove shaped like a drum, and air conviction pipes. But in this case the pipes are built into the drum skin and pull cool air from the floor, heat it while it is drawn around the belly and sides of the stove, and release it above the stove. These stoves, called Free Flow Stoves, are available in four sizes, from a 15-lb, 26-in × 33-in 5000 to 10,000 BTU unit that takes 16-in logs and costs about $360 to a 325-lb stove with a 15-in diameter door that accepts 30-in logs. I have not run this stove but the design seems excellent: a large-diameter door in relation to the stove size minimizes wood cutting and splitting.

Business operation For more information on the stove and for names and addresses of dealers near you, contact Nor 42,

Ltd., PO Box 100, Richford, VT 05476; (514) 243-0193. Definitely worth a close look.

Catalytic Stoves
Vermont Iron Stove Works, Inc.
299 Prince St.
Waterbury, VT 05676
(802) 244-5254

Even though I am not crazy about glass door woodstoves or manufacturers that dress up their products by emblazoning nicknames across the front, Vermont Iron makes such a stove, called The Elm, with plain or catalytic burners, that is a stunner. It even has a metal elm tree mounted directly in front of the glass door, which should really bother me, but it seems only to contribute to the absolutely unique design. The Elm is a round-bodied stove with gently splayed legs and a sculpted, liplike ash apron. The wide-diameter access door has a convex, double glazed window positioned above a butterfly draft control. The firebrick-lined chamber directs the flame path to the back of the stove before returning it to a Corning catalytic combuster and on to the flue. This addition increase combustion efficiency 20 percent and reduces creosote by 90 percent and air pollution by 75 percent. Incidently, this company also manufactures iron-framed, wood slat park benches.

Business operation Vermont sells nationally through mail order and dealers. It will provide dealer names on request, plus illustrated product brochures and very detailed information substantiating the effects of the Corning catalytic burner.

Pricing The noncatalytic Elm is about $550 for a stove with 18-in log capacity, $600 for 24-in log capacity, and $650 for 36-in log capacity. The catalytic Elm is about $800 for a stove with the 18-in log capacity and $850 for 24-in log capacity. Write for a good look at this one.

Central Wood Heat
Essex Thermodynamics Corporation
PO Box 817
Essex, CT 06426
(203) 767-2651

This firm manufactures a large chamber, woodburning, central heating system. The furnace is designed as a downdraft gasifier-combustor, which means that a small fire at the bottom of the wood load bakes the wood in a controlled atmosphere inside the combustion chamber (sort of a misnomer in this case) that is short on oxygen. This produces a highly flammable gas, which is drawn down through the bed of coals, mixed with oxygen, and burned in a refractory chamber. This final combustion occurs at about 2000 degrees F before the gases are cooled in a water jacket, which creates low smoke and low creosote exhaust. Depending on your cost for wood, this system can be very cost efficient.

Business operation Essex will provide illustrated product sheets, specs, and full test data on request.

Fireplaces/Inserts/Chimneys
Preway, Inc.
1430 Second St. North
Wisconsin Rapids, WI 54494
(715) 423-1100

Preway is a major manufacturer of free-standing, built-in, and insert fireplace equipment, all of which is widely distributed. It also supplies a complete line of prefabricated

fireplace flues, all UL listed, triple-wall piping. For many do-it-yourselfers this is the best and the safest alternative.

Business operation Preway fireplaces can be seen at home centers, hardware chains and building supply outlets. Most dealers have extensive product literature, although the company will provide what you can't find locally, including a thorough brochure on chimneys. It covers special pipe for mobile home installations, low slope and A-frame roofs, cleanouts, firestop spacers—all you need to install complete flues without any masonry.

Furnace and Stove Parts/Repair
Heckler Bros.
464 Steubenville Pike
Pittsburgh, PA 15205
(412) 922-6811

Heckler is a unique firm providing parts for hundreds of different furnaces, boilers, cookstoves, and ranges. It has patterns for manufacturing castings for Williamson and Economy coal furnaces and sells firebrick and grates for a wide variety of coal-fired heating plants.

Business operation Heckler will provide quotes on specific repair parts. Be prepared to give details like brand name, model number, or other identifying characteristics. It works retail and through the mail.

Masonry Stoves
Basilio Lepuschenko
RFD 1, Box 589
Richmond, ME 04357

Also referred to as Russian or Finnish stoves because this type of design has been used in the colder regions of Europe for over 500 years, these brick designs have multiflue chimneys, i.e., a fire set at the bottom of the hearth moves to the back of the brick column (overall dimensions for a three-flue design may be approximately 2 ft wide, 3½ ft deep, and 6½ ft high), then up to the top of the brick box, down into a second chamber, back up, and so on, until it is released into the final, full height flue. The idea has been used in many metal wood stoves where a baffle plate directs the flame path to the rear of the stove before bringing it back to the front and over the baffle plate before exiting. Mr. Lepuschenko designs and builds these masonry stoves locally and sells plans so you can tackle the job yourself.

Business operation The book offered has a detailed text, cloudy photos, and amateurish drawings that take a little work to understand. Yet I would gladly forgive this because the necessary detail is there—except that the author wants $11 for the 30-page pamphlet. It's just too much for what you get, but what you get has value, so you decide. The advantages of this system include extremely high efficiency (reported up to 90 percent because of the exceptionally long flame path), low creosote levels because of the complete burn, and also a lot of heat for a little wood.

Maine Wood Heat Company
RFD 1, Box 640
Norridgewock, ME 04957
(207) 696-5442

Albie and Cheryl Barden of Maine Wood Heat offer services in consulting, design, hardware, materials, and construction of masonry heaters to owner-builders and contractors. They have two standard sets of plans (both $12) for an end-loading horizontal flue Russian Heater, and for a front-loading open fire option Finnish Heater. They also have plans for bake ovens, cookstoves, and small heaters on special request. They are preparing a catalog of end-loading doors, airtight cleanout doors, and other specialties, along with a book published by Rodale Press on masonry heaters.

Multifuel Furnaces

Tekton Corporation (HS Tarm)
Conway, MA 01341
(413) 369-4367

Tekton is the sole North American distributor for HS Tarm multifuel boilers. It sells to plumbing and heating wholesalers through distributors in about twenty states. Elsewhere it sells direct to consumers. Tarm boilers are unique because they can burn oil, gas, wood, and coal and have taps for electrical hookups and resistance heating. The boiler has a firetube heat exchanger for wood and coal combustion, separate heat exchanger for oil or gas (and, obviously, a separate combustion chamber), and is available with a tankless coil for heating domestic water.

Business operation Tekton provides toll-free numbers for consumers who want information: (800) 628-9327; (800) 282-7719 in Massachusetts only. They will send a distributor list, product spec sheets, and several reprints from *Popular Mechanics*, which featured this furnace in a story about 4 years ago. An interesting system that enables you to burn the fuel that is most economical, no matter how much costs of different fuels fluctuate.

Prefab Fireplaces

Martin Industries
301 E. Tennessee St.
PO Box 128
Florence, AL 35631
(205) 767-0330

Martin manufactures several models of prefabricated fireplaces that are designed for energy-tight houses. Since any combustion process requires oxygen, tight houses either leak a lot to support combustion, or the combustion robs the house interior of oxygen. Martin fireplaces take this problem into account. Their "Octa-Therm" models have three sets of ducts running into and around the combustion chamber: fresh-air inlet ducts from the outside foundation wall; warm-air outlet ducts above the fireplace; and return ducts near the hearth. The system works somewhat like a conventional furnace by drawing outside air for combustion and cool room air for reheating around the double-wall fireplace, which is released back into the room with the heat radiated from the fire. Martin also makes several blowers, insulated flue pipe, and other accessories.

Business operation Call or write the company for information on dealers in your area, and for product brochures that fully illustrate the energy-efficient fireplaces. Martin's 38-page installation manuals are clear and comprehensive.

Recirculating Fireplace
Majestic Company
1000 E. Market St.
Huntington, IN 46750
(219) 356-8000

Majestic manufactures built-in, recirculating air fireplaces that look pretty much like conventional fireplaces but can be installed without masonry work, with close fire to combustible tolerances and with some improvement in energy efficiency. Some 30 models are available through close to 300 distributors and about 5000 independent dealer outlets nationwide, in Canada, and several countries overseas.

Business operation Majestic will respond to inquiries (and asks for 50¢ for costs) with a performance report on fireplace efficien-

cies, an installation planer, and products catalog. Their Warm Majic fireplace system has been rated 41 to 43 percent efficient by the Wood Heating Alliance.

Reconditioned Wood and Coalstoves
Bryant Steel Works, Inc.
Thorndike, ME 04986
(207) 568-3663 or 3665

If you like old wood and coalstoves, particularly if you know they have been checked inside and out and reconditioned to make them safe and efficient without altering their appearance, you will probably write to Bea Bryant and ask for brochures. When they arrive you will start to gape, and groan and ooh and ahh. The selection is stunning. Bryant Steel is a family-owned business that does fabrication and other work. Since 1970 it has been restoring and selling antique cast iron cookstoves. Five years ago Bea Bryant sold one cookstove from the mass she had been collecting for years. Last year she sold over 600, many to museums, shops, and restorations and many to energy-conscious homeowners who also tend to go weak in the knees looking at a rare old Ideal Atlantic kitchen stove. Bryant Steel has 200-plus stoves in stock, takes each one apart, sandblasts where necessary, welds cracks, and reblacks.

Business operation Bea Bryant writes, "We try to help people find what they want and need. We do mail order from all over the world, crate and ship."

Pricing You're too late to get in at the bottom, but who knows where the prices will go. Antique Queen Atlantics that sold for $300 only a few years ago are close to $1000 now. Write for pictures and quotes on Home

Clarions, Glenwood N's, Ideal Clarion parlor heaters, and much more.

Shop Heater/Splitting Maul

Sotz Corporation
13600 N. Station Rd.
Columbus Station, OH 44028

In business for twenty-six years, Sotz has stuck to two products, advertised nationally, and sells via mail order. Their shop heater comes in kit form and consists of all equipment necessary to turn a standard 55-gal drum into a reasonably efficient woodstove. This includes door and frame, draft control, and hardware. Double stoves that use two drums can also be adapted with the Sotz kits. As the literature reads, "Before you spend $500 or $600 on a wood heater try the Sotz heater for under $60. If within one year you don't agree it outperforms any wood heater money can buy or (within ten years) if the kit cracks, warps, or burns up, your money will be refunded, including shipping charges." Talk about confidence in the product. Sotz's "Monster Maul" (about $25) is a V-shaped, steel head and steel handle splitter that is similarly guaranteed.

Business operation For a complete and totally entertaining look at both products, ask for a copy of *The Sotz News*, a twelve-page newsletter with all sorts of information on the products, and testimonials.

Soapstone Woodstove

Woodstock Soapstone Company, Inc.
Rte. 4, Box 223
Woodstock, VT 05091
(802) 672-5133

Woodstock makes one product, a woodstove with cast iron frame and large soapstone panels. The side and top-loading model appears to have something missing at first glance because the front panel of the stove is a plain, uninterrupted piece of smooth stone. This airtight stove has a firebrick lining, nicely detailed black ironwork against light gray soapstone. On a full charge of wood, burning time is estimated at 10 to 12 hours, enough to heat betwen 7000 and 10,000 sq ft with a capacity of 45,000 BTUs per hour. The double-wall soapstone construction stores a lot of heat and regulates heat output naturally. In this sense the stove operates more like a conventional furnace with a thermostat. The Woodstock Soapstone accepts 17-in long logs, measures 28 in × 26 in × 20 in and weighs 432 lb.

Business operation Woodstock stoves are sold through a small number of dealers and factory direct via mail order. Woodstock's informative catalog is sent on request at no charge. An extremely unusual (although classic nineteenth-century) design, with no technical wizardy or elaborate flame path. It should be seen.

Stove Kits

Country Craftsmen
PO Box 688
Corvalis, OR 97339
(503) 758-8111

This firm sells the components needed to turn a 10- to 30-gal drum into a working woodstove. The basic kit consists of a cast iron door frame and door (with built-in draft adjustment), cast iron flue flange, steel legs, and connecting hardware. Accessories include a steel top plate for cooking. No welding is required.

Business operation The company would

like an SASE with requests for product information.

Pricing   Cost is approximately $50.

Wood and Coalstoves

Jøtul U.S.A., Inc.
343 Forest Ave.
PO Box 1157
Portland, ME 04104
(207) 775-0757

Jøtul stoves have been produced since 1853 in Norway. They are among the best-looking stoves available in this country, beautifully enameled, cleanly detailed, frequently with bas-relief sculpture of animals and pastoral scenes on the fire door or the side of the combustion chamber. Jøtul now has an extensive dealer network nationwide where you can get a look. Aside from the classic rectangular log burner, two other models deserve your attention. Number 507B is a 3-ft high, slightly tapered coal burner with three doors for access and cleaning, a cranking ash grate, and firebrick-lined lower chamber, and it puts out, under draft control, from 12,400 to 42,400 BTUs. The red orange enamal finish is outstanding. Not as beautiful but technically fascinating, Jøtul's new 201 Turbo is only 20-in deep, 13½-in wide and 32-in high, yet with a compressed flame path that is supercharged with secondary air inlets it turns out 30,000 BTUs and is rated to run at 70 percent efficiency, which is exceptional.

Business operation   These stoves should be seen, and the company will help by sending you a completely illustrated series of product brochures. Jøtul also sells a book, *A Resource Book on the Art of Heating with Wood*, for $1. The Turbo, by the way, has a really nice, spring-loaded, hickory handled

door operator, integral ash pan, small round monitor window—neat stuff.

Woodstoves

Agape Antiques
Box 225
Saxtons River, TV 05154
(802) 869-2273

Agape offers completely restored parlor stoves, like ornate Glenwood Oaks, and kitchen ranges. In addition, it has many new castings for old Glenwood stoves, so don't despair if something breaks. Local repair services that can do welding without defacing the design can offer one solution. New reproduction parts may be a better alternative.

Business operation   Agape sells nationally and will respond to inquiries with an illustrated brochure showing large, clear reproductions of five Glenwood models.

Pricing   Item by item.

The Coalbrookdale Company
522 Parkway View Dr.
Pittsburgh, PA 15205
(412) 787-1988

Some companies have a history worth telling. The Coalbrookdale foundry was started in 1707 when Abraham Darby took out a patent for casting iron pots in sand. In 1709 he was the first with another breakthrough —smelting iron with coke instead of charcoal. In 1770 one of his successors, Abraham Darby III, built the first iron bridge: the stunning, 100-ft arch span over the Severn River in Shropshire, England, using 50-ft, 6-ton, iron ribs cast in sand at the foundry. The Coalbrookdale Company was the first to cast iron wheels and rails. In 1801 it assembled and tested the world's first steam railway locomotive. The company brochure is a treat to look at, fun to read, and sent me to the encyclopedia for more information on several occasions. This is a glimmer of the history behind Coalbrookdale's woodstoves. They are not what you'd call popularly priced, but they are stunning. Their "nasturtium" seats and benches, cast from original nineteenth-century patterns, also will get to you. Anyway, the top of the line Darby stove lists for $1250—ouch—and then you find out why: 55,000 BTUs per hour output; 14-hour burn on wood; 24 hours on coal; heats up to 10,000 sq ft area; double, all-cast skin for radiant and convected heat production; shaker grate for coal or wood support without replacement grates; sculpted top grate that tilts up so you can use the inner skin as a warmer or simmering surface; front-loading, window-pane, glass-backed doors; primary and secondary draft control (four in all); firebrick liner, etc. Smaller models start at about $400. Georgous work.

Cornwall Coal and Supply Company, Inc.
Station Rd., Box D
Cornwall, NY 12518
(914) 534-3650

A New York area—authorized dealer for the double-wall, Coalbrookdale wood stoves. Several models are on display for a close-up look. See preceding entry for details on these beauties.

Upland Stove Company
PO Box 338
Greene, NY 13778
(607) 656-4156

Upland currently offers three American-made cast iron woodstoves: a 50,000-BTU front loader, a 45,000-BTU front loader particularly suited for fireplace conversions, and a 33,750-BTU rectangular log burner. All are airtight. All have integral baffles to create S-shaped flame paths that force more heat to radiate through the cast iron before the gases enter the flue. Materials are all cast iron, Class 30 gray or better. The two large front loaders weigh about 300 lb. The smaller log burner is about 150 lb. Both large stoves feature small, side-loading doors with circular grate draft controllers.

Business operation Upland responds to inquiries with attractive, informative product sheets, including detailed specs, wood capacity, burn times, etc. It welcomes calls and has staff on hand to answer questions.

Vermont Castings, Inc.
Prince St.
Randolph, VT 05060
(802) 728-3111

Vermont Castings makes four stove models: the Defiant, Vigilant, Resolute, and Intrepid. These stoves have capacities ranging from 25,000 BTUs per hour to 60,000 on the Defiant, which is rated to heat up to 10,000 cu ft (that's like a 20-ft × 25-ft room with 20-ft ceilings). Although the prices are not low ($500 for the small Intrepid and $700 for the Defiant, both without accessories or extra features like blue or green paint finish), all stoves made by Vermont are high quality with excellent detailing, highly efficient draft controls, and flame path design.

Business operation The company's literature is comprehensive with very detailed installation directions, explicit directions for fire safe installation near protected and unprotected walls, hook ups to existing fireplaces, and more. This excellent, fully illustrated package of literature is sent at no cost in response to consumer inquiries.

Solar, Wind, and Hydro

Greenhouse Materials

Gro-Tek
RFD 1, Box 518A
South Berwick, ME 03908
(207) 676-2209

Gro-Tek is a full-service supply house of quality tools, supplies, and information for greenhouses. They carry a full line of fans, glazing materials including an interesting woven plastic, thermal storage units, thermostats, books, and blueprints. They also offer consultation services and design/construction services.

Business operation Their products are available nationally via mail order. Their new, expanded catalog is available for 50¢. See if you can get hold of a sample of their woven polyethylene glazing material (9.5 mm thick; tested to avoid cold cracking down to −110 degrees F), and their reflective fabric called Foylon, a heat reflector and moisture barrier available in 54-in widths with an R-value of 2.2.

Hydroplants

Alaska Wind and Water Power
PO Box G
Chugiak, AK 99567
(907) 688-2896

Alaska Wind and Power is an original equipment manufacturer (that means it manufactures equipment that is sold by other companies) for several small-scale hydroplants, Yanmar diesel engines, and EnerTech wind generators. The company has developed a new 12½-in diameter Pelton Wheel (stainless steel) with nozzle diameters from 1⅞ to 3¾ in. It offers 9-in Pelton wheels (and plans for the housings) for do-it-yourselfers who want to build their own systems and full engineering consulting services for homebuilt turbine systems. Getting power from water is a complicated business. However, this firm has really good, basic literature on measuring the fall and quantity of water and excellent power tables that let you calculate what you have and what you can get in the way of power using different kinds of turbines. (Their tables appeared in *Popular Science* in May 1977.)

Business operation The company's introductory hydropower brochure is available for $2 and includes a data sheet to simplify your calculations.

Pricing Pelton wheel castings are: 9-in bronze casting bored for 1½-in shaft, $375; 18-in steel casting mounted on a $1^{15}/_{16}$-in shaft, $650; ready-to-run turbines in housings rangs from about $2000 up to $50,000, according to capacity.

Measuring Instruments

Dodge Products, Inc.
PO Box 19781
Houston, TX 77024
(713) 467-6262

Dodge makes a limited selection of sophisticated instruments to monitor and measure solar heating materials and systems: a solar intensity meter ($65) that can measure the performance of solar voltaic panels, lenses, and concentrating mirrors, and measure the transmission loss through transparent material; a solar sensor ($180) designed to provide an electrical signal proportional to solar insulation; panel meters; solar recorders; and more.

Business operation Write for product information sheets that describe performance and calibration specs with price list.

Solar Design
Soltice Designs
Box 2043
Evergreen, CO 80439
(303) 674-1597

Soltice provides custom design services for residential and commercial applications as well as long- and short-term consulting, site analysis to help owners and builders determine what kind of solar systems or designs will work for them (if any), and performance evaluation, i.e., monitoring the thermal and economic performance of solar system. In addition, Soltice offers several d-i-y solar plans for attached greenhouses, domestic hot water systems, and solar forced-air heating systems, all for a very reasonable amount (about $20 each on average). For serious folks, Soltice has complete solar house plans, information on small-scale ethanol fuel plants, and other appropriate technology goodies.

Business operation A comprehensive brochure, available on request, covers the plans in detail with illustrations and lists a series of slide packages on subjects such as the construction and operation of solar food dryers, an economic analysis of five basic types of solar greenhouses, and more. Soltice has interesting, thorough material. Worth a look.

Solar Design/Consulting
Ensar Group Energy and Design Services
3710 Hwy. 82
Glenwood Springs, CO 81601
(303) 945-6503

This company provides a wide range of energy-related services dealing with both conventional and alternative hardware systems. Formerly called Solar Pathways, Ensar now operates or has a controlling interest in the following companies:

Ensar, Inc., which deals mainly in energy consulting, working with computer models and integrating architecture and engineering requirements.

Insulshutter, Inc., manufactures insulated shutters and skylight louvers and is beginning to include windows fabricated with Heat Mirror transparent insulation.

Alpen Products, Inc., is a separately incorporated firm making insulated glass and several types of sophisticated glazing ranging from solar heating to solar control products.

Sunspool, Inc., in Palo Alto, makes drain down valves and other solar-related hardware.

Details, product information, and addresses for the companies above can be obtained by writing Ensar at the address beginning this entry. Examples of their projects with energy-saving results and more are available on request.

Solar Equipment
Sunworks
PO Box 3900
Somerville, NJ 08876
(201) 469-0399

Sunworks manufactures collectors, mounting racks, evacuated tube collectors, closed loop drain back systems, solar fluids, complete pool heating systems, and more.

Business operation Technical product sheets are sent on request.

Solar Louver Controls
Bramen Company, Inc.
PO Box 70
Salem, MA 01970
(617) 745-7765

Bramen imports and distributes Thermofor Controls, made in England for the last 25 years or so. These small lever devices are designed to operate greenhouse vent panels, cold frame tops, or other sash *without* electricity. A gas-loaded, temperature-sensitive cylinder provides the power. And it can be adjusted to start opening a greenhouse vent anywhere from 55 to 85 degrees F, and can be turned off for manual operation. Another big advantage of this hardware is the slow, ambient temperature modulation achieved as the unit reacts to gradual temperature changes; you are likely to get a relatively constant greenhouse temperature instead of a flip-flop from hot to cool as motorized vents wind open and shut. The 15-lb force, is designed to raise 30-lb hinged vents up to 18 in—plenty for cooling. The operating cylinder is warrantied for 5 years and may be mounted inside or outside.

Business operation Available at many greenhouse, garden supply houses, and also direct from the distributor listed above. Illustrated brochures that include construction details for cold frames are sent on request.

Pricing Single vent operators start at about $50.

Solar Louvers/Absorbers/ Accessories

Zomeworks Corporation
PO Box 25805
Albuquerque, NM 87125
(505) 242-5354

Zomeworks has a really interesting group of products, not the standard array of collectors. Its emphasis is on practical applications and minimal hardware, i.e., you don't have to be a technician or engineer to figure out what the system is, how it works, and sometimes even more important, how to install it. For instance, it carries Sunbender shields that capture and concentrate heat from low winter sun (by as much as 200 percent),

which makes them ideal for cold frames; also, they have sun angle calculator devices (like a sundial with a reading screen held above it at an angle) and solar tracker stands for photovoltaic panels to maximize exposure during the day. The systems of most interest, however, particularly to greenhouse owners, and homeowners who have a lot of glass, are first, an absorber fin system (called Big Fin), and second, an insulated louver system called Skylid. These panels (also ideal for large skylights) are self-operating as the sun exposure effects their responsive weight-shifting system. Two types are available: an airfoil pattern and a flat honeycomb core (the airfoil model is filled with fiber glass insulation). The patented product can be made to special sizes on request. Big Fin is a system of absorber plates, really large aluminum fins with a U-shaped center that enables them to be fitted onto ¾-in copper piping. The fins can be cut to fit between greenhouse window mullions or left long to cover an entire wall.

Business operation Zomeworks sells to individuals and contractors, and writes, "Our prices are the same for everyone." Product sheets with specs are sent on request.

Solar Products

Solar Components Corporation
PO Box 237
Manchester, NH 03105
(603) 668-8186

The Solar Components catalog (for $3) covers the spectrum of solar products in some 75 pages, including collectors, installation accessories, absorber plates, fixed and movable insulation, air and liquid circulators, storage containers, hardware and electrical equipment—a lot to look at. It covers products from many manufacturers; Sun-Lite storage tubes and air storage pods, Grumman heat exchangers, etc. The company claims its store in Manchester is the nation's largest solar retail outlet.

Business operation You can order the catalog at the address above; place orders toll-free at 1 (800) 258-3072.

Solar Usage Now, Inc.
420 E. Tiffin St.
Box 306
Bascom, OH 44809
(419) 937-2226

Solar Usage sells primarily through its mail-order catalog, *The People's Solar Source Book*. Along with tips on energy saving, tax advantages and the like, it covers an array of solar-related products (also sold through 150 independent SUN energy stores nation-wide). Products include complete domestic hot water heating kits with collectors, tank, and controls (about $1400); finned tube heat exchangers; heat exchange coils; iso-cyanurate pipe insulation; exterior mounted hot air panels; and even small solar ovens. The 1983 sourcebook is available at the above address for $5.

Solar Products/Evaluation

Solar Products, Inc.
2419 20th St.
Rockford, IL 61108
(815) 397-0536

Solar Products provides two kinds of service. First, it sells collectors, pumps, controllers, heat exchangers, storage tanks and other solar hardware through its catalog, direct to consumers. Second, it offers consulting services on solar-related energy saving, for instance, sizing solar pool heating systems and domestic hot water and space heating applications, including printouts with heat load calculations on the client's house. In this regard, most of its customers are in the upper midwest states. Catalog sales are nationwide.

Wind Power and Photovoltaic Systems

Windlight Workshop
PO Box 6015
Santa Fe, NM 87501
(505) 982-2624

This firm supplies consultation services, design help, and mail order in the field of solar-powered electric systems. It designs systems that "make direct and efficient use of DC battery power without expensive inverters—often using less than one-quarter of the energy consumed/wasted by typical AC appliances." Part of its consultation work includes advising which appliances to buy and how to wire a new home to use these systems.

Business operation The company requests "at least" return postage to cover requests for basic information and $2 for details. Its service is primarily for homesites without utility power service. Via mail order, it may be able to supply hard-to-find DC power supplies. Try an SASE with inquiries on its mail order and design services first.

Retrofitting Equipment

Add-On Fireplace Damper

Lyemance International
141 N. Sherrin Ave.
PO Box 6651
Louisville, KY 40206
(502) 896-2441

Most fireplaces have about a 50 percent efficiency rating, i.e., half the heat produced goes up the chimney. What's worse, as the fire burns low, goes out, and the hot air draw decreases, the open flue continues to draw the recently produced heat out of the house. Glass doors are one answer. Another is this kind of top sealing, add-on damper, which keeps heat in as well as rain and snow out. The damper is operated by a cable running down the flue. The best part, though, is that it mounts on top of the chimney, so it is a practical way to upgrade the efficiency of older flues, built without a damper, without ripping your fireplace apart to install a conventional damper at the fireplace throat.

Business operation   Lyemance does not sell direct to consumers. It probably should as the unit certainly could be shipped. However, B. C. Lyemance writes, "We sell nationwide and throughout Canada to dealers and distributors only. We will forward literature to consumers, along with a list of all our dealers and distributors in their state." Lyemance currently sells as well through the Sears Roebuck catalog.

Air Exchangers
Mitsubishi Electric Sales America, Inc.
3030 E. Victoria
Compton, CA 90221
(800) 421-1132 (Toll-free)

First you spend a lot of money adding insulation and vapor barriers and caulking and weatherstripping, then you start crawling around on your hands and knees for lack of oxygen. It may not get that bad, but if you take a good whiff of the air inside a wonderfully efficient, energy-tight house you may find that it needs improvement. So guess what? You get to spend a little more money on an air to air heat exchange ventilator. This firm manufactures several models, one that weighs only 6 lb and pushes 23.5 CFMs

of air with a heat exchange efficiency of 65 percent, and one that installs in your ceiling or crawl space and handles over 60 CFMs at 60 percent heat exchange efficiency.

Business operation   If you write the manufacturer in California, it will send you the name of a local dealer who can provide brochures and specs on the products. In some cases this type of system is the most reasonable answer to condensation problems, less expensive to operate than a dehumidifier with a compressor.

Air to Air Heat Exchangers
Memphremagog Heat Exchangers Inc.
PO Box 456
Newport, VT 05855
(802) 334-5412

Responding to a problem caused by super-tight, super-insulated homes, this company makes air exchange systems designed to supply healthy air, while eliminating excess humidity and stale air from tight houses. The principle is quite simple: as stale air is let out of the house, its warmth is transferred to fresh air coming in, or at least some of its warmth. The company estimates that three-quarters of the heat in the exhausted air is recaptured this way. The boxlike unit is designed for basements and crawl spaces, even a closet where there is a minimum clearance of 20 in to the floor.

Business operation   A pamphlet illustrating the exchange system, hardware, clearances and dimensions is sent on request.

Pricing   Without fans the basic unit is about $600; with fans, defrost controller, and utility finish case about $700. The basic control package with on/off/auto switch, one remote time switch, remote dehumidistat, and remote pilot light is $115.

Barrel Stove Conversions
Enderes Tool Company, Inc.
PO Drawer 691
Albert Lea, MN 56007
(507) 373-2396

Although this company manufactures hand tools for professionals and do-it-yourselfers, the item that caught my attention is its kit for turning surplus barrels into functioning and reasonably efficient woodstoves. Available by mail order for approximately $60, the kit consists of a set of legs, door assembly, and flue outlet starter for a standard 55-gal drum. Some companies sell slightly fancier versions of this system as finished stoves; one in particular (Sotz) sells a two-stage system with the second barrel on top of the first used as an afterburner. No, you probably don't want to use the Enderes kit for a barrel stove in your living room. But it is a low-cost answer to heat in a shop, for example.

Catalytic Combustor
Corning Glass Works
Corning, NY 14831
(607) 974-9000

Voted "Product of the Year" by *National Wood Stove and Fireplace Journal*, Corning's combustor, unfortunately, cannot be added to existing stoves or simply fitted into existing flue pipes. But when they are incorporated into the design of woodstoves (with a bypass in case they clog), the specially coated honeycomb configuration lowers the ignition point of smoke from its normal burning temperature of about 13,000 degrees F to about 500 degrees F, which literally reburns the smoke before it gets into the flue. Three nice things happen when your stove has a catalytic combustor: air pollution is reduced by up to 75 percent, creosote buildup is reduced by about 90 per-

cent, and heating efficiency is improved by up to 20 percent. No significant problems have yet surfaced for this new product. Corning tests show the units can maintain effectiveness as long as 10,000 hours of continuous burning.

Note: A few manufacturers are offering retrofit devices that incorporate combusters to be added at the start of the flue pipe, just above your stove. Write Corning for recommendations and be careful about what you buy and how you attach it.

Business operation Corning will send product brochures and complete test reports, question and answer sheets, and more on request.

Catalytic Stack Reclaimer
Clean Energy, Inc.
83 S. Groffdale Rd.
Leola, PA 17540
(717) 656-2011

The idea of catalytics for woodstoves is to get an afterburn from exhaust gases, which provides more useful heat and cleaner exhaust. The manufacturer states this add-on box, which fits in line with your flue pipe, replacing a short section, will burn 85 to 90 percent of the creosote that would otherwise accumulate. The 41-lb unit has a thermostatically controlled fan and measures 16 in $\times$ 12 in $\times$ 18 in. Details are sent on request.

Ceiling Fans
Casablanca Fan Company
182 S. Raymond Ave.
PO Box 37
Pasadena, CA 91109
(213) 960-6441

Casablanca makes many different ceiling fans. Their Centennial model has solid bronze decorative fittings, etched rosewood blades, and hand-cut crystal light shades, all done in a limited signed and numbered production run of 5000. Most of the fan designs have real character, albeit intricate and ornate. Also, they make 16 different kinds of blades in teak, walnut, cane, and more; 25 different kinds of lamp shades for fans with fixtures attached below the motor housing. Their catalog covers it all. The owner's manual is 18 pages, filled with photographs and illustrations, covering electrical safety, mounting locations for maximum energy efficiency, installation and wiring, including optional wiring applications, plus troubleshooting and specs. It leaves nothing out. Too bad most companies don't take this kind of care with the customers who buy their products.

Business operation   Casablanca has about 1000 retail outlets across the country where you can get product information. The company will handle inquiries direct, and offers a toll-free line: (800) 423-1821; in California only, (800) 352-8515.

Delaware Electric Imports
111 S. Delaware Ave.
Yardley, PA 19067
(215) 493-1795

Delaware imports TAT ceiling fans. The large, plain unit (no redwood blades and elaborate brass plating) has a 56-in sweep, draws 80 watts at full speed of 280 rpms, and pushes 18,00 cfm's of air at full speed. A five-speed control with wall-mounted regulator is included. A light kit is optional. These efficient, no-frills units are sold mostly to contractors and hardware retailers, also through some mail-order catalogs, for shops and industrial plants with high ceilings where significant energy savings are possible when some of the warm, expensive air at the top

of the room is pushed back down where the people are. At the retail level, Delaware sells mainly through wood- and coalstove dealers. Its president, W. Cunliffe, writes, "We believe our company is the only one pipe cutting, wiring, and assembling the fans according to the customer's locations and ceiling height."

Business operation   You can write for product literature and specs that are free on request.

Robbins & Myers, Inc. (Hunter Fans)
Comfort Conditioning Division
2500 Frisco Ave.
Memphis, TN 38114
1 (800) 238-6872

Robbins & Myers makes more than 50 models of Hunter fans that are available with some 100 accessories, such as decorative ceiling plates and light kits to mount just below the blade spindle. The basic design has remained the same since 1903 (the company was founded in 1886). Paddles are available in colors, with wood finishes, cane inserts, from 38- to 52-in diameters.

Business operation   Through the toll-free line consumers can reach Hunter's "fan doctor" any weekday. The company's catalog includes sizing information and installation requirements. Independent service centers are located in most major cities. If they do not have product catalogs write the company at the address above or use the toll-free line. Form CF-75 provides a full listing of products and features. Hunter estimates that a fan can make a 78-degree room feel like 72 degrees when used with air conditioning. Savings are equally significant when warm air at ceilings is brought down where the people are during the winter.

Chimney Lining

Chimney Relining International, Inc.
PO Box 4035
Manchester, NH 03108
(603) 668-5195

Permaflu is a system for restoring chimneys without reconstructing them. It works on angular and straight flues and the work can be done from outside the house. The idea is disarmingly simple: you snake a flexible tube down the flue, inflate it to form a smooth, uniform shape, then pour a special fire resistant lining material around it, between the tube and the chimney walls; release the form and you have a new, safe flue. Permaflue material has been tested to temperatures in excess of 2100 degrees F and is evaluated in BOCA Research Report No. 82–23. The company will provide a brochure and the names of authorized contractors in your area on request.

Energy House
PO Box 4035
Manchester, NH 03108
(603) 669-5136

Energy House produces Z-Flex Stainless Flexible Chimney Liner, useful for safety's sake on any flue, and particularly for relining crooked flues in older homes where straight pipe sections just will not work. Z-Flex components include mounting collars for masonry flue top connections, length connectors, T-sections, and fireplace adaptors, all tied together with flexible flue that can be bent even to 90 degrees while remaining structurally sound and airtight. Standard 25-ft lengths are definitely usable by do-it-yourselfers who are comfortable working from the roof. The liner is recommended with all fuels except coal. Temperature resistance has been measured in excess of 2100 degrees F.

Business operation Write to the address above for a brochure that covers product details. The company should also be able to steer you to a retailer who handles their products in your area.

Fireplace Inserts

Thermograte, Inc.
2785 N. Fairview Ave.
St. Paul, MN 55113
(612) 636-7033

Think of all the money that went into building the fireplace in your home. Then think how much heat it is probably sending straight up the flue. Many modern, deep-well fireplaces are only 40 or 50 percent efficient. Thermograte manufactures several inserts that close off the face of the fireplace, with solid airtight doors or operator glass doors, and also improve efficiency by drawing cool air near the fire floor up and around the back of the fire chamber inside pipes before releasing the warmed air above the fireplace opening. This solves several problems with conventional fireplaces, namely, that they may draw some 20,000 cu ft of heated room air up the chimney every hour and that they continue to funnel out warm air even when the fire has died and is no longer contributing heat. Independent tests rate Thermograte as keeping 84 percent of warm room air from disappearing up the flue.

Business operation Thermograte sells nationally through dealers but will sell direct if they do not have your area covered. Their Model 2000 is carried in many building supply chains. Write for full, illustrated product sheets, or call 1 (800) 328-0882 toll-free.

Furnace Test Equipment

Bacharach Instruments
301 Alpha Dr.
Pittsburgh, PA 15238
(412) 782-3500

This firm makes both elaborate, laboratory-quality can become critical simply because as simple temperature and humidity indicators. Try to get hold of two of its excellent booklets, No. 4006, *Gas Burner Combustion Testing*, and No. 4011, *Oil Burner Combustion Testing*. They give fully detailed and sensible (even readable) explanations of the tools, equipment, and procedures of testing combustion efficiency, information generally reserved for professional consumption.

Business operation Bacharach sells through a national network of distributors. The company will send the distributor list (and the two booklets mentioned above) if you can't locate a dealer in your area.

Gas Sensor

Stanley Solar & Stove Company
610 Front St.
Manchester, NH 03102
(603) 669-4500

In light of new supertight homes in which air quality can become critical simply because whatever you've got in there is likely to stay there for a while, it is not surprising that several new products to measure and monitor that air have appeared. The Home Gas Sentry has a carbon monoxide sensitivity to 425 ppm and capacities to detect multiple gas concentrations well below levels that are dangerous. Such a system may be particularly valuable to homeowners who regularly use coal, kerosene, and gas. The unit operates on normal house current.

Business operation A product brochure is available on request. Cost is about $40.

High Performance Windows

The Southwall Corporation
3961 E. Bayshore Rd.
Palo Alto, CA 94303
(415) 962-9111

Although the new material manufactured by Southwall is not yet in homes the way double and even triple glazing is, it may be soon because, according to test reports, Heat Mirror has a significantly higher R value; that is, it keeps much more of the heat you pay for inside where you can use it. The system uses a transparent polyester film suspended between two panes of glass so it is roughly equal to triple glazing in trapped air space. But the film is coated to allow most longer waves of solar radiation to pass through while preventing shorter waves from passing back out. The company reports an R value of 4.3, which is a dramatic improvement over single thickness glass (about R= .9), over double glazing (about R=1.8), and even over triple glazing (about R= 2.9).

Business operation Because the product is relatively new, your best bet is to write or call the manufacturer direct for product information, spec sheets, and local availability.

Pricing Costs is generally greater than for double glazing.

Set-Back Thermostats

Clark & Company, Inc.
Drawer C-1000
Underhill, VT 05489
(802) 899-2971

Clark's literature is straightforward about the special cases, and only those special cases, in which its products are suitable. For instance, it says that when a heated or air-conditioned space is occupied on a regular schedule (like an office building, for example), a standard clock thermostat is fine. But when occupancy is not regular, clock thermostats have limitations, and their cost goes up as the number of options needed to meet all conceivable schedules are added on. Henry B. Clark, president of the company, relates the simplicity of Clark controls to the way people respond to wood stove heat. "The occupant of the room determines if it is too hot or too cold. If the room is vacant, the wood fire has been allowed to die down, therefore there is a minimum waste of heating energy." The Clark thermostats (for oil, gas, and electric systems) can be set to return to reduced (set-back) levels once every 30 minutes and up to once every 12 hours. Touch the control button, and the cycle is restarted. This way, constant temperature is not called for unless you are in the room, and want it, and call for it. If you regularly use a part of the house for, say, 4 or 5 hours at a time, you might set the dial for 5 hours, and save fuel costs when you leave.

Business operation Write for information on local distribution. The company will sell direct if you can't find a retailer. Free information is sent on request. A sensible energy-saving idea.

Honeywell
Inquiries Supervisor
Honeywell Plaza MN12-4118
Minneapolis, MN 55408
(612) 931-4186

Honeywell, which makes many kinds of electronic controls, has come out with a series of set-back thermostats particularly for do-it-yourself installations. In fact, Marc Renner of Honeywell writes, "Surveys show 60 per-cent of consumers consider installing their own thermostats." And Honeywell will send you information on their line of four thermostats that fit this bill. The most elaborate (Model T8200) has a programmable keyboard, LCD clock, and capacity for multiple functions, 5- and 7-day programs, provisions to change or skip programs, and temperature setbacks of 5, 10, or 15 degrees.

Business operation Honeywell controls are sold nationally at retail outlets, and by contractors. The company will supply any product information requested. The set-back thermostats are covered in Catalog No. 50–6769.

Johnson Controls, Inc.
2221 Camden Court
Oak Brook, IL 06521
(312) 654-4900

Johnson manufactures controls for heating, ventilating, and air-conditioning appliances. It makes a mechanical (not electrical) vent damper that works as heat reaches a bimetal plate. The flex caused by hot exhaust opens the plate fully within 15 seconds. The unit is made of stainless steel but requires relatively clean combustion (not a lot of soot and ashes in the flue pipe) to operate properly. Johnson also makes several set-back thermostats and an electronic gas ignition control that lights the pilot only when heat is called for. This system is standard on many new high-efficiency furnaces because constant burning pilots can account for 5 percent of your gas bill. Johnson also makes a retrofit package for older gas furnaces.

Business operation Johnson controls are sold through heating dealers and contractors exclusively. If you cannot get product literature from them, write the company, Attention: Marketing Communications Department, at the address above.

Thermostats/Controls

Jade Controls
PO Box 271
Montclair, CA 91763
(714) 985-7273 (California, Hawaii, and
    Alaska call collect)
(800) 854-7933 (Toll-free except states
    above)

Jade manufactures many types of heating
and cooling controls, including thermostats,
gas cock safety valves, millivolt generator
replacements, evaporator cooler controls,
and pilot light kits. Of particular interest to
energy-conscious consumers is their digital,
automatic set-back thermostat for heating
and cooling systems that offers constant display of time and temperature, four heat and
four cooling settings to be programmed in
a 24-hour period, automatic rereading and
display every 15 seconds, and other sophisticated features.

Business operation   Using the toll-free or
collect service offered by Jade, you can get
information on local retail sources, and, as
John Firestone, vice-president for sales and
marketing, writes, "We will be happy to
answer any question whether it be where to
purchase an item or technical questions on
how to install a product." Illustrated product
literature is sent on request.

Ventilation

Kool Matic Corporation
1831 Terminal Rd.
PO Box 648
Niles, MI 49120
(616) 683-2600

Many new homeowners have found that the
tighter the house, the stuffier the air. All
houses have to breathe. Kool Matic manufactures ventilating equipment so you can let
air in and out in an energy-efficient manner.
It makes roof-mounted attic ventilators to
clear out superheated summer air and decrease air-conditioning loads; gable-mount
ventilators; a ventilator hidden in a cupola;
and whole-house vent systems.

Business operation   Kool Matic will send
complete catalog sheets with product specs,
motor sizes, and costs on request, plus a list
of distributors in your area.

Pricing   Whole-house vent systems, which
include wall or ceiling grille, timer, and
speed control, range from about $300 to
$500 depending on capacity.

Woodburning/Energy Saving/ Kitchen Goods

The Plow & Hearth, Inc.
PO Box 560
Madison, VA 22727
(703) 948-7010

This very nice catalog carries quality woodburning and wood handling equipment,
energy-saving devices, general hand tools,
and more. They have a retail store in Madison (north central Virginia) and sell nationally via mail order. Generally a limited,
thoughtful selection of interesting goods, including many nonstock items you will not
see in most mail-order catalogs.

Business operation   Mail order by phone
at (703) 948-6873 works Monday through
Friday from 9:00 to 5:00. The catalog is
available for $1.

Pricing   A few of the nifty items include:
water heater set-back timer, $42; cast iron
woodstove kettles, $35 to $49, and a lot
more.

TRADE ASSOCIATIONS

Fire Prevention/Protection

National Fire Protection Association
(NFPA)
Batterymarch Park
Quincy, MA 02269
(617) 328-9230

The NFPA is *the* place to go for information about all phases of fire prevention, protection, and fighting, although a caution must accompany the latter: fire fighting is a complicated business for professionals, and even though it is a natural reaction to fight a house fire when it breaks out, to protect your family and your property, all fire fighting professionals advise you to get out and leave the job to them. That said, there is still a lot to know about fires. The NFPA produces the National Fire Codes, a set of about 250 standards and codes on fire safety. And many consumers are confused because state, county, and local fire codes may supersede these national codes and each other. For example, portable kerosene heaters are outlawed in New York City, allowed in some single-family dwellings, but not in some multiple dwellings outside the city, and banned in some townships but not in others. The NFPA, which has a lot of valuable literature for consumers and fire professionals, notes that "with woodstoves and coal-burning stoves gaining in popularity, people should be especially careful with these installations." In this regard, two pieces of their literature are appropriate: "Home Heating Fact Sheet," and "Save Home Energy the Firesafe Way."

Business operation You can write the address above for a complete list of publications. Ask also for their information on a new trend in home fire protection, residential sprinkler systems.

Gas Appliance Information

Gas Appliance Manufacturers Association
(GAMA)
1901 N. Fort Myer Drive
PO Box 9245
Arlington, VA 22209
(703) 525-9565

GAMA, a cosponsor of the Major Appliance Consumer Action Panel, represents manufacturers who make over 90 percent of all residential gas appliances made in the United States. In addition to business and statistical services to its members, GAMA responds to consumer inquiries about appliances, buying guides, and so forth, and maintains an advisory liaison between its members and consumers who have complaints that cannot be reconciled at the retail level.

Gas Heat Information

American Gas Association
1515 Wilson Blvd.
Arlington, VA 22209
(703) 841-8400

Here is a source of voluminous consumer and technical information on all aspects of residential gas use. AGA sets standards in the field, particularly for appliances under the Blue Star Certification Program. Happily for consumers it has a reputation for being a nit-picker. Write for their list of publications, including two particularly useful though technical 75-page manuals: *Fundamentals of Gas Combustion* (a thorough survey of the field) and *Fundamentals of Gas Appliances*, which is a well-illustrated book covering cooking appliances, water heating, space heating, outdoor grills, clothes dryers, and more.

Home Appliance Information

Association of Home Appliance
  Manufacturers
2 N. Wacker Dr.
Chicago, IL 60606
(312) 236-2921

AHAM is a respected industry group providing a wealth of consumer information, particularly detailed heating and cooling load estimate forms (outlines that help you decide how much heating and cooling you need) that may equal or surpass the thoroughness exercised by many heating and cooling contractors. The forms make provision for your type of building construction, insulation, glass area, and other details, from which it is possible, after some mathematics, to come up with accurate BTU ratings for mechanical equipment. Write for the forms and publication list.

Oil Heat Information

National Oil Jobbers Council
1707 H St. NW, Suite 1100
Washington, DC 20006
(202) 331-1078

This organization is in the forefront of the heated (pardon the pun) and sometimes virulent public relations war between the oil and gas industries. With incredible amounts of money at stake, and a rash of oil-to-gas conversions in the last few years, a letter informing the council that you are thinking of switching should net an impressive array of data designed to inform you of oil's great benefits, much of it detailed and informative. Just remember to give the other side a chance to make its case before you make up your mind.

PROFESSIONAL SOCIETIES

Air-Conditioning Contractors

Air-conditioning Contractors of America
  (ACA)
1228 17th St. NW
Washington, DC 20036
(202) 296-7610

ACA represents professional air-conditioning contractors who have the expertise to plan and install central air-conditioning systems. It will provide the name of an affiliated contractor in your area and brochures on general consumer information. ACA requires only one year of field experience for membership, although some local chapters specify two years.

Heating and Cooling Contractors

Mechanical Contractors Association of
  America
5530 Wisconsin Ave. NW, Suite 750
Washington, DC 20015
(202) 654-7960

This organization will provide names of contractors in your area and consumer information on standards of practice for mechanical contractors; standardization of materials in the industry; safety; and other issues such as the scope of apprenticeship training programs.

Write for the publication list, remembering that this is an engineering group, not a consumer group; you may need a paddle to get through some of the language.

Heating-Cooling Engineers
American Society of Heating,
    Refrigeration, and Air-conditioning
    Engineers (ASHRAE)
1791 Tullie Circle NE
Atlanta, GA 30329

ASHRAE has some 30,000 members and 125 local chapters. It conducts 87 technical committees to research and establish industry guidelines for such things as equipment, installation, and maintenance, in the fields of heating, ventilation, and air-conditioning. ASHRAE provides referrals to engineers in your area and valuable guidelines to help consumers calculate heating and cooling loads, determine air quality, and more.

Plumbing, Heating, Cooling Contractors
National Association of Plumbing-
    Heating-Cooling Contractors
1016 20th St. NW
Washington, DC 20036
(202) 331-7675

Representing close to 10,000 contractors in nearly 500 local groups, this organization has a standing committee on apprenticeship training that can provide useful guidelines for those seeking a high degree of expertise and professionalism as do-it-yourselfers. Write for its list of publications, including many technical films that demonstrate, for example, plumbing practice.

GOVERNMENT AGENCIES

Climate/Solar/Storms
U.S. Department of Commerce
National Oceanic and Atmospheric
    Administration (NOAA)
Environmental Data and Information
    Service
National Climatic Center
Federal Building
Asheville, NC 28801

A bonanza of information on all aspects of climate for serious homesteaders, those in very rural areas, seacoasts, or sites with severe weather—or for people like me who are simply interested.

NOAA has booklets on tsunamis, the great ocean waves, with incredible pictures, computer simulations, even a travel time chart for the waves, and a storm surge booklet that has a North Atlantic hurricane-tracking chart in it. This stuff is fabulous, takes a little work and some imagination to apply directly to specific sites, but is worth it, particularly for those folks I mentioned above. You can write for free, detailed reports on wind chill, computing and using degree-day information, local climate data, and more. Other publications are for sale. Write for the list. A little known, abundant source of specific, technically supported, practical environmental information.

Home Weatherization

Department of Energy
Division of Weatherization Assistance
    Programs
Conservation and Renewable Energy
Washington, DC 20585
(202) 252-2207

The Weatherization Assistance Program was
established by Title IV of the Energy Conservation and Production Act of 1976
(Public Law 94–385). The emphasis is to
provide low-income households with help in
energy conservation. To date, about 1.3
million homes have had some form of
weatherization improvement under this program, and DOE estimates the savings that
result are the equivalent of some 4.8 million
barrels of fuel oil a year.

Business operation Write the above address for information on eligibility and application instructions. Applications are
granted according to a priority rating system
based on need and whether the applicant is
handicapped or elderly. Much of the work
done is caulking and insulating. Other work
includes furnace upgrading, installing vapor
barriers, clock thermostats, water heater insulation, and the like. The maximum expenditure per household is generally $1000.

Renewable Energy

Conservation and Renewable Energy
    Inquiry and Referral Service
U.S. Department of Energy
PO Box 8900
Silver Spring, MD 20907
(800) 523-2929 (Toll-free)

Formerly known as the National Solar Heating and Cooling Information Center, this
branch of DOE provides information about
a variety of energy systems and technologies
for both residential and commercial applica-

tions. Call toll-free or try a letter to get hold
of its publications list and a rundown on
specific services.

Small-Scale Energy Technology

National Center for Appropriate
    Technology (NCAT)
PO Box 3838
Butte, MT 59702
(406) 494-4572

The heading above should have listed the
U.S. Department of Energy. But due to
budget cuts, their Small-Scale Technology
Branch, which manages the Appropriate
Technology Program, no longer can provide
funding for grants to develop AT systems.
However, funds are still available (at least
for a while) for monitoring and disseminat-
ing information about ongoing projects. The
information is available through the National
Center listed above, which should by now
have finished its series of fifteen how-to
publications and training guides based on the
projects funded by the DOE program. AT is
the link between dwindling fossil fuels and
the power source of the future, whether
nuclear, solar, wind, or whatever. And it is
possible that AT is the future, whether anyone comes up with a safe, abundant fuel
source or not.

State Utility Commissions

Following is a state by state listing of utility
commissions. They are important to you because they regulate the rates you pay for gas
and electricity, and in some states, water and
transportation. Many offer complaint handling services and may be spurred to conduct
investigations when a number of complaints
are received on the same issue. You should

contact them before making a decision about switching fuels, going solar, or investing in new equipment. Efficiency and payback periods, selling excess power back to utility companies, and other questions can, at least in part, be determined by present and projected policies at these commissions. Also, some states have utility consumer advocates who may represent you before the commission, investigate utility service, and more. To find out if your state has this consumer service, contact the National Association of State Utility Consumer Advocates, c/o Florida Public Counsel, Room 4, Holland Building, Tallahassee, FL 32304; (904) 488-9330.

Alabama Public Service
   Commission
PO Box 991
Montgomery, AL 36130
(205) 832-3421

Alaska Public Utilities
   Commission
1100 MacKay Building
338 Denali St.
Anchorage, AK 99501
(907) 276-6222

Arizona Corporation
   Commission
1210 W. Washington St.
Phoenix, AZ 85007
(602) 255-3931

Arkansas Public Service
   Commission
400 Union Station
Markham and Victory Sts.
Little Rock, AR 72201
(501) 371-1453

California Public Utilities
   Commission
California State Building
350 McAllister St.
San Francisco, CA 94102
(415) 557-1487

Colorado Public Utilities
   Commission
500 State Services Building
1525 Sherman St.
Denver, CO 80203
(303) 866-3154

Connecticut Public Utilities
   Control Authority
State Office Building
165 Capitol Ave.

Hartford, CT 06115
(203) 566-7384

Delaware Public Service
   Commission
1560 S. DuPont Hwy.
Dover, DE 19901
(302) 678-4247

District of Columbia Public
   Service Commission
Cafritz Building
1625 Eye St. NW
Washington, DC 20006
(202) 727-1000

Florida Public Service
   Commission
101 E. Gaines St.
Fletcher Building
Tallahassee, FL 32301
(904) 488-1234

Georgia Public Service
   Commission
162 State Office Building
244 Washington St. SW
Atlanta, GA 30334
(404) 656-4501

Hawaii Public Utilities
   Commission
1164 Bishop St., Suite 911
Honolulu, HI 96813
(808) 548-3990

Idaho Public Utilities
   Commission
Statehouse
Boise, ID 83720
(208) 334-3143

Illinois Commerce Commission
Leland Building
527 E. Capitol Ave.

Springfield, IL 62706
(217) 782-7295

Indiana Public Service
   Commission
901 State Office Building
Indianapolis, IN 46204
(317) 232-2715

Iowa State Commerce
   Commission
State Capitol
Des Moines, IA 50319
(515) 281-5309

Kansas State Corporation
   Commission
State Office Building
Topeka, KS 66612
(913) 296-3323

Kentucky Public Service
   Commission
730 Schenkel La.
PO Box 615
Frankfort, KY 40602
(502) 564-3940

Louisiana Public Service
   Commission
One American Place, Suite 1630
Baton Rouge, LA 70804
(504) 342-4404

Maine Public Utilities
   Commission
State House
Augusta, ME 04333
(207) 289-3831

Maryland Public Service
   Commission
American Building
231 E. Baltimore St.
Baltimore, MD 21202
(301) 659-6000

Massachusetts Department of
Public Utilities
100 Cambridge St.
Boston, MA 02202
(617) 727-3500

Michigan Public Service
Commission
Mercantile Building
6545 Mercantile Way
PO Box 30221
Lansing, MI 48909
(517) 373-3244

Minnesota Public Utilities
Commission
780 American Center Building
160 E. Kellogg Blvd.
St. Paul, MN 55101
(612) 296-7124

Mississippi Public Service
Commission
Walter Sillers State Office
Building, 19th Floor
PO Box 1174
Jackson, MS 39205
(601) 354-7474

Missouri Public Service
Commission
Jefferson Building
PO Box 360
Jefferson City, MO 65101
(314) 751-3243

Montana Public Service
Commission
1227 11th Ave.
Helena, MT 59601
(406) 449-3017

Nebraska Public Service
Commission
301 Centennial Mall South
PO Box 94927
Lincoln, NE 68509
(402) 471-3101

Nevada Public Service
Commission
505 E. King St.
Carson City, NV 89701
(702) 885-4180

New Hampshire Public Utilities
Commission
8 Old Suncook Rd.

Concord, NH 03301
(603) 271-2452

New Jersey Board of Public
Utilities
1100 Raymond Blvd.
Newark, NJ 07102
(201) 648-2026

New Mexico Public Service
Commission
Bataan Memorial Building
Santa Fe, NM 87503
(505) 827-2827

New York Public Service
Commission
Empire State Plaza
Albany, NY 12223
(518) 474-7080

North Carolina Utilities
Commission
430 N. Salisbury St.
Dobbs Building
Raleigh, NC 27602
(919) 733-4249

North Dakota Public Service
Commission
State Capitol Building
Bismarck, ND 58505
(701) 224-2400

Ohio Public Utilities
Commission
375 S. High St.
Columbus, OH 43215
(614) 466-3016

Oklahoma Corporation
Commission
Jim Thorpe Office Building
Oklahoma City, OK 73105
(405) 521-2267

Oregon Public Utility
Commissioner
300 Labor and Industries
Building
Salem, OR 97310
(503) 378-6666

Pennsylvania Public Utility
Commission
PO Box 3265

Harrisburg, PA 17120
(717) 783-1740

Rhode Island Public Utilities
Commission
100 Orange St.
Providence, RI 02903
(401) 277-3500

South Carolina Public Service
Commission
111 Doctors Circle
PO Box 11649
Columbia, SC 29211
(803) 758-3621

South Dakota Public Utilities
Commission
Capitol Building
Pierre, SD 57501
(605) 224-3203

Tennessee Public Service
Commission
C1–120 Cordell Hull Building
Nashville, TN 37219
(615) 741-3125

Texas Public Utility
Commission
7800 Shoal Creek Blvd.,
Suite 400N
Austin, TX 78757
(512) 458-0100

Utah Public Service Commission
330 E. Fourth South St.
Salt Lake City, UT 84111
(801) 533-5518

Vermont Public Service Board
120 State St.
State Office Building
Montpelier, VT 05602
(802) 828-2319

Virginia State Corporation
Commission
Jefferson Building, PO Box 1197
Richmond, VA 23209
(804) 786-3608

Washington Utilities and
Transportation Commission
Highways-Licenses Building
Olympia, WA 98504
(206) 753-6423

West Virginia Public Service
  Commission
Capitol Building, Room E-217
Charleston, WV 25305
(304) 348-2182

Wisconsin Public Service
  Commission
432 Hill Farms State Office
  Building
Madison, WI 53702
(608) 266-1241

Wyoming Public Service
  Commission
Capitol Hill Building
320 W. 25th St.
Cheyenne, WY 82001
(307) 777-7427

Technical Energy Information
  Department of Energy
  Technical Information Center (TIC)
  PO Box 62
  Oak Ridge, TN 37830
  (615) 576-1308

This agency offers a unique service particularly suited to consumers who want detailed information on a specific subject but don't know where to get it. If you send TIC the specific topic that interests you, it will respond with a limited bibliography and source list on the subject. It's up to you to pursue and evaluate these sources. Be specific to get results that are meaningful.

CONSUMER EDUCATION

Appropriate Technology
  The Mother Earth News
  PO Box 70
  Hendersonville, NC 28791

Mother Earth News has taken a step few organizations do; it has established an open testing ground for the ideas and final, practical applications of its self-sufficiency doctrines. It is called Mother's Eco-Village, occupying 622 acres in the mountains near Hendersonville. It is a showplace for both elaborate and simple projects for do-it-yourselfers, all of which have appeared in the magazine. Eco-Village runs an ongoing series of "show-how" demonstrations covering earth-sheltered housing, wind power, log construction, cordwood construction, and a lot more.

Business operation   One year of 6 issues of *Mother Earth News* is $18. Daily admission to Eco-Village is $6 for adults, $4 for children 12 to 20 (few 20-year-olds will appreciate that description). Admission is free for ages 11 and under. Information including illustrated brochures of village activities and demonstrations is sent on request. This is the only place I have found where you can get a close look at so many self-sufficiency disciplines. Worth investigating.

Energy Audits/Conservative Planning

Energy Program Housing Council
121 N. Fitzhugh
Rochester, NY 14614
(716) 546-3700

Among the many services offered to Monroe County residents by the Housing Council (funded by the Monroe County Community Development Administration) is free energy counseling, which takes the form of a house call (usually for about 2 hours), during which professionals cover typical energy audit subjects. The Energy Program also conducts workshops and maintains bulletins on energy conservation, air to air heat exchangers, indoor air pollution, and more.

Business operation Services are provided free to owners and renters living in Monroe County.

Energy Conservation

Center for Energy Policy and Research
New York Institute of Technology
Old Westbury, NY 11568
(516) 686-7578

The Center stays abreast of all aspects of energy technology, with particular emphasis on conservation and alternate energy systems. In 1978 it established the Energy Extension Service, a kind of clearinghouse on energy-related information, serving professionals, academics, and home consumers as well. Currently, it publishes a monthly bibliography of selected materials on energy conservation, renewable energy systems, and the like. You can write for subscriptions to the address above.

Renewable Energy Information Service

Conservation and Renewable Energy
    Inquiry and Referral Service
PO Box 8900
Silver Spring, MD 20907
(800) 523-2929
(800) 462-4982 (Pennsylvania only)
(800) 523-4700 (Alaska and Hawaii
    only)

You will find this service indispensable for information above active and passive solar, photovoltaics, wood heat, small scale hydroelectricity, bioconversion, alcohol fuels—in short, all the leading issues of renewable energy and conservation. It exists to further the spread of information on the topics above.

You can get in touch with these people at no cost and get all kinds of brochures, fact sheets, excellent bibliographies on specific energy subjects, and individual tailored responses. They also provide referrals to trade associations, state and local groups working in the field, federal agencies, private consultants, professional associations, and other special interest groups that may be able to help you. And what's nice is that this service is operated by the Franklin Research Center for the U.S. Department of Energy (at least for new, whole they have a budget), and, therefore, makes no product endorsements and has no axe to grind. As an example, their Solar Water Heating Bibliography lists about eight books(like the excellent *Homemade Hot Water Systems* listed in this book), four research reports, a series of pamphlets, five groups that sell do-it-yourself plans, and about fifteen recent articles on the subject—not bad for the cost of a stamp, even better for a toll-free call. If you have any interest in these energy issues *do not* pass up this source. It's excellent, a gold mine.

Solar Greenhouses (SGA)

Solar Greenhouse Association
34 N. Gore
Webster Groves, MO 63110
(314) 962-4176

SGA is a not-for-profit, member-supported organization, but not a trade association representing solar manufacturers. Its purpose is to educate in depth serious members of the organization in the skills of designing and building functional solar greenhouses and other solar installations. The emphasis, as you might expect, is on energy conservation but includes information on self-sufficiency, for instance, how to grow plants for food, even in the winter. Here are a few of its more interesting activities: its technical staff regularly prepares programs, workshops (the hands-on-variety), and even tours of solar greenhouses built by its members. Many of these activities are available only for those in the St. Louis area. SGA provides other services for members across the country. For instance, it has prepared code-approved building plans for sale; books; and a newsletter.

Business operation Membership dues in SGA are $10 per year to receive the newsletter and attend local meetings, $30 per year for its plan selection, book, and membership fees for those who cannot attend the workshops and tour.

Solar Hot Water

The Passive Solar Institute
PO 722
Bascom, OH 44809

This organization is a good source for specific, detailed information on hot water solar systems—not the high-technology, high-priced variety, but the small-scale, build-it-yourself variety. Probably the best way to start with this source is by asking for information on their Integral Passive Solar Water Heater Book ($11.50). It details simple systems (buildable for about $500 or less and a long weekend's worth of labor) called *batch heaters*—a simple plumbing system carrying water through a south-glazed box. This source has a good book list and can provide further solar sources such as manufacturers of tanks, plan services, a passive solar catalog ($12.50) with details on retrofitting, air to air heat exchangers, and a lot more. Worth a query, particularly if you appreciate a small-scale, practical approach.

Solar Owner-Builder Services

Cornerstones Energy Group, Inc.
54 Cumberland St.
Brunswick, ME 04011
(207) 729-5103

Cornerstones was founded in 1976 as an owner-builder school. And as interest in solar design increased, Cornerstones added more courses and more services, including special courses for solar design and retrofit professionals, an extensive bookstore (all titles are sold by mail order as well), design and consulting services, complete building plans, energy audit software, and training programs.

Business operation For complete course descriptions (some last only a few days, some several weeks) write Cornerstones. Students have built many energy-efficient homes and solar greenhouses during their training. *Cornerstones Journal* covers topical energy news, a few projects in great detail, and carries updated information on course schedules.

Superinsulation

New Alchemy Institute
237 Hatchville Rd.
East Falmouth, MA 02536

New Alchemy is a nonprofit research and education center founded to develop ecological approaches for providing food, energy, and shelter. It offers a good book list and a series of seminars on superinsulation —the art of trying to keep just about all of the heat you produce. One-day seminars are offered for homeowners who want to go a step beyond the old hat advice about caulking and deatherstripping. More detailed weekend seminars cover project costs, heat load calculations, vapor barriers, and get "hands on" installation and construction details. Weekend seminars run about $100.

Business operation   Write for a free brochure giving seminar details, and request a copy of its publications list.

READING AND REFERENCE

Alternate Energy

Alternate Sources of Energy Magazine
Milaca, MN 56353

A bimonthly, educational, scientific survey of energy issues covering solar, wind, and water power, biofuels, insulation and energy conservation. Treatment includes plans, new products, research, and trends. Published by Alternate Sources of Energy, Inc., a nonprofit, tax-exempt organization dedicated to the development and use of renewable energy sources.

Pricing   This is the only drawback. At $15 a year for 6 issues ($2.95 each at the newsstand), one wonders how much Alternate Sources pays for printing and office space to remain nonprofit. It offers your money back if you're not happy with the first issue.

At Home with Alternative Energy, by
    Michael Hacklemann
Peace Press Inc.
3828 Willat Ave.
Culver City, CA 90230

A practical, nonthreatening book (no endless tables and formulas) that covers solar, wind, wood, water, and methane energy and goes into code compliance, backup heating, and other everyday concerns that are ignored in many books on the subjects. The photos are great; the illustrations weak but clear enough. A nice, up-to-date survey of AT energy systems; about $13.

Environmental Action Resource Service
    (EARS)
Box 8
Farisita, CO 81037
(303) 746-2252

The EARS catalog (for $1) carries an extensive listing of books, with capsule descriptions and a few illustrations on solar and wind energy and all appropriate technologies. Steve Wachterman, coordinator for EARS, writes, "EARS is a nonprofit organization working for rational energy and environmental policies. We have distributed many books, pamphlets, and graphic materials to individuals, schools, libraries, government agencies, and citizen organizations through our mail-order service." Its selection is very good, covering biomass, utility energy policy, and teaching materials. EARS, the organization's acronym, is carried over into the organization's symbol—the gigantic-eared antelope jack rabbit—chosen because of its superb adaptations to desert life.

Alternate Technology

META Publications
PO Box 128
Marblemount, WA 98267
(206) 853-8807

Modern Energy & Technology Alternatives (META), is a retail mail-order clearinghouse for books on appropriate technology, alternative energy, house construction, and related topics. They gather titles from domestic and foreign publishers and have an extensive, thoughtful selection. Their list covers planning, solar buildings, biofuels, sun, wind, and water systems, tools and machines, metalwork, water supply, food and health, land use, and more. Drop into the middle of any subject listing and you find a nice combination of indispensable classics (like Ramsey & Sleeper's *Architectural Graphics* in planning), and lesser known references (like ASHRAEs *Fundamentals Handbook*). Sarah Huntington, of META, sums up the ideas behind this list: "Although the government is dragging its bureaucratic heels in supporting such things as passive solar construction and superinsulated houses, the people on the street see the benefits to themselves as well, perhaps, as seeing the collective benefit to society and the conservation of energy. These people are eager to get information on what they can do and how to do it. These are the people we serve."

Business operation The publication list is free, although they would appreciate a SASE for return postage.

Climate Analysis

Climates of the United States, by John L. Baldwin
Superintendent of Documents, U.S. Government Printing Office
Washington, DC 20402
(No. 003–017–00211–0)

Valuable for any builder or buyer, particularly for those who plan to relocate in a different region of the country where they are unfamiliar with weather patterns. This 113-page book ($2.50) includes records, averages, and more of wind, temperature, sun, and rain. You can find charts and maps of all sorts of details, for instance, average cloudiness (technically called mean daily sky cover sunrise to sunset) month by month, and even temperature ranges month to month. Interesting, and a good deal at the price.

Appropriate Technology Energy Projects

Small Farm Energy Project Newsletter
Small Farm Energy Project
PO Box 736
Hartington, NE 68739

This bimonthly newsletter ($8 a year for subscriptions) covers energy improvements and efficiency particularly related to the operation of small-scale farms. However, many of the projects that are reported in detail have wider applications: simple solar roofing construction using low-cost corrugated panels, up-to-date reports on irrigation systems, and more. Try a copy. The information is purely practical; very informative, even if you don't live on a farm.

Energy Saving

New Hampshire Energy Saving Manual,
    by James W. Morrison
Arco Publishing

A more up-to-date edition may become available. In any case, you can adjust the costs for oil, gas, and so forth in the book to suit current conditions. The manual is one of the few treatments on energy saving that does get into mathematics, payback periods, R values, etc., without reverting to undecipherable tables and technical gobbledygook. It is a workbook, requiring some effort to benefit from the technically supported common sense.

Furnace/Boiler Replacements

Environmental Protection Agency (EPA)
Office of Planning and Evaluation
401 M St. SW
Washington, DC 20506
(202) 557-7743

In a time of volatile fuel costs and a constant stream of new, high-efficiency heating appliances, consumers are faced with the question of when it makes sense to replace their furnaces. If you own an 80-year-old "octopus" hot-air system running at 50 percent efficiency, the answer is obvious. But there are a lot of gray areas explored in great detail in an EPA report, *An Analysis of the Economics of Replacing Existing Residential Furnaces and Boilers with High-Efficiency Units.* With a catchy title like this you know you are in for some heavy-duty but informative reading.

Gas Furnace Efficiency

Environmental Protection Agency (EPA)
Office of Public Awareness
401 M St. SW, Room W311
Washington, DC 20460
(202) 755-0700

Write for EPA's informative, illustrated booklet, *Get the Most from Your Gas Heating Dollars* (Publication No. IERL–RTP–D–252), particularly valuable for its detailed photographs of properly and improperly tuned gas flames—all in glowing color so you can make valid comparisons between what you have and what the booklet shows you should have. For a more technical treatise, write the EPA Library Service at the above address for a copy of *Guidelines for Adjustment of Atmospheric Gas Burners for Residential and Commercial Space Heating and Water Heating.* A little light reading before bedtime.

Heating Efficiency

National Bureau of Standards
U.S. Department of Commerce
Center for Building Technology
Washington, DC 20234

Write for an informative, illustrated brochure, *Making the Most of Your Home Heating Dollars* (Publication No. C13–53–8), a general guide to home heating efficiency.

Oil Furnace Efficiency

Department of Energy (DOE)
Office of Energy Information
12th St. & Pennsylvania Ave. NW
Washington, DC 20585
(202) 634-5610

Write for an informative, illustrated brochure, *How to Improve the Efficiency of Your Oil-Fired Furnace*, which covers tune-up procedures for existing systems. Ask for Publication No. DOE/OPA–0018. A more general brochure, *Get the Most from Your Oil Heating Dollars* (Publication No. IERL–RTP–P–298), on roughly the same topic is available from EPA, Office of Public Affairs, Research Triangle Park, NC 27711.

Passive Solar

The Passive Solar Institute
PO Box 722
Bascom, OH 44809
(419) 937-2225

The Passive Solar Institute offers a selection of books on such subjects as passive solar water heating, superinsulation, home plans and specifications, and solar space heating.
Business operation A book list is available on request.

Self-Help Information

CoEvolution Quarterly and *Whole Earth Catalog*
Box 428
Sausalito, CA 94966

The Whole Earth Catalog is probably the best starting point if you are beginning to get interested in some of the fields in this book such as what are some of the companies in the field, what kinds of magazines and books are available on the subject. Leaving a lot out, some of the fields covered are:

alternative construction, solar, wind, and water power, construction equipment, tools for building, repairing, crafts of all descriptions, logging, self-sufficient living and more, plus access to tools and information on waste systems, land management, musical instrument making, and computers—it really covers a lot of ground. I use it a lot and love using it, even though it is spotty; some of the views and reviews are absorbing, full of telltale indicators, while some are quite brief and tell you no more than the company or book or whatever exists. Sometimes that's enough. Generally, though, the product and book entries are considerably shorter than most of the entries in this book. Still, a monumental research effort; well presented, worthwhile. If you bought this book you'll probably like it. (Costs $16 now.)

Solar Design

A Golden Thread, by Ken Butti and John Perlin
Cheshire Books

From an interesting analysis of passive solar design incorporated into Greek towns 2500 years ago, to President Eisenhower waving a radioactive wand to inaugurate the opening of America's first nuclear power plant in 1954, this book traces the evolution of solar architecture and technology. If that sounds a bit stodgy you've got the wrong impression. Many illustrations, drawings, old newspaper clippings, old ads for "new and revolutionary" solar heaters, details of the "House of Tomorrow" designed for the 1933 World's Fair, and a lot more makes a fascinating journey. Oddly, one of the strongest impressions I got was how much of what is new now (or called new) is, in fact, a design retread, frequently a more complicated, high-tech version with not much extra to offer. Extremely readable;

full of ideas; a bargain for close to 300 well-illustrated pages at about $11.

The Solar Decision Book of Homes, by
    Richard H. Montgomery
John Wiley & Sons

This is a very thorough step by step guide with worksheets that starts with the fundamentals of solar radiation and proceeds to calculating available solar energy; estimating fuel costs; evaluating passive solar home design, orientation, and collection and distribution system; and analyzing several basic styles of building with solar efficiency in mind. A thorough 300-plus-page book with more than enough fodder to chew before making a major solar decision.

Solar Heating and Cooling, by Jan F.
    Kreider and Frank Kreith
    McGraw-Hill

A highly recommended, very technical analysis of solar energy use covering sun angles, radiation principles, flat plates, concentraters, computerized monitoring. Not a do-it-yourself book but loaded with background data that can be useful. Try the library first and be willing to look past the formulas. One of the sources for the invaluable declination and solar time charts of the Smithsonian Meteorological Tables, which can be used to determine exactly when and at what angles the sun will hit the structure you are designing.

Solar Energy Availability
Solar Energy Map
    ENMAP Corporation
    PO Box 4430
    Boulder, CO 80306

For those interested in solar design, passive or active, who find the Smithsonian and similar graphic tables of solar declination a bit complicated, ENMAP's large (about 2½ ft × 4 ft) map of the United States and parts of Canada is presented more like a conventional weather map, with solar availability, degree days, and more laid out for 240 cities.

Sun Angles
Sun Angles for Design, by Robert Bennett
6 Snowden Rd.
Bala Cynwyd, PA 19004

Covering all sites from the equator to 60 degrees north latitude, this book of charts can be used to accurately predict where the sun will be at any particular time. Thus it is possible to plan for kitchen windows to get the greatest possible benefit from morning sun or a wall of sliding glass doors on a southern Florida house to receive the least amount of direct sun to minimize air-conditioning costs. Unlike the Smithsonian graphics, which are ingeniously displayed, the Bennett Sun Angle Charts are more commonsensical, covering territory in 2-degree jumps, listing sample cities, and logical "head on" horizon to zenith sun track displays; $6.

A Reporter's Guide to Utility Ratemaking
American Gas Association, 1982
1515 Wilson Blvd.
Arlington, VA 22209

This interesting booklet (available through many local utility companies) covers and explains the process by which utility companies, public service commissions, and, supposedly, consumers, get to the bottom line on the monthly bill. Rate bases, utility expenses, preliminary rate hearings, and more are explained in detail.

Woodstoves
The Woodstove Directory
Energy Communications Press
PO Box 4474
Manchester, NH 03108
(603) 622-8206

If you are in the market for a woodstove, this is an excellent place to start looking. The annual directory has hundreds of listings arranged helpfully with a few paragraphs from the manufacturer and specifications. You won't find hands-on tests or editorial evaluations but will see each stove illustrated. In addition, the issue contains several articles. Cost is $3.50 for the 250-plus-page magazine at the address above.

PLUMBING
AND
ELECTRICAL

PRIVATE FIRMS

Water Supply

Alternate Source Hot Water
Blazing Showers
PO Box 327
Point Arena, CA 95468

Behind the bizarre misnomer is a small alternate energy company manufacturing three types of water heaters that use the heat of your woodstove or fireplace. All use coiled copper pipe as a heat exchanger—appropriate heating technology that you may be able to make yourself following plans in one of many home heating do-it-yourself books or magazines. Its stovepipe heat exchanger (for 6-, 7-, and 8-in pipe) with entry and exit fittings, has 15 ft of pipe. Its firebox heater is a 10-ft coil fitting an 8-in × 5-in space inside the stove and includes ¾-in pipe fittings, a punching tool, and hole seals. Its custom fireplace/firebox exchanger is a flat grid of black iron pipe (either 5½- or 8-in high) with the length built to your specs. These or your own pipe coil systems can be connected to gas or electric hot water heaters. Blazing Showers makes an antisiphon adaptor for this purpose. Bear in mind that any obstruction will affect the draft and may cause problems unless you move up one flue size or down one coil diameter size. Yet, a time tested energy-saver like this, when used with the same temperature, pressure, and safety valves of modern water heating systems, may make and store up to 20 gal of hot water per hour.

Business operation Shipping charges are modest. Write for details, or start by ordering *Handmade Hot Water Systems* (for $4.95, refunded against the price of a heat exchanger if you order.

Pricing All exchangers are $55 to $70. The storage tank adapter is just under $20.

Water Treatment
Culligan U.S.A.
One Culligan Pkwy.
Northbrook, IL 60062
(312) 498-2000

"Hey, what's his name." This is his name. You hear it regularly on television and radio advertisements. But behind the somewhat abrasive commercials is an extremely large company distributing water treatment equipment in 91 countries through over 1000 franchised dealers in the United States and Canada. It makes, installs, and services three basic types of systems: softening equipment that works on the principle of ion exchange to remove calcium and magnesium deposits that make water "hard" (symptoms are scale deposits on fixtures, curding instead of frothy bubbling when water is mixed with soap); water treatment equipment, for ion removal, pH balancing, controlling odor and sediment, hydrogen sulfide (the incredibly unpleasant rotten egg smell), nitrate and sulfate reduction, and more; and drinking water systems that work on the principle of reverse osmosis filtering.

Business operation You'll find the name Culligan in most Yellow Pages under Water Conditioning, or you can write to the Consumer Affairs Director at the above address for the nearest dealer. Initial water tests are frequently free. Full product information is available free for the asking.

Well Drilling

DeepRock Manufacturing Company
2200 Anderson Rd.
Opelika, AL 36802
1 (800) 633-8774
(205) 749-3377 (Call collect from
    Alabama, Alaska, Hawaii, Canada)

DeepRock sends one of the most distinctive packages of product information you are likely to see from any company. It concerns their well-drilling machinery, which is a small-scale, one-man machine. A Tecumseh motor provides the power and can be hand held or mounted on the company's "power mast" frame. An 18 : 1 gearbox turned by the 3-hp engine generates 200 rpm. Pipe sections are threaded together as needed while a drilling pump (theirs or yours) supplies water to the line. With the weight of the engine behind the pipe, you can stand back and watch until it is time for another pipe length. The company sells pilot and reamer bits, screen and casing, pipe lengths with threaded couplings, a swivel attachment for your garden hose that keeps the water flowing and the hose stationary as the drill rotates, plus other accessories.

Business operation The Hydra-Drill information kit is simply wonderful: blow by blow photographs from packages of parts to flowing water. A full-color brochure showing all parts and explaining how to order the right package for your site, an informative brochure on water sources, quality, supply, and more, and the kicker—a flexible 33⅓ LP record of case history interviews, conducted over the phone, so that the people interviewed come across as neighbors, people down the street.

Pricing The engine, power mast rigging system (with pulley system for lifting the motor and attaching new pipe sections), and power swivel connection for garden hose is sold as a kit for about $500. Bits are about

$35; what appears to be PVC casing $35 for ten 5-ft sections. Call toll-free for information.

Windmills/Pumps

Dempster Industries, Inc.
Beatrice, NB 68310
(402) 223-4026

Dempster offers a solid variety of windmill-driven and hand pumps. Its windmills, requiring oiling and maintenance only once a year, are available with steel fans from 6 to 14 ft in diameter to match towers available from 22 to 40 ft high. It also manufactures hand and windmill force pumps, pump cylinders, plungers and checks for deep well cylinders, and hardware for hose connections, bushings, pipe clevises, and more.

Business operation Complete, straightforward, well-illustrated literature is available on request.

Pricing Complete windmills range from about $860 for a 6-ft vane model with engine, mast pipe, wheel, vane assembly and vane stem. Weight is 312 lb. A similarly complete 14-ft model weighing just over 1000 lb costs about $5700.

Plumbing Fixtures

Brass Fixtures/Fittings/Hardware

Sign of the Crab
8101 Elder Creek Rd.
Sacramento, CA 95824
(916) 383-2722

It costs $2, but it is an ooh-ahh catalog, with one of the most stunning covers I've seen—a large, solid brass crab, incredibly detailed, in a splash of water on a black background. Another goodie: the inside cover has a message from Francis E. Strom, the owner, welcoming his son (the new executive vice-president) and his son-in-law (new sales vice-president and father of the toddler in the bathtub on the back cover). How could you go wrong here? Anyway, the full-color catalog offers some gadgets and gizmos, like a 19-in high replica of a Mark V diver's helmet, a good selection of brass bells, barometers, clocks, door knockers and handles and letter boxes, plus a lot of bathroom brass: exposed brass piping, faucets, etc. Really nice stuff.

Business operation Sign of the Crab's main office has a showroom and nine other retail outlets across the country can be located by writing the headquarters at the address above. The brass "watering can" shower heads, hammered brass bar sinks, and wall-mounted glass holders are something to see.

Decorative Fixtures
M. Wolchonok & Son, Inc.
155 E. 52 St.
New York, NY 10022
(212) 755-2168

Wolchonok is a major distributor of furniture hardware. The company handles a modular polished chrome furniture framing system, the clip-together type that can be attached to make coffee table frames. Wolchonok carries decorative hardware a step further to include a full line of artistic brass plumbing valves and faucets, including Victorian porcelain and brass fittings, as well as ultramodern sculptured chrome and Lucite fittings.

Business operation The company sells wholesale and retail locally and will ship goods. I asked them what help, information, and literature, consumers could receive by contacting them. The reply was straightforward: "They state their problems—and we'll solve them." Write for catalogs or, if you are in New York, wander in.

Drain-Cleaning Tools
General Wire Spring Company
1101 Thompson Ave.
McKees Rocks, PA 15136
(412) 771-6300

General Wire manufactures drain-cleaning augers, both hand and power-operated. It sells through plumbing supply houses in the United States and Canada, mostly to contractors and other professionals. Most of the equipment is a lot more than you need for an occasional job on the kitchen sink. But the hand augers and the smallest of the power units will suit the task. (Some have wonderful names like Sewermatic and Sewerooter Senior.) If you do have recurring drainage problems, however, you might look into the company's water ram. It is a small cylinder that is pressurized by a hand pump (the pressure is metered), then discharged through a nozzle that is surrounded by a rubber stopper. Generally, you have to stop-up overflow drains and any other air-vent outlets to get the effect of a hydraulic wave, really a shock wave of water triggered by the blast of compressed air. It's a very practical system (I have used a similar tool from another manufacturer) that does an excellent job without chemicals. The only drawback is that too much of a blast will tend to find the weak spots in your plumbing system, say, one of the solder connections, and pop it open.

Business operation Write for General Wire's Catalog HO–CC–80, or for full spec sheets on specific products.

Faucets and Fittings

U.S. Brass, Wallace Murray Corporation
901 10th St.
Plano, TX 75074
(214) 423-3576

U.S. Brass makes Aqua-Line Washerless Faucets, Quest polybutylene piping and fittings, and EZ Plumb prepackaged water and gas connectors and plumbing fittings. The latter brand line is found in many home centers and building supply houses and is one of the ways inexperienced do-it-yourselfers can get started doing some of their own plumbing work. Of particular interest is a new washerless faucet (Aqua-Line L1100, L1300, and L1400) that can be installed without tools of any kind.

Business operation U.S. Brass offers (free for now) an excellent booklet called *Faucet Replacement Guide.* In 24-plus, well-illustrated pages and detailed, practical instructions, it covers how to remove old faucets, replumb new fixtures and offers troubleshooting tips. A good piece of literature. Ed Pincu, U.S. Brass' advertising manager, will send you one if you send your request to this address: PO Box 37, Plano, TX 75074. Write "Customer Service" on the envelope.

Faucets and Valves

The Chicago Faucet Company
2100 S. Nuclear Dr.
Des Plaines, IL 60018
(312) 694-4400

Even though Chicago Faucet restricts sales to wholesalers only, and even though it would rather not be contacted directly by consumers, it is included here because its product line of faucets and valves for residential and commercial applications (in-cluding the most sophisticated equipment for hospitals and laboratories), is so extensive and some of it is absolutely beautiful. Solid brass faucets and fittings, particularly those in their catalog called *The Renaissance Collection* are used extensively in serious restoration work. Professionals in the field should write for Catalog N, the complete product listing.

Business operation If you get stuck locally, the company will refer calls to plumbing distributors who handle its products in your area.

Fixtures—General

U.S. Plumbing Products (American
    Standard)
PO Box 2003
New Brunswick, NJ 08903
(201) 885-1900

American Standard is a common specification on architectural plans (frequently listed as "American Standard or equal"), which means the products are generally solid and reliable, widely available, and offered in a great range of styles and sizes. The Director of Consumer Affairs for American Standard is ready to supply product sheets with specs on request. And you might want to ask for its publication called *Lifestyle Bathrooms*—yes, it seems you do have to maintain appearances even when you are taking care of bodily functions. My guess is that this catalog is an attempt to outdo Kohler, known for lavish product presentations. (Kohler was the first to show a lot of skin on its models.) It's got a rundown on bath products in the back, but in the front—there's Rome and a sunset bursting above sunken tubs and bidets set in cobblestone and a dove perching on a faucet handle. It's mind-blowing.

Homestead Waste Systems
Enviroscope Corporation
PO Box 2933
Newport Beach, CA 92663
(714) 645-4400

Enviroscope manufactures lightweight plastic plumbing systems that do not use water for normal operation. And they do not use chemicals. Instead, waste material is digested by aerobic bacteria to an earthlike compost. Efficiency is increased with an electric heat source, although it is not required. The company also makes a sludge separator, tubing, vents, and all parts and equipment necessary for installation. The system has received Seal Number 8543 from the National Sanitation Foundation.

Business operation The company will send you test reports, parts lists, operation literature, and ordering information free on request. The literature explains in detail the operation of aerobic decay, maintaining a carbon-nitrogen balance, with adequate air flow and heat for waste processing, capacity, and more.

Pricing The smaller system (two-person household) is about $1000 including all installation parts and equipment. The larger system is about $1400 on the same basis.

Minimal Water Closets
Western Builders Co-Op, The
    Environmental Concern
2150 Pine Dr.
Prescott, AZ 86301
(602) 445-6351

Western Builders Co-Op imports Ifö Cascade plumbing fixtures from Sweden. Two things about them are distinctive. Some models operate with only a 3-liter tank— about four times more efficient than a con-

ventional water closet. Several other models (all are less expensive than the 3-liter model) use 6 liters, which is still highly efficient. Also, the fixtures are obviously Swedish design, cleanly bulbous, if that's possible, with an integral tank top and lifting flush knob that resembles the top of a tea cozy. (Now you'll have to write for the brochure, just for a look, right?) The polished vitreous china WCs (and bidets and basins) are available in white, a variety of earth tones and muted greens, and a few deep tones. The appearance is similar to a nicely finished gelcoat fiber glass.

Business operation Write for a color catalog and price list. The company has a policy of making a $10 donation from its profits to one of seven environmental groups (CoEvolution, New Alchemy, etc.) with your first order.

Pricing The 3-liter Cascade is about $375 in white; 6-liter Cascade about $300 with visible trap (made of china and appearing as part of the design rather than part of the plumbing), $390 with concealed trap. Seat, supply inlet, stainless steel anchor bolts, rubber seal, and an adaptor for retrofit are included.

Modern Fixtures
Kohler Company
Kohler, WI 53044
(414) 457-441

Kohler is a leader in bath fixture design. That sounds like pure advertising copy, but in this case it is true. Its catalog has consistently been first with dramatically sculptured sunken tubs, home spas and whirlpools, and true innovations like the Kohler Environment and Habitat, which are basically mini-rooms with controls for sun, steam, wind, music, and water, all programmable. These units are quite expensive and also unique. And Kohler has consistently produced dramatic colors that might have been considered ahead of their time—items like hot orange toilets and dark green, severely elliptical basins. Kohler's products are definitely *American* modern. Also, its catalogs are distinctive for the amount of flesh that appears on the male and female models. I would love to be privy to some of the conversations between client and ad agency on just how many more (or fewer) whirlpool bubbles should appear around the breast. The photographs are often right on the edge, certainly a lot closer than any catalog I've ever seen that had anything to do with construction.

Business operation Kohler's extremely elegant consumer catalog is available from local dealers or direct from Kohler for $2. In some 40 pages it gives a good look at its range of products. Kohler's product sheets and installation literature is first-rate. Elegant, high-quality products, including fiberglass moulded fixtures with excellent gelcoat finishes. Worth a look.

Organic Waste Treatment
Clivus Multrum USA, Inc.
14A Eliot St.
Cambridge, MA 02138
(617) 491-5820

Clivus Multrum is probably the best-known organic waste treatment system for residential applications. The complete system, which starts at a reasonably conventional-looking toilet and ends at a large, interior, furnacelike storage cabinet, is a self-contained, waterless, odorless treatment process capable of handling all organic wastes. It does not use chemicals or heating elements and has no polluting discharge. The com-

pany estimates that it can save up to 40,000 gallons of water per year in an average home. The strange company name, Clivus Multrum, translates from Swedish as "inclining compost room"—hardly quaint, but accurate. One large composting tank can serve toilets and a waste inlet from the kitchen, and requires conventional roof venting. Wastes are mixed in the chamber and allowed to decompose in the oxygen-rich environment, while water vapor and carbon dioxide are vented. Decomposition reduces waste volume by about 90 percent, leaving fertile organic compost that is safe to handle, odorless, and of obvious value for gardening. This type of system requires careful investigation. Check your local plumbing codes as well.

Business operation The firm sells nationally through a network of dealers and sales representatives. Its literature is excellent. Write for its comprehensive guide, *Planning Installation and Operation for Residential Applications*.

Pricing Complete systems to serve five people year round (tank height is 72 in) is about $4000; nine-person capacity system is about $4500.

Plumbing Fixtures for Older Homes
A*Ball Plumbing Supply
1703 W. Burnside
Portland, OR 97209
(503) 228-0026

A complete source of bathroom plumbing fixtures and accessories, concentrating on Victorian-period fixtures like a solid oak, high-tank toilet with polished brass flush tube, white china bowl, and oak seat, which A*Ball manufactures itself. A*Ball's illustrated catalog is an interesting combination of old and new (shower fixtures in solid brass for claw and ball tubs, plus whirlpool-fitted fiber glass tubs), and particularly fun if you like the wonderfully bulbous, teardrop sleekness of Chicago valves with porcelain escutcheons and lever handles imprinted "HOT" and "COLD." A*Ball provides thorough help for cleaning and maintaining polished brass, dull nickel, and polished chrome plumbing; it also sells cleaners, polish, and an epoxy reglazing compound for porcelain called Tubcote. Accessories include grab bar components, towel hooks, wire racks, and cast aluminum Victorian register grates. Help can be had on meeting plumbing codes with older fixtures.

Business operation This is a wholesale and retail source selling locally and by mail order with modest shipping charges.

Pricing The high-tanker in oak is about $500, including all parts for installation. The low, wall-hung commode in oak is about 10 percent less.

Tankless Water Heaters
Chronomite Laboratories, Inc.
21011 S. Figueroa
Carson, CA 90745
(213) 320-9452

This company's literature starts off with a very intriguing claim: a $500 investment in its in-line, water temperature booster (used for dishwater and possibly the clothes washer's hot water plumbing lines) will provide up to a $3500 return in 10 years. Included in the calculation is a tax break for energy-saving equipment and the premise that your current water heater is set somewhere between 150 and 160 degrees F. The idea is that you turn the water heater ther-

mostat down to 110 to 120 degrees F, and install the booster only for, say, your dishwasher. The small unit (about 1 sq ft of space is needed under your sink) uses electricity to boost the water temperature in a pipe coil. It requires 20 psi to operate and has a maximum temperature capacity of 190 degrees F. I'm not sure of the arithmetic; the numbers may not work out so delightfully in every case. And if your water heater is up at that slightly outrageous setting, you can save money by bringing it back to 115 degrees F, say, without a booster. Also, some models of dishwashers come with an in-line super heater. Certainly, the product is interesting as a kind of mini–water heater for a remote, low-use sink, for example.

Business operation The company will send an informative product sheet on request.

Pricing Suggested retail is $180. Installation is estimated at about $320.

Tub/Shower Kits
Plaskolite, Inc.
1770 Joyce Ave.
PO Box 1497
Columbus, OH 43216
(614) 294-3281

Plaskolite manufactures shower stalls, tub-wall and shower wall kits, inside-mount storm windows and acrylic safety glazing, window well covers, and the like. The plumbing kits are one alternative for remodelers faced with deteriorated and decaying tile walls who do not have the money or the room, for a new, moulded fiber glass enclosure.

Business operation Selling retail through a national distribution system, Plaskolite offers product brochures and information on local retail outlets on request.

Valve Repair

O'Malley Valve Company
4228 Eighth Ave. South
St. Petersburg, FL 33711
(813) 327-6817

Many homeowners make the mistake of thinking that a leaking faucet is a broken faucet that must be replaced. Sometimes a new washer stops the leak. When it doesn't the trouble is very likely a problem called a worn seat. Remember that the faucet is a valve. It opens and closes. That means moving parts that operate under some pressure and friction and hence wear. When they wear a lot, the contact between the valve stem and the valve seat is not good enough to stop the flow of water. So instead of getting a new faucet, O'Malley offers faucet repair kits (seat regrinding tools) in a variety of sizes. Its master set (retail for $150) has some fourteen cutters up to 2-in diameters for all Jenkins-type disc valves and conical cutters for plug or ball–type valves. Also it sells two-cutter kits for as little as $2 and $3.

Business operation O'Malley sells in home centers and other retail outlets nationwide. An illustrated catalog and price list is available free from the address above.

Victorian Bath Products

Barclay Products
PO Box 12257
Chicago, IL 60612
(312) 243-1444

Barclay is a mail-order company specializing in a wide variety of plumbing products, both new and old designs. Its Victorian and turn-of-the-century reproductions include claw-footed bath tubs, towel racks, and brass fixtures. Also, it sells several models of convertible showers, including setups that allow a shower to be added to older, showerless tubs.

Business operation Sells nationally via mail order. A free catalog is sent on request, and the marketing manager writes that personnel are available to provide expert advice and do-it-yourself tips on all plumbing questions.

Electrical System

Electrical Supplies/Specialties

Leviton Manufacturing Company, Inc.
Consumer Products Division
59–25 Little Neck Pkwy.
Little Neck, NY 11362
(212) 229-4040

Although Leviton sells only wholesale, its consumer products catalog covers such a complete collection of plugs and sockets, switches, cordsets, and fuses that it is worth writing for, just to see what's available.

Business operation Leviton wiring products are widely available in hardware stores and home centers.

Electronics/Motors Surplus Supplies

C & H Sales Company
2176 E. Colorado Blvd.
Pasadena, CA 91107
(213) 681-4925

Who knows where they get it all, but C and H has thousands of items (and the catalog does not list them all even though it is 112 pages long). All are surplus in one way or another. They may be purchased from discontinued inventories, removed from units that have never been used, or in some cases removed from functioning equipment. The company says all equipment is fully tested and offers a 10-day full credit policy if you are not satisfied. Just to give you a sense of what they have: sixty-one different kinds of small blowers, including a 15 cfm Gould fan (11 watts, single phase, 2900 rpm, about 3 in × 3 in × 2 in, for $2.95); eighty-one different kinds of DC motors, including several from GE, Globe, Oster, Electrolux (and you thought when the motor went you had to throw the appliance away); batteries; heating elements; hydraulic cylinders; heat shrink tubing; a wide range of optics, including a few really esoteric items such as aerial cameras and beam splitters; a reasonable selection of small precision hand tools (tweezers, snips, etc.); pressure gauges; pumps; all kinds of solenoids and switches and transistors; plus, just when you think you've found the limitation of the selection, a page of universal joints.

Business operation As far as I can tell the catalog is still free—quite a good deal. Mail-order sales are made nationwide. There is a minimum order of $20.

to be on the floor where a fire broke out in one of the electric panel-board rooms. I remember vividly hearing guys yelling for people to get away, seeing electrician supervisors come running across the unpartitioned concrete floor, and seeing an electrician come shooting out of the small room backward as the room seemed to make a popping sound and turned bright white for an instant. The room continued to pop quietly, and the electrician struggled to his feet and seemed all right. Everybody was ordered off the floor, and when I checked it out the next day, everything was back to normal. Having witnessed this, I have never put a penny in a fuse holder, and I don't pull out appliance cords by tugging on the cord either. This is a long way of saying that Bussmann is nearly synonymous with the word "fuse." It makes all kinds for all situations; for the 30 million VA load of the Superdome in New Orleans and for your puny little 15 AMP circuits.

Business operation The common varieties are available in most hardware stores. To get a look at the specialties and to learn just about everything worth knowing about fuses, Bussmann has a book called *Electrical Protection Handbook* (for $5). It will send you free a safety brochure that is worth reading called *Fuse Facts and Tips.*

Fuses

Bussmann, Division McGraw-Edison
   Company
PO Box 14460
St. Louis, MO 63178
(314) 394-2877

Way back when I was an apprentice and working on the barely closed-in building opposite Madison Square Garden, a 30-story office building in New York City, I happened

Surplus Tools/Equipment/ Machinery

Airborne Sales Company Inc.
8501 Stellar Dr.
PO Box 2727
Culver City, CA 90230
(213) 870-4687

Airborne started as a government surplus mail-order house over thirty years ago. Their

90-page catalog includes a lot of hydraulic equipment, parts, motors, actuators, cylinders, and the like, but also a typically crazy-quilt surplus selection: aircraft instruments, compressors, engines, fans, filters, fire extinguishers, hose, levels, log splitters, pulleys, hand tools, welding supplies, winches. Some stock is new surplus, some used.

Business operation Airborne's illustrated catalog is sent on request.

Timing Controls

Intermatic, Inc.
Intermatic Plaza
Spring Grove, IL 60081
(815) 675-2321

Intermatic is the world's largest manufacturer of all kinds of timing controls, both electronic and electromechanical, for home and industry. When you see 24-hour timers with labels that say Sears, Wards, Penney, Radio Shack, Ace Hardware, True Value Hardware, and other such well-known names, they are made by Intermatic. If this is news to you—that giant retailers don't actually manufacture all the products they sell—you qualify as a truly naïve consumer. Intermatic also sells retail through many catalog outlets. Probably their most useful device for owners and renters alike, is the simple, very inexpensive 24-hour timer. You can use it to control appliances—something as simple as turning off the TV so it doesn't run all night after you fall asleep halfway through the late movie. Also, a few timers can be set up to turn on and off lights, radios, TV's and more to simulate occupancy even when you're not home. This very basic burglary protection turns out to be quite effective. Basic Intermatic timers I have used have proven to be reliable and a good

buy, particularly if you use your imagination to save on energy costs.

Business operation Although Intermatic has no special consumer department, they are responsive to consumer inquiries. Paul Saxton, vice-president of marketing, writes, "They [consumers] can talk to anyone in the company from the president on down."

Wind and Water Power Alternators

Zepher Wind Dynamo Company
PO Box 241
Brunswick, ME 04011
(207) 725-6534

Zephyr manufactures direct-drive alternators to be used in wind powered systems. The permanent magnet alternators operate at very low speed and produce a three-phase alternating current corresponding to rpm's. Although its alternators are designed specifically for wind systems, the low speed makes them adaptable to direct drive applications without the efficiency loss and added maintenance of gearing. Although Zephyr does not yet make complete wind systems, the following companies do, using Zephyr's VLS-PM alternators: Aesthetic Power Systems, 644 Main St., Bally, PA 19503; Sol-Air Track Company, PO Box 1247, Elizabeth, WV 26143; Diversified Energy, PO Box 303, Bremen, IN 46506; and Windstar Corporation, 1930 Winner St., Walled Lake, MI 48088.

Business operation Zephyr will supply limited information on products at no charge and offers an *Original Equipment Manufacturers Owners Manual* covering detailed theory, wiring diagrams, and the like, for $8.50. All units are sold direct from the factory in Maine.

Pricing Three units are available currently, ranging from $1400 to $4500. Rectifier/regulators are also available.

Winddriven Generators

Natural Energy System, Unltd. (NES)
130 Albert St.
Box 69832
Rochester, NY 14606
(716) 458-9402

Elektro wind generators, made in Switzerland and distributed in this country by NES, combine upwind design, self-feathering blades for overspeed control, three-phase, brushless AC alternator, automatic shutdown and restart, folding tail, and setup for stand alone use or connection to a grid using a synchronous converter. A booklet detailing these machines in great length is available for $10. Product sheets are sent on request. This company also handles a limited range of other solar and energy products.

Wind Systems Equipment

Natural Power, Inc.
New Boston, NH 03070
(603) 487-5512

Natural Power offers an interesting catalog filled predominantly with wind equipment, from air speed indicators and monitoring equipment to complete system controls. Also shown is a modest number of similar products for solar systems. In addition Natural Power builds custom instrumentation and controls.

Business operation Although much of its information is technical, you might want to start by asking for two of the company's booklets, which it offers at no charge: one, called *Wind Power*, is a brief preamble to the subject; another is a condensed product chart. If the company does not make a control or instrument you need, it will steer you to a source that can help.

Wind Systems/Generators

Enertech Corporation
Box 420
Norwich, VT 05055
(802) 649-1145

Enertech makes two utility interface wind systems. That means they can be connected directly to the electrical system in your building so that the windmill and your utility company lines can provide electrical power at the same time. The more current you generate at the mill, the slower your meter turns. Sometimes it plain stops. Then you get into the complicated question of selling power back to the utility company, or storing it. The Enertech 1800 is tested to produce 120 kilowatt hours (kwh) a month under average wind speeds of 8 mph. At 10 mph it produces 240 kwh; at 12 mph, 360 kwh; at 14 mph, 480 kwh. Enertech's Model 4000 windmill produces approximately 2.2 times as much power under the same conditions: 270 kwh at 8 mph, etc. Efficiency and payback depends on your conditions, and to measure them, Enertech also sells a wind odometer that can measure average wind speeds on a daily, weekly, or monthly basis. Working on a 6-volt battery (and workable from −40 to 140 degrees F), the small odometer mounts on a 50-ft telescope mast that may be rented (with the odometer) from Enertech. It makes sense, obviously, to do this before buying a complete system.

Pricing The 1800 system typically costs $6000 to $10,000 installed. The 4000 system typically costs $11,000 to $16,000. Forty percent is IRS tax deductible. Some states offer incentives as well. Write for free brochures, or send $2 for brochure and full technical specifications. Currently Enertech has six dealers across New York State.

Lighting Fixtures

Antique Lighting
St. Louis Antique Lighting Company
PO Box 8146
St. Louis, MO 63156
(314) 535-2770

The St. Louis Company manufactures solid brass reproductions of antique lighting fixtures, including chandeliers, table lamps, and wall sconces. They also restore antique light fixtures and do custom design work.

Business operation St. Louis's extensive catalog is available for $3, and includes complete prices and full-page black and whites of the fixtures that show exactly what you're getting. For restoration buffs, you may be interested in the daisy ruffle and diamond daisy glass shades, two sizes of snowflake shades, elegant satin floral and basket weave shades, off center, single fixture chandeliers, and a few truly incredible designs such as a cast bronze "lily lamp"—literally with the base of a water lily, complete with bronze stems climbing the lamp stem to end in small leaves. The catalog is refreshingly blunt about this remarkable product: "These lamps are individually cast, signed, and numbered. They are such a pain in the neck to make that we make as few as possible. Call or write for details." An amazing collection all around, expensive ($36 for a satin floral glass shade) with some fixtures like the more elaborate chandeliers running to $500 and above. Stunning nonetheless;

worth a look, although the $3 will keep some people away, I'm afraid.

Modern Fixtures
George Kovacs Lighting, Inc.
24 W. 40 St.
New York, NY 10018
(212) 944-9606

George Kovacs is one of the most innovative and prolific manufacturers of lighting fixtures. It sells clocks as well. Everything it does is modern; some of it is ultramodern, done by leading modern designers. It sells all varieties of fixtures: clip-ons, goose necks, swivels, balancers, you name it.

Business operation Kovacs has a decorator showroom and a retail showroom in Manhattan and a mail-order division that ships nationwide. If you like modern furnishings and would like to see ways of shedding light that you never dreamed of, write for its catalogs.

Pricing Kovacs is not cheap. The least expensive fixture is about $25; many are $100, $200, $300, and up. Several, in the imposing, elegant catalog are over $500.

Recessed/Track Lighting
Lightolier
346 Claremont Ave.
Jersey City, NY 07305
(201) 333-5120

Lightolier has been in business for 80 years, which may account for the fact that most of its products are not ultramodern track and recessed fixtures. It manufactures chandeliers, bath and vanity lighting, and many hanging fixtures as well—not exactly reproductions but more like development houses that have been around for awhile and are surrounded by regrown trees and bushes that were leveled for construction. (Is that "older contemporary"?) The product line is extensive and presented in a thorough book called *The Light Book* (available for $3). There is a $5 coupon inside so you get more than your money back with an order. Two small brochures, one on down lighting and one on track lighting (each for 25¢, which always strikes me as very silly—what are you supposed to do, send them a check for a quarter?) are less detailed but worth getting if the company will send them along gratis. Lightolier manufactures several unique fixtures along with its mainstream products—things like an extremely thin track strip for undercounter use and nightlight-type bulbs to mount in it; also, framing projector lamps that can spotlight a painting, for example, and only that painting. Rick Liotta, Lightolier's public relations manager writes, "New decorative fluorescent units are also generating interest because of the energy-saving properties of fluorescent lighting." Some fixtures are as much as 80 percent more efficient than conventional incandescent lighting. ("Generating" is Rick's pun, not mine, thank you.)

Restoration Lighting Fixtures

Alcon Lightcraft Company
1424 W. Alabama
Houston, TX 77007
(713) 526-0680

Alcon's brochure shows a small sampling of their Victorian lamp fixtures. All are polished and lacquered brass with (at least in the brochure) tulip shaped milk glass shades. Selling mostly to restorers and restaurateurs, Alcon has now assembled a catalog showing homeowners their wares. Although they carry many stock items, most of their work

is custom, done to specifications. They also carry antique lamps and lamp parts. All wiring, less bulbs, is included, and the fixtures are set up to mount to modern electrical boxes.

Business operation Alcon sells wholesale, retail locally in Houston, and via mail order. Write for ordering instructions (no COD's or personal checks) and a complete price list.

Pricing Starting at approximately $60 for wall sconces, their curly arm (it does a 360 running from the brass wall plate to the tulip shade) is currently $57.50. Two-pole, curly arm ceiling fixtures are about $125. Larger, four-pole ceiling fixtures are $225 and up.

Authentic Designs
330 East 75th St.
New York, NY 10021
(212) LE5-9590

Mr. Krauss, who hand-fashions the 250-plus varieties of wall lamps and chandeliers in this shop, has one antique original—a tin, eighteenth-century, wooden-stemmed, twelve-armed chandelier he bought for $2700. Prices at Authentic Designs are more realistic than that. But the selection of fixtures is great, and all are replicas of antiques, museum pieces, and fixtures found in restorations, replicas except that they are electrified to hold small, "candle" bulbs. If that distresses you, you can order a lamp without wiring for a 15 percent discount. Pieces are turned out one at a time from solid brass, using solid maple turnings. No lacquer or polish is added. Pewter plating is available also.

Business operation The retail store displays a wide selection. A catalog (for $3) is really a small, 64-page book with hundreds of photographs, plus price list and ordering information.

Pricing The list I saw had two 20 percent price changes stamped on the top, so I would ask for current prices. Many of the chandeliers are, or at least were, in the $250 to $400 range.

> Roy Electric Company, Inc.
> 1054 Coney Island Ave.
> Brooklyn, NY 11230
> (212) 339-6311

Roy Electric are licensed electrical contractors working in the New York City area, particularly on older brownstones and other homes where the wiring and the fixtures require special skills. Over the years it has accumulated a stock of antique lamps; gas, oil, and early electric fixtures with sconces and brackets; and unusual pieces of fixture art. These fixtures are restored in the shop and sold mostly to decorators, contractors, and the like but also to the public.

Business operation Roy sells wholesale, retail locally, and via mail order. It will supply an illustrated catalog showing dozens of fixtures and will answer questions on the phone.

PROFESSIONAL SOCIETIES

Electrical Contractors

> National Electrical Contractor's
>   Association (NECA)
> 7315 Wisconsin Ave.
> Washington, DC 20014
> (301) 657-3110

NECA's 6000-plus members include installation, repair, and service contractors covering wiring, equipment, and appliances. The association maintains committees on codes and standards and publishes the NECA Standard of Installation, which is wise to use as a standard for writing contracts in this field. In fact, it is set up so some of its provisions can be included in residential wiring contracts. Write for NECA's list of publications and price list.

Safety Inspections for Wiring

> International Association of Electrical
>   Inspectors (IAEI)
> 802 Busse Hwy.
> Park Ridge, IL 60668
> (312) 0696-1455

Over 14,000 members of IAEI include state, federal, industrial, utility, and insurance electrical inspectors affiliated for the purpose of promoting safe electrical wiring, and compliance with the national electrical code. A source for the complete code, available for $8.25 on the last price list.

GOVERNMENT AGENCIES

Construction Training Programs

U.S. Department of Labor, Bureau of
Apprenticeships and Training
601 D St. NW, Room 5000
Washington, DC 20213
(202) 376-6585

This department approves professional training programs offered by, for example, the International Brotherhood of Electrical Workers. Outlines of these programs can serve as guides for aspiring do-it-yourselfers seeking a high level of expertise and professionalism. Also, major contractors who participate in an approved program just may be turning out better-quality work.

Inspection of Installations

New York Board of Fire Underwriters
85 John St.
New York, NY 10038

This is the only independent electrical inspection board left in the United States. Worth contacting prior to electrical work in New York and for inspection guidelines you can apply to work done elsewhere. Many areas have inspections by local building departments, even when the inspector was a builder and not an electrician, or worse yet, by private, profit making inspection firms working on a commission basis.

Soil/Water/Environment

U.S. Dept. of Agriculture, Soil
Conservation Service (SCS)

PO Box 2890
Washington, DC 20013

In 1935 Congress established the SCS as a reaction to the erosion of topsoil from much of America's farmland. Now the SCS covers three areas: soil and water conservation, natural resource surveys, and rural community protection and development. They provide an almost overwhelming amount of different services to landowners, groups, communities, and states, working through some 3000 districts that roughly follow county lines. Nearly every county in the country has a branch of the SCS, found in the phone book under the "Government" listing. And every state has a state conservationist. In addition, the SCS maintains four technical service centers and technical staff and resources at the national level.

Your local office is best equipped to tell you the details of local programs. Generally they cover the following: watershed protection, flood prevention, technical and financial assistance to landowners to reclaim abandoned surface-mined coal lands, appraise soil and water resources, give assistance to owners concerning land management, pollution control, and water quality, and conduct snow surveys for water supply forecasting, environmental education, and more.

Business operation Check with your local office or write the national headquarters for a publications list. Generally, the titles are thorough and interesting and cover a fascinating collection of subjects: house drainage, grass and tree growing, pond design, evaluating soil on building sites, "inviting birds to your home": windbreak design, and much more. A rich resource.

CONSUMER EDUCATION

Information and Services

Appropriate Technology for Building; Water Use

Intermediate Technology Development
  Group (ITDG) of North America, Inc.
777 United Nations Plaza
New York, NY 10017
(212) 972-9877

The ITDG was established in 1979. Its work, generally in the field of appropriate technology, centers in four areas: distributing AT information, initiating small-scale enterprises, trying to include AT training in the technical training programs of colleges, and hooking up their AT effort with other groups worldwide. They hold detailed workshops periodically in different parts of the country, on such subjects as low-cost solar hot water heaters.

Business operation Write for their publications list, which includes many titles on housing, such as manuals for small building construction using locally available materials, biogas manuals, and titles on cookstove technology, water supply, and waste systems.

Waterlines is their journal of appropriate water supply and sanitation ($14 per year for 4 issues). Write for subscription information to: ITDG Publications Office, PO Box 337, Croton-on-Hudson, NY 10520.

Water Quality/Supply

Water Information Center, Inc.
The North Shore Atrium
6800 Jericho Tpk.
Syosset, NY 11791
(516) 921-7690

The center offers extensive practical and technical information on water, particularly groundwater, and a twice-monthly newsletter called *The Groundwater Newsletter*, a distillation (sorry) of technical reports, articles, press releases, private and government reports, and more.

Business operation A catalog of publications is available on request. The newsletter is $97 a year in the United States, $117 in Canada.

Water Resources

Water Resources Center
University of California at Davis
Davis, CA 95616

The center is an organized research unit serving all campuses of the University of California and working with faculty and staff scientists on many water research issues. Many of its publications are available from the National Technical Information Service (5285 Port Royal Rd., Springfield, VA 22161), and a publications list is available free from the center. It covers such subjects as wilderness water quality, consumer evaluation of the quality and cost of domestic water, and other far more esoteric issues. Also free is an interesting condensation called *What We Can Do Before the Well Runs Dry*, a summary of a report on residential water condensation, which has many very practical, nonscientific suggestions for water use, equipment. and more. If your water is metered, you will be interested to know some of the facts brought out in this report: if all family members turn off the tap while brushing their teeth it saves between 5 and 10 gal of water a day; a 20-minute car wash uses between 200 and 600 gal of water. Worth writing for.

Wind-Electric Machinery
Earthmind
4844 Hirsch Rd.
Mariposa, CA 95338

These folks have "unlisted" their phone number because they are an understaffed, nonprofit, education and research corporation that doesn't have enough time for phone calls from information-hungry consumers. They spend their time developing natural energy sources, specifically wind-electric machinery and S-Rotors, restored Windchargers, and particularly Jacobs windplants. Other projects include working on the design of electric vehicles, electric heat systems, and preparing several books and publications that describe the systems, how to install them, use them, and maintain them.

Business operation Send an SASE for the Earthmind book list.

Practical Training

Heating/Cooling Training
Commercial Trades Institute (CTI)
1500 Cardinal Dr.
Little Falls, NJ 07424
(201) 256-4512

CTI is a vocational home study school offering courses in air-conditioning, refrigeration, heating, and solar technology. The courses include a substantial amount of tools and materials, plus workbooks that take you through the lessons.

Business operation On request CTI sends out a pretty thorough brochure describing the school, tools, courses, the works. And it adds that its staff does not include salespeople who will come knocking on the door with a hard sell. The school is operated under the direction and approval of the New Jersey Commissioner of Education.

Pricing Total tuition, which includes materials, is $895. Financing may be available. Duration is adjustable to suit your needs and schedules.

Electrician's Skills
International Brotherhood of Electrical
    Workers (IBEW)
1125 15th St. NW
Washington, DC 20005
(202) 833-7000

Write for addresses and phone numbers of a local chapter near you and request from them literature on electrical wiring apprentice programs—a good source of information on acquiring skills and the technical knowledge needed to plan a residential wiring system. Note that union apprentice programs in this field generally entail 4 years of field work supported by classroom study.

READING AND REFERENCE

Compost Toilets
*Compost Toilets: A Guide for Owner-
    Builders*, by Robin Adams et al.
National Center for Appropriate
    Technology (NCAT)
PO Box 3838
Butte, MT 59701

Although composting toilets have been re-
garded as only for the most dedicated re-
cyclers, in many states and townships (even
in out of the way places like northern New
Hampshire) environmental codes are so
strict that conventional septic systems can
run $5000 or more—and that's for a mod-
est rural home that may cost $30,000 in-
cluding the land. This 54-page book from
NCAT takes a hard look at composting systems, including what it is like to live with
the raw sewage. While many company pamphlets stress ease of operation, they tend
to talk around the plain fact that you have
a large container of noxious and potentially
hazardous waste down in the cellar. A good
source to check before you are swept away
by alternative and appropriate promises.
Costs about $2.

Creek Water
Protecting Creeksheds, by E. Wayne Say
    and Allan Dines
U.S. Department of Commerce
National Technical Information Service
5285 Port Royal Rd.
Springfield, VA 22161

This informative, 24-page book ($6.50 from
NTIS), subtitled *Analysis and Action*, is a
primer in preserving creekbeds and their
surroundings, protecting them from the ef-

fects of housing development, working with
local government officials to achieve these
goals, and more. It is a condensation of the
authors' extensive, 234-page report that includes many case history studies and a review of literature in the field. Field reports
stem from work done by the authors first
hand on creek sheds around the Great Lakes.

Do-It-Yourself Solutions
Poor Man's Catalogue, by Johnny
    Blackwell
St. Martin's Press, 1981

Plumbing and wiring are included with a lot
more—energy projects, lawn and garden
work, photography—all geared to get a lot
of results from a good idea without spending a lot of time or money. For instance,
the poor man's bird feeder is a simple tin
can with the lid attached at one edge and
wrapped around a small piece of branch to
serve as a perch. The book is loaded with
ideas. Some are marginal, many are ingenious and useful, and most will get you
thinking—like making a loop out of your
hacksaw blade, attaching it to a pole, and
using the hand-made tool as a weed hacker.
About $6; useful and entertaining too.

Energy Audit
The Home Energy Audit, by Richard H.
    Montgomery
John Wiley & Sons, 1983

Basic home energy audits are available from
most utility companies. This book guides

you through your own audit. It does it thoroughly in almost 200 pages with worksheets, efficiency ratings, and retrofitting guidelines.

Hot Tubs and Spas
Hot Tubs, Spas, and Home Saunas, by
Jack McDowell
Sunset Books, Lane Publishing

Although the designs in many of the Sunset how-to books tend to be prosaic, hot tub design is so basic that the tendency to turn a simple outdoor barbecue into a space age appliance can't get started. The drawings and plans are well-detailed, although cutting staves and hooping tubs yourself is quite a task. The plumbing part of the job is not complicated with PVC running to and from the pumps.

Hot Water Supply
Handmade Hot Water Systems
Garcia River Press

This is a wonderfully practical book for those who are willing to do a little work to heat their domestic water as long as they are working to burn wood for heat. The $5 is well spent as the book is filled with clear drawings and does not skimp on the details you need to know about, go off on an alternate energy binge, or yell softly (as too many of these books do) from a soapbox. The book will help you design, fabricate, and install a simple piping system that will pull heat from your stove. Coiled piping in some form is the basic ingredient, and all the technology required is about as appropriate as appropriate technology can get. Write Art Sussman for more details, if needed, at the address above.

Hydroponics
Beginner's Guide to Hydroponics, by
James Sholto Douglas
Sterling Publishing

Hydroponics is the science (and sometimes the art) of growing plants without soil by feeding them with water and fertilized mixtures. This book is a good place to start if you're interested; it covers the kinds of equipment, plumbing, water supply, amount of regular attention, and more needed to set up and maintain a hydroponic system— even a small, portable bed that can be moved to different light exposures in the house.

Lighting
The Lamp and Lighting Book, by Thelma
R. Newman
Crown Publishers, 1976

With a good mix of technical, design, and how-to information, this large, well-illustrated book covers table and standing lamps and ceiling and wall fixtures. It includes detailed step by step coverage of shade making, stained glass fabrication, wiring, and a close look at available lamp parts and their assembly. Because a fair amount of space is devoted to specific designs, try to get a look at the library. The styles, although they range from Colonial classic to acrylic modern, may not suit your tastes.

Photovoltaic Systems
Photovoltaics, by Paul D. Maycock and
Edward N. Stirewalt
Brick House Publishing
34 Essex St.
Andover, MA 01810

Photovoltaics covers the process of turning solar radiation directly into electricity. If the idea is made practical it will do away with steam and water generators, with all the middleman, energy-processing equipment that pulls power from a waterfall or a controlled nuclear reaction and transforms it (losing quite a bit along the way) into usable electric power. This book is an excellent primer on the complicated field, starting with the basics of semiconductors and how the photovoltaic process works depending on the materials used. It includes manufacturers, information sources, and even a fascinating series of predictions: by 1986 photovoltaic systems will be widely used on private homes across the country delivering power direct from the sun at a cost of 5¢ to 10¢ per kilowatt hour. The authors also predict that up to 30 percent of the country's electric energy needs can be provided by these systems by the year 2000. The simple, direct method will get into the residential power mainstream sooner or later. This book tells why it will be sooner.

Plumbing Design/Standards
National Plumbing Code Handbook, by
    Vincent T. Manas
McGraw-Hill Book Company

This large and detailed volume is based on the National Plumbing Code (ASA A40.8) and edited by the executive secretary of the coordinating committee that developed the code. It is not light reading, nor readable, nor usable for common, home how-to plumbing questions. Its value lies in the comprehensive treatment of design possibilities and standards, i.e., the proper sequence for percolation tests and minimum standards for disposal fields.

Plumbing How-To
Do-It-Yourself Plumbing, by Max Alth
Harper & Row, 1975

Generated by *Popular Science* books, this is an extremely practical book, covering common and uncommon repairs, with a solid section on the design of plumbing systems and code compliance. True to the magazine format, seemingly simple operations like cutting and connecting PVC piping are laid out in picture/caption sequences, leaving no doubts about proper procedure. About $15.

Rainwater Collection
*Feasibility of Rainwater Collection
    Systems in California*, by David Jenkins
California Water Resources Center
    Report No. 173
California Water Resources Center
University of California at Davis
Davis, CA 95616

Most homes do not have rain barrels beneath the roof drainpipe, even though it used to be quite common, and even though rainwater is as soft (mineral free) as water gets and is silky smooth and generally excellent for washing. This small pamphlet (55 pages) graphically shows the complicated relationships between month by month rainfall, storage capacity, and demand, from which it is possible to design a rain collection system that does not run dry.

Residential Plumbing
Plumbing
Time-Life Books

This book offers very basic but generally practical information on household plumbing, even to the point of illustrating several ways to patch small pipe leaks temporarily and clearing frozen pipes and drain pipe obstructions. Well-illustrated coverage is detailed on the standard residential projects (replacing a worn faucet stem, for example) but unfortunately is light on the fine points of basic skills (soldering, for instance).

Residential Wiring
Basic Wiring
Time-Life Books

One of the better Time-Life how-to books, this one starts with the absolute basics of how power gets from the utility to your home, explaining volts, amps, and watts thoughtfully and continues through required tools and materials, circuits, switches, outlets, outdoor wiring and lighting. As most of the Time-Life books do, it covers several specific improvement projects (doubling up a duplex receptacle, installing a dimmer, and the like). Detailed how-to drawings, overblown in many of the books in this series, are helpful at this scale where it is important to get the right wire lead onto the right terminal head.

Rural Water Supply
Water Supply for Rural Areas and Small Communities, by Edmund G. Wagnor and J. N. Lanoix
World Health Organization Monograph No. 42
WHO Publications Center USA
49 Sheridan Ave.
Albany, NY 12210

This interesting 340-page report covers small-scale appropriate technology water systems and tells you where you are most likely to find groundwater, the sources that are most economical to tap, and more. Written initially for use in third world nations, this book is straightforward and particularly useful for homesteaders and homeowners in out-of-the-way places who need to tap springs or dig shallow wells.

Septic Systems
Septic Tank Practices, by Peter Warshall
Doubleday, 1979

This is more than a how-to book because it has a definite point of view, contending that it is more sensible in the long and short run to treat sewage on the site and that it is not fair for homeowners to be forced to connect to town sewers that run by their houses. With that in mind, note that coverage includes construction and maintenance of residential septic systems and recycling. A practical book with tips that stem from field experience. About $4.

Small Engines and Motors
The Power Guide, by Peter Fraenkel
Intermediate Technology Development Group North America
PO Box 337
Croton-on-Hudson, NY 10520

The Power Guide is a comprehensive, 240-page catalog of windmills, diesel and steam engines, and small engines of every variety. Listing specialty manufacturers worldwide, the book includes companies that make products to specs and gives a quick synopsis of their products, capacities, and methods of operation. About $15 from ITDG and a good initial source showing the field of small-scale power plants.

Solar Information Updates
Sun Times
Solar Lobby
1001 Connecticut Ave. NW
Washington, DC 20036

Solar Lobby works on Congress and the government in Washington lobbying for solar and energy programs, product standards, and more. *Sun Times* is the group's monthly newsletter sent to members ($15 a year for membership) free every month. The newsletter regularly covers what's happening in the field and is a good way to keep track of recent solar findings and literature.

Water Conservation
Residential Water Conservation,
    by Murray Milne
California Water Resources Center
    Report No. 35
U.S. Department of Commerce
5285 Port Royal Rd.
National Technical Information Service
Springfield, VA 22161

This gargantuan manual (close to 500 large-format pages costing $32) covers virtually every possible water-saving procedure and device used in residences; includes manufacturers; listings of reports and other sources of information on the subject; and excellent planning and analysis of water use in addition to the end-use details. One of the most interesting and graphic presentations (reprinted in the *Whole Earth Catalogue* if you want to take a look) is a flow chart (pardon the pun) of water use showing how the daily average per capita water consumption of 140 gal can be reduced to 75 by re-using "gray" water (already used for showers, dishwashing, etc.) for waste systems and more. With proper treatment, the 45 percent

(some 32 gal) used daily for toilets can be supplied in part by some of the 49 gal used daily indoors. And by the way, cooking and drinking accounts for only about 3 gal of the total water consumed. An interesting, detailed manual from one of the best sources on water through the National Technical Information Service.

Water-Generated Power
*Harnessing Water Power for Home
    Energy,* by Dermot McGuigan
Garden Way Publishing
Charlotte, VT 05545

This modest book (about 100 pages) is an appropriate technology tour of simple water harnessing devices, i.e., all kinds of waterwheels that convert water power to electrical power. The book clearly tells what different conditions (rate of water flow and amount of drop) are capable of producing and where to find waterpower equipment. Cost is about $6.

Water Pumps and Windmills
*The New Alchemy Water Pumping
    Windmill Book,* by Gary Hirschberg
Brick House Publishing, 1981
34 Essex St.
Andover, MA 01810

This thoroughly illustrated book covers water system design; sources, design, and installation of commercial windmill systems; and detailed plans for sailwing water pumpers, including nitty-gritty particulars of assembly, parts sources and sizes, and maintenance. About $5.

Water System Design
Planning for an Individual Water System
American Association for Vocational
   Instructional Materials
Engineering Center
Athens, GA 30602

This book is enlivened by great illustrations (people in action instead of exploded, theoretical views) that devotes 156 pages to the design and installation of residential water systems, including how to dig your own well with or without power equipment, a thorough look at electric pumps, and interesting designs such as a diverter valve system at roof downspouts that allows for roof washing, then diversion of rainwater into a cistern. About $8 from a good source for many different kinds of how-to information.

Wind Electrical Systems
Wind Power, by Donald Marier
Rodale Press, 1981

A comprehensive, 350-page paperback on wind power systems at the residential level, with understandable information on evaluating a site and installing the right equipment, this book also deals with codes, maintenance, and more.

Wind Energy
Wind Power Digest
Wind Power Publishing
PO Box 700
398 E. Tiffin
Bascom, OH 44809
(419) 937-2299

Wind Power Digest is a quarterly consumer publication with some 80 pages of stories and technical information on products and designs. It is a magazine for real enthusiasts who will eat up the kilowatt output charts. Typical issues cover new products in detail, developments in all phases of wind power around the world, trade shows, government research, and more. It's thorough.

Business operation   A year's subscription is $12. Orders are accepted at this toll-free number: 1 (800) 537-0985. Individual issues are $3, and one would give you a reasonable survey of what's new and what's happening in this field.

Windmills
Wind-Catchers, by Volta Torrey
Stephen Greene Press, 1976
Brattleboro, VT 05301

A very nice background book for anyone interested in wind power, *Wind-Catchers* covers European and American windmill design and operation from their beginnings. And although radical-design, vertical-axis turbines are covered in the last few chapters, the real fun comes from the "radical" designs of the early inventors—a merry-go-round, vertical fan mill used to pump water on a Nebraska farm in 1898 and post mills built by colonists in the early 1600s; all done with the people behind the machines, their trials and tribulations, included.

Wiring
Wiring Simplified,
   by H. P. Richter and W. C. Schwan
Park Publishing

Although you may not believe the title (and if you don't or are generally paranoid about electricity call an electrician), straightforward explanations and illustrations here cover residential wiring from the service on in. The illustrations, although simplified versions of the real thing, do show more detail than most; enough reality is included so that you can use the screw heads and little bends shown in the drawings as signposts. Helpful; clear; about $3.50.

Wood Heat Equipment and Practice
Wood Heat, by John Vivian
Rodale Books

An extremely functional first book for wood heat people that covers the kinds of wood, how they burn, how they split, how to lay fires, and how to repair and clean all types of woodburners and chimneys. Endless practical tidbits are offered and clear, friendly illustrations help a lot. The style here approaches what really useful how-to books should strive for—written like a letter from an experienced, helpful friend; over 400 pages; about $10.

Wood Heat Maintenance
Be Your Own Chimney Sweep,
    by Christopher Curtis and Donald Post
Garden Way Publishing

Thousands of woodstoves, fireplace inserts, and other auxiliary heating plants have gone into existing homes, where many were simply plugged into an existing chimney or flue. And that's on top of all the new installations. In every case regular cleaning is probably the most important part of operating wood heat systems (and coal too) safely. This short book (100 pages) covers the subject in detail and lists sources for all the wire brushes, extension rods, and patented cleaning systems you might want to use.

Woodstove Design and Building
Woodstove Construction, by Al Ulmer
Small Farm Energy Conservation Project
Federation of Southern Cooperatives
PO Box 95
Epes, AL 35460

This 50-page manual details do-it-yourself design and construction of two stoves. They are similar in principle to the operation of the Enderes oil barrel equipment and the Sotz shop heater, using a double drum design (one for combustion and one as an efficient heat exchanger). The detailed plans take you through construction step by step. Cost estimates for materials are about $100. You do have to know how to weld to follow the directions.

INDEX